CAMBRIDGE URBAN AND
ARCHITECTURAL STUDIES

3. URBAN MODELLING

CAMBRIDGE URBAN AND ARCHITECTURAL STUDIES

GENERAL EDITORS

LESLIE MARTIN
Emeritus Professor of Architecture, University of Cambridge

LIONEL MARCH
Professor, Department of Systems Design, University of Waterloo, Ontario, and University Lecturer, Department of Architecture, University of Cambridge

VOLUMES IN THIS SERIES

1. *Urban Space and Structures*, edited by Leslie Martin and Lionel March
2. *Energy, Environment and Building*, by Philip Steadman
3. *Urban Modelling*, by Michael Batty
4. *The Architecture of Form*, edited by Lionel March

Urban Modelling

Algorithms, Calibrations, Predictions

MICHAEL BATTY

CAMBRIDGE UNIVERSITY PRESS

CAMBRIDGE

LONDON · NEW YORK · MELBOURNE

CAMBRIDGE UNIVERSITY PRESS
Cambridge, New York, Melbourne, Madrid, Cape Town, Singapore,
São Paulo, Delhi, Dubai, Tokyo

Cambridge University Press
The Edinburgh Building, Cambridge CB2 8RU, UK

Published in the United States of America by Cambridge University Press, New York

www.cambridge.org
Information on this title: www.cambridge.org/9780521134361

First published 1976
This digitally printed version 2010

A catalogue record for this publication is available from the British Library

Library of Congress Catalogue Card Number: 75–41592

ISBN 978-0-521-20811-6 Hardback
ISBN 978-0-521-13436-1 Paperback

Preface

During the last decade, urban modelling has generated a momentum in Britain which has been unparalleled anywhere else in the world. In one sense, it is perhaps surprising that so 'North American' a phenomenon as the building of mathematical models of cities and regions should have caught the interest of researchers in Britain; in hindsight, this is all the more remarkable given the rather uncertain prospect for the first generation of urban models constructed in the early 1960s in North America, which preceded and promoted the British experience. Yet conditions in Britain have especially favoured urban modelling in recent years. Both the theory and practice of modelling have been stimulated by the development of an explicit 'Systems Approach' to urban research and land-use planning, and the presence of a highly developed institutional planning system has been of enormous significance in providing a natural focus for research efforts in this field. The importance of the planning system in fostering such research cannot be stressed too much, for the continuing demand by planners for better tools to explore urban problems has helped to increase the relevance of urban modelling research; and it has meant that urban models have been largely built as aids to conditional prediction, rather than solely as aids to a greater understanding of urban phenomena.

This book is a direct outcome of my contact with this movement since 1967. It reflects my particular interests in urban modelling and it attempts to synthesise some of my research writings over this period. Although I have organised the book around what I believe is a consistent framework which developed along with my research, I leave it to the reader to make his own interpretations of the material presented here. Clearly this book is not intended to be a comprehensive treatment of urban models, and thus it is no substitute for a review of the field. But I have tried to emphasise the process of modelling rather than the models *per se* and in this sense the treatment is of more general import. However, my personal biases, which are reflected in the book, date back to earlier interests.

I was much influenced by my undergraduate schooling in the Department of Town and Country Planning in the University of Manchester, and

v

I was fortunate in being taught by a strong and impressive but diverse group of people led by Roy Kantorowich. Although my interests were originally and continue to be in the three-dimensional attributes of cities, I was frustrated by the lack of explicit method in planning, and thus I became interested in the so-called systems approach which was being advocated in the department by George Chadwick and Brian McLoughlin. In particular, I owe George Chadwick a great debt, for it was he who persuaded me into research rather than professional practice. My initial research into design method evolved into an interest in the system being designed and I was supported and guided during these early days by George Chadwick, whose perspective on this field has helped me formulate a realistic research strategy.

Although a little of the work reported in this book was carried out in Manchester, most of it was made possible by an appointment in the Urban Systems Research Unit at Reading University. In 1968, Peter Hall obtained a substantial grant from the Centre for Environmental Studies in London, and then set up the Unit at Reading to undertake urban modelling research. An optimistic and ambitious programme was initiated and much of the work which is reported here stems from my personal involvement in this programme. From my experience with the Unit, I learnt the conventional wisdom that theory is barren without practice, and a great enthusiasm for modelling was sobered by the realisation that in Georgescue-Roegen's phrase 'there is a limit to what we can do with numbers, as there is a limit to what we can do without them'.

Many people have helped me in writing this book and it goes without saying that I wish to thank all of them. But some have played a very special role. From my Manchester days, I have mentioned the influence of George Chadwick and Brian McLoughlin but my friend and colleague Duncan Thomas, who subsequently took an alternative path to landscape architecture, had a great feeling for this area and he taught me a great deal. Dave Foot deserves a special mention, for not only did he teach me my rudimentary but essential knowledge of computer programming but he continues to guide me in the arts of the possible in urban modelling. At Reading, Erlet Cater, Roger Sammons, Eric Cripps and Jane Read have all helped me to clarify my ideas, and the influence of my M.Sc. students over the years has been considerable; indeed, Chapter 9 is the outgrowth of a project originally started by the 1971–2 M.Sc. students in Urban and Regional Planning at the University of Reading. Stewart Mackie of the Local Government Operational Research Unit originally collaborated on Chapter 8, and Ian Masser of the University of Liverpool on Chapter 10. I am especially indebted to these authors for letting me include work which they were instrumental in implementing. I realise that I have also been a perpetual nuisance to the staff of the Computer Centre at Reading. Urban modelling is a young field and enthusiasm often outstrips common sense especially in the area of computation. Thus I am greatly indebted to Tony Hewitt and his staff for the generous amount of computer time and programming advice they have given. All of these things would not have been possible at Reading without the support of Peter Hall, whose boundless energy and enthusiasm for the field has been a great source of inspiration.

I must also mention several people who have helped me on technical questions: Dick Baxter, Andrew Broadbent, Martyn Cordey-Hayes, Marcial Echenique, Geoff Hyman and Alan Wilson. All of these people have taken time out from their own researches to advise me on different points and I am grateful to them. Lionel March has helped me considerably over publication and I must thank Sheila Dance who drew the diagrams, Ann Watts for much of the early typing and Jennifer Preston for typing the manuscript. My wife Sue has helped me on all aspects of the book and only she knows the frustration of putting up with an untidy academic whose home is littered with papers. I dedicate this book to her.

Kitchener-Waterloo, Ontario   MICHAEL BATTY
October 1974

Acknowledgements

Some material in this book has been previously published in the form of journal articles. The author gratefully acknowledges the following editors and publishers for permission to use and revise this material here: Josephine P. Reynolds, editor of the *Town Planning Review* published by Liverpool University Press, for some material in Chapter 4 originally published in Vol. 41, pp. 121–47, 1970; Alan G. Wilson, editor of *Environment and Planning* published by Pion Press, for some material in Chapters 5, 6 and 7, originally published in Vol. 2, pp. 95–114, 1970, Vol. 3, pp. 411–32, 1971 and Vol. 4, pp. 205–33, 1972; Alan G. Wilson, editor of *London Papers in Regional Science* published by Pion Press, for some material in Chapter 12 originally published in Vol. 3, pp. 44–82, 1972; Peter G. Hall, editor of *Regional Studies* published by Pergamon Press, for some material in Chapters 5 and 8 originally published in Vol. 4, pp. 307–32, 1970 and Vol. 7, pp. 351–66, 1973; Sumner N. Levine, editor of *Socio-Economic Planning Sciences* published by Pergamon Press, for some material in Chapter 10 originally published in Vol. 7, pp. 573–98, 1973; and Margaret Cox, editor of the *Town Planning Institute Journal* published by the Royal Town Planning Institute, for some material in Chapter 4, originally published in Vol. 55, pp. 428–35, 1969.

Contents

List of Figures

List of Tables

It is said that science will dehumanise people and turn them into numbers. That is false, tragically false...

Science is a very human form of knowledge. We are always at the brink of the known, we always feel forward for what is to be hoped. Every judgement in science stands on the edge of error, and is personal. Science is a tribute to what we know although we are fallible.

Dr Jacob Bronowski in
The Ascent of Man, London,
1973

Introduction

Thomas Kuhn (1962), in his stimulating book *The Structure of Scientific Revolutions*, advances and demonstrates the theory that the history of science is not characterised by a gradual accretion of knowledge, as is assumed by the community at large, but is dominated at any one time by a set of fundamental ideas or a paradigm which can only be changed by scientific revolution. Most scientists spend their lives working within the recognised limits of the paradigm and only when anomalies become too significant to disregard will scientists endeavour to search for a new paradigm. This view of science is appealing and is readily endorsed by a study of major revolutions in thought such as those due to Newton and to Einstein. Moreover, there appear to exist a hierarchy of paradigms from the most general to the most specific. Kuhn's ideas can also be traced in the social sciences although such paradigms are more difficult to identify and somewhat more ill-defined than the paradigms of science.

Because the paradigms of social science are so elusive and so pervasive, scientific revolution is less easy to recognise in these fields. Yet it appears that during the last two decades, the study of man in general and the social sciences in particular have been affected by a profound transformation in approach and method akin to a scientific revolution. Although it is too soon to take a long view, the last two decades have seen the emergence of more rigorous argument in social science characterised by some semblance of experimental design and a much greater realisation of the nuances and biases of the subject matter. There is little doubt that the development of large-scale computational facilities has made these new approaches both possible and necessary. Despite the present-day view that technology presents more of a hindrance than a help to resolving the dilemma of man, it is worth remembering that many of the newer and perhaps more exciting developments in science and social science are inextricably linked to the rise of the modern computer. Nowhere is this more evident than in those fields dealing with the phenomena of man in social as well as biological and physical terms – in the fields where psychology, linguistics, computer science and engineering merge in the quest to develop 'artificial intelligence'. Immense strides have recently been made in these fields which are totally dependent on the computer, and the optimism and conviction of their scientists suggests that man is firmly set on the road to establishing what Simon (1969) has called '*The Sciences of the Artificial*'.

Urban modelling, the subject of this book, is an integral part of this revolution in thought in which the boundaries between traditional disciplines are blurring in response to the need for interdisciplinary co-operation. In short, the field of urban modelling is concerned with de-signing, building and operating mathematical models of urban phenomena, typically cities and regions. There are many reasons for the development of such models: their role in helping scientists to understand urban phenomena through analysis and experiment represents a traditional goal of science, yet urban modelling is equally important in helping planners, politicians and the community to predict, prescribe and invent the urban future. In education too, in its narrowest and widest senses, urban modelling can help by demonstrating the limitations of theory and the potential of simulation.

This quest is truly interdisciplinary, drawing directly and by analogy from all the sciences, and making use of mathematics, that best-developed language of science. But there are inevitable dangers in the development of such a field and two distinct dangers can be immediately recognised. First, in an era when the body of 'new' knowledge is as great or greater than the body of 'existing' knowledge, there are severe difficulties in evaluating the relevance of new theories, techniques or methodologies. There is a further dilemma in that those who know the least about the subject matter are often expected to ponder and evaluate its relevance to education, and that those who know the most about any line of research are often the least willing to speculate on its importance. These comments are not only applicable to urban modelling but to all areas of knowledge where the traditional boundaries are changing in response to new lines of inquiry. Yet perhaps the second danger is more serious. In any field where new modes of thought are not built up from knowledge already acquired in that field, it is likely that the new ideas become the prerogative of very few; this is evident in the development of urban modelling where the use of mathematical technique favours those who have acquired skills not in the social but in the physical sciences. This danger cannot be over-estimated and it is well to keep in mind the old adage 'In the country of the blind, the one-eyed man is king.' Thus the approach in this book is tentative and is pursued with the view that it will take many years to evaluate the true relevance of urban modelling: hopefully this work might contribute a little to this longer term endeavour.

A new analytical tradition

Prior to these new developments in social science hinted at above, the traditional form of theory-building and testing revolved around classical analysis. For example, in economics, one of the first areas where theory was formulated in mathematical terms, analysis was usually restricted to mathematical manipulation in the quest to determine the relevance of the theory. Similarly in locational analysis, theories explaining city size and form were tested primarily using mathematical deduction. This classical tradition, although still existing today in various forms and still having some importance, has been largely supplanted by a more conscious process of theory development and testing through modelling, utilising the power of the computer to store and manipulate the large number of observations essential to the process of model design. Apart from the discipline which has come from developing a more explicit scientific method in social science, the computer has also made possible the design of theories and building of models from simple modules whose interaction through replication has produced an added dimension of complexity, commensurate with the mechanisms at work in urban and regional systems.

Although this new analytic tradition represents a breakthrough, it is more exploratory than the old; in some senses, it is less sensitive and less elegant, more ambitious and more straightforward. Its reliance on computation gives it a bias towards the 'number crunching' or 'sledge hammer' approach to theory-building. Yet it has also brought greater opportunities to social science in that many more researchers can participate in the process of theory-building. It has, in short, brought science and mathematics to the realm of everyday affairs. But with these advantages have come a harder, less tolerant evaluation of these new ideas in practice, thus implying that these tools can never be solely valued for their pedagogical use. As this book will hope to establish, a great deal can be learned from urban modelling but one of the dilemmas which will appear time and time again in these pages concerns the content of what is learned. Many critics of urban modelling hold the view that model-builders are learning more and more about their models but less and less about the real world which they are attempting to model. Such a view will always provide food for thought but it illustrates that model-builders walk a fine line between theoretical acceptability and practical feasibility. Outside these narrow limits, respectability is lost and so precarious an existence is perhaps untypical of other fields. Nevertheless, this is part of the challenge which makes this field so exciting and although it is too soon to establish principles for urban modelling, there are some ground rules which dominate the present state of play.

Ground rules for urban modelling

Simplicity is the hallmark of any good theory and apparent complexity is often simplicity in disguise. Many of the models to be introduced here reflect this observation, and the idea that more complex models can be constructed out of building blocks based on simple postulates, is a theme which is recurrent throughout this book. As far as possible, this rule has been adhered to and it is unlikely that readers will accuse the author of over-complexity, more likely the reverse. A second rule reflects the related idea of parsimony. Simon and Chase (1973) elaborate on this rule in stating: 'If, in order to explain each new phenomenon, we must invent a new mechanism, then we have lost the game. Theories, gradually modified and improved over time, are convincing only if the range of phenomena they explain grows more rapidly than the set of mechanisms they postulate.' This rule of parsimony relates to a further rule based on the idea of using Occam's razor to prune unnecessary embellishments to theories and models which seek to mystify rather than explain.

The rule of clarity is especially important in urban modelling. It is essential to lay bare the assumptions upon which such models are founded for only then can any attempt at objective evaluation be made. Much of the early literature in this field coming from North America is shrouded in mystique. The fact that so much of the early development of the field was pioneered by researchers working in a private rather than public capacity has added further to the confusion, and like many recent developments in social science, these ideas have often been dismissed by social scientists as 'sorcery' (Andreski, 1972) and by physical scientists as precocity. But perhaps the most important rule of all relates to compromise, that quality which removes much of the glamour from both theory and practice. In what follows, there is little mathematical elegance in the classical sense, and little of the pure empiricism which characterises present-day planning and government for such qualities must be impossible to synthesise in any complete sense. Thus, a strong element of pragmatism is coupled with a desire to build strong theory. The strategy to achieve this however has some fairly unconventional turns and it is because of these twists that some apologies need to be offered, especially to mathematicians, in advance.

Apologies to mathematicians: terminology and notation

The approach to urban modelling adopted here lies toward the end of the spectrum beginning at theory and research and terminating at practice and development. Thus most of the mathematics is of a finite kind with special emphasis upon algorithms, accounting frameworks and some rough and ready numerical analysis. There is little of the more elegant analysis characterising the calculus or statistical distribution theory, although there are small chunks of such analysis generally included in referring readers to other work. This is pragmatic mathematics reflecting a pragmatic approach and those with an eye to formal mathematics may encounter equation systems and explanations which set their teeth on edge. Nevertheless, all of the equation systems given in this book are in a form which makes their programming for a large-scale computer comparatively straightforward without recourse to any intermediate form; at least, all of these equations have been programmed from these descriptions, at one time or another and in various computer languages, by the author.

With regard to terminology, much will be familiar to those working in the fields of statistics and operational research from which a wide variety of terms have been drawn. Hopefully, no new terms have been devised in this book although readers might recognise a North American influence for much of the early work in this field originated in the United States. Terminology is introduced gradually as each idea is developed and definitions are given where necessary. In a similar way, the mathematical notation used is defined when introduced but is constantly redefined to keep the reader continually aware of the problem. An attempt has been made to keep notation completely consistent throughout the book, but because of the very large number of variables and parameters introduced, some redefinition is necessary in parts. In particular, the pre- post- sub-super-scripting of variables has been mainly restricted to the integer range, $i, j, \ldots, n$, and because of the narrowness of this range, certain redefinitions are occasionally necessary. However, key variables such as population, employment, distance, etc. are given a constant notation throughout the book. High-level computer language notation has been avoided.

An outline of the book

Among the many themes around which this book is organised, the strongest relates to the process of model design reflected in the subtitle as *Algorithms, Calibrations, Predictions*. Each chapter emphasises specific parts of the process of model design from theory through to operation and prediction in a planning context. Yet there are several subsidiary themes, three of which stand out. The material included in each chapter and the relation of the chapters to one another reflect a very approximate chronological order of research which is also embodied in a second theme concerned with the level of complexity. The material introduced proceeds from the simple to the more complex, a progression which matches the order in which various problems were defined and tackled. For example, this theme involves progression from partial to general, from aggregated to disaggregated, and from static to dynamic modelling. A third theme is less dominant but relates to the phenomena being modelled. An attempt has been made to include models of a wide range of urban systems and subsystems dealing with residential location, shopping, transport and, to a lesser extent, industrial location.

The first chapter is devoted to providing a context for urban modelling and a classification of models in terms of their origins, traditions, early history in North America, and scope. In the second chapter simple models of urban subsystems based on both the generation and allocation of activities are introduced and are assembled into systems of equations for more general models in Chapter 3. In Chapters 4 and 5, the task of getting such models operational is outlined using two examples from the British subregions of Central Lancashire and Nottinghamshire–Derbyshire. But the more important role of these two chapters is to demonstrate how these models can be used in a planning context, in impact analysis and in the evaluation of alternative plans.

Chapters 6–9 are concerned with developing and resolving problems of operational modelling concerning calibration and spatial system design, first identified in Chapters 4 and 5. The problem of calibration is explored tentatively in Chapter 6 using a shopping model, and in Chapter 7, the calibration problem is treated as a problem of non-linear optimisation, demonstrated by shopping and transport models. These calibration techniques are applied to a more general model of the Northampton subregion in Chapter 8 which also serves to introduce problems of zoning and the relationship between the system and its environment which is treated extensively in Chapter 9.

Chapters 10–12 attempt to extend the models of the previous chapters in two ways: by disaggregation of variables such as population and by the design of dynamic models which explicitly treat the concept of time. In Chapter 10, a series of disaggregated residential location models based on explicit ideas about the housing market are developed and tested on the Reading subregion. Chapter 11 sets the context for dynamic modelling by reviewing the concepts involved in making models dynamic and by introducing certain hypotheses relevant to the behaviour of urban systems. Finally, Chapter 12 presents a design for a dynamic model which is explored and tested on the Reading subregion. From these various experiences conclusions are then drawn which comment on the limitations of urban modelling but more optimistically suggest ways in which the potential of urban modelling might be realised in future work.

1. *The art of urban modelling*

The art of urban modelling, which has evolved during the last decade, is part of a much wider revolution in thought within the social sciences, a revolution which began in North America over twenty years ago and which is continuing apace today. In the quest to infuse both rigour and quality into disciplines such as sociology, political science and urban studies, social scientists have turned to fields such as modern physics in the hope that powerful analogies might exist, thus pointing the way to more sophisticated and relevant theories of human behaviour. In the early years of this endeavour, the emphasis was on abstraction in the form of simple theories of social and economic organisation although the importance of testing such theories was quickly realised and the concept of modelling the system and manipulating the model in the hope of gaining new insights became firmly established. Models of social and economic systems involving the essential idea of simplifying reality to a point at which it is understandable hardly embody new ideas, but the formalisation of what was previously implicit involves a realisation that modelling is fundamental to the rigorous development of all the social sciences. It is in fact this realisation which distinguishes modern social science from its ancestry.

The development of urban research which is closely linked to urban modelling is founded upon the conviction that urban phenomena exhibit a degree of complexity which only formal study can hope to unravel. The complexities and ambiguities surrounding the mechanisms sustaining and altering the modern city have become more and more difficult to understand as urban society has become more diverse, more mobile and more diffuse. Thus, urban modelling has developed as a direct response to such complexity although such developments have also been tied to advances in large-scale computation without which urban modelling could never really have begun. Modern theories of the city such as those involving the spatial organisation of land use and related activities and the economic behaviour of different locators in the city require symbolic models in their testing and refinement against real world data; such use of models as media through which the science of urban organisation can

1

be refined and evolved represents the first important role for urban modelling, a role which is a relatively pure expression of the goal involving the search for a greater understanding of urban phenomena.

There is a second and perhaps more fundamental role for urban modelling and this involves the use of urban models in physical planning. Indeed, the short history of urban modelling which is to be outlined in this first chapter suggests that most of the large-scale numerical models already developed in an urban or regional context were based on the notion that better forecasting could only result through their use. In some senses, the two roles for models just outlined are both required in planning studies, and frequently the need to use models in forecasting can be an essential complement to models designed to achieve a better understanding of reality, and the reverse is also true. Most of the models referred to in this book are based on the requirement that such models need to be operational: that these models can be implemented using real data on large-scale computers and can thus be manipulated in both analytical and predictive contexts. This is in contrast to a large number of models which are essentially theoretical in nature, such as those models explaining the structure and behaviour of urban markets. Although these models are critical to the development of computer simulation models, for all intents and purposes in this book, they will be regarded as theories upon which the art of urban modelling is based.

Science and design in urban modelling

The need to produce more coherent and suggestive theories of urban structure and growth has been the prerogative of urban researchers drawn from the fields of urban economics, geography and sociology as well as planning, architecture and engineering. As in most branches of the physical sciences, the development of theory is implicitly based upon the commonly accepted cycle of scientific method involving hypothesis formulation, observation, experiment and hypothesis refinement, tasks which can be and have been carried out in more or less any order. Urban modelling involving the construction of models based on particular hypotheses is largely concerned with the experiment and refinement stages of the cycle in which the theory or hypothesis is translated into a testable form. A most pertinent definition of an urban model formulated by one of the sages of the field, Britton Harris, is based upon this scientific focus. Harris (1966a) defines an urban model as 'an experimental design based on a theory', thus recognising the role of modelling in the search for a relevant understanding of urban structure.

Yet it is necessary to dispel the myth that urban modelling and indeed, any branch of scientific endeavour, is mechanistic and technocratic. The popular view of science is based on the notion that science is an inevitable outcome of rigid narrow thinking, but that is far from the truth. Science like any other area of knowledge is largely based upon insights which occur through intuitive processes (Medawar, 1969). Despite Poincaré's dictum that 'discovery favours the prepared mind', many an analysis of the history of science, for example that by Kuhn (1962) described briefly in the introduction, reveals that science does not progress continuously and mechanistically but advances in discrete jumps based on fundamental insights and intuition. The idea of science as a process of conjecture, then refutation of problems, followed by tentative solutions, error-elimination and the redefinition of problems (Popper, 1972) is reflected in the development of urban theories and models as will be illustrated later. But perhaps the most important change which has taken place in the development of urban theory and modelling in the last decade is in the gradual switch which has occurred away from inductive style towards deductive analyses. Stronger grounding in *a priori* theory building has been largely responsible for this change but the development of facilities for large-scale computation has also helped this trend.

It is no exaggeration to state that electronic computers have made urban modelling possible. The testing of urban theories requires such an enormous amount of data concerning the most simple of hypotheses describing the workings of cities, that such experiment is only possible on large-scale computers. Thus the big number crunching exercises characteristic of urban models are now a reality. Furthermore, the hybrid nature of urban models in terms of their somewhat crude mathematical design often involves solution procedures which are approximate, which in short involve iteration. Such trial and error solution procedures represent the forte of the high-speed computer, thus enabling solutions to problems, which hitherto would probably never have been formulated and certainly never resolved, to be found. A further note on the development of urban theory is relevant here: urban models now represent the means for testing theory in a spatial context, and it appears that many of the newer theories of urban phenomena are model-based. No longer is it satisfactory simply to propose theories to be tested by others. More empirical support is required in formulating theory, and this has led to new developments in urban theory going forward under the guise of urban models. Thus urban modelling is not just a reflection of urban theory formulated elsewhere; it is now an essential part of theory in the fields of urban economics, geography and planning.

The rationale for developing models of the urban system is equally as strong in the fields of urban design and physical planning. The idea of designing a working model of the city with the notion that future plans for the city can be simulated and evaluated on the computer is an appealing and immensely exciting concept. The analogy between such computer application and the physical scientist's laboratory has been drawn many times (McLoughlin, 1969), and the use of such models in an experimental context seems to provide one of the foundation stones in the development of urban science. Yet despite the optimism of the planners concerned with the use of models in this way, the role of models in planning remains extremely crude and has never been systematically thought through. Such models appear to fit into any of the stages of the planning process – into planning analysis, the design of alternative plans, their evaluation and even their implementation – and thus the role of existing models can be tentatively ascribed as neutral. Certainly questions of the effect of models on design and optimisation in planning have hardly been broached although there are signs that designers are now coming to grips with the role of modelling in this field (Martin and March, 1972). The relationship between the use of models in hypothesis testing and in a predictive, possibly prescriptive context involves an inevitable source of conflict in the empirical development of this field. In some senses, every application of a model is unique and requires special adaptation to the problem in hand, and thus there is an element of hypothesis testing in every predictive model design. Such conflicts have been and continue to be a feature of urban model development. To trace the implications of these problems, however, it is first necessary to dig a little deeper into the origins of urban modelling, thus charting its recent history and setting the context for a more technical appreciation.

The Quantitative Revolution and the Systems Approach

The revolution in the social sciences and in related fields such as geography and the sciences of the built form which began in the late 1950s, was founded on the belief that progress in the development of knowledge could best be achieved by rigorous theory-building rather than by loose speculation. There was a genuine feeling among researchers that the benefits of the physical sciences would be bestowed upon the social sciences if more fundamental approaches could be developed. But this view was also coloured by the desire of social scientists to achieve a degree of respectability in the eyes of their fellow scientists and in the community at large. This change in approach which has pervaded almost every social science during the last two decades has been referred to in various ways, but two of the best-known clichés summing up these developments are termed the 'Quantitative Revolution' and the 'Systems Approach'.

The Quantitative Revolution is clearly demonstrated in the development of modern geography where concern for describing the nature of geographical space has involved the widespread use of mathematical and statistical description. The geometry of space and the statistical variation of spatial phenomena in locational terms have formed the basis for a new science of human geography, quite different in method and scope from the rather introverted regional geography which it has replaced. For example, the development of spatial abstractions such as idealised urban economic landscapes has led to the use of sophisticated mathematical analysis in the search for relevant theory. In economics, too, the descriptive tradition has been almost totally replaced during the last thirty years by analytical approaches which seek to explain, as well as describe the mechanisms governing the behaviour and structure of economic institutions and organisations.

The Systems Approach, on the other hand, appears to have been more formally adopted by disciplines whose content is less amenable to quantitative description. In response to the blurring of disciplinary boundaries in science and the realisation that many sciences use the same basic methodology, this approach was spurred on by the obvious relevance of *General System Theory* (Von Bertalanffy, 1971), and *Cybernetics* defined by Wiener (1948) as 'the science of control and communication in the animal and the machine', to almost every facet of human existence. Furthermore, the success of Operations Research as a common quantitative medium for analysis of a host of different 'human' problems was regarded by many as the arm of General System Theory which made the subject operational and usable in practice. The idea of systems being described in terms of structure and behaviour, in terms of input and output, and the notion of purposeful control of such systems in terms of negative and positive feedbacks, appeared to many social scientists an ideal description of their systems of interest and thus the approach has come to be used in more-or-less all of the social sciences.

The appeal and relevance of the system model can be formally traced through the work of Easton (1965) and Deutsch (1963) in political science, through Parsons (1952) to Buckley (1967) in sociology and less formally in a proliferation of works in economics, social psychology and geography. An excellent review article by McLoughlin and Webster (1970) lists pertinent literature from the social sciences and the reader is referred to this for further study. The Systems Approach however has been highly explicit in the fields of planning and design where the concept of control as well as system is of utmost importance. In physical planning, researchers and academics have been acutely conscious of the somewhat pragmatic nature of the subject and its lack of theory, and this has proved to be fertile ground upon which the Systems Approach has grown. Recently, this approach has been formally embodied in theoretical texts by Mc-Loughlin (1969), Catanese and Steiss (1970) and Chadwick (1971) who have all brought their particular blend of Systems Theory to planning. Moreover, it is clear from these works that these authors regard urban modelling as one, if not the most important, medium through which the Systems Approach can be implemented in practice. In some senses, this is *a posteriori* reasoning for the origins of urban modelling go back further than the formal expression of planning as a Systems Approach.

The origins of urban modelling

The pioneer developments in urban modelling came almost exclusively from North America where two traditions were fused in response to the need for more systematic planning and better forecasting. Increasing car ownership during the 1940s and early 1950s led to the growing realisation that cities with their traditional physical form could simply not cope with the new mobility. Out of these problems came the first transportation studies in which planners and engineers sought to understand and solve congestion and by the late 1950s, the rudiments of the transportation planning process had been established. Part of this process involved fore-casts of future trip generation and its spatial distribution and to meet these needs, trip generation was modelled using linear regression analysis, and distribution was modelled using the 'gravity model', so called because of its analogy with Newton's Law of Gravitation. These modelling tech-niques were widely used and in the absence of evidence to the contrary, these techniques appeared successful in that they were fairly manageable and simple to operate. Yet the transportation studies neglected many important questions concerning land use and it was inevitable that trans-port engineers should attempt to take such questions into account by extending their ambit to encompass land-use forecasting. The interrelation-ship between traffic and land use was a subject of much practical and academic debate during these years and the pioneering work of Mitchell and Rapkin (1954) in their book *Urban Traffic: A Function of Land Use* did much to convince engineers and planners of the need for integrated land-use and transportation planning.

The immediate success in operational and academic terms of transporta-tion planning and modelling naturally led those concerned to begin to think about the possibility of building land-use models, and by 1960 several such models were under construction. But another tradition apart from transport planning had an effect upon such developments and this concerned research activity in urban and location economics. Two important research projects involving theoretical models of urban structure were nearing completion at this time. The intra-urban location model designed by Wingo (1961), and the similar but slightly more theoretically oriented economic model proposed by Alonso (1960) established an economic theory for urban systems, comparable to existing theories of economic location in regional systems. These models together with other more empirically based research in urban economics being initiated at the RAND Corporation (Kain, 1962) had a profound influence on the development of the first generation of urban models in the early 1960s, and this work is so important that it warrants further explanation.

The synthesis achieved by Alonso and Wingo at this time grew out of certain simple and long-established ideas concerning location and the price of space around a market centre due to Von Thunen (Hall, 1966). In 1826, Von Thunen suggested that around a market centre, the rent paid for agricultural land plus the cost of transporting agricultural produce from the land to the market would equal a constant value. At the margin of development, rent would be zero and the total cost incurred to the producer would be equal to the transport cost to the market. From this statement, it is not hard to deduce that rent would decline with distance from the market centre, and subsequent empirical evidence bore out this simple result. Von Thunen's work was largely neglected in the subsequent years although it became apparent that not only rents but other activities such as population density and trip-making also declined with distance from the centre (Clark, 1951). Wingo's achievement was to design a model based on Von Thunen's work but integrating detailed transport costs and explaining population density, and Alonso took this work a stage further by setting the whole model within the micro-economic theory of consumer behaviour based on utility-maximisation. A major restriction of these analyses concerned the fact that only one centre could be treated – the monocentric assumption; but it was clear that the trip-distribution model which treated many centres was consistent with these theoretical models and thus the way lay open for ambitious land-use modelling integrating theoretical elegance with operational feasibility.

A short history of first generation urban modelling

The first generation urban models were designed and implemented in North America mainly during the years 1959–68, years which coincided with the launching of large-scale land-use–transportation studies in major metropolitan areas. There are some excellent reviews of model construction during this period and in particular the reader is referred to the work of Lowry (1968), Harris (1968), Kilbridge, O'Block and Teplitz (1969),

Brown, Ginn, James, Kain and Straszheim (1972) and Lee (1973) who have all provided useful summaries of the modelling experience. Boyce, Day and McDonald (1970) in a fine review of metropolitan plan-making also present pertinent material on the planning environment within which these modelling projects were initiated; although this section will draw on these works, the discussion is in no way a substitute for reference to these reviews but is an interpretation of the most important facets of the North American modelling experience.

One of the striking features of urban modelling during these years was the almost exclusive development of models in practical planning situations. Apart from the work of Chapin and his colleagues in North Carolina (Chapin, 1965), most of the fundamental research into urban modelling was carried out under the auspices of metropolitan planning agencies or consultants, a situation probably due in part to the practical need for better forecasting, the continuing tradition of transportation modelling and the availability of federal funds. Yet an extensive variety of approaches was utilised involving a diverse selection of techniques ranging from linear regression and gravity modelling to mathematical programming. Emphasis on theory ranged from the pragmatic to the pure, and the approach to modelling from the most partial to the most general. The models can best be grouped according to the techniques used. Conventional and well-established linear statistical techniques were used as a basis for several models, in particular the Greensborough model (Chapin and Weiss, 1962), the EMPIRIC model of the Boston Region (Hill, 1965) and the Baltimore and Connecticut models (Lakshmanan, 1964, 1968). Non-linear models such as the Delaware Valley (Penn–Jersey) Activities Allocation model (Seidman, 1969) were constructed in a similar fashion and most of these attempts reflected a somewhat inductive approach to modelling with little *a priori* theory. In contrast, the many models built around the gravity model suggested a more deductive approach in which specific mechanisms at work in the urban system were simulated. The Pittsburgh model (Lowry, 1964) and its successors, the Pittsburgh Time-Oriented Metropolitan Model (TOMM) designed by Crecine (1964) and the Bay Area Projective Land Use Model (PLUM) designed by Goldner (1968) as well as the Upper New York State model (Lathrop and Hamburg, 1965) are good examples of the gravity modelling approach, an approach which appears in retrospect to have produced the most successful urban models during this time.

Models based on mathematical programming such as the residential-location model originally proposed for Penn-Jersey by Herbert and Stevens (1960) and subsequently developed by Harris (1972) at the University of Pennsylvania, and the South East Wisconsin Land Use

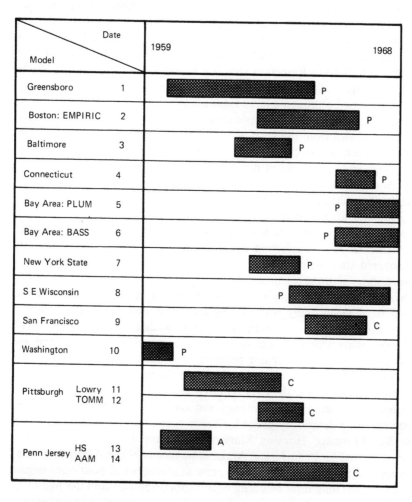

REFERENCES TO MODELS:
1 :	Chapin and Weiss, 1962,	8 :	Schlager, 1965, 1966,
2 :	Hill, 1965,	9 :	Robinson *et al.*, 1965,
3 :	Lakshmanan, 1964,	10 :	Hansen, 1959,
4 :	Lakshmanan, 1968,	11 :	Lowry, 1964,
5 :	Goldner, 1968,	12 :	Crecine, 1964,
6 :	Wendt *et al.*, 1968,	13 :	Herbert and Stevens, 1960,
7 :	Lathrop and Hamburg, 1965,	14 :	Seidman, 1969.

A: abandoned; C: calibrated; P: used in prediction.

Fig. 1.1. Urban modelling projects in North America during the 1960s.

Plan Design models built by Schlager (1965, 1966) show how optimisation techniques can be used in urban modelling although there has only been limited success with these techniques. More hybrid modelling schemes such as the Bay Area Simulation Study (BASS) initiated by Wendt *et al.* (1968), and the San Francisco Housing Market Model (Robinson, Wolfe, and Barringer, 1965) which attempt to link several different techniques were also tried although a large measure of arbitrariness is often a feature of such schemes. Figure 1.1 presents a chart of model developments in North America from the years 1959–68, and from this chart, it is evident that the peak in modelling activity occurred in the early- and mid-1960s. Although only a sample of models developed during these years is presented on the chart, most of the important applications described in easily available publications are included.

Although a great deal was learnt from the first generation of urban modelling, the experience was somewhat unprecedented in that several fundamental factors affecting the whole process of modelling were only discovered after the model construction had begun. Reactions to the relative failure of these early models differ quite widely: for example, Lee (1973) considers the experience to have been a salutary warning of the dangers of technocracy whereas Ingram, Kain and Ginn (1972) regard these early attempts as vindicating the view that modelling is a large complex affair which requires far more resources than were then and are now available. The first major problem confronted by most of the early models involved questions of size. Many of the models were so ambitious in terms of their scale, the data required and computer time and capacity needed, that real time and money ran out and the models were then abandoned or drastically pruned. Classic examples of such failures were the San Francisco Housing Market Model and the original Herbert–Stevens model for Penn-Jersey. At the same time in North America, disillusionment with technology began to grow as planners and politicians began to realise that long-term planning of transportation and land use had little or nothing to do with more immediate problems of poverty and inequality. One by one the funds available for such long-term projects were diverted to more critical and pressing problems. Optimism among model-builders and planners turned to pessimism and bitterness and after the mid-1960s 'sharp criticism forced the movement to go underground' (Lee, 1973).

It is easy to blame excessive ambition, lack of time and money, and changing priorities for the failures in first generation urban modelling, but the quality and limitations of the models also had a great deal to do with the situation. At the beginning of the decade, urban modelling seemed to present a means for cutting through and tackling the complexity of the modern metropolis. Lee (1973) sums it up nicely in the following way: 'Everything seemed to be an urban problem, and everything seemed interrelated; the whole world was a jumble of secondary and iterative side effects. Some way of integrating it all was needed without giving anything up. . .and computers and models held out this promise.' But the modellers failed to recognise the limitations of their models in helping to sort out ill-defined planning problems. Such models based on fairly well-defined formal structures had to rely upon fairly sparse theory, thus often appearing arbitrary and somewhat mechanistic in structure. The ill-defined nature of reality and the lack of behavioural content combined to limit the use of models to a much greater extent than was realised at the time. As many land-use–transportation studies were model-based, such limitations had severe repercussions upon the projects as a whole.

A more fundamental problem of urban modelling was realised at this stage. The problem of observing the mechanisms of cause and effect in urban systems is compounded by the fact that such observation is clouded by a host of different factors. It is unusually difficult to test specific theories in the social sciences for it is impossible to hold all variables but one constant and trace the effects on the system. This is a problem which is basic to theory in the social sciences and there is little doubt that it is the major limitation on urban modelling. The problem was only partly faced during the first generation of modelling for it was obscured by the other, more immediate difficulties outlined above. A further problem, which will only be alluded to here and dealt with in greater detail in later chapters, concerns the use of these models in planning. The question of modelling, optimisation and design was never really considered in most studies, and land-use–transportation plans were largely based on trend projection, thus implicitly endorsing an assumed optimality, in the eyes of the planners and modellers, of the present situation. The lessons from this first generation experience are hard and long and provide the basis for a detailed investigation of the role of models in planning. But before this is done, it is worth while outlining the variety of possible urban models through classification schemes, thus introducing, at the same time, some of the terminology essential to further discussion of urban modelling.

Classification and terminology

Hardly a book or paper is written on urban modelling which does not contain some reference to a classification of models. Useful classifications are provided in the review papers cited earlier and these schemes reveal the difficulties of devising classes which are mutually exclusive of each other and the difficulties caused by having to place a model in one particular class or another. Before embarking on a simple classification for models, it is worth reflecting upon these problems and recognising that the value of classification is in terms of abstraction and simplification, not only in terms of constructing a taxonomy for families of models. The proposed classification is based upon the author's experience in urban modelling rather than upon any particular theoretical stance, and thus, the scheme is likely to reflect personal biases and interpretations. Moreover, the classes are based upon dichotomous groupings which reflect extreme limits, and consequently, many of the models discussed here will fall between classes. Therefore, the essential purpose of this classification is to introduce certain concepts and techniques rather than providing an exhaustive set of boxes into which individual models can be placed.

A simple distinction between *substantive* issues based upon the system being modelled and *design* issues reflecting techniques and styles of modelling serves as the basis for the classification. It is worth dealing with these two issues in turn, then integrating them into the overall classification. With regard to substantive issues, a distinction between *partial* and *general* models is useful. In the sense implied here, partial models deal with models which simulate one subsystem of the urban system whereas general models attempt to simulate two or more subsystems. For example, the retail shopping model designed by Lakshmanan and Hansen (1965) is taken to be a partial model whereas the Upper New York State model (Lathrop and Hamburg, 1965) which simulates residential, retail, and industrial subsystems is clearly general. Although traffic (trip-distribution) models are not usually included in discussions of land·use modelling, in this context such models would be partial.

A second important substantive distinction relates to the behavioural focus of the model. Most of the urban models discussed here are based upon *non-optimising behaviour*, in the sense that activities locate in a non-optimum way. Yet certain types of model attempt to simulate *optimising behaviour*; for example, the Penn-Jersey residential location model designed by Herbert and Stevens (1960) was based upon an operational statement of the land market drawn from Alonso's theory which assumed that consumers maximised their utility. This model was set up to maximise the consumers' aggregate rent-paying ability, the proxy for utility. This distinction in terms of optimisation relates to other notions such as the normative or non-normative emphasis in classification and the continuum from descriptive to predictive to prescriptive modelling. Classifications based upon these concepts have been constructed by various researchers (Harris, 1968; Lowry, 1965) but these distinctions really reflect the role of the model, as a descriptive tool useful in understanding and as a tool used as a predictive or even prescriptive generator in the planning and design processes. For some time social scientists have distinguished between these two roles implying that different models would be required for each but it appears that the concept of optimisation can be applied to all models, thus opening up the possibility that any kind of urban model has potential within the design process. If this argument is accepted then urban models can be regarded as independent of any optimum or normative framework. For example, the land-use plan design model built by Schlager (1965) in which urban development is allocated by linear program, thus minimising total location cost, is based upon a very crude model of the urban system but incorporating a sophisticated optimisation routine. This is in contrast to models such as the Pittsburgh model (Lowry, 1964) which are less crude simulations of reality but with no optimisation characteristic whatsoever.

A third substantive distinction which has been widely debated during the short history of urban modelling relates to the question of time. Whether or not a model reflects *static* elements of urban structure or *dynamic* elements depends largely upon the theory around which the model is based. Most urban economic and geographic theory is static, describing structure at one cross-section in time or at best, comparative static incorporating some long-term and often imputed equilibrium. Therefore most urban models simulate the static observable structure of cities. Yet the Systems Approach has brought in its wake the concept of dynamics in that any system has a structure, and a behaviour which changes the structure through time. It is interesting to note that those urban models which are dynamic or quasi-dynamic in character, are based on much more meagre rations of theory than their static equivalents; the model designed by Forrester (1969) and regression-based models such as the EMPIRIC (Hill, 1965) bear out this observation. A final substantive distinction concerns the classic economic divide between *micro* and *macro*. Questions of spatial scale immediately come to mind in this regard, and the term *urban* rather than regional, city, or land-use model has been chosen in this book precisely to neutralise these questions of scale. Yet micro and macro also relate to the level of activity aggregation. The most micro of urban models involve theories attempting to explain the behaviour of individuals whereas macro-models deal with groups, institutions or larger aggregations of activity. In this sense, the distinction is based on micro- and macro-economic considerations, and is often a useful general indicator as to the amount of data required for calibration of an urban model.

Design characteristics of urban modelling mainly involve technical factors concerning the mathematical formulation and solution procedures used. There are many possible classifications for the field of mathematics is rich in concepts, and thus, only those most familiar to the author and those which involve the models described here will be used. A division into *linear* and *non-linear* models based upon the intrinsic non-linearity or otherwise of the equation systems involved is relevant. But there are limitations to this distinction: a model might be both linear and non-linear at different levels of specification or in its different parts. For example, the discrete state, discrete time ergodic Markov process can be solved as a system of linear difference equations although the equations describing its transition probabilities might be non-linear. However, this classification is useful for most of the statistically-based regression models are linear in contrast to the intrinsic non-linearity of gravity-type models. Another distinction due to Harris (1968) is in terms of whether or not the system is solved *simultaneously* or *sequentially*. This frequently relates to whether or not the model is static or dynamic for in static models, cross-sectional relationships require simultaneous solution whereas temporal behaviour is clearly sequential. However simultaneous relationships often have to be solved sequentially in an iterative or trial and error fashion due to the intractable structure of the system. Lowry's Pittsburgh model provides such an example, for a stable distribution of activities cannot be derived simultaneously but is the result of an iterative process in which outputs are fed back as inputs until a convergence limit is attained.

Classification according to the solution procedure can also be framed as *analytic* solution or *simulation*. Analytic solution procedures do not involve any form of iteration: such procedures are relatively direct in comparison with simulation in which the solution is gradually reached in stages. Clearly, analytic solution and simulation often relate to simultaneous and sequential processes. Typically, the parameters of simultaneous linear systems can be derived analytically whereas sequential models such as those involving time based on linear difference equations, are solved recursively or sequentially by simulation. In actual fact, most of the urban models to be introduced here involve some degree of simulation in that they are based upon hybrid algorithms, and thus they are often referred to as simulation models, although this usage is somewhat more general than the precise technical interpretation of the term. The final distinction presented here relates to classification of model variables, and follows conventional mathematical terminology. Variables are often classified as dependent or independent of each other in the system; more specifically, variables might be *exogenous* to the system, that is originating outside the system or *endogenous*, that is predicted by the system itself. Each of the models mentioned earlier could be classified using the distinctions outlined above. This is sometimes a difficult task and although it can be quite illuminating, the reader is referred to the seminal papers of

Lowry (1965), Harris (1968) and Wilson (1968) where the first generation urban models are reviewed in these terms. In later chapters, models will be mainly referred to using the notion of partial and general, static and dynamic generalisations which seem to be the most important features of the models introduced in this book.

The process of model design

Harris's definition of a model as 'an experimental design based on a theory' contains the essence of the model-building process. In theory, urban models are designed according to a formal process which can be stated in the following terms: hypothesis formulation; observation, data collection, programming; calibration, parameter estimation; testing, verification, evaluation; prediction. This process is self-explanatory and embodies elements similar to other design processes such as architectural and engineering design (Asimow, 1962). It contains a strong theme relating to the scientific method in which hypotheses are conjectured and refuted by experiment, by new observation but most importantly by insight. Most modelling ventures coincide to some degree with this formal process but as with any seemingly closed system, it must be seen within a wider context. The basic question involving the choice of theory upon which the hypothesis and model is structured and the goal of refuting the hypothesis by calibration, testing, verification and evaluation is meaningless if seen as one single project: the choice of hypothesis rests on a more fundamental paradigm which in any one period of time, governs developments in the field (Kuhn, 1962). The same comment applies to refinement or refutation of the hypothesis: only through time can a model be 'verified' in any conventional sense of the word, and thus the terms used here to describe the modelling process may appear somewhat presumptuous; this is reason enough for the reader to be a little tolerant of terminology in a field as new as this one.

If it is hard to disentangle longer-term goals from shorter-term attempts at hypothesis testing and evaluation, it is equally hard to separate out the model design process from wider processes such as planning and urban design. It appears that for any one process, it is always possible to find a meta-process within which the original process sits, thus implying a hierarchy of processes like a set of Chinese boxes. This is particularly difficult when it comes to extracting scientific method from model design and model design from plan design. This problem has been admirably discussed by Chadwick (1971) who contrasts the similarities and differences between the search for truth in a scientific sense, the solution of problems in an empirical sense, the design of artifacts in a mechanical sense, and the planning of adaptive teleological systems to which the designer belongs. An attempt to contrast urban model design with science on the one hand and planning on the other is presented diagrammatically in Figure 1.2. Between these three processes lie shifts in outlook and goals which are encountered when trying to find a common thread linking all three. Suffice it to say that urban model design draws from and hopefully contributes to both planning and science, and thus elements of these two streams are to be found implicitly and explicitly throughout the field of urban modelling.

Model design and plan design

The process of model design within the meta-process of plan design has already been discussed and the role of existing models in planning was ascribed as neutral. This conventional wisdom is based upon the notion that analysis, design and evaluation of any urban or regional system can be aided and amplified through modelling. Although few would dispute the need to design a model relevant to each particular stage of the planning process, in actual fact similar models have been proposed and used at every stage. The role for modelling in understanding and analysis is perhaps the most straightforward but the use of models in forecasting, design and evaluation needs careful and sensitive foresight. This difficult

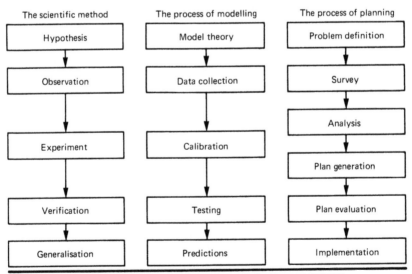

The many feedbacks which can occur during these processes are
too complex to portray and thus have been excluded.

Fig. 1.2. Scientific method, planning method and the method of model design.

and hazy area involving the balance between what can and should be optimised in planning and the restrictions on optimum values imposed by the existing reality are somewhat perilous subjects to negotiate with models. Often, control over the model's input may not coincide with the elements which can and should be controlled by the plan and this has repercussions which are difficult to resolve.

In the analysis and understanding stages of the plan design process, urban models can be calibrated and evaluated against the system of interest and the propriety of the model can be thus determined. As the model can be seen as a mechanism which generates a response to a particular stimulus, such responses being determined by the structure of the model, it is largely up to the planner as to whether or not such stimulus-response mechanisms serve to help in design or plan-evaluation. If the planner judges the stimulus to be capable of control, and the responses not, then the model might be an eminently useful design tool. If the planning process is seen as a process of matching and integrating optimality with reality, then the model might be more useful as an evaluation tool. For example, Echenique, Crowther and Lindsay (1972) have used a simple urban model to predict a series of indicators measuring the accessibility of activities to one another. For a series of new town plans, the model is applied and indicators predicted and compared with the set of indicators predicted from a naturally evolving town. In this way, an implicit evaluation of the efficiency of a series of urban forms is made.

Apart from the use of models to sketch the implications of alternative plans, the use of such models in a conditional sense has been widely exploited (Lowry, 1965). In particular, models designed to test the impact of a major change in the urban system on the existing structure have been used; such impacts are usually predicted in a one-shot fashion to some often unspecified future date by which time the system is assumed to have reacted and moved to a new equilibrium. This long-term impact analysis can be useful both for assessing the effect of large-scale changes and for assessing the sensitivity of the model. Moreover, it suggests that the real use of these models in prediction is not in any absolute way but in a relative fashion contrasting different possibilities. In terms of the planning process, a final note should be made of the suggested use of such models in implementation, specifically in monitoring the trajectory of the system. Much has been made of these suggestions by planners with little experience of modelling, and it does appear that although these sentiments are laudable, urban models are as yet too crude to apply in this fashion. In time the planning process may become more systematic and the models easier to develop, but until then, the hope of using models in monitoring will very much remain in the realms of speculation.

This whole question of model design and plan design is fraught with difficulties, often due to a lack of understanding between model-builders and planners. Indeed, Lee (1973) sees one of the major stumbling blocks with regard to the development of first generation models as due to the fact that model-builders had little appreciation of the planners' design tasks whereas planners had little idea of the model-builders' limitations in constructing models with a comprehensive capability. This problem is probably more severe in North America than in Britain, where there is a strong tradition of planning as a design science. Yet the problem exists and only the education of planners and model-builders in each others' science and art will help resolve these conflicts.

Style in urban modelling

The fact that so many different traditions and disciplines are reflected in urban modelling means that many different styles have developed. In particular, the styles originating from engineering and economics are quite different and worthy of some comment. The engineering style is perhaps deterministic and typically mechanistic, with less emphasis upon theory and more upon operationality. Thus, there is a certain measure of arbitrariness in such models which has led to poignant criticism and the accusation that modelling is technocracy. In contrast, the style characteristic of economics, in particular of micro-economics, is found in much more theoretical, less operational models of the, urban system. Such models tend to be less comprehensive than their mechanistic counterparts and they are dominated by the search for behavioural underpinnings. A variety of models has developed around these two major traditions, many of them attempting to build upon both traditions and styles, although there are very few models which appear to have captured an essence of theory together with an operational formulation. Hopefully, this synthesis is being attempted in developments in Britain (Batty, 1972a) and in the second generation wave of models at present being constructed in North America. Some of the models presented in later chapters of this book will attempt to capture some of this flavour.

Differences in approach are often transmitted as differences in presentation and formulation of the model. The engineering tradition has led to many models being expressed as algorithms rather than systems of equations in formal algebra. Theoretical economic models of the urban system are usually expressed in such formal terms, but several hybrid models especially those based upon linear regression, are treated in statistical terms. This diversity in style ranging from systems analysis to formal algebraic presentation has led to an openness of mind in urban modelling which is a rare combination of circumstances in any field. Some synthesis has been attempted, for example in the work of Wilson (1970*a*) and in the work of Ingram *et al.* (1972), but there is an urgent need for comparative work. Too often this synthesis has reflected a blunt coupling or stringing together of models, thus laying open such schemes to criticism based on error propagation and arbitrariness. Progress can only occur through more sensitive integration where both theoretical and operational criteria are considered.

In the quest to improve urban models, advances are needed in both theory and practice, in research and development. An attitude of mind in which the intrinsic difficulties of modelling ill-defined systems are recognised must be cultivated, in contrast to the extreme prejudice which has dominated the development of the field in the last decade. In some senses urban modelling represents the frontier between the clash of cultures, science versus art, and the clash of temperaments, rigour versus speculation. In these terms urban modelling must be regarded as both science and art, a combination which although not new must now be regarded as essential in the application of the phenomena of science to the phenomena of man. One of the major goals of this book is to try to weave a middle way between the theory and practice of urban modelling. The presentation of modelling ideas will be organised in the following chapters from the simple to the more complex, which necessarily means from partial to general, from static to dynamic, from aggregated to disaggregated. In the next two chapters, the elementary theories and algorithmic forms of several well-established partial and general modelling strategies will be explored, as a necessary preliminary to the operational development of such models in later chapters.

2. *Models for generating and allocating urban activities*

This chapter is perhaps the most important in this book, for here the foundations are laid upon which all the urban models to be discussed in later chapters are built. Many of the techniques and theories central to this approach to urban modelling are presented here in their most elementary form and this chapter also suggests how certain principles of model design described in the first chapter can be applied. The models to be developed are partial rather than general in two senses. First, several of these models attempt to simulate the structure and behaviour of single subsystems of the urban system such as the residential or retail sectors of activity although these models may account for the influence of other sectors on the particular sector of interest. The general approach to modelling adopted in this book begins with such partial models and treats these models as the basic *building blocks* used to construct more general and more complex models. Second, some of the models presented are more general, thus dealing with two or more subsystems of the urban system, but are partial in the sense that these models simulate only one facet of the system; some of the models described treat the generation of urban activities independently from the location of these same activities, and are therefore partial in this respect.

Another distinction needs to be made here between static and dynamic approaches to modelling. Although this has already been discussed in the previous chapter, it is important to emphasise that most of the models dealt with in this book are essentially static in that they describe the structure of the urban system at one cross-section in time. As all the variables pertaining to such models are measured at the same instant of time, the various mathematical forms associated with these models are not notated with regard to time. A further point needs to be made concerning the types of equation systems developed in this chapter. Such equation systems for partial models are relatively simple and can usually be understood without resort to various mnemonics such as flow charts. This is in direct contrast to the equation systems of the next chapter which are complex, and such a progression from simple to complex follows the process of constructing more general models from partial models.

20

Apart from the categories into which urban models can be classified outlined in the previous chapter, an understanding of models can be developed from two specific standpoints which, although somewhat arbitrary, do find an expression in practice. Models can be discussed in terms of the *generation* or the *allocation* of activities or land uses in the urban system. This distinction reflects the way in which the spatial dimension is handled; in considering models which generate or derive activities from other activities, the spatial dimension is implicit, whereas in treating models which allocate activities, space is explicit for activities which are allocated to different subdivisions of the space. To show that this distinction is not as unrealistic as might first appear, two examples are pertinent. The general regional input–output model (Isard *et al.*, 1960) is a model which is designed solely to generate activities, and although this generation occurs in a space such as a region, such activities are not allocated within the space. On the other hand, the residential model of Greensborough (Chapin and Weiss, 1968) is designed to allocate a given residential population to discrete subdivisions of a town. The residential population is not generated by the model but is exogenous to the simulation.

There are of course several models which both generate and allocate activities but, in general terms, such models are usually more complex than models which only generate or allocate. Although this division between generation and allocation serves to simplify the presentation of urban models, it also reflects ways in which various hypotheses or theories about the workings of the urban system are derived. More complex models are formed not only by synthesising partial models of different urban subsystems but also by integrating methods for allocating and generating activities. In this chapter, the distinction between models which generate and models which allocate is rigidly maintained and this helps to highlight the way in which very different hypotheses about the system are built up. In the next chapter, however, the distinction between generation and allocation is relaxed as more complex models are built up from these partial models. But first, before these partial models are described, it is worth while providing a general orientation to the approach taken in developing various hypotheses and theories concerning the workings of the urban system.

An approach to urban systems theory

In outlining this approach, the classical distinction between macro-analysis and micro-analysis as it is perceived in economics is retained, for this distinction helps to clarify the argument. This approach to modelling follows the tradition of economics in the broadest possible sense, and in particular of macro-economics. The theories which form the basis of the models presented here mainly relate to economic relationships within the urban system which are described statistically; for example, hypotheses such as those governing the patterns of trip-making behaviour, and the processes whereby changes in activities affect other activities, are measured using methods of statistical analysis. This approach is in contrast to the micro-economic viewpoint where the causes and effects of urban structure and behaviour are more rigorously sought. The micro-theoretical approach is often richer and more complex than the macro-approach although it is usually easier to develop macro-theory which can be tested in a formal sense against the real world.

It is important not to overplay this distinction between macro and micro for many theories appear to contain elements of both approaches. Perhaps a more fruitful way of describing these approaches to analysis is through the concept of aggregation. The concept of aggregation can be applied to the way in which the urban system is treated in time and space as well as in terms of its critical variables. Many researchers, notably theoretical geographers such as Berry (1964), have identified the key features of urban theory in terms of the system's attributes or variables, and its spatial and temporal dimension. The theories and models discussed here can be described in these terms according to their level of aggregation. Concerning the attributes of the urban system such as its structural characteristics – activities and land uses, the theories are highly aggregated; activities such as residential or retail populations are not partitioned by income or economic group or by indices such as social class. In terms of the spatial dimension, the theories are disaggregated rather than aggregated, for the space to which the theory or model refers is partitioned into subspaces or zones. However, the particular level of spatial aggregation is usually determined by various operational characteristics which are discussed in later chapters. With regard to the temporal dimension, theories and models which treat time both in an aggregated and in a disaggregated way are presented: most of the models to be described are static but later these models are made dynamic by disaggregation of the temporal dimension.

A general approach to the classification of theories and models which exhibits a close correspondence to this argument has been suggested by Lowry (1968). In reviewing urban development models, Lowry suggests 'a theory of the urban land market in paradigm'. By the term paradigm, Lowry means a conceptual frame of reference useful for contrasting and comparing models of the urban system. Lowry's approach to modelling presents the urban system as a mechanism for resolving conflict between various groups who require land for their various purposes. The paradigm is specifically related to the processes for resolving such conflict by clearing the market of any excess demands or supplies of land. Lowry defines the urban system as consisting of sites and establishments and transaction periods – the necessary prerequisites to the operation of the land market. By aggregating sites to locations, establishments to activities and transaction periods to discrete time units, Lowry shows how many different models can be compared using the paradigm. In this view, there is no conflict between macro or micro, or between aggregate and disaggregate, for different theories and models simply express different ways of building up an understanding of the urban system.

This approach to urban modelling is certainly partial in the sense that only one of many approaches is developed but there are important reasons why such a macro approach has been adopted. To construct operational models, such an approach appears at the present time to be most relevant although eventually other approaches may gain the ascendency: this is a matter for future research. Yet although this approach is partial, the treatment of the urban system is intended to be as comprehensive as possible. Most of the major subsystems, residential, retail, manufacturing and transport, are modelled singly and jointly in this book. Of the few attempts at organising the diverse elements of the urban system into comprehensive theories, the work of Chapin (1965) is of relevance. Chapin's approach to the study of spatial phenomena is based on two complementary abstractions: the first involves a behavioural interpretation of the urban system and focuses on the definition of activities and interactions. Any set of particular activities and their associated interactions is called an *activity system* and Chapin defines activities as within-place interactions. This view is similar to the view of activity allocation developed later in this chapter which considers activities as summations or integrations of interaction. The second abstraction concerns the physical adaptation of these activity systems. Space is adapted to accommodate these activities, and channels are constructed to contain the interactions between these activities. Chapin also relates this descriptive classification to the processes of change through time, the concept of lags between the location and spatial adaptation of these activities, and the changes in interactions and channels.

Many of the theories presented in the following pages are elementary and obvious. The construction of intricate and complex theoretical structures is not a feature of this macro-approach for here the emphasis is upon the development of hypotheses which can be efficiently modelled in an operational context. Consequently, there is little discussion of theory *per se* and the origins of such theories are only briefly indicated. The focus is upon the techniques used to model theory and upon the analy-

tical methods necessary to fit hypotheses to the real world. To introduce
such theories of the urban system, methods for generating urban activities
will be described first.

The generation of urban activities

The generation of urban activities is sometimes considered as part of that
body of techniques known as forecasting. Such forecasts usually treat
space implicitly and are time-dependent in the sense that activities are
generated or derived from other activities during some period of time.
Probably the best-developed forecasting techniques in a planning context
are those used to derive estimates of population and such techniques are
usually based upon the following relationship

$$P(t+1) = (1+b-d+m)P(t) = qP(t). \tag{2.1}$$

Population $P(t+1)$ is generated at time $t+1$ from population at time t
called $P(t)$ using a growth factor q. This factor is derived from the birth
rate b, the death rate d and the net migration rate m. There are many
forecasting schemes based on equation (2.1) and the reader can find
a detailed treatment in the works of Keyfitz (1968), Rogers (1968), and Rees
and Wilson (1976). Population-forecasting models of this type will not
be considered further for, in this chapter, methods for generating activities
at one cross-section in time are required.

The type of model described in this section relates the population sector
to the employment sector at any particular point in time. Unlike population-forecasting methods, such models are based on the assumption that
both sectors are necessary to explain the structure and behaviour of the
urban system. The employment sector is subdivided into a *basic* sector
and a *non-basic* or *service* sector and the approach implied by these
distinctions is known as *economic base theory*. The basic sector of employment is usually defined as export-oriented employment, embracing
industries and production processes in which the final product is exported
out of the particular system of interest. It is assumed that the location of
basic industries is not dependent upon other activities in the system and
that the overall growth path of the system is directly linked to change in
the basic sector. Such industries have been called by Alexandersson (1956)
city-forming in contrast to the city-serving industries of the service sector.
As the name suggests, the service sector depends upon the basic sector
and upon the population sector in that this sector provides the services
for these other sectors. Furthermore, the location of these service industries
is assumed to relate to the locational patterns of other sectors.

There are many problems of defining and measuring the economic base and a useful discussion of these problems is given in a paper by Massey (1973). Although this problem will not be discussed in any detail in this book, it will be considered further in later chapters, particularly Chapters 4 and 5. For the purposes of this chapter, it is sufficient to note the distinction between service and basic employment. An elementary form of the economic base hypothesis can be succinctly stated by the following functions

$$P = f(E),$$
(2.2)

$$S = f(P).$$
(2.3)

In (2.2), population P is expressed as some function of total employment E and in (2.3), service employment S is some function of population. Equations (2.2) and (2.3) highlight the essential structure of the economic base method and an explicit form for this hypothesis is derived if linear functions are adopted. The hypothesis can now be completely stated in three equations

$$P = \alpha E, \quad \alpha > 1,$$
(2.4)

$$S = \beta P, \quad 0 < \beta < 1,$$
(2.5)

$$E = E^b + S.$$
(2.6)

Equations (2.4)–(2.6) are the fundamental identities of the economic base hypothesis which must hold in any closed system of regions or towns. Equation (2.6) is an accounting relation in which E^b is basic employment. The constants α and β have the following interpretation. Rearranging (2.4), it is clear that α must be an inverse activity rate defined as

$$\alpha = \frac{P}{E}.$$
(2.7)

In a similar fashion, β is called a population-serving ratio which is defined as

$$\beta = \frac{S}{P}.$$
(2.8)

There are two major methods for analysing the identities of the economic base hypothesis. First, there is a direct method of analysis which is called the analytic form and second, there is an indirect method which is called the expanded form. These two methods of analysis will now be discussed in turn.

The analytic form of the economic base method

The objective of economic base method is to express the derived variables of population and service employment in terms of basic employment.

By substituting (2.6) into (2.4), population can be expressed as

$$P = \alpha E = \alpha E^b + \alpha S. \tag{2.9}$$

Rearranging (2.9) and expressing service employment S in terms of population from (2.5), population can be generated from basic employment in the following way

$$P - \alpha \beta P = \alpha E^b, \tag{2.10}$$

$$P = \alpha E^b (1 - \alpha \beta)^{-1}. \tag{2.11}$$

Equation (2.11) is usually referred to as the reduced form of (2.4) and, in a similar way, reduced forms can easily be calculated for (2.5) and (2.6) (Beach, 1957). In (2.11), the term $(1 - \alpha \beta)^{-1}$ acts as a scalar which converts basic population αE^b to total population P in one step. In short, this is the multiplier which contains both the direct and indirect effects of changes in basic employment on other activities. From the previous definition, it is obvious that $(1 - \alpha \beta)^{-1} > 1$ when $0 < \alpha \beta < 1$. The commonsense of this assertion is seen by expanding $\alpha \beta$ from (2.7) and (2.8)

$$\alpha \beta = \frac{P}{E} \frac{S}{P} = \frac{S}{E}, \quad 0 < \frac{S}{E} < 1.$$

The multiplier in (2.11) acts in exactly the same way as the income multiplier in macro–economics (Allen, 1967) and this economic base multiplier is similar to the multiplier in input–output economics (Artle, 1961) which is examined later.

It is possible and indeed desirable to disaggregate the service sector further in this simple model into consumer services S_1 and producer services S_2. As services refer both to employment and to population, it is reasonable to suppose that this distinction is realistic. There are now four rather than three fundamental identities; equation (2.4) is as before, and (2.5) and (2.6) are rewritten as

$$S_1 = \beta_1 P, \quad 0 < \beta_1 < 1, \tag{2.12}$$

$$S_2 = \beta_2 E, \quad 0 < \beta_2 < 1, \tag{2.13}$$

$$E = E^b + S_1 + S_2. \tag{2.14}$$

β_1 and β_2 are population-serving and employment-serving ratios respectively. By undertaking a similar process of manipulation and substitution to that outlined above, a new reduced form is derived,

$$P - (\alpha \beta_1 + \beta_2) P = \alpha E^b, \tag{2.15}$$

$$P = \alpha E^{\mathrm{b}}[1 - (\alpha\beta_1 + \beta_2)]^{-1}. \tag{2.16}$$

By dividing (2.16) by α, total employment E can be generated, and by multiplying E by β_2 and adding the product of β_1 and (2.16), total service employment S is derived. The multipliers in (2.11) and (2.16) are equivalent; in other words

$$\alpha\beta_1 + \beta_2 = \alpha\beta,$$

as can easily be shown by making the appropriate substitutions. The indirect effects of the multiplier are implicit in the above equations yet it is possible to derive the multiplier by tracing through these indirect effects explicitly. In the next section, the expanded form of the economic base method demonstrates the process which is generated by these indirect effects.

The expanded form of the economic base method

From an input of basic employment E^{b}, the indirect effects of this input on other activities can be traced by applying the identities (2.4), (2.12) and (2.13) in a sequential fashion. First, basic population $P(1)$ can be derived from basic employment using (2.4)

$$P(1) = \alpha E^{\mathrm{b}}. \tag{2.17}$$

The consumer services associated with $P(1)$, called $S_1(1)$, and the producer services relating to E^{b}, called $S_2(1)$, are calculated using (2.12) and (2.13) respectively

$$S_1(1) = \beta_1 P(1) = \beta_1 \alpha E^{\mathrm{b}}, \tag{2.18}$$

$$S_2(1) = \beta_2 E^{\mathrm{b}}. \tag{2.19}$$

Adding (2.18) and (2.19) gives the first increment of service employment $S(1)$

$$S(1) = \beta_1 \alpha E^{\mathrm{b}} + \beta_2 E^{\mathrm{b}} = E^{\mathrm{b}}(\alpha\beta_1 + \beta_2). \tag{2.20}$$

This sequence of operations in (2.17)–(2.20) is now repeated by generating a second increment of population $P(2)$ associated with $S(1)$. Second increments of producer and consumer services are then derived from $P(2)$ in a similar manner. These equations are listed below, thus demonstrating the iterative nature of this process

$$P(2) = \alpha S(1) = \alpha E^{\mathrm{b}}(\alpha\beta_1 + \beta_2), \tag{2.21}$$

$$S_1(2) = \beta_1 P(2) = \beta_1 \alpha E^{\mathrm{b}}(\alpha\beta_1 + \beta_2), \tag{2.22}$$

$$S_2(2) = \beta_2 S(1) = \beta_2 E^{\mathrm{b}}(\alpha\beta_1 + \beta_2). \tag{2.23}$$

Adding (2.22) and (2.23) and rearranging gives

$$S(2) = \beta_1 P(2) + \beta_2 S(1) = E^b(\alpha\beta_1 + \beta_2)^2. \qquad (2.24)$$

Working through this process it is clear that the increment of population or service employment on any iteration m can be derived using the following recurrence relations

$$P(m) = \alpha E^b(\alpha\beta_1 + \beta_2)^{m-1}, \qquad (2.25)$$

$$S(m) = E^b(\alpha\beta_1 + \beta_2)^m. \qquad (2.26)$$

To calculate total employment E, basic employment E^b and the increments of service employment $S(m)$ must be summed,

$$E = E^b + (\alpha\beta_1 + \beta_2)E^b + (\alpha\beta_1 + \beta_2)^2 E^b + \ldots + (\alpha\beta_1 + \beta_2)^m E^b. \qquad (2.27)$$

Then as $m \to \infty$, total employment E and total population P can be expressed as follows

$$E = E^b \sum_{m=0}^{\infty} (\alpha\beta_1 + \beta_2)^m, \qquad (2.28)$$

$$P = \alpha E^b \sum_{m=0}^{\infty} (\alpha\beta_1 + \beta_2)^m, \qquad (2.29)$$

where $(\alpha\beta_1 + \beta_2)^0 = 1$. Examining (2.28) and (2.29) as $m \to \infty$, it is clear that these summations converge to a limit for $0 < (\alpha\beta_1 + \beta_2) < 1$ as shown previously. Therefore

$$\lim_{m \to \infty} (\alpha\beta_1 + \beta_2)^m = 0. \qquad (2.30)$$

In (2.28) and (2.29) there is a converging geometric series whose summation can be expressed analytically as

$$\sum_{m=0}^{\infty} (\alpha\beta_1 + \beta_2)^m = [1 - (\alpha\beta_1 + \beta_2)]^{-1}. \qquad (2.31)$$

Although the convergence implied by (2.31) is intuitively obvious, formal proofs can be found in most books on elementary algebra (Parry-Lewis, 1964). Substituting (2.31) into (2.28) and (2.29) gives the analytic expressions for total employment and population which were derived in the previous section

$$E = E^b[1 - (\alpha\beta_1 + \beta_2)]^{-1}, \qquad (2.32)$$

$$P = \alpha E^b[1 - (\alpha\beta_1 + \beta_2)]^{-1}. \qquad (2.33)$$

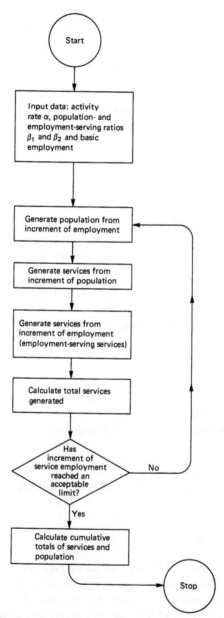

Fig. 2.1. The sequence of operations in generating population and services from basic employment.

The equivalence of the analytic and expanded forms of the economic base method is obvious from a comparison of (2.33) with (2.16).

The sequence of operations contained in equations (2.17)–(2.29) is easily grasped from the flow chart presented in Figure 2.1. This flow chart shows the essential structure of the solution method: the importance of this diagram cannot be overemphasised, for this method of presenting the economic base hypothesis forms the basis of several models presented in later chapters. Both the analytic and expanded forms of method are used as part of more general models in Chapter 3, but in terms of the expanded form, it is important to investigate the rate at which the procedure converges. If the rate of convergence is slow, it may be necessary to speed up the process by approximation.

To examine the rate of convergence, the actual percentage and the cumulative percentage of activity generated at any iteration m can be derived. Taking first the population $P(m)$ as a percentage of total population P, this percentage called ψ can be written as

$$\psi = \frac{P(m)}{P} = (\alpha\beta_1+\beta_2)^{m-1}[1-(\alpha\beta_1+\beta_2)]. \qquad (2.34)$$

Equation (2.34) can be simplified to

$$\psi = (\alpha\beta_1+\beta_2)^{m-1}-(\alpha\beta_1+\beta_2)^m, \quad 0 < \psi \leqslant 1. \qquad (2.35)$$

If the same process is carried out with the service employments, identical equations to (2.35) are derived. The cumulative percentage of population called Ψ can be calculated by summing the total increments generated up to iteration m and dividing by total population. The expression for Ψ is as follows

$$\Psi = \frac{\sum\limits_{k=0}^{m} P(k)}{P} = \sum\limits_{k=0}^{m-1}(\alpha\beta_1+\beta_2)^k[1-(\alpha\beta_1+\beta_2)]. \qquad (2.36)$$

Equation (2.36) can be simplified to

$$\Psi = 1-(\alpha\beta_1+\beta_2)^m, \quad 0 < \Psi \leqslant 1. \qquad (2.37)$$

Equations identical to (2.37) can also be derived for the cumulative percentage of service employments. From equations (2.34)–(2.37), convenient convergence limits for the iterative process can be worked out. For example, it is clear from (2.37) that the percentage error ξ between the predicted and actual quantity of activity is

$$\xi = (\alpha\beta_1+\beta_2)^m. \qquad (2.38)$$

Given any ξ within which convergence of the process is required, then the minimum number of iterations m to achieve this can be directly calculated by transforming (2.38) as follows

$$m = \frac{\ln \xi}{\ln (\alpha\beta_1 + \beta_2)}. \tag{2.39}$$

Equation (2.39) is an extremely useful expression for finding out how quickly the process converges.

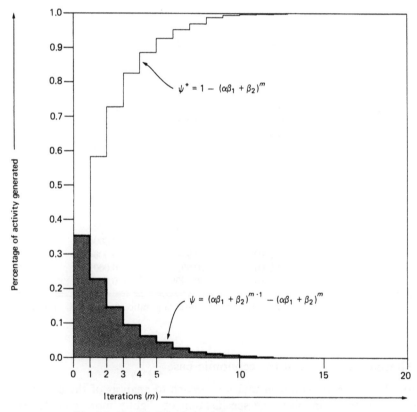

Fig. 2.2. Graphical analysis of the economic base method.

Before this section is concluded, it is worth while examining the convergence properties of a real example. Using data from the Reading subregion, a plot of equations (2.35) and (2.37) is made in Figure 2.2. As can be seen from this graph, these simple difference equations converge quite rapidly. Table 2.1 records data pertinent to this example and also lists the percentages and error term computed from equations (2.35), (2.37) and (2.38).

TABLE 2.1. *Convergence of the expanded form of economic base method*

Iteration m	Percentage ψ from (2.35)	Cumulative percentage Ψ from (2.37)	Error ξ from (2.38)
1	0.3520	0.3520	0.6479
2	0.2282	0.5801	0.4198
3	0.1478	0.7279	0.2720
4	0.0957	0.8237	0.1762
5	0.0620	0.8857	0.1142
6	0.0402	0.9260	0.0739
7	0.0260	0.9520	0.0479
8	0.0168	0.9689	0.0310
9	0.0109	0.9798	0.0201
10	0.0070	0.9869	0.0130
11	0.0045	0.9915	0.0084
12	0.0029	0.9945	0.0054
13	0.0019	0.9964	0.0035
14	0.0012	0.9977	0.0022
15	0.0008	0.9985	0.0014
16	0.0005	0.9990	0.0009
17	0.0003	0.9993	0.0006
18	0.0002	0.9995	0.0004
19	0 0001	0.9997	0.0002
20	0.0001	0.9998	0.0001

NOTE: activity rate $\alpha = 2.9941$, population-serving ratio $\beta = 0.2164$, multiplier $(1-\alpha\beta)^{-1} = 2.8405$.

Alternative models of the economic base

An alternative yet complementary approach to analysis of the economic base hypothesis involves the specification of slightly more complex relationships which are usually fitted using statistical methods. Where comparisons of several different regions or towns are required in terms of the economic base relation, linear regression analysis is often used and the models are formulated accordingly. The work of Weiss and Gooding (1968) provides a useful example of such an approach. Weiss and Gooding formulate a simple two-equation economic base model in the following way; they use (2.6) which is repeated below and a variant of (2.13)

$$E = E^b + S, \qquad [(2.6)]$$

$$S = a + gE. \qquad (2.40)$$

a and g are parameters of the equation. The reduced forms for (2.6) and for (2.40) are derived by substitution and are given as

$$E = a(1-g)^{-1} + E^b(1-g)^{-1}, \qquad (2.41)$$

$$S = a(1-g)^{-1} + gE^b(1-g)^{-1}. \qquad (2.42)$$

From (2.41) and (2.42) it is clear that $(1-g)^{-1}$ is the multiplier; Weiss and Gooding suggest that such a model can be fitted using regression analysis, although they maintain that it is preferable to fit (2.42) rather than (2.41) to data so that the bias caused by including basic employment in total employment is avoided.

As a further example of this approach, Isard and Czamanski (1965) have fitted a more complex economic base model to data for several different-size classes of a North American city. The identities for this model are listed below with the accounting relation (2.14) repeated

$$P = a_1 + g_1 E, \qquad (2.43)$$

$$S_1 = a_2 + g_2 P, \qquad (2.44)$$

$$S_2 = a_3 + g_3 E^b, \qquad (2.45)$$

$$E = E^b + S_1 + S_2. \qquad [(2.14)]$$

a_1, a_2, a_3, g_1, g_2 and g_3 are parameters of the model. Isard and Czamanski have fitted a reduced form of this model by regressing population against basic employment and have found that the population multiplier varies widely between different classes of city. However, more constant multipliers were derived by fitting the model to marginal changes in population and employment over a ten-year period. These kinds of analyses illustrate fairly elementary approaches to the use of economic base analysis but many researchers have attempted to improve the economic base hypothesis by the use of input–output analysis.

Artle (1961) has shown that there are obvious relationships between economic base and input–output analysis, and these are worth stating here. The general input–output model organises the production–consumption process into intermediate and final products or demands; intermediate products are required to produce final products and such processes set up commodity flows between the various sectors of the economy. In relation to economic base theory, the products may be measured in terms of employment required in each sector but often products are measured in neutral indices such as monetary units. The economy might be divided into K sectors and the gross output or product of sector i called x_i can be written as

$$x_i = \sum_{j=1}^{K} x_{ij} + y_i, \tag{2.46}$$

where x_{ij} is the commodity flow from sector i to sector j $(i, j = 1, 2, ..., K)$ and y_i is the final product in sector i. The commodity flow x_{ij} can be expressed as a proportion of gross output x_j by

$$a_{ij} = \frac{x_{ij}}{x_j}. \tag{2.47}$$

The proportions a_{ij} are usually called the technical input–output coefficients and indicate the quantity of product i required to produce one unit of product j. Using (2.47), equation (2.46) can be rewritten as

$$x_i = \sum_{j=1}^{K} a_{ij} x_j + y_i. \tag{2.48}$$

As in economic base analysis, it is possible to derive a reduced form for (2.48) expressing x_i in terms of the final product y_i.

It is more convenient to write the input–output equation using matrix notation, for the basic structure of the model can thus be clearly observed. Rewriting (2.48) in matrix terms gives

$$\mathbf{x} = \mathbf{A}\mathbf{x} + \mathbf{y}, \tag{2.49}$$

where $\mathbf{x}$ and $\mathbf{y}$ are $K \times 1$ column vectors of gross output and final product respectively and $\mathbf{A}$ is a $K \times K$ matrix of technical coefficients. The reduced form of (2.49) can be derived as

$$\mathbf{x} = (\mathbf{I} - \mathbf{A})^{-1} \mathbf{y}, \tag{2.50}$$

where $\mathbf{I}$ is a $K \times K$ identity matrix. The inverse matrix $(\mathbf{I} - \mathbf{A})^{-1}$ is the input–output multiplier which shows the direct and indirect output requirements per unit of final product. The similarity between economic base and input–output analysis is demonstrated by a comparison of (2.50) with (2.11). The input–output model has become the basis of more general techniques of urban analysis such as social accounting and activity analysis and in Chapter 3 this method of analysis is further discussed in relation to urban modelling. All the necessary concepts involved in the generation of activities have been introduced and in later chapters, these ideas will be taken further. In the following sections, models for allocating activities to the zones of an urban system, will now be outlined.

The allocation of urban activities

To introduce the concept of allocation, it is worth while starting by defining certain terms and notation. The terms allocation and location are used interchangeably in the text, and the process of allocating or locating urban activities involves the placement of activities in different subdivisions or zones of the spatial system. Spatial interaction is defined as the flow of activity between different zones and the summation of various flows or interactions gives rise to the location of activities, as will become clear below. All variables which refer to different zones are subscripted by *i* or *j* or both; for example, the general flow of activity between zones *i* and *j* is called T_{ij}, where the subscripts fall in the ranges $i = 1, 2, ..., I$, and $j = 1, 2, ..., J$. Summation over *i* or *j* throughout the whole range is defined below as

$$\sum_{j=1}^{J} T_{ij} = T_{i1} + T_{i2} + T_{i3} + ... + T_{iJ},$$

$$\sum_{i=1}^{I} T_{ij} = T_{1j} + T_{2j} + T_{3j} + ... + T_{Ij}.$$

Throughout the rest of this book, where the range of summation is not explicitly indicated, summation is implicit over the whole range.

Perhaps the best-known model of spatial interaction is the gravity model, so called because of its analogy with the Newtonian concept of gravity. The traditional gravity model is based on the hypothesis that the interaction between any two masses varies directly with the product of the masses and inversely with some measure of the spatial separation or cost between the two masses. The model has an interesting history in the social sciences having been adapted to many kinds of spatial phenomena and the reader is referred to an excellent article by Carrothers (1956) for a review of some early versions. A general form of the gravity model can be stated as

$$T_{ij} = GO_i D_j f(c_{ij}). \tag{2.51}$$

T_{ij} is the interaction between zone *i* and zone *j*, O_i is the activity in the origin or production zone *i*, D_j is the activity in the destination or attraction zone *j*, $f(c_{ij})$ is some function of generalised travel cost or impedance between *i* and *j*, and *G* is a constant of proportionality. A well-known form for the function of generalised travel cost has been an inverse power function of distance

$$f(c_{ij}) = d_{ij}^{-\lambda},$$

where λ is a parameter of the function and d_{ij} is the distance between *i* and *j*. The model has been applied widely, using this inverse power function, especially in geographic research, and Olsson (1965) argues that it is preferable to treat this form of model as a type of regression analysis. By manipulating and transforming the inverse power model, a linear form of equation is derived which can be fitted using linear statistical method

$$\ln \left(\frac{T_{ij}}{O_i D_j}\right) = \ln G - \lambda \ln d_{ij}. \qquad (2.52)$$

The gravity model is closely related to the potential model first introduced by Stewart (1947). The potential model is based on an attempt to measure the 'potential' of any activity which is exerted on surrounding activities. Stewart first outlined the concept in relation to the potential of population but the model has since been applied to other kinds of spatial phenomena (Stewart and Warntz, 1958).

A form of the potential model can be derived from the gravity model if equation (2.51) is summed over j. By summing interaction over j, the 'potential' amount of interaction at i is calculated.

$$\sum_j T_{ij} = GO_i \sum_j D_j f(c_{ij}). \qquad (2.53)$$

The potential at i per unit of activity in zone i, called V_i, is calculated as

$$V_i = \frac{\sum_j T_{ij}}{O_i} = G \sum_j D_j f(c_{ij}). \qquad (2.54)$$

This measure of potential has been called a measure of competition by Wilson (1970a) and forms the basis of the normalising factors in the modern gravity model. In fact, the first attempts at allocating activity to zones of the urban system were based on simple measures of potential; for example, in the model designed by Hansen (1959), new residential activity is allocated in proportion to a weighted index of employment potential.

A general framework linking spatial interaction and location models has recently been designed by Wilson (1970a) and the importance of this framework is based on the consistent way in which the level of constraint on interaction and location is treated. From this framework has come the development of a family of spatial interaction and related models (Cordey-Hayes and Wilson, 1971) but perhaps the most interesting way of interpreting this approach is through the concept of accounting. The matrix of interaction can be displayed as a table of trips whose rows and columns refer to the zones of the urban system. The summation of the trips across the columns or down the rows leads to estimates of activity originating or terminating in different zones, and such a table of accounts is presented in Table 2.2. There can be many different degrees of constraint on the origin or destination of activities in such a schema, and Wilson (1970a) has provided a systematic approach to classifying the family of models which is set up by this framework.

TABLE 2.2. *The interaction matrix as a table of accounts*

Destination zones...	1	2	3	...	j	...	J	$\sum_j T_{ij}$
Origin zones								
1	T_{11}	T_{12}	T_{13}	...	T_{1j}	...	T_{1J}	O_1
2	T_{21}	T_{22}	T_{23}	...	T_{2j}	...	T_{2J}	O_2
3	T_{31}	T_{32}	T_{33}	...	T_{3j}	...	T_{3J}	O_3
.	.	.	.	.	.	.	.	.
.	.	.	.	.	.	.	.	.
.	.	.	.	.	.	.	.	.
i	T_{i1}	T_{i2}	T_{i3}	...	T_{ij}	...	T_{iJ}	O_i
.	.	.	.	.	.	.	.	.
.	.	.	.	.	.	.	.	.
.	.	.	.	.	.	.	.	.
I	T_{I1}	T_{I2}	T_{I3}	...	T_{Ij}	...	T_{IJ}	O_I
$\sum_i T_{ij}$	D_1	D_2	D_3	...	D_j	...	D_J	$\sum_i \sum_j T_{ij} = T$

A family of spatial interaction models

The concept of a family of spatial interaction models is also due to Wilson (1970a, 1971a) and this discussion leans heavily on his work. The family of models has also been related in a general sense to variants of the gravity model as used, for example, in geographic analysis and in transportation planning, and Cordey-Hayes and Wilson (1971) demonstrate how models such as the intervening-opportunities model can be regarded as special cases within this family. Following Wilson (1970a), four models within the family are characterised and the discussion is centred around the degree of constraint to which each model is subject.

The traditional gravity model presented in equation (2.51) represents an extreme case in the family; the model is called *unconstrained* for there are no constraints on the origin or destination of activities in the urban system. For convenience, equation (2.51) is repeated

$$T_{ij} = GO_i D_j f(c_{ij}). \qquad [(2.51)]$$

However, the model is usually subject to an overall accounting constraint of the form

$$\sum_i \sum_j T_{ij} = T, \tag{2.55}$$

where T is the total amount of interaction in the system. In other words, although the origin and destination of activity is in no way constrained, the model is constructed so that the predicted amount of total interaction is equal to the observed amount. To evaluate the constant G, (2.51) is summed over i and j and substituted into (2.55) giving

$$G = \frac{T}{\sum_i \sum_j O_i D_j f(c_{ij})}. \tag{2.56}$$

Although (2.51) has been developed in analogy with Newton's gravity equation, Isard *et al.* (1960) have developed a version of this unconstrained model using a probabilistic approach.

At the other extreme in the family, there is the *production-attraction* constrained model which is essentially a distribution model. The model has to satisfy constraints on both the origins and destinations, and in terms of Table 2.2, the column and row sums have to be satisfied by the model. These constraints can be stated as follows

$$\sum_j T_{ij} = O_i, \tag{2.57}$$

$$\sum_i T_{ij} = D_j, \tag{2.58}$$

and note that

$$\sum_i \sum_j T_{ij} = \sum_i O_i = \sum_j D_j = T.$$

The appropriate model satisfying constraint equations (2.57) and (2.58) is written as

$$T_{ij} = A_i B_j O_i D_j f(c_{ij}). \tag{2.59}$$

In this case the terms A_i and B_j, which are called balancing or normalising factors, replace the constant G in (2.51). A_i and B_j can be found by summing (2.59) over j and i respectively, and these terms are evaluated as

$$A_i = \frac{1}{\sum_j B_j D_j f(c_{ij})}, \tag{2.60}$$

$$B_j = \frac{1}{\sum_i A_i O_i f(c_{ij})}. \tag{2.61}$$

The production-attraction constrained model has been used extensively as a trip-distribution model in transportation planning and many variants of this model exist. Good examples of this model are the Bureau of Public

Roads model (Bureau of Public Roads, 1968), the SELNEC traffic model (Wagon and Hawkins, 1970), and the time function iteration model (Furness, 1965).

Between these two extremes in the family of models lie many models which are subject to some constraints but not others. Two important types can be identified: the *production-constrained* gravity model and the *attraction-constrained* gravity model. The production-constrained model is subject to constraint equation (2.57) and is written as

$$T_{ij} = A_i O_i D_j f(c_{ij}), \tag{2.62}$$

$$A_i = \frac{1}{\sum_j D_j f(c_{ij})}. \tag{2.63}$$

As there are no constraints on the destination of activity in (2.62), then in general the predicted and actual amounts of activity in j are not equal, that is

$$\sum_j T_{ij} \neq D_j.$$

In a similar way, the attraction-constrained model is only subject to constraint equation (2.58), and the model is written as

$$T_{ij} = B_j O_i D_j f(c_{ij}), \tag{2.64}$$

$$B_j = \frac{1}{\sum_i O_i f(c_{ij})}. \tag{2.65}$$

These two models in (2.62) and (2.64) are usually referred to as location models, for by summing the model equations over the constrained zone subscripts, the amount of activity locating in different zones can be calculated. In the partially constrained models presented above, the constraints to which these models are subject refer to the full set of origin and/or destination zones. It is however possible to develop models which are only constrained over certain sets of zones and to illustrate such a model, the production and partly attraction-constrained model developed by Wilson (1969a) for the residential subsystem will be outlined. An outline of this model is helpful here for, in Chapter 3, this partially constrained model is embedded in a more complex urban model.

To ensure a general treatment, the set of zones is divided into two subsets Z_1 and Z_2. Z_1 refers to that subset of zones in which the quantity of activity is constrained by physical limitations on location such as capacity constraints or by policy decisions. Z_2 is the subset of zones which is not affected by such constraints. Then

$$Z = Z_1 \cup Z_2,$$

where Z is the total set of zones in the urban system, and from the definitions, it is clear that

$$\varnothing = Z_1 \cap Z_2,$$

where $\varnothing$ is the empty set. The constraints on activity can now be written using this notation

$$\sum_{j \in Z} T_{ij} = O_i, \quad i \in Z, \tag{2.66}$$

$$\sum_{i \in Z} T_{ij} = D_j, \quad j \in Z_1. \tag{2.67}$$

Equation (2.66) is the usual production constraint but note that (2.67) refers only to the subset of zones Z_1. Two linked submodels, one for each subset of zones, can be developed to account for constraint equations (2.66) and (2.67). First, for the case where $j \in Z_1$

$$T_{ij} = A_i B_j O_i D_j f(c_{ij}), \quad i \in Z, \quad j \in Z_1, \tag{2.68}$$

and second, for the case where $j \in Z_2$

$$T_{ij} = A_i O_i D_j f(c_{ij}), \quad i \in Z, \quad j \in Z_2. \tag{2.69}$$

Although equations (2.68) and (2.69) have an identical form to (2.59) and (2.62), the balancing factors A_i and B_j are slightly different, thus accounting for the differences in the constraints. Making the relevant summations and rearrangements, the balancing factors are evaluated as

$$A_i = \frac{1}{\sum_{j \in Z_1} B_j D_j f(c_{ij}) + \sum_{j \in Z_2} D_j f(c_{ij})}, \quad i \in Z, \tag{2.70}$$

$$B_j = \frac{1}{\sum_{i \in Z} A_i O_i f(c_{ij})}, \quad j \in Z_1. \tag{2.71}$$

There are other kinds of partially constrained models, accounting for trips external to the system for example; several of these models will be discussed in Chapters 8 and 9 and the book by Wilson (1970a) contains a detailed discussion of related developments. Having outlined the family of spatial interaction models, it is now appropriate to discuss the various location models which are part of this family, in greater depth, and to outline certain applications which have been made.

Location models based on gravity and potential models

Already the potential model has been mentioned in the context of location models, and one of the first attempts at modelling the urban system was

made by Hansen (1959) using such a model. Hansen's model is designed
to allocate the change in the residential population called ΔP, in a specific
time period, to zones of an urban region in proportion to a weighted measure of employment potential. Hansen assumes that employment potential
reflects the hypothesis that more people tend to live near their workplace
but Hansen recognises that land availability is also a factor which affects
residential location. As land availability increases, the potential for residential location is likely to increase, and Hansen weights employment
potential by land availability. The model has the following form

$$\Delta P_j = GL_j \sum_i E_i d_{ij}^{-\lambda}, \tag{2.72}$$

where ΔP_j is the new increment of population in j and E_i is the employment in i, L_j is the land available in j for residential development, d_{ij} is
the distance between i and j, G is a constant of proportionality and λ is
a parameter. Equation (2.72) is subject to the constraint

$$\sum_j \Delta P_j = \Delta P, \tag{2.73}$$

and the constant G can be evaluated by summing (2.72) over j and substituting into (2.73)

$$G = \frac{\Delta P}{\sum_i \sum_j E_i L_j d_{ij}^{-\lambda}}. \tag{2.74}$$

This method of allocating activity is mathematically equivalent to summing the interaction estimates given by the unconstrained gravity model
presented in (2.51). The potential model has also been used as part of
larger modelling frameworks, and in Chapter 3 its use in the original
Pittsburgh land-use model designed by Lowry (1964) will be outlined.

An attraction-constrained gravity model has been formulated by Wilson
(1969*a*) for problems of residential location. The model computes interaction between residential origins and workplace destinations, and is subject to the following constraint

$$\sum_i T_{ij} = E_j. \tag{2.75}$$

A simple form of model satisfying (2.75) is derived as an interaction model
with a negative exponential function of travel cost

$$T_{ij} = B_j W_i E_j \exp(-\lambda c_{ij}), \tag{2.76}$$

$$B_j = \frac{1}{\sum_i W_i \exp(-\lambda c_{ij})}. \tag{2.77}$$

In equations (2.76) and (2.77), W_i is a measure of locational attraction of the residential zone i. Residential population can be found by summing (2.76) over j and scaling by an inverse activity rate α

$$P_i = \alpha \sum_j T_{ij} = \alpha W_i \sum_j B_j E_j \exp(-\lambda c_{ij}). \qquad (2.78)$$

This type of model is explored further in the next chapter, where it is formulated as a production-constrained model.

Perhaps the best-known example of a production-constrained model is the retail location model first applied by Lakshmanan and Hansen (1965) to Baltimore and derived by Huff (1963) and Casey (1955) from the work of Reilly (1929). The model allocates consumer expenditures from residential zones i to shopping centres j subject to the constraint

$$\sum_j S_{ij} = c_i P_i. \qquad (2.79)$$

S_{ij} are the sales made by vendors in j to consumers in i, and c_i is the *per capita* expenditure on consumer goods in i. The model is formulated

$$S_{ij} = A_i c_i P_i W_j^{\lambda_1} d_{ij}^{-\lambda_2}, \qquad (2.80)$$

$$A_i = \frac{1}{\sum_j W_j^{\lambda_1} d_{ij}^{-\lambda_2}}. \qquad (2.81)$$

W_j is a measure of shopping centre attraction in j and λ_1, λ_2 are parameters of the model. In the original version of the model by Lakshmanan and Hansen, λ_1 was set to unity. Sales in shopping centre j can be calculated by summing (2.80) over i

$$S_j = \sum_i S_{ij} = W_j^{\lambda_1} \sum_i A_i c_i P_i d_{ij}^{-\lambda_2}. \qquad (2.82)$$

In Chapter 6, this shopping model is explored in some detail and several applications in Britain are compared. A useful review of the problems in developing such models is contained in the report by NEDO (1970).

The final model to be discussed in this section is called the intervening-opportunities model, first suggested by Stouffer (1940) in a study of residential migration. Stouffer argued that a person's propensity to migrate was not necessarily dependent upon the distance between two zones i and j but more likely to be directly proportional to the opportunities perceived at a destination j and inversely proportional to the number of intervening-opportunities between i and j. Stouffer's hypothesis was formulated as

$$T_{ij} = G \frac{D_j}{V_{ij-1}}. \qquad (2.83)$$

G is a constant of proportionality and V_{ij-1} is the number of intervening-opportunities between i and j and is defined in terms of the opportunities at any zone j as

$$V_{ij-1} = \sum_{k=i}^{j-1} D_k,$$

where the summation $i \rightarrow j-1$ is over the zones falling on the travel path between i and j. Since Stouffer's original hypothesis, the model has been extended theoretically by Schneider (1959) and Harris (1964) and the form of the model is now usually given as

$$T_{ij} = A_i O_i \left[\exp(-\lambda V_{ij-1}) - \exp(-\lambda V_{ij}) \right]. \qquad (2.84)$$

The normalising constant A_i is likely to be near unity if the model is applied to a bounded region with small external interaction. Wilson (1969a) has also shown that (2.84) can be approximated by a production-constrained gravity model of the form

$$T_{ij} = A_i O_i \lambda D_j \exp(-\lambda V_{ij-1}). \qquad (2.85)$$

So far, this chapter has been largely concerned with presenting a variety of allocation models and little has been said on the methods used to construct such hypotheses. In the next section, several methods for constructing these kinds of model will be briefly discussed.

Methods for constructing spatial interaction models

The purpose of this section is to introduce various methods and concepts which have been devised to construct theories and models of spatial inter-action and location; no formal presentation of these methods is attempted for only the conceptual development of such techniques is required. The models which have already been discussed, have been presented without recourse to any theoretical derivation, for such models have been stated heuristically. An example suffices to demonstrate the difference between the approach adopted and more formal methods. The various constraints or normalising factors introduced into many of the spatial interaction models described above are designed to ensure that the models satisfy different sets of constraints. The precise form of these factors was calculated by standard mathematical techniques of substitution and rearrangement of variables and equation structures. However, there exist more formal approaches which attempt to interpret the elements of such models as part of more rigorous theories.

The first of these methods which has been used quite widely in interpretation, if not in derivation of spatial interaction models, is largely due to Huff (1963). Huff interprets production-constrained location models in terms of probability and he uses concepts from utility theory to explain the substantive content of such models. Huff assumes that any person living in a zone i perceives a certain utility U_{ij} in travelling to any zone j, and that this utility can be expressed as a percentage of the total utility of travelling to all zones j. Such an assumption suggests that every person in the system has a certain probability p_{ij} of making a trip from i to j which can be written as

$$p_{ij} = \frac{U_{ij}}{\sum\limits_j U_{ij}}, \quad 0 < p_{ij} < 1, \quad \sum\limits_j p_{ij} = 1. \tag{2.86}$$

In the case of a shopping model, for example, the utility of travel between i and j could be hypothesised to be directly proportional to some index of shopping centre attraction $W_j^{\lambda_1}$ and inversely proportional to a function of cost or time incurred by travel between i and j, $d_{ij}^{-\lambda_2}$. Then the probability in (2.86) can be rewritten as

$$p_{ij} = \frac{W_j^{\lambda_1} d_{ij}^{-\lambda_2}}{\sum\limits_j W_j^{\lambda_1} d_{ij}^{-\lambda_2}}. \tag{2.87}$$

The shopping model presented earlier in (2.80) and (2.81) can now be written in terms of probabilities using (2.87)

$$S_{ij} = c_i P_i p_{ij} = c_i P_i \frac{W_j^{\lambda_1} d_{ij}^{-\lambda_2}}{\sum\limits_j W_j^{\lambda_1} d_{ij}^{-\lambda_2}}. \tag{2.88}$$

Just as Huff has interpreted the probability of interaction as a relationship between specific and total utility, Wilson (1970a) has described the balancing factors of spatial interaction models as measures of competition. In the case of the shopping model, the denominator of the right-hand side of (2.88) can be regarded as a measure of the competition of all shopping centres acting on the decision to shop in a particular centre. Isard et al. (1960) have also derived the unconstrained interaction model using a probabilistic approach which seeks to modify a hypothetical pattern of trips by introducing the effect of spatial cost or distance; the reader is referred to Isard's work for further details.

A completely new and general theoretical derivation of the gravity model based on the concept of entropy as used in statistical mechanics has recently been put forward by Wilson (1970a) and this method is quickly becoming the basis of the accounting framework for spatial interaction modelling, discussed earlier. The method is based upon a definition of the states and distributions which characterise the system of interest and Wilson's argument can be illustrated in relation to the interaction matrix shown in Table 2.2. A state of the system is defined as an assignment of individual persons to the pairwise links in the system which does not violate any of the constraints on movement. In terms of Table 2.2, many different sets of individuals can be assigned to make up the trip volume T_{ij} on any link without changing this volume. The pattern of trips in the system is called a distribution, and it is clear that many states are associated with each distribution. On the assumption that each state is equi-probable, the method is based on finding the most probable distribution of trips subject to any constraints.

The equation describing the frequencies of different trip distributions can be interpreted as an entropy of the system, and Wilson's method is referred to as the method of entropy-maximising. Entropy is maximised subject to accounting constraints such as those in (2.57) and (2.58) and also subject to a constraint on the cost of travel C. In the case of the production-attraction constrained model, this constraint is of the form

$$\sum_i \sum_j T_{ij} c_{ij} = C,$$

and in the case of production- or attraction-constrained models, this cost is offset by a measure of locational benefit W_j^*

$$\sum_i \sum_j T_{ij} (c_{ij} - W_j^*) = C.$$

The models which result from this maximisation procedure are similar to the family of models outlined earlier but the general function of travel cost is replaced by a negative exponential function, and the balancing factors have a mathematical interpretation. Perhaps the most important contribution which this theory makes involves the role of the constraint equations. To the model-builder, such equations represent the amount of information known about the system, and thus the approach is sufficiently general to mean that consistent models can be generated in situations where information about the problem is limited.

Although the original application of this approach was in the field of transport, Wilson has extended the method in two directions; first, disaggregated interaction models for the transport and residential sectors have been proposed and second, the method has been used to derive models which are consistent within an overall accounting framework. Wilson has developed a comprehensive set of models dealing with residential location behaviour. These models disaggregate employees by occupation and industry, and housing by physical type; furthermore, constraints are developed relating to the household budget available for housing, and such constraints bring into these models explicit data about wage rates and rents. In Chapter 10, such disaggregated models will be explored in greater depth in a practical context. In a wider sense, Wilson has shown how his approach can be used to design models which are consistent with accounting frameworks, such as those implicit in input–output analysis. These developments have been synthesised in a useful book by Wilson (1970a) and the reader is strongly advised to refer to this work which is complementary to much of the material presented in this chapter. Other methods for deriving spatial interaction models which are linked to the entropy-maximising method have been used; for example, interaction models can be derived using statistical techniques such as the method of maximum-likelihood and in Chapter 7, some of these alternate techniques will be discussed in the context of model calibration.

Alternative approaches to spatial allocation

Although most of the allocation models to be developed here are based on the concept of spatial interaction, there are other approaches to allocation and for completeness, two important processes need to be noted. In the terminology of the previous chapter, spatial interaction models are non-optimising in contrast to certain optimising models which have been used in allocation. Perhaps the best-known optimising model is based on the technique of linear programming and the structure of such a model can be clearly seen in relation to a production-attraction constrained interaction model. The model described above in (2.57)–(2.61) can be expressed as a problem in linear programming in which it is required to find a distribution of non-negative trips T_{ij} which minimise the cost of transportation C. Like the spatial interaction model, the linear programming model is subject to $I+J$ constraints of the following form

$$\sum_{j=1}^{J} T_{ij} = O_i, \quad O_i > 0, \quad i = 1, 2, ..., I, \tag{2.89}$$

$$\sum_{i=1}^{I} T_{ij} = D_j, \quad D_j > 0, \quad j = 1, 2, ..., J. \tag{2.90}$$

The objective function which is to be minimised subject to (2.89) and (2.90) can be stated as

$$C = \min \sum_{i=1}^{I} \sum_{j=1}^{J} T_{ij} c_{ij}. \tag{2.91}$$

The particular type of linear programming problem given in (2.89)–(2.91) is called a transportation problem and if such a problem is formulated consistently, a unique optimal solution to the problem has a maximum of $I+J-1$ variables (T_{ij}) different from zero (Hadley, 1962).

Linear programming has been used in several cases to allocate urban activities but there are some fundamental problems involved in applying the technique. Apart from problems caused by the linearity and additivity assumptions, the fact that only $I+J-1$ variables are positive in any solution to problems of the type given above is somewhat unrealistic for urban systems. In the case of a trip model, only a small proportion of the total links in the system would have positive trips. However, great strides are being made in adapting such models to more realistic problems and linear programming techniques are likely to become more widespread in urban allocation in the future. Yet there is no dearth of linear programming models and several applications can be mentioned. The Detroit model, designed by Ingram *et al.* (1972) at the National Bureau of Economic Research, employs a linear programming model to allocate employees to residential areas. The original Penn-Jersey housing market model proposed by Herbert and Stevens (1960) and since modified by Harris (1972) is based on a linear program which allocates persons to housing by maximising aggregate rent-paying ability; this model has been fitted to data from Hartford, Connecticut and to the Los Angeles region (Harris, Nathanson and Rosenberg, 1966). The Harris–Herbert–Stevens model is also the basis of a more general linear programming model which allocates several types of employment and population to zones of an urban system by maximising a generalised welfare function (Ben-Shahar, Mazor and Pines, 1969).

Another class of models used to allocate urban activities is based on linear models which are usually fitted by regression analysis. Such models are typically used when the model-builder has little *a priori* information on which to base a structured hypothesis. A good example of the use of this technique is in the Greensborough model (Chapin, Weiss and Donnelly, 1965) where population was allocated using a function of the following form

$$P_j = a_0 + \sum_{k=1}^{n} a_k X_{kj}. \qquad (2.92)$$

X_{kj} is a measure of some independent variable X_k in zone j, and a_k and a_0 are parameters of the model. In the Greensborough model, several tests were made to find the best combination of the independent variables X_k which explained the maximum amount of variance in the residential population. A final set of four independent variables was culled from an initial set of sixteen, and these four variables were based on accessibilities to work, to elementary schools, to the nearest major highway and to the availability of sewerage facilities. Other models such as the EMPIRIC model (Hill, 1965) are based on linear forms of allocation equation and the use of such equations in allocating basic employment to zones is examined in Chapters 11 and 12 in the context of dynamic modelling.

So far only allocation models dealing with the residential, retail or service and transport sectors of the urban system have been outlined, and no models allocating basic employment have been presented. There are considerably fewer models of the basic sector, for this sector of activity is not easy to model in a formal sense because its locational requirements are difficult to specify quantitatively. A useful review of some basic employment models which have been developed in North America is presented in a paper by Massey (1969) and the main feature of these models seems to rest on the distinction between growth and decline of various types of employment which have been treated by separate submodels. Several of the models have been based on linear forms such as that given in (2.92).

In concluding this chapter, it is worth summarising the main themes which have been developed. From discussion of models to allocate urban activities, these activities have been mainly regarded as summations or integrations of activity flows or interactions. The distinction between allocation and generation, which has served to introduce many partial models, will no longer be retained in Chapter 3 when these partial models are stitched together to form more general models. The stitching process involved in the next chapter will attempt to set the simple equation systems of this chapter in more complex structures which will later be developed as operational models.

3. *Urban models as systems of equations*

The fundamental concern of this chapter is with the design of equation systems for urban models. Equation systems will be discussed and presented in terms of the assemblage of partial models and with regard to methods for effecting fast and efficient solutions to the modelling problem. The synthesis of various partial models described in the previous chapter into more general models involves questions of assessing the degree to which the model's structure reflects the workings of the urban system, for such questions are basic to an evaluation of the model's relevance. Although various equation systems may be excellent structural analogues of the real world, such systems are sometimes intractable and therefore of little use in operational modelling. In contrast, there are models based on systems of equations which imply efficient solution methods but are poor analogues of reality. Looked at in this light, the problem of model design is to invent equation systems which are good representations of reality and which are soluble in a fast and efficient way.

Although the models to be outlined here all spring from the approach to urban systems theory outlined in the last chapter, there is still a wide diversity in modelling styles which have been developed within this narrow field. Of interest here is the fact that style is usually reflected by the way in which the model is assembled as a system of equations. Before such models are presented however, it is worth while stating and defining certain pertinent characteristics of equation systems: the following commentary is in no way exhaustive and must not be regarded as a comprehensive summary of the factors influencing the design of equation systems, for the intention of this section is solely to introduce certain features pertaining to the urban models discussed later in this chapter.

The design of equation systems

Perhaps the most basic distinction between equation systems involves the various methods used in solving such systems. Harris (1968) has identified both simultaneous and sequential methods of solution and, in terms of the classification given in Chapter 1, equation systems which are solved

49

simultaneously use analytic solution methods, whereas sequential solution methods are based on simulation. As pointed out previously, there is another interpretation of simultaneous and sequential methods which involves questions of statics and dynamics. It is logical to suppose that static models which attempt to describe the structure of the urban system at one cross-section in time are formulated as systems of simultaneous equations, whereas dynamic models are formulated using sequentially linked equations. Although static models may attempt to describe the location of various activities simultaneously, frequently such systems are not tractable using analytic methods, and sequential iterative methods must be employed. In this chapter, both types of method are illustrated in connection with the design of static models.

There is a classic rule of model design which although obvious, is essential to the design of any equation system. A necessary but not sufficient condition for the solution of a system of equations states that there must be as many equations as unknowns. This condition is best seen in the solution of simultaneous equations, and the condition is elaborated in most books on elementary and linear algebra (Hadley, 1961; Stephenson, 1961). There are of course other conditions involved in the solution of equation systems relating to interdependence and consistency within the set of equations. These matters will not be pursued here but they are briefly mentioned at a later point in this chapter. Although it is often a trivial matter to check by a count of equations and unknowns, whether or not the equation system is determined, this is sometimes a useful method to highlight the structure of the equation system. In three of the models introduced here, a count of equations and unknowns is made, although these equation systems are presented in a way which makes their determination fairly obvious.

Systems of simultaneous equations which cannot be solved using standard linear methods, such as the Gauss–Jordan method or Cramér's rule, can often be solved by sequential methods such as iteration. Methods of iteration involve the calculation of new and hopefully better solutions to a problem based on information obtained from earlier solutions. In this chapter, first-order iteration is used to obtain solutions to several of the models, and such an iterative process can be written as

$$x_{m+1} = f(x_m),$$

where x_{m+1} is the solution derived on iteration $m+1$ which is some function of the solution on the previous iteration m. Whether or not such a procedure converges depends upon the particular properties of the equation system under study; such concepts of convergence will be examined for each of the equation systems presented later. A further important distinction which was made in Chapter 1 is relevant here; the distinction between linear and non-linear equation systems usually affects the method of solution. Linear systems can generally be solved using standard methods whereas non-linear systems are more difficult to handle, and often require extensive iteration.

Linear equation systems have been extremely well developed in economic analysis for problems involving demand and supply, and econometricians have built up a large body of statistical technique involved in fitting such equation systems to data. There are many treatments of the classic econometric problem of correctly identifying and specifying the variables to be included in such systems and it is of interest to note that there is a class of urban models which has been based on such econometric methods. The EMPIRIC model of the Greater Boston region is the model around which several similar linear models have been developed (Hill, 1965), and an excellent discussion of the problems in developing this kind of model is contained in an article by Masser, Coleman and Wynn (1971). To show the particular forms of model which have been developed, a simple two-equation model is presented below.

$$\Delta P_j = a_0 + a_1 \Delta E_j^b + a_2 X_j + \epsilon_p,$$
$$\Delta S_j = b_0 + b_1 \Delta P_j + b_2 X_j + \epsilon_s.$$

ΔP_j, ΔS_j and ΔE_j^b are changes in population, service employment and basic employment respectively, in zone j over a given time period, X_j is an exogenous variable measured in zone j, a_0, a_1, a_2, b_0, b_1 and b_2 are coefficients which are estimated by some statistical method, and ϵ_p and ϵ_s are the respective error terms for the population and service employment equations. If ΔE_j^b is exogenous to the model, then this simple econometric model reflects the economic base hypothesis explained in Chapter 2 and it can be regarded as the econometric equivalent of the Lowry model presented later in this chapter. This model has been formulated as a triangular or recursive system (Walters, 1968; Christ, 1966) and the coefficients can therefore be estimated using Ordinary Least Squares.

These kinds of econometric model will not be discussed further in this book, but it is important to note that such models are formulated as fairly simple systems of equations to which fast and efficient solution methods can be applied. Such models reflect very simple hypotheses about the functioning of the urban system, much simpler in fact than the hypotheses contained in the models to be presented here which are structurally more complex and somewhat harder to solve. In contrast to the econometric urban models, the models presented here are non-linear and techniques of solution and calibration are based on methods such as iteration and search.

There are two ways in which the partial models of the last chapter can be assembled into more general models and these reflect the relative strengths of the coupling together of submodels. Firstly, there are models which are built up as a series of allocation models and these models are referred to as *loosely-coupled*. In such cases, the partial models are simply arranged in sequence with some simple link between each submodel. Secondly, there are models which are *strongly-coupled* in the sense that the generation of activities is used as a device to link the partial models. Such generation models are in themselves strongly-coupled and different partial models can be mapped onto their structure. In loosely-coupled models, constraints on the location of activity are usually easier to handle than in strongly-coupled models and although most of the models dealt with here are strongly-coupled, the first model to be presented is by contrast loosely-coupled.

An opportunity-accessibility model

An urban model allocating different activities to zones of a region and based on Stouffer's concept of intervening-opportunities has been designed and tested in Upper New York State by Lathrop, Hamburg and Young (1965). The model is designed to allocate activities given at a set of origin-centres in the region to a set of destination-locations. There is no submodel dealing with the generation of these activities which are loosely-coupled through the intervening-opportunities concept. The activities are allocated according to a particular order in which activities are ranked by their ability to compete with one another. Given M activities each referred to as O^m, the structure of the model can be presented as

$$O^1 \to O^2 \to \ldots \to O^m \to \ldots \to O^M,$$

where the arrows indicate the order in which activities are allocated. Opportunities are defined as the product of available land and the density of activity, and as each activity is allocated, available land is reduced and the opportunity surface is recomputed. Therefore, the first activity has the greatest choice of locations in the region and the last activity has the least choice.

The structure of this type of model can best be presented as a formal system of equations and the following outline is based on the description given by Lathrop and Hamburg (1965), and by Walker (1968). The set of activities at each origin centre i, O_i^m is exogenous to the model and each activity is allocated to destination-locations j. Without loss of generality, it is assumed that the total number of origin zones I is equal to the total number of destination zones J, and that these sets are in one–one correspondence. For any activity O^m, the opportunity surface is first derived by computing intervening-opportunities on the minimum time path for each i–j link in the system

$$V_{ij-1}^m = \sum_{k=i}^{j-1} \delta_k^m L_k(m). \tag{3.1}$$

V_{ij-1}^m is the cumulative number of opportunities for activity m between i and j, δ_i^m is the density of activity m in zone k expressed in unit area, and $L_k(m)$ is the land available in zone k on iteration m of the model. It is important to note that the superscript m refers to activity type whereas the bracketed postscript (m) refers to the iteration; as a different activity is allocated on each iteration, these indices are in practice equivalent. The activity O_i^m is allocated using the intervening-opportunity model devised by Schneider (1959), presented previously as equation (2.84). Then

$$T_{ij}^m = A_i^m O_i^m \exp\left(-\lambda V_{ij-1}^m\right)\{1 - \exp\left[-\lambda \delta_j^m L_j(m)\right]\}, \tag{3.2}$$

$$A_i^m = \frac{1}{[1 - \exp\left(-\lambda V_{ij}\right)]}. \tag{3.3}$$

T_{ij}^m is the flow of activity m from i to j and (3.2) and (3.3) are simplifications of (2.84). The total quantity of activity m locating at j, called D_j^m, is found by summing (3.2) over i

$$D_j^m = \sum_i T_{ij}^m, \tag{3.4}$$

and the land required for D_j^m called L_j^m is found by applying an inverse density function to (3.4)

$$L_j^m = (\delta_j^m)^{-1} D_j^m. \tag{3.5}$$

The land available for activity allocation on the next iteration $m+1$ is found by subtracting (3.5) from the land presently available

$$L_j(m+1) = L_j(m) - L_j^m. \tag{3.6}$$

To ensure that (3.6) is never negative, the land available is checked as follows. If

$$L_j(m+1) < 0, \tag{3.7}$$

then

$$L_j(m+1) = 0. \tag{3.8}$$

The model now proceeds to allocate activity O^{m+1}; $L_k(m+1)$ is substituted for $L_k(m)$ in equation (3.1), and (3.1)–(3.8) are reiterated until all activities have been allocated. A flow chart of this procedure is presented in Figure 3.1.

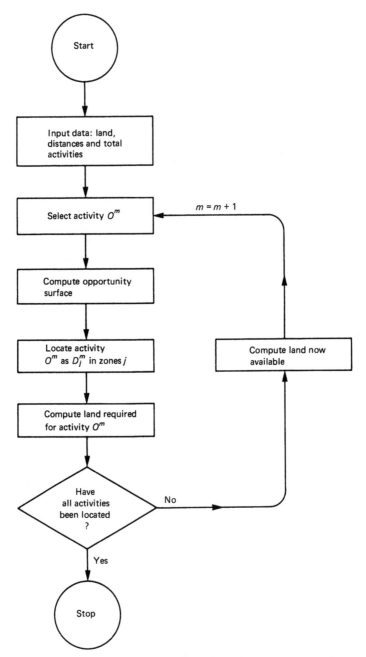

Fig. 3.1. Generalised flow chart of the Lathrop–Hamburg opportunity-accessibility model.

It is clear that the coupling of activities is accomplished through (3.6) above and that this coupling is the device used to establish the 'pecking order' assumed by each activity. Although this competitive order may partially reflect the mechanics of the urban land market, the method used to allocate activities is somewhat rigid and the equation system is much more of a solution method than an analogue of the workings of an urban system. Although the model could be elaborated in several ways, for instance by refining the constraints procedure or by incorporating a sub-model to predict densities, this simple form has already been used to evaluate a wide range of land-use strategies in the Buffalo–Niagara Falls area. A version of this model has also been used by the Cleveland–Seven Counties Transportation Study (Walker, 1968) and in this particular application, the opportunity surface was derived from rank-ordered indices of accessibility computed from a potential formula similar to (2.54). Both non-residential and residential land uses were allocated by the model and a set of 'passive' land uses such as transportation, local open-space etc. were calculated as a simple proportion of the allocated uses. The paper by Walker (1968) contains a worked example of this model.

These models have been used to allocate the changes in activity rather than the total stocks of activity in Upper New York State and Cleveland, although it is conceivable that total stocks could be allocated. Further developments of this framework, however, are likely to involve stronger couplings between the various activities and some means to generate such activities. The models presented hereafter all attempt to integrate methods of allocation with means for generating these same activities.

The Lowry model

One of the first models to couple the generation with the allocation of urban activities was designed by Lowry (1963, 1964) for the Pittsburgh urban region. The Lowry model, as it has come to be called, organises the urban space-economy into activities on the one hand, and land uses on the other. The activities which the model defines are population, service employment and basic (manufacturing and primary) employment, and these activities correspond to residential, service and industrial land uses. The model's major operations are carried out at the level of activities and these activities are translated into appropriate land uses by means of land-use/activity ratios. The division of employment into service and basic sectors is required because the model uses the analytic form of the economic base method, as described in Chapter 2, to generate service employment and population from basic employment. It is worth while repeating the definitions of these activities. Basic employment is defined as that employ-

ment which is associated with industries whose products are exported outside the region, whereas the products of service employment are con-
sumed within the region. It is assumed that the location of basic industry
is independent of the location of residential areas and service centres, and
although this assumption appears to be weak, it is taken as a point of
departure in the Lowry model.

Besides deriving population and service employment, this model also
allocates these activities to zones of the urban region. Population is
allocated in proportion to the population potential of each zone and
service employment in proportion to the employment or market potential
of each zone. Constraints on the amount of land use accommodated in
each zone are also built into the model. The model ensures that population
located in any zone does not violate a maximum density constraint which
is fixed on every zone. In the service sector, a minimum size constraint is
placed on each category of service employment, and the model does not
allow locations of service employment to build up which are below these
thresholds. Service employment is disaggregated into three types: neigh-
bourhood, local or district, and metropolitan, each reflecting a different
scale of activity in the urban region.

Having located the various activities in accordance with the predetermined constraints, the model also tests the predicted distribution of population against the distribution used to compute potentials to find out
whether the two distributions are coincident. Lowry argues that it is necessary to secure consistency between these distributions because the model
uses distributions of population and employment to calculate the potentials which indirectly affect the predicted location of these same variables.
Consistency is secured by feeding back into the model predicted population and employment and reiterating the whole allocation procedure until
the distributions input to the model are coincident with the outputs.

To firm up the structure of this model and to emphasise the solution
method adopted by Lowry, the model will be presented as a formal system
of equations. This interpretation of the model adopts a different notation
from that used in the original formulation, and this particular notation
and method of presentation used, is necessary so that the various models
outlined in this chapter can be contrasted. The model divides up the
spatial system into four sets of zones which differ in regard to the constraints imposed. Z_1 is the set of zones in which there are no locational
constraints, Z_2 the set in which there are only residential constraints, Z_3
the set in which there are only service constraints and Z_4 the set in which
there are both residential and service constraints. During the operation
of the model, zones may be continually shifting between these four sets
if the locational constraints are violated. The diagram opposite shows

an abstracted division of the spatial system into these four sets.

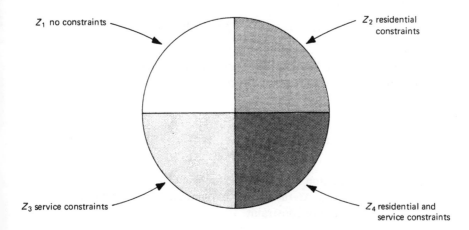

The total set of zones is called Z and, from the definitions above,

$$Z = \bigcup_{s=1}^{4} Z_s.$$

It is also obvious that the intersection of these four sets is equal to the empty set $\varnothing$

$$\varnothing = \bigcap_{s=1}^{4} Z_s.$$

Each variable will be defined as it appears in the text, although the notation is the same as in the previous chapter; the index m refers to the inner iterations of the model necessary to ensure that the locational constraints are satisfied, whereas the index n refers to the outer iterations necessary to ensure a stable co-distribution of input and output variables. At the start of the model's operations, $m = 1$, and $n = 1$, and it is important to note that $Z = Z_1$, and that $Z_2, Z_3, Z_4 \subseteq Z_1$. Also total employment in zone i, $E_i(1)$ is equal to the basic employment E_i^b, and the total land for service uses $L_j^r(1)$ is equal to zero. The zonal subscripts i and j fall in the range $i,j = 1, 2, ..., I$, and the superscript k is in the range $k = 1, 2, ..., K$.

Total population is first calculated using the analytic form of economic base relationship given in Chapter 2 as

$$P(m) = \alpha\sum_i E_i^b(1-\alpha\sum_k \beta^k)^{-1}, \quad i \in Z. \tag{3.9}$$

P is the total population in the region, α is the inverse activity rate and

β^k is the ratio of service employment k to total population, called here the kth population-serving ratio. Total land use available for housing $L_j^h(n)$ is now calculated from

$$L_j^h(n) = L_j - [L_j^u + L_j^b + L_j^r(n)], \quad j \in Z. \tag{3.10}$$

L_j is the total amount of land in each zone and the superscripts u and b on L_j denote unusable land and land used for basic industry respectively. Population is allocated to zones in proportion to a normalised population potential defined as

$$P_j(m,n) = P(m) \frac{\sum_i E_i(n) f^1(c_{ij}),}{\sum_i \sum_j E_i(n) f^1(c_{ij})}, \quad i \in Z, \quad j \in Z_1, Z_3. \tag{3.11}$$

$P_j(m,n)$ is the population allocated to zone j, and $f^1(c_{ij})$ is a function of generalised travel cost. At this point, population in each zone must be tested against the density constraint. If

$$P_j(m,n) \geqslant \delta_j L_j^h(n), \quad j \in Z_1, Z_3, \tag{3.12}$$

then
$$P_j(m,n) \in Z_2, Z_4. \tag{3.13}$$

δ_j is a density coefficient which converts $L_j^h(n)$ into population. In the constrained sets Z_2 and Z_4, population is set equal to the maximum population allowed. The index m is increased to $m+1$ and

$$P_j(m+1,n) = \delta_j L_j^h(n), \quad j \in Z_2, Z_4. \tag{3.14}$$

The population to be reallocated is found by taking the constrained population in Z_2 and Z_4 from total population

$$P(m+1) = P(m) - \sum_j P_j(m+1,n), \quad j \in Z_2, Z_4. \tag{3.15}$$

Then, $P(m+1)$ is substituted into (3.11), and (3.11)–(3.15) are reiterated until

$$P_j(m+1) \leqslant \delta_j L_j^h(n), \quad j \in Z. \tag{3.16}$$

When equation (3.16) is satisfied, the allocation of population is in accord with the residential constraints. m is set equal to 1, and service employment in each class k, S^k, is now calculated

$$S^k = \beta^k \sum_j P_j(m,n), \quad j \in Z. \tag{3.17}$$

Service employment is now allocated to each zone i, S_i^k, in proportion to an employment or market potential defined as

$$S_i^k(m,n) = S^k \frac{\sum_j g^k P_j(m,n-1)f^2(c_{ij}) + q^k E_i(n)}{\sum_i \sum_j g^k P_j(m,n-1)f^2(c_{ij}) + \sum_i q^k E_i(n)}, \quad i,j \in Z. \quad (3.18)$$

On the first iteration of the full model ($n = 1$), $P_j(m,n-1)$ is equal to the observed population P_j. g^k and q^k are empirically-determined coefficients showing the relative importance of population and employment in the index of market potential. $f^2(c_{ij})$ is a function of generalised travel cost. The quantity of service employment located in i must now be tested against the minimum size constraint $\min S^k$. If

$$S_i^k(m,n) \begin{cases} < \min S^k, \text{ and} \\ = \min_i S_i^k(m,n), \quad i \in Z, \end{cases} \quad (3.19)$$

then

$$S_i^k(m,n) \in Z_3, Z_4, \quad (3.20)$$

and

$$S_i^k(m+1,n) = \begin{cases} 0, i \in Z_3, Z_4, \\ S^k \dfrac{S_i^k(m,n)}{\sum_i S_i^k(m,n)}, \quad i \in Z_1, Z_2. \end{cases} \quad (3.21)$$

$S_i^k(m+1,n)$, $i \in Z_1, Z_2$ is substituted into equation (3.19), and (3.19) and (3.20) are reiterated until

$$S_i^k(m+1,n) \geqslant \min S^k, \quad i \in Z. \quad (3.22)$$

At this point in the model, all activities have been allocated. The index n is increased to $n+1$, and service employment is converted to land use, using the ratios e^k,

$$L_i^r(n+1) = \sum_k e^k S_i^k(m,n), \quad i \in Z. \quad (3.23)$$

A test for residential land availability on the next iteration is now required. If

$$L_i^r(n+1) \geqslant L_i - (L_i^u + L_i^b), \quad i \in Z, \quad (3.24)$$

then

$$L_i^r(n+1) = L_i - (L_i^u + L_i^b), \quad i \in Z. \quad (3.25)$$

Total employment is now calculated as

$$E_i(n+1) = E_i^b + \sum_k S_i^k(m,n), \quad i \in Z. \quad (3.26)$$

The predicted distribution of population $P_j(m,n)$ must be tested against the distribution $P_j(m,n-1)$ which is used to compute the market potentials. The aim is to generate a consistent distribution of input and output variables and if the predicted distribution is within a certain limit ξ_p of the input distribution, the two distributions are judged to be consistent. In other words,

$$P_j(m,n) = P_j(m,n-1) \pm \xi_p, \quad j \in Z. \tag{3.27}$$

If (3.27) is not satisfied, then $L_i^r(n+1)$ and $E_i(n+1)$ are substituted into (3.10) and (3.11) respectively, and (3.8)–(3.26) are reiterated until (3.27) is satisfied. A similar test on the predicted distributions of employment $E_i(n)$ and $E_i(n-1)$ could also be incorporated in like manner. At the beginning of each outer iteration of the model, the inner iteration m is set equal to 1, and $Z_1 = Z$ as before. A diagrammatic interpretation of this sequence of operations is presented in Figure 3.2. The model has been presented following the method used to solve the equation system but it is worth while listing the major equations, thus high-lighting the essential structure of the model. In Table 3.1, seven equations are listed and a count of the number of equations in the expanded system is made. By counting the number of endogenous variables in equations (3.9)–(3.27), it is clear that the number of equations equals the number of unknowns and the system is therefore determined. The method used to establish consistency between input and output variables is a device used to reflect the simultaneous nature of relationships in the system, thus emphasising the strong coupling between the submodels.

TABLE 3.1. *Structural equations of the Lowry model*

Equation number	Form of equation	Number of equations
(3.9)	$P(m) = \alpha \sum_i E_i^b (1 - \alpha \sum_k \beta^k)^{-1}, \quad i \in Z$	1
(3.10)	$L_j^h(n) = L_j - [L_j^u + L_j^b + L_j^r(n)], \quad j \in Z$	I
(3.11)	$P_j(m,n) = P(m) \dfrac{\sum_i E_i(n) f^1(c_{ij})}{\sum_i \sum_j E_i(n) f^1(c_{ij})}, \quad i \in Z, \ j \in Z_1, Z_3$	I
(3.17)	$S^k = \beta^k \sum_j P_j(m,n), \quad j \in Z$	K
(3.18)	$S_i^k(m,n) = S^k \dfrac{\sum_j g^k P_j(m,n-1) f^2(c_{ij}) + q^k E_i(n)}{\sum_i \sum_j g^k P_j(m,n-1) \ f^2(c_{ij}) + \sum_i q^k E_i(n)}, \quad i,j \in Z$	KI
(3.23)	$L^i(n+1) = \sum_k e^k S_i^k(m,n), \quad i \in Z$	I
(3.26)	$E_i(n+1) = E_i^b + \sum_k S_i^k(n,n), \quad i \in Z$	I

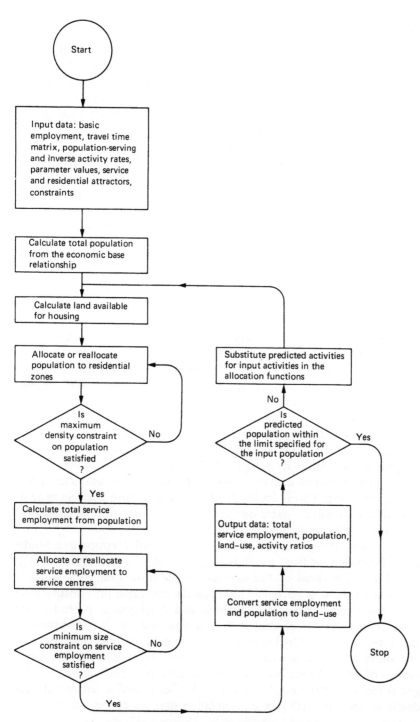

Fig. 3.2. Generalised flow chart of the Lowry model.

The model outlined above is based on a widely accepted theory of spatial structure, and is perhaps one of the best expressions of the paradigm governing the development of the field of urban modelling alluded to in the Introduction. The economic base mechanism which is used to derive service employment and population from basic employment, and the allocation of activities according to potentials reflect important determinants of spatial structure. Although it is obvious that the model is based on a highly simplified interpretation of the urban system, the model is so organised as to permit further disaggregation of its variables. This flexibility means that the detailed structure of the model can be closely matched against available data, and this is frequently a critical factor in spatial forecasting. In North America, several land-use models have been proposed which take the development of this model further, and at this stage it is worth while reviewing some of these as they provide additional insights into the theory and application of the model.

Development of the Lowry model

The first development of Lowry's model was made by the CONSAD Research Corporation as part of the Pittsburgh Community Renewal Program (Crecine, 1964). This model, called the Time Oriented Metropolitan Model (TOMM), adopted the basic structure of the model outlined above but also permitted a disaggregation of population into different socio-economic groups. It was felt that by disaggregating the model in this way, the explanatory power of the model would be increased. Furthermore, this model was restructured to account explicitly for the time element in forecasting. In using the Lowry model for forecasting, there is an assumption that *all* activities respond to changes in potential in a given projection period. This is obviously not the case because a certain proportion of activity will be stable during the forecast interval. The model was therefore revised to account for such inertia.

At present, three versions of the Time Oriented Metropolitan Model exist. Following on from the Pittsburgh version, Crecine (1968) has suggested a further revision. The structure of the revised model is basically the same as the original model although the allocation mechanisms have been made more realistic. Population and employment potentials are fairly crude measures of locational attraction, and Crecine has proposed that these be replaced by linear equations relating site rent, transport cost and other site amenities such as the availability of schools. The latest version of the model has been calibrated to data from East Lansing, Michigan (Crecine, 1969), and the model is also being used as an educational device in the METRO gaming simulation exercise at the University of

Michigan (Crecine, 1967). The model is used to show participants in the game the consequences of their decisions in terms of the spatial distribution of population and employment. This modelling effort is discussed in more detail in Chapter 11, when problems of building dynamic urban models are encountered.

Another major development of the Lowry model in which the potential models are replaced by gravity models has been suggested by Goldner (1968). Goldner's model, called the Projective Land Use Model (PLUM) has been designed for the San Francisco region, specifically for the Bay Area Transportation Study Commission, and this model allocates services and population using intervening-opportunity models. Instead of disaggregating the population or service sector, Goldner disaggregates the parameters for each of the nine counties in the Bay Area. Goldner also builds into his model zone specific activity rates and population-serving ratios to account for differences in population and employment structure. This necessitates the introduction of additional sets of scaling factors to adjust zonal populations and employment so that these activities sum to their respective regional totals.

Perhaps the most important development of the Lowry model is a theoretical one. Garin (1966) has reinterpreted the Lowry model in two ways; first, the potential models have been replaced by production-constrained gravity models and second, the expanded form of the economic base mechanism has been substituted for the analytic form. In this way, Garin has succeeded in strengthening the coupling between allocation and generation, and this model is presented formally in the following sections. At this point, it is worth while outlining the procedure used by Garin's model in simple terms as an introduction to the particular developments described later. The structure of the model can be presented as

$$E^b \to P \rightleftharpoons S,$$

where basic employment E^b is the primary input starting the process of generating population P and service employment S. These activities P and S are dependent upon each other in the following sense.

From a given distribution of basic employment, the model first finds the residential location of these workers who are employed in the basic sector, and then finds the population associated with this employment by application of an inverse activity rate. The first increment of service employment is derived from this basic population using a population-serving ratio, and this employment is then allocated to service centres. These workers require residential locations and this leads to a further increment of population and in turn to a further increment of service employment and so on. Continued application of this sequence of operations results in the derivation of smaller increments of population and service employment, and eventually a threshold is reached below which any further increments are small enough to ignore. This process is then said to have converged; the values of the inverse activity rate, and population-serving ratio ensure that these increments of population and service employment sum to their respective totals.

A version of Garin's model which incorporates constraints on allocation is presented in the following section. This model demonstrates the way in which the expanded form of the economic base method is used as a framework for synthesising the partial models of spatial allocation; the particular model outlined does not treat land uses explicitly, although it would be a simple task to translate activities into land uses using simple land-use/activity ratios as in the original Lowry model.

An Activity Allocation model

The full model will be outlined using a notation and presentation similar to that used earlier. An index m denotes the value of a variable on the inner iteration of the model. This inner iteration is used to derive the increments of service employment and population from basic employment. This differs from the Lowry model in which the sum of these increments was derived analytically using the economic base relation in (3.9). The outer iteration, denoted by the index n is used to ensure that the model satisfies the locational constraints. The previous notation will be used, and further notation will be defined when necessary.

At the start of the model's operations, $m = 1$, $n = 1$ and $E_i(1, n)$ is equal to E_i^b. The weight $B_j(n)$, $j \in Z$ on residential attraction is set equal to 1 and the weight on service centre attraction $Q_i(n)$, $i \in Z$ is also equal to 1. All zones belong to Z_1 at this stage. First, the basic employees $E_i(1, n)$ are distributed to their zones of residence

$$T_{ij}(m, n) = A_i(n) \, B_j(n) \, E_i(m, n) \, f^1(D_j, c_{ij}), \quad i, j \in Z, \qquad (3.28)$$

$$A_i(n) = \frac{1}{\sum_j B_j(n) \, f^1(D_j, c_{ij})}, \quad i, j \in Z. \qquad (3.29)$$

$T_{ij}(m, n)$ is the number of workers employed at i and living at j, and $f^1(D_j, c_{ij})$ is a function relating the attraction D_j of area j to the generalised cost of travel c_{ij} between i and j. The population living at j is found by summing (3.28) over i and applying the inverse activity rate α

$$P_j(m, n) = \alpha \sum_i T_{ij}(m, n), \quad i, j \in Z. \qquad (3.30)$$

The population at j demands to be serviced and the number of service employees demanded, $H_j(m,n)$ is found by applying the population-serving ratio β

$$H_j(m,n) = \beta P_j(m,n), \quad j \in Z. \tag{3.31}$$

In this outline of the model, the service sector is not disaggregated; in terms of the original Lowry model, $\beta = \sum_k \beta^k$. The service employees demanded at j now have to be distributed to their places of work

$$S_{ij}(m,n) = R_j(n) H_j(m,n) Q_i(n) f^2(D_i, c_{ij}), \quad i,j \in Z, \tag{3.32}$$

$$R_j(n) = \frac{1}{\sum_i Q_i(n) f^2(D_i, c_{ij})}, \quad i,j \in Z. \tag{3.33}$$

$S_{ij}(m,n)$ is the number of service employees working at i demanded by the population at j, and $f^2(D_i, c_{ij})$ is a function relating the attraction of service centres to the generalised cost of travel.

Service employment in i, called $S_i(m,n)$ can be calculated by summing (3.32) over j

$$S_i(m,n) = \sum_j S_{ij}(m,n), \quad i,j \in Z, \tag{3.34}$$

and this increment of service employment becomes the input of employment to be allocated on the next iteration of the model $m+1$. In other words

$$E_i(m+1,n) = S_i(m,n), \quad i,j \in Z. \tag{3.35}$$

At this point, the first increments of population and service employment have been generated. It is now necessary to allocate service employees to zones of residence, and $E_i(m+1,n)$ is substituted for $E_i(m,n)$ in (3.28). Equations (3.28)–(3.35) are reiterated until

$$\sum_i E_i(m+1,n) \leqslant \xi_e, \quad i \in Z, \tag{3.36}$$

and

$$\sum_j P_j(m,n) \leqslant \xi_p, \quad j \in Z. \tag{3.37}$$

ξ_e and ξ_p are limits below which further increments of service employment and population are small enough to ignore. Total population and employment predicted by the model are now approximately equal to their respective totals and these totals are calculated from

$$P_j(n) = \sum_m P_j(m,n), \quad j \in Z, \tag{3.38}$$

$$E_i(n) = \sum_m E_i(m,n), \quad i \in Z. \tag{3.39}$$

By summing equations (3.38) and (3.32) over m, matrices giving the interactions between workplace and residential areas and between residential
areas and service centres can be calculated. Zonal inverse activity rates
$\alpha_{ij}(n)$ and population-serving ratios $\beta_{ij}(n)$ can also be calculated and
these ratios help to highlight the effectiveness of the model's allocation
procedures

$$\alpha_{ij}(n) = \frac{P_j(n)}{E_i(n)}, \quad i = j, \quad i, j \in Z, \tag{3.40}$$

$$\beta_{ij}(n) = \frac{\sum_{k=2}^{m} E_i(k,n)}{P_j(n)}, \quad i = j, \quad i, j \in Z. \tag{3.41}$$

At this point, tests must be made on the allocation of activities to find
out whether the density constraints on population or the minimum size
constraints on service employment have been violated. First, if

$$\frac{P_j(n) - \delta_j L_j^h}{\delta_j L_j^h} > \xi_c, \quad j \in Z, \tag{3.42}$$

then

$$P_j(n) \in Z_2, Z_4. \tag{3.43}$$

Second, if

$$[E_i(n) - E_i^b] < \min S, \quad i \in Z, \tag{3.44}$$

then

$$[E_i(n) - E_i^b] \in Z_3, Z_4. \tag{3.45}$$

If equations (3.42) and (3.44) do not hold for any zone, then the constraints are satisfied and the simulation terminates. However, if (3.42)
and (3.44) do hold then

$$B_j(n+1) = \begin{cases} B_j(n) \dfrac{\delta_j L_j^h}{P_j(n)}, & j \in Z_2, Z_4, \\ 1, & j \in Z_1, Z_3, \end{cases} \tag{3.46}$$

and

$$Q_i(n+1) = \begin{cases} 0, & i \in Z_3, Z_4, \\ 1, & i \in Z_1, Z_2. \end{cases} \tag{3.47}$$

$B_j(n+1)$ and $Q_i(n+1)$ are now substituted into (3.28), (3.29) and (3.32),
(3.33) respectively and the whole system of equations from (3.28) to (3.47)
is reiterated until

$$\frac{P_j(n) - \delta_j L_j^h}{\delta_j L_j^h} \leqslant \xi_c, \quad j \in Z, \tag{3.48}$$

and

$$[E_i(n) - E_i^b] \geqslant \min S, \quad i \in Z_1, Z_2. \tag{3.49}$$

The sequence of operations in this model is presented in Figure 3.3.

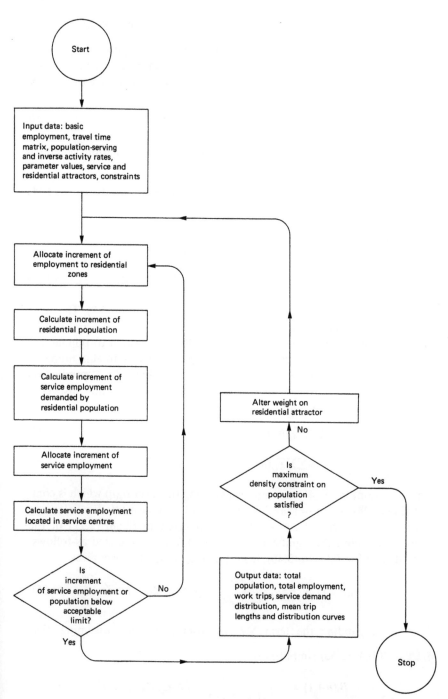

Fig. 3.3. Generalised flow chart of the Activity Allocation model.

Examination of the model reveals that the total population generated approximates the population predicted by the economic base relationship given in (3.9). By summing (3.30) over j, the following recurrence relation can be derived

$$\sum_j P_j(m,n) = \alpha\sum_i\sum_j T_{ij}(m,n) = \alpha(\alpha\beta)^{m-1}\sum_i E_i(1,n), \quad i,j\in Z. \quad (3.50)$$

Then summing (3.50) over the iterations m, total population generated in the model is given by

$$\sum_j P_j(n) = \sum_m\sum_j P_j(m,n) = \alpha\sum_i E_i(1,n)\sum_m (\alpha\beta)^m, \quad i,j\in Z. \quad (3.51)$$

Using the argument and assumptions in the section on the expanded form of the economic base hypothesis in Chapter 2, it is clear that the term $\sum_m (\alpha\beta)^m$ converges to $(1-\alpha\beta)^{-1}$ as $m\to\infty$. Then population is given by

$$\sum_j P_j(n) = \alpha\sum_i E_i(1,n)(1-\alpha\beta)^{-1}, \quad i,j\in Z, \quad (3.52)$$

which is formally identical to the population estimate in (3.9). The argument showing that service employment converges is similar and can be deduced from the fact that employment is linearly related to population.

A comment on the method of applying constraints to this model is warranted. The residential location model is subject to a production constraint on the numbers of workers leaving any zone, and also constraints on the maximum population density allowed in any zone. Formally

$$\sum_m\sum_j T_{ij}(m,n) = \sum_m E_i(m,n), \quad i,j\in Z, \quad (3.53)$$

$$\alpha\sum_m\sum_i T_{ij}(m,n) \leqslant \delta_j L_j^h, \quad i,j\in Z. \quad (3.54)$$

The constraint in (3.54) is accomplished using the term $B_j(n)$ which is computed in (3.48). To show that this term is similar to the attraction balancing factor in the partially constrained model given in (2.68)–(2.71) in the previous chapter, the significant part of (3.46) is manipulated as follows. Substituting for $P_j(n)$ in (3.46), from (3.50) and (3.51) above, gives

$$B_j(n+1) = B_j(n)\frac{\delta_j L_j^h}{\alpha\sum_i T_{ij}(n)}, \quad j\in Z_2, Z_4, \quad i\in Z. \quad (3.55)$$

Then by expanding the term $\sum_i T_{ij}(n)$ from (3.28) and assuming that $\delta_j L_j^h = f(D_j)$, (3.55) simplifies to

$$B_j(n+1) = \frac{1}{\alpha\sum_i A_i O_i f(c_{ij})}, \quad j\in Z_2, Z_4, \quad i\in Z. \quad (3.56)$$

If (2.71) is substituted into the right-hand side of (3.56) then

$$B_j = \alpha B_j(n+1), \quad j \in Z_2, Z_4, \tag{3.57}$$

and it is clear that $B_j(n+1)$ plays the same role as B_j in the production-attraction constrained gravity model. No formal proof for the convergence of $B_j(n)$ is offered here and in certain circumstances convergence may not occur, especially if zones are being continually switched from the sets Z_2, Z_4 to Z_1, Z_3. Also, the amount of land available for housing in the system can influence the speed of convergence. If

$$\sum_j \delta_j L_j^h \gg \sum_j P_j(n),$$

then convergence can be fast but if the amount of available land approaches the population to be allocated, the system may not converge in a reasonable time.

In the service centre location model, constraints on the numbers of service employees demanded by the population in each zone, and the minimum size constraint on the location of service employment are satisfied. Formally,

$$\sum_m \sum_i S_{ij}(m,n) = \sum_m D_j(m,n), \quad i,j \in Z, \tag{3.58}$$

$$\sum_m \sum_j S_{ij}(m,n) \begin{cases} = 0, & i \in Z_3, Z_4, \\ \geqslant \min S, & i \in Z_1, Z_2. \end{cases} \tag{3.59}$$

These constraints can usually be satisfied by the model but (3.59) is dependent upon the procedure used to ensure that the density constraints in the residential model are met. In concluding discussion of this model, a list and count of the major equations serve to highlight the model's structure. Table 3.2 presents such a list and the model is determined, for the total number of endogenous variables is equal to the total number of equations. The structure of this model is explored further in the following section where the system of equations is presented in simultaneous form.

There are three important differences between this model and the Lowry model. First, this model uses interaction models of a gravity type to allocate activity, in contrast to the potential functions used by Lowry. This means that trips between home and work and between home and service centre are calculated explicitly. Besides the obvious advantages of generating this information, it means that calibration procedures such as those used in trip-distribution studies, can be employed in fitting the model as is demonstrated in Chapters 6, 7 and 8. Second, the method of securing consistency between the input and output distributions used by Lowry, is not embodied in the equation system described here. Assuming that

population and employment were used as proxies for locational attraction
in the model, it would be a simple matter to feed back these variables in
the outer iteration of the model. However, this considerably complicates
calibration procedures and the difference between the inputs and outputs
might not be sufficient to warrant using this option. Third, there is more
emphasis on activities than on land use in the model. Although land use
enters the model through the maximum density constraint on population,
there is no priority given to the location of service employment as in the
Lowry model. This is largely due to the scale for which the model is intended; if the maximum density constraint on population is likely to affect
the amount of service land use, then the model could be easily extended
by adding the appropriate procedures.

TABLE 3.2. *Structural equations of the Activity Allocation model*

Equation number	Form of equation	Number of equations
(3.28)	$T_{ij}(m, n) = A_i(n)B_j(n) E_i(m, n) f^1(D_j, c_{ij}), \quad i, j \in Z$	I^2
(3.30)	$P_j(m, n) = \alpha \sum_i T_{ij}(m, n), \quad i, j \in Z$	I
(3.31)	$H_j(m, n) = \beta P_j(m, n), \quad j \in Z$	I
(3.32)	$S_{ij}(m, n) = R_j(n) H_j(m, n) Q_i(n) f^2(D_i, c_{ij}), \quad i, j \in Z$	I^2
(3.35)	$E_i(m+1) = S_i(m, n), \quad i, j \in Z$	I
(3.46)	$B_j(n+1) = \begin{cases} B_j(n) \dfrac{\delta_j L_j^h}{P_j(n)}, & j \in Z_2, Z_4 \\ 1, & j \in Z_1, Z_3 \end{cases}$	I
(3.47)	$Q_i(n+1) = \begin{cases} 0, & i \in Z_3, Z_4 \\ 1, & i \in Z_1, Z_2 \end{cases}$	I

The Garin–Harris matrix formulation

Although the model presented by Garin (1966) has already been discussed, a major feature of Garin's work involved a demonstration of the
convergence properties of the Lowry model in its expanded form using
the algebra of matrices. At about the same time, Harris (1966b), in a remarkable paper contrasting the equilibrium-seeking characteristics of
urban models, also formulated the Lowry model in matrix terms thus

revealing the simultaneous nature of the model's structure. The Activity Allocation model of the previous section can be rewritten using matrix notation and this presentation follows the Garin–Harris formulation, apart from the specification of locational constraints which are incorporated into the model. It is of interest to note that several researchers have favoured matrix notation in presenting versions of this model (Echenique, Crowther and Lindsay, 1969a; Goldner, 1968; Stradal and Sorgo, 1971) and this matrix model has already formed the basis of an efficient computer programming strategy in operational use (Batty, 1969).

As the model is operated through both inner and outer iterations, vectors referring to the inner iteration are subscripted by the index m and vectors and matrices referring to the outer iteration are subscripted by the index n, as in the model of the previous section. Before the model is introduced, two probability interaction matrices are defined. First, an $I \times J$ matrix $\mathbf{T}_n$ describes the probability that a worker who is employed in i lives at j. From (3.28), each probability $t_{ij}(n)$ is calculated as

$$t_{ij}(n) = \frac{B_j(n) f^1(D_j, c_{ij})}{\sum_j B_j(n) f^1(D_j, c_{ij})}, \quad 0 \leqslant t_{ij}(n) \leqslant 1, \quad \sum_j t_{ij}(n) = 1, \quad i, j \in Z.$$

Second, a $J \times I$ matrix $\mathbf{S}_n$ describes the probability that a person living in i will demand to be serviced at centre j. Then in analogy with (3.32), each probability $s_{ij}(n)$ is calculated as

$$s_{ij}(n) = \frac{Q_j(n) f^2(D_j, c_{ij})}{\sum_j Q_j(n) f^2(D_j, c_{ij})}, \quad 0 \leqslant s_{ij}(n) \leqslant 1, \quad \sum_j s_{ij}(n) = 1, \quad i, j \in Z.$$

The $1 \times J$ row vector $\mathbf{p}_{mn}$ and the $1 \times I$ row vector $\mathbf{e}_{mn}$ describe the population and employment distributions generated on the iterations m, n of the model.

Starting with the distribution of basic employment called $\mathbf{e}_{1n}$, a distribution of basic population $\mathbf{p}_{1n}$ is found by distributing employees to their residence zones using the matrix $\mathbf{T}_n$ and multiplying the result by the $J \times J$ scalar matrix of activity rates called $\boldsymbol{\alpha}$. Then

$$\mathbf{p}_{1n} = \mathbf{e}_{1n} \mathbf{T}_n \boldsymbol{\alpha}. \tag{3.60}$$

The service employees demanded by $\mathbf{p}_{1n}$ called $\mathbf{e}_{2n}$ are calculated by applying the $J \times J$ scalar matrix of population-serving ratios $\boldsymbol{\beta}$ and these employees are distributed to service centres using the matrix $\mathbf{S}_n$. Formally,

$$\mathbf{e}_{2n} = \mathbf{p}_{1n} \boldsymbol{\beta} \mathbf{S}_n = \mathbf{e}_{1n} \mathbf{T}_n \boldsymbol{\alpha} \boldsymbol{\beta} \mathbf{S}_n. \tag{3.61}$$

To simplify the presentation, a matrix A_n is defined from

$$A_n = T_n \alpha \beta S_n.$$

The service employees calculated in (3.61) have to be distributed to their residence zones and the associated population demands further increments of service employment. These are calculated in a similar manner to (3.60) and (3.61) by

$$p_{2n} = e_{2n} T_n \alpha = e_{1n} A_n T_n \alpha, \tag{3.62}$$

$$e_{3n} = p_{2n} \beta S_n = e_{1n} A_n^2. \tag{3.63}$$

From (3.60) to (3.63) for any iteration m, the following recurrence relations can be derived using a similar argument to that in deriving equation (3.50). Then

$$p_{mn} = e_{1n} A_n^{m-1} T_n \alpha, \tag{3.64}$$

$$e_{mn} = e_{1n} A_n^{m-1}. \tag{3.65}$$

The increments of population and employment generated in (3.64) and (3.65) can be summed over the subscripts m to derive totals. Taking the summation of employment, a $1 \times I$ row vector of total employment e_n is calculated as

$$e_n = e_{1n}(I + A_n + A_n^2 + \ldots + A_n^m), \tag{3.66}$$

where I is an $I \times I$ identity matrix. The summations for total population and employment can be written in shorter form as

$$p_n = e_{1n} \sum_{m=0}^{\infty} A_n^m T_n \alpha, \tag{3.67}$$

$$e_n = e_{1n} \sum_{m=0}^{\infty} A_n^m, \tag{3.68}$$

where A_n^0 is taken to be the $I \times I$ identity matrix I. Comparing the series representation of population and employment in (3.67) and (3.68) with (3.51) and with (2.25) and (2.26), it appears likely that these series will converge to the zero limit.

No formal proof for convergence of the matrix series is offered here, for good proofs are given by Garin (1966) and also by Hadley (1961). The series in (3.67) and (3.68) can be written as

$$(I - A)^{-1} = \sum_{m=0}^{\infty} A_n^m, \tag{3.69}$$

if and only if

$$\lim_{m \to \infty} A_n^m = 0. \tag{3.70}$$

Using (3.69), the equations for population and employment in (3.67) and

(3.68) now become

$$\mathbf{p}_n = \mathbf{e}_{1n} \, (\mathbf{I} - \mathbf{A}_n)^{-1} \mathbf{T}_n \boldsymbol{\alpha}, \tag{3.71}$$

$$\mathbf{e}_n = \mathbf{e}_{1n} \, (\mathbf{I} - \mathbf{A}_n)^{-1}. \tag{3.72}$$

Equations (3.71) and (3.72) are particularly important for the inverse $(\mathbf{I} - \mathbf{A}_n)^{-1}$ is similar to the input–output matrix in (2.50), and this inverse contains both the direct and indirect effects of basic employment in any zone i on total employment in any zone j. Furthermore, (3.71) and (3.72) have been derived analytically by Harris (1966b), thus revealing the simultaneous nature of the equation system. Perhaps the most important aspect of these results is the fact that (3.71) and (3.72) can be used to predict the distribution of population and employment in a direct fashion. As many modern computer installations have efficient library routines for manipulating and inverting matrices, the use of (3.71) and (3.72) can speed up the programming and reduce computational time, and lead to more efficient operation of the model. Although (3.71) and (3.72) dispense with the need for the set of inner iterations m, the outer iteration n used to ensure that the locational constraints are satisfied, is still needed. After (3.71) and (3.72) have been calculated, the model utilises the constraints procedure given in (3.42)–(3.49) above; new values for $B_j(n+1)$ and $Q_j(n+1)$ are predicted from (3.46) and (3.47) and a new matrix $\mathbf{A}_{n+1}$ is formed. $\mathbf{A}_{n+1}$ is substituted into (3.71) and (3.72) and this procedure is repeated until the locational constraints are satisfied.

The errors resulting from the series expansion of population and employment to any power m as in (3.66) can be calculated in a similar way to the error in (2.38). To calculate the maximum error, the norm of the matrix $\mathbf{A}_n$, called $N(\mathbf{A}_n)$, is defined.

$$N(\mathbf{A}_n) = \max_j \sum_i a_{ij}(n),$$

where $a_{ij}(n)$ is now an element of $\mathbf{A}_n$. The norm is usually defined as the maximum value of the sum of the absolute values of a_{ij} in any column j but, in this case, $a_{ij} \geqslant 0$ from a previous definition. It is interesting to note here that if $N(\mathbf{A}_n) < 1$, then this fact can be used to prove convergence of the series in (3.67) and (3.68). Such a proof was developed by Waugh (1950) to demonstrate the convergence properties of the Leontieff input–output model. The maximum percentage error ξ which arises from the summation in (3.66) to any power m can be shown to be

$$\xi \leqslant N(\mathbf{A}_n^m) \leqslant [N(\mathbf{A}_n)]^m. \tag{3.73}$$

The right-hand side of (3.73) constitutes an appropriate upper bound for the error ξ. Then the minimum number of iterations m required to bring the model to a given error ξ is

$$m \geq \frac{\ln \xi}{\ln [N(\mathbf{A}_n)]},$$ (3.74)

and Waugh (1950) has shown that if the error called ξ^* is in absolute rather than percentage terms, the minimum number of iterations m can be calculated from

$$m \geq \frac{\ln \xi^* + \ln [1 - N(\mathbf{A}_n)]}{\ln [N(\mathbf{A}_n)]}.$$ (3.75)

Using the matrix formulation, the model can be easily manipulated to demonstrate its potential. For example, if the vector of population $\mathbf{p}_n$ was already given, together with the probability and scalar matrices, it is theoretically possible to find vectors of total and basic employment by rearranging (3.71) and (3.72). Equation (3.71) is rewritten below for convenience

$$\mathbf{p}_n = \mathbf{e}_{1n}(\mathbf{I} - \mathbf{A}_n)^{-1} \mathbf{T}_n \boldsymbol{\alpha}.$$ [(3.71)]

Multiplying both sides of (3.71) by the inverses of $\mathbf{T}_n$ and $\boldsymbol{\alpha}$ gives an estimate of total employment from population

$$\mathbf{e}_n = \mathbf{p}_n \boldsymbol{\alpha}^{-1} \mathbf{T}_n^{-1} = \mathbf{e}_{1n}(\mathbf{I} - \mathbf{A}_n)^{-1}.$$ (3.76)

Basic employment can be calculated from (3.76) as

$$\mathbf{e}_{1n} = \mathbf{p}_n \boldsymbol{\alpha}^{-1} \mathbf{T}_n^{-1}(\mathbf{I} - \mathbf{A}) = \mathbf{p}_n \boldsymbol{\alpha}^{-1} \mathbf{T}_n^{-1} - \mathbf{p}_n \boldsymbol{\beta} \mathbf{S}_n,$$ (3.77)

and from (3.77) it is clear that the vector of service employment $\mathbf{S}_n$ is

$$\mathbf{s}_n = \mathbf{p}_n \boldsymbol{\beta} \mathbf{S}_n.$$ (3.78)

Harris (1966b) argues that population and service employment are likely to be extremely sensitive to the probability distribution matrices $\mathbf{T}_n$ and $\mathbf{S}_n$, and that negative values of population and service employment might result in extreme conditions. In a development of this model in Central and North East Lancashire described in the next chapter, equations (3.76) and (3.77) were used to find the impact of given distributions of population on employment. To satisfy (3.77), the vector of basic employment included both large negative and positive elements due to the peculiar behaviour of the inverse $\mathbf{T}_n^{-1}$, and in all cases severe difficulties were encountered in operating the model in this way. Such problems represent important areas for further research.

A model of urban stocks and activities

The final model to be presented in this chapter is based on a modification of Garin's formulation and is being developed by a team at the Centre for

Land Use and Built Form Studies in the University of Cambridge. In contrast to the Activity Allocation model, this model is designed to operate at the town scale, hence the emphasis on both stocks and activities. Garin's model has been extended in two ways: first, a submodel is used to allocate stocks in terms of floorspace to zones, and it is assumed that the stocks model simulates, albeit very crudely, the 'supply' side of the urban land market. Second, the model uses these stocks of floorspace as constraints on the demand for space by different activities; as the activities begin to fill up the zones, the amount of available space is reduced and any excess activity is reallocated to other zones. This model is more strongly coupled than any of the models presented previously; the amount of available floorspace is used as a measure of attraction on each iteration of the model, and as this floorspace is reduced, so is the measure of locational attraction.

The model has been fitted to several British towns (March, Echenique and Dickens, 1971) and a version has been applied to the Santiago Metropolitan area (Echenique and Domeyko, 1970). The detailed equation system is presented in two papers by Echenique *et al.* (1969*a*, 1969*b*) in an application to the town of Reading. Although the equation system presented below follows the Reading model, certain details concerning the application of the constraints differ slightly; as in the previous presentation, the index m refers to the iterations used in applying the expanded form of economic base method but the index n refers now to an *inner* iteration used to effect locational constraints. The zonal subsets, Z_g, are not explicitly presented in this model in contrast to previous outlines of equation systems in this chapter.

The model is started by allocating total floorspace F_j to zones of the system; this is the stocks model which has the following form

$$F_j = \pi \sum_i E_i(1) \frac{f(L_j, c_{ij})}{\sum_j f(L_j, c_{ij})}. \tag{3.79}$$

$E_i(1)$ is basic employment in i, L_j is the total land available for urban uses in j and π is a ratio of total floorspace to basic employment in the system. The amount of floorspace available on the first iteration for services and population called $F_j(1)$ is calculated as

$$F_j(1) = F_j - \pi^b E_j(1), \tag{3.80}$$

where π^b is the floorspace standard for basic employment. Note that it may be desirable to relate π^b to specific zones if floorspace standards vary widely within the class of basic employment. Hereafter, available floorspace is written more generally as $F_j(m)$, thus relating to any iteration m of the model. Then on iteration m, the measure of locational attraction D_j

in the residential sector is set equal to available floorspace

$$D_j = F_j(m),\tag{3.81}$$

and population $P_j(m)$ generated from the increment of employment $E_i(m)$ is calculated using a production-constrained gravity model with a form similar to the model in (2.62) and (2.63)

$$P_j(m) = \alpha \sum_i T_{ij}(m) = \alpha \sum_i E_i(m) \frac{f^1(D_j, c_{ij})}{\sum_j f^1(D_j, c_{ij})}.\tag{3.82}$$

The locational attraction D_i in each service centre i is now calculated as

$$D_i = \sum_{k=1}^{m} E_i(k) + \frac{F_i(m)}{\omega},\tag{3.83}$$

where ω is the service floorspace standard expressed as the ratio of floorspace to service employment.

At this stage, the model enters a somewhat more complicated loop in which the floorspace constraints are satisfied and service employment is allocated. This inner iteration is referred to by the index n but note that on the first of these iterations $n = 1$, the overflow population $P_j^h(m,n) = 0$. Then residential floorspace $F_j^h(m,n)$ is calculated as

$$F_j^h(m,n) = \kappa[P_j(m) - \sum_{k=1}^{n} P_j(m,k)],\tag{3.84}$$

where κ is the floorspace standard for the residential population. Service employment $S_i(m,n)$ is derived by distributing the service employees demanded by the population to service centres using an attraction-constrained gravity model equivalent to the model in (2.64) and (2.65)

$$S_i(m,n) = \beta \left[P_j(m) - \sum_{k=1}^{n} P_j(m,k) \right] \frac{f^2(D_i, c_{ij})}{\sum_i f^2(D_i, c_{ij})}.\tag{3.85}$$

The floorspace generated by (3.85) called $F_i^r(m,n)$ is calculated as

$$F_i^r(m,n) = \omega S_i(m,n),\tag{3.86}$$

and a test is now made to ensure the total floorspace generated can be accommodated by the available floorspace. If

$$F_j^h(m,n) + F_j^r(m,n) > F_j(m),\tag{3.87}$$

then service employment is assumed to take priority and a population overflow $P_j(n, m+1)$ is calculated as

$$P_j(m,n+1) = \frac{F_j^h(m,n) + F_j^r(m,n) - F_j(m)}{\kappa}.\tag{3.88}$$

This overflow has generated both floorspace and services and to produce consistent distributions of floorspace, population and services, $P_j(m, n+1)$ is substituted into (3.84), and (3.84)–(3.86) are repeated. Two iterations of this procedure suffice to ensure that the constraints are satisfied, but if some constrained equilibrium is sought, further iteration of the sequence (3.84)–(3.88), excluding (3.87), is necessary.

The overflow population $P_j(m, n+1)$ must be reconverted into employment which is allocated together with service employment on the next iteration $m+1$. To obtain a consistent distribution of employment associated with the overflow population, an equation similar to (3.76) must be used. Reverting to matrix notation for clarity, the vector of overflow employment $\mathbf{e}$ is obtained from the overflow population $\mathbf{p}$ by

$$\mathbf{e} = \mathbf{p}\alpha^{-1}\mathbf{T}^{-1}, \tag{3.89}$$

where α^{-1} and $\mathbf{T}^{-1}$ are the appropriate inverse matrices defined from the

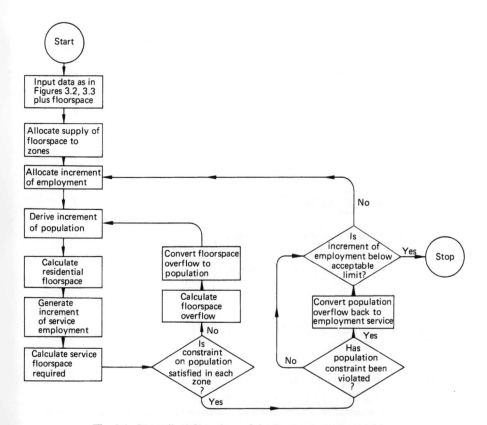

Fig. 3.4. Generalised flow chart of the Stocks–Activities model.

scalar matrix of activity rates and the residential probability distribution matrix respectively. Employment to be allocated on the next iteration $m+1$ is calculated as

$$E_i(m+1) = S_i(m,n) + E_i, \tag{3.90}$$

where E_i is from the vector $\mathbf{e}$ in (3.89). Available floorspace on iteration $m+1$ is also calculated as

$$F_j(m+1) = F_j(m) - [F_j^h(m,n) + F_j^r(m,n)]. \tag{3.91}$$

$F_j(m+1)$ and $E_i(m+1)$ are substituted into (3.81) and (3.82) respectively and the equations (3.81)–(3.91) are reiterated until the increments of population and employment fall within prespecified limits such as those given in (3.36) and (3.37). The reader can easily satisfy himself that this system of equations converges to these limits.

TABLE 3.3. *Structural equations of the Stocks–Activities model*

Equation number	Form of equation	Number of equations
(3.79)	$F_j = \pi \sum_i E_i(1) \dfrac{f(L_j, c_{ij})}{\sum\limits_j f(L_j, c_{ij})}$	*1*
(3.80)	$F_j(1) = F_j - \pi^b E_j(1)$	*1*
(3.81)	$D_j = F_j(m)$	*1*
(3.82)	$P_j(m) = \alpha \sum_i E_i(m) \dfrac{f^1(D_j, c_{ij})}{\sum\limits_j f^1(D_j, c_{ij})}$	*1*
(3.83)	$D_i = \sum\limits_{k=1}^{m} E_i(k) + \dfrac{F_i(m)}{\omega}$	*1*
(3.84)	$F_j^h(m, n) = \kappa \left[P_j(m) - \sum\limits_{k=1}^{n} P_j(m, k) \right]$	*1*
(3.85)	$S_i(m, n) = \beta \left[P_j(m) - \sum\limits_{k=1}^{n} P_j(m, k) \right] \dfrac{f^2(D_i, c_{ij})}{\sum\limits_i f^2(D_i, c_{ij})}$	*1*
(3.86)	$F_i^r(m, n) = S_i(m, n)$	*1*
(3.88)	$P_j(m, n+1) = \dfrac{F_j^h(m, n) + F_j^r(m, n) - F_j(m)}{\kappa}$	
(3.89)	$\mathbf{e} = \mathbf{p}\alpha^{-1} \mathbf{T}^{-1}$	*1*
(3.90)	$E_i(m+1) = S_i(m, n) + E_i$	*1*
(3.91)	$F_j(m+1) = F_j(m) - [F_j^h(m, n) + F_j^r(m, n)]$	*1*

Various constraint procedures can be designed for this type of model, and that shown above is only one of many possible methods. A flow diagram of the model's operations is presented in Figure 3.4 and, as in the two previous models, the major equations are listed in Table 3.3. From this table it is clear that the number of equations is equal to the number of unknowns and therefore the model is determined. This model differs from the Lowry model and the Activity Allocation model for the outputs of the model are quite separate from the inputs. Therefore, a procedure such as the one used by Lowry (1964) to obtain consistency between inputs and outputs is not required. In this sense, the model is more complete than any of the previous descriptions, for only available land is used to start the process of generating measures of locational attraction. Thus the implied circularity built into the Lowry and Activity Allocation models through the measures of locational attraction, is avoided.

A family of urban models

The Activity Allocation and the Stocks–Activities models presented above form the basis for a family of urban models originating from the parent Lowry model. There have been many developments of these kinds of model in Britain in recent years and it is useful to refer to the major applications and specific adaptations of these models in particular areas. Although detailed reviews of this family of models are presented elsewhere by Goldner (1971) and by the author (Batty, 1972a), this section will attempt to highlight the critical differences between various applications. Models have been developed around both the Activity Allocation and Stocks–Activities models and in general, the Activity Allocation model has been used at the subregional-metropolitan scale while the Stocks–Activities model has been applied to the town scale.

The models built for the Bedfordshire subregion by Cripps and Foot (1969a) and by the author for the Central and North East Lancashire subregion described in the next chapter are direct applications of Garin's model. The Activity Allocation model based on Garin's version but incorporating locational constraints has been developed for Nottinghamshire–Derbyshire described in Chapter 5, for Northamptonshire described in Chapter 8, for Severnside (Turner, 1970a) and for Merseyside (Masser, 1970). A model designed for the Tyne–Wear region (Bone, 1971) is based on the Activity Allocation model but constraints have been handled in a manner akin to the original Lowry model. In the South Hampshire region, Caulfield and Rhodes (1971) have developed an Activity Allocation model with population disaggregated by socio-economic group, and in which the constraints are handled in a similar way to the Stocks–Activities model. A model designed for Cheshire by a team at the Centre for Environmental Studies (Barras, Broadbent, Cordey-Hayes, Massey, Robinson and Willis, 1971) is based on Garin's model although considerable refinements have been made to the allocation models and much attention paid to the definition and design of the spatial zoning system.

The Stocks–Activities model has been applied to several towns by a team at the Centre for Land Use and Built Form Studies in Cambridge. The model originally developed for Reading has been built for Stevenage, Milton Keynes and for the proposed new town of Hook (Echenique et al., 1972) and the model has also been used to evaluate alternative plans for Cambridge (Booth, 1970a, 1970b). The outputs from this model have been transformed into indices measuring the relative 'performance' of certain aspects of urban structure based mainly on concepts of accessibility, and such indices have been used to provide a guide in evaluating the relative merits of different urban forms.

Table 3.4 lists these applications and shows the number of zones adopted by each model. Apart from the differences in the structure of developments in this family of models in North America and Britain, there are two other distinct differences. In Britain the main emphasis has been on developing land-use models for systems of interdependent cities, whereas in North America many of the models have been developed for more complicated

TABLE 3.4. *A comparison of some urban models*

Region or town	Type of model	Number of zones	Reference
Bedfordshire	Garin's version	130	Cripps and Foot (1969a)
Cambridge	Stocks–Activities	180	Booth (1970a)
Central Lancashire	Garin's version	51	Chapter 4
Cheshire	Garin's version	150	Barras et al. (1971)
Hook	Stocks–Activities	35	Lindsay (1971)
Merseyside	Activity Allocation	29	Masser (1970)
Milton Keynes	Stocks–Activities	168	Echenique et al. (1972)
Northamptonshire	Activity Allocation	50	Chapter 8
Notts.–Derbys.	Activity Allocation	62	Chapter 5
Reading	Stocks–Activities	130	Echenique et al. (1969a)
Severnside	Activity Allocation	40	Turner (1970a)
South Hampshire	Activity Allocation	134	Caulfield and Rhodes (1971)
Stevenage	Stocks–Activities	49	Echenique et al. (1972)
Tyne–Wear	Activity Allocation	136	Bone (1971)

metropolitan areas. This difference in scale means that the average zone size used in these models is considerably larger in Britain. Furthermore, the British versions have used fewer zones and this appears to be due to limitations on the size of the computational facilities available and the lack of data for the development of these models.

This chapter has demonstrated how fairly elementary ideas can be linked together in systems of equations which form sets of hypotheses or models of urban systems. Despite the fact that the models discussed here all originate from the concepts developed in Chapter 2, these are sufficiently diverse to show how different changes in emphasis can alter the model structure. In the next two chapters, the Activity Allocation model presented above will be applied to two subregions, thus raising a host of practical issues concerning model design, calibration and prediction. An attempt will be made in these next two chapters to describe the total process of model design without getting involved too deeply in detailed development problems, but establishing the background for a thorough exploration of the calibration and zoning problems in later chapters. Yet it is also important to judge the worth of these kinds of model in a predictive context at an early stage, and therefore these two chapters are primarily concerned with demonstrating the use of such models in the land use planning process.

4. *Subregional model design: impact analysis*

One of the principles adhered to in this book involves the notion that urban modelling can best be illustrated by both theoretical and practical demonstrations, one following on from the other. Rather than presenting the book in two distinct parts based on theory and practice, an attempt has been made to follow mathematical description by operational development; thus, this chapter is concerned with making operational one version of the Activity Allocation model outlined in the previous chapter. A much simplified but total process of model design is described here with the initial emphasis upon an elementary design and calibration for the model. The place of such a model in the physical planning process is also described, and this application to a planning problem is perhaps the least complicated of all applications, being based upon the concept of using the model to analyse the impact of major changes in urban structure. This kind of impact analysis which seeks to trace the implications of a fundamental change in spatial structure on an otherwise static system, represents a relatively straightforward use of an urban model in that the model is essentially regarded as a tool to identify problems rather than potential. The form of this analysis will be described after the calibration of the model has been discussed.

Although the models discussed here are referred to as urban, their application is to metropolitan subregions which have mainly urban but some rural components. However, the implication is that such models are best suited to simulating urbanised situations and the subregion of Central and North East Lancashire, the subject of this chapter, provides one such example. In Figure 4.1, a diagram of the locations of all the subregions modelled in this book is presented, and it is immediately apparent from the most cursory glance at this map that the subregions in question are mainly fringe areas to the extensive metropolitan areas of North West, South East and Midland England. The fact that none of the models presented here deal with the more complex parts of such regions is significant and implies that these models are easier to build on less complex systems, a fact which will become apparent in the following pages.

The structure of the operational model

The model described in equations (3.28)–(3.49) has been fitted to the Central Lancashire subregion and this section serves to define certain details of this model structure. In particular, it is necessary to define the attraction–deterrence allocation functions in (3.28), (3.29) and (3.32), (3.33). In the following presentation, the sets to which each zone belongs are not explicitly notated, thus implying that the equations given apply to all sets. The residential and service allocation functions are defined as

$$f^1(D_j, c_{ij}) = P_j^* \, d_{ij}^{-\lambda_1},$$
$$f^2(D_i, c_{ij}) = S_i^* \, d_{ij}^{-\lambda_2},$$

Fig. 4.1. Location of the subregional modelling projects
outlined in subsequent chapters.

where P_j^* is observed population in zone j, S_i^* is observed service employment in zone i, and λ_1 and λ_2 are parameters of these functions to be
estimated numerically by the calibration. The choice of functions of
inverse distance as proxies for the generalised travel costs is arbitrary
although based on conventional use (Carrothers, 1956). Yet the seemingly
tautological specification of locational attractions by observed values of
variables the model is required to predict, needs some explanation. This is
the *locational attraction* problem which will be referred to again in some
detail in Chapter 8, and which is also discussed by Broadbent (1970a). The
use of observed values of population and service employment is purely
due to convenience, in that other measures which describe locational
attraction at any cross-section in time are difficult to specify and measure.
Most alternative measures, when they have been available, have been
highly correlated with these observed variables (Davies, 1970), and have
thus made little difference to the simulation in practice.

In the model designed for Central Lancashire, no constraints on the
location of population and service employment were imposed. In fact,
the model was programmed using the matrix equations (3.71) and (3.72),
and Table 3.4 classifies the model as a straight application of the model
due to Garin (1966). In terms of the equation system beginning at (3.28),
only equations (3.28)–(3.41) were used: the values for $B_j(1)$ and $Q_i(1)$
were set at 1 for all i and j, and the constraints in (3.42)–(3.49) were not
invoked. The logic of running this model unconstrained is important; the
less constraints there are on the model, the less are the number of variables
exogenous to the model and, therefore, the greater the predictive power
of the model. Constraints are generally only introduced for extraneous
reasons based on policy or for pragmatic reasons based on the performance
of the model, as in the constraints introduced in the Nottinghamshire–
Derbyshire model described in the next chapter.

Zone and data requirements

The first model built used a zoning system based on the 29 Local Authority
areas in Central and North East Lancashire; but the attempt was
abandoned soon after it became clear that the irregularity and non-
homogeneity of these areas as zones for the model precluded a good fit
ever being achieved between the predicted and observed populations.
Rural districts were very large and irregular in shape and several of them
included suburban development around the main towns of Preston, Blackburn and Burnley. These zones were not functional units in terms of
localised economic activity, for they were based on fairly arbitrary divi-
sions in the subregion; the extreme variation in the density of population

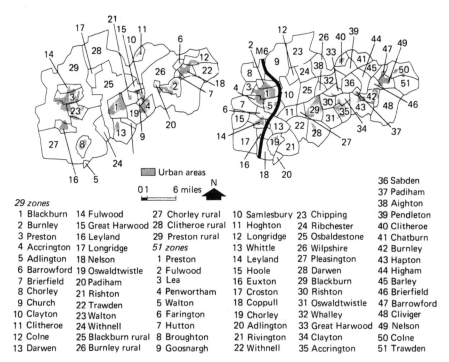

Fig. 4.2. Zoning systems for the Central Lancashire subregion.

29 zones

1 Blackburn	14 Fulwood	27 Chorley rural	10 Samlesbury	23 Chipping	36 Sabden
2 Burnley	15 Great Harwood	28 Clitheroe rural	11 Hoghton	24 Ribchester	37 Padiham
3 Preston	16 Leyland	29 Preston rural	12 Longridge	25 Osbaldestone	38 Aighton
4 Accrington	17 Longridge	*51 zones*	13 Whittle	26 Wilpshire	39 Pendleton
5 Adlington	18 Nelson	1 Preston	14 Leyland	27 Pleasington	40 Clitheroe
6 Barrowford	19 Oswaldtwistle	2 Fulwood	15 Hoole	28 Darwen	41 Chatburn
7 Brierfield	20 Padiham	3 Lea	16 Euxton	29 Blackburn	42 Burnley
8 Chorley	21 Rishton	4 Penwortham	17 Croston	30 Rishton	43 Hapton
9 Church	22 Trawden	5 Walton	18 Coppull	31 Oswaldtwistle	44 Higham
10 Clayton	23 Walton	6 Farington	19 Chorley	32 Whalley	45 Barley
11 Clitheroe	24 Withnell	7 Hutton	20 Adlington	33 Great Harwood	46 Brierfield
12 Colne	25 Blackburn rural	8 Broughton	21 Rivington	34 Clayton	47 Barrowford
13 Darwen	26 Burnley rural	9 Goosnargh	22 Withnell	35 Accrington	48 Cliviger
					49 Nelson
					50 Colne
					51 Trawden

in these areas meant that the positioning of a zone centroid, which could be used in the computation of inter-zonal distances, was almost impossible. To offset these problems, certain criteria were defined which could be used to disaggregate the subregion into regular units. Physical factors, density of population, dominant land use, similarity in zonal size: these were some of the factors applied when the subregion was redefined into 51 distinct zones. Figure 4.2 provides a comparison of the two zoning systems developed.

A combination of several factors meant that this model had to be constructed at a far higher level of zonal aggregation than the Pittsburgh model (Lowry, 1964). Primarily, the supply of data fixed an upper bound on the number of zones which could be used but also the size of the sub-region with its several fairly independent settlements, the need to simulate interurban trips, and the simple structure of the model omitting density and minimum size constraints lead to somewhat large zones resulting in a better calibration yet still at a level of detail necessary to study the problem of impact. Not least in this discussion of zone size is the question of the allocation functions to be used. As outlined in the previous section, it was decided to use conventional gravity models in the calculation of the distribution probabilities, and experience suggests that such functions can best be fitted to fairly large areas in which irregularities in the mass of population or economic activity tend to cancel each other out (Isard *et al.*, 1960).

Compiling the inventory of data necessary for the operation of the model took up a fair amount of time at the calibration stage. The division into basic and non-basic employment was made from Employment Exchange Area data at mid-1965. Basic employment is usually defined as employment which is not dependent upon the local economy for siting and access. This is export-oriented industry exogenous to the system under study. Although it is difficult to classify basic and non-basic employment with complete accuracy, the primary and manufacturing sectors of the Standard Industrial Classification (S.I.C., 1–17) correspond to basic employment here. Non-basic employment is dependent upon the local economy for its markets and consumers, and this service-oriented employment was classified under the service sector of the S.I.C. (18–24). Population from the 1961 Census of Population was up-dated to 1965 using a cohort survival programme and these projections were checked against independent estimates (MHLG, 1968). Another data source consisted of work trips from the Workplace Tables of the 1961 Census of Population.

The data were then distributed to the 51 zones already defined. Disaggregating these data, which were collected in the 29 Local Authority and 12 Employment Exchange areas, was facilitated by the finer grained information on population by parishes. Proportions of basic to non-basic employment had to be retained from the Exchange Area data and their transformation into these smaller zones inevitably involved a series of errors. This process of disaggregation was a lengthy task as continual refinement and redefinition of the data had to be sought so that unavoidable errors could be minimised. The most unsuccessful yet probably the most important part of this data refinement involved the decomposition of work trips between zones. It is essential to have independent data on trips for any interaction model, but these data were too coarse to provide observations against which to fit the allocation functions. Therefore, an attempt was made to decompose the trips between the 51 zones although the attenuating effect of distance could not be brought to bear on this reallocation. The inverse activity rate (population/total employment) and the population-serving ratio (non-basic employment/population) were also calculated from the data. The major characteristics of this subregion are presented in Table 4.1.

TABLE 4.1. *Major characteristics of the
Central Lancashire subregion*

Total number of zones	51
Total land area in square miles	392
Average land area per zone in square miles	7.6863
Total population	724063
Average population per zone	14197
Population density in persons per square mile	1847
Basic employment	172874
Total employment	313165
Ratio of basic to total employment	0.5517
Ratio of inter-zonal to intra-zonal work trips	0.5059

Required for this model is a matrix of inter-zonal distances or travel times to be used in the computation of the distribution functions. After locating the zone centroids, a planar graph of the route network was drawn. Time-distances for private car, varying over the type and condition of the road system and modified by terminal traffic speeds at centroids, were measured on the direct paths of this graph and provided input to a Shortest Route Programme based on the Cascade Algorithm (Farbey, Land and Murchland, 1967). This subprogramme is in fact built into the main body of the computer programme used in calibrating the model, and the matrix of interzonal time-distances is set up within the computer each time the model is run; thus the data requirements for the model were extremely manageable.

Calibration as statistical estimation

In calibrating urban models, there are two major problems necessary to resolve. First, there is the problem of defining 'best' statistics which measure the goodness of fit of the model to reality in a meaningful way. Second, having derived such 'best' statistics, there is the problem of developing efficient methods for finding 'best' values for the model's parameters; such values are usually chosen by finding the optimum fit of the model in terms of the 'best' statistics. With regard to the two parameters λ_1 and λ_2 of the activity allocation model, a number of statistics which measure the correspondence of various observed and predicted endogenous variables, have been chosen arbitrarily. At this early stage, the statistics were taken from conventional linear methods involving measures such as the correlation coefficient and chi-square test. In later chapters, particularly in Chapter 7, theoretical methods for deriving 'best' statistics will be explored, but here the emphasis is on fitting or calibrating the model in fairly rough and ready terms, thus avoiding the use of more sophisticated methods.

Four statistics are used in this chapter and the next and each of these statistics has been applied to several different distributions such as population, employment, work trips and so on. The following statistics are defined for the population distribution but can be extended to any other distribution. Define the population mean

$$\bar{P} = \sum_j P_j/J = \sum_j P_j^*/J,$$

where P_j and P_j^* are the predicted and observed values of population in zone j given previously. Note that J is the total number of zones associated with these population distributions. The first statistic is the standard deviation of the predicted distribution σ and of the observed distribution σ^*. Then for the predicted distribution

$$\sigma = \left[\frac{\sum_j (P_j - \bar{P})^2}{J} \right]^{\frac{1}{2}}.$$

The standard deviation for the observed distribution is calculated in like manner. The correlation coefficient r can now be defined using the means and standard deviations as

$$r = \frac{\sum_j (P_j - \bar{P})(P_j^* - \bar{P})}{J\sigma\sigma^*}.$$

The third statistic which is known as the root mean square error ζ is defined by Hill, Brand and Hansen (1965) as

$$\zeta = \left[\frac{\sum_j (P_j - P_j^*)^2}{J} \right]^{\frac{1}{2}},$$

and the fourth statistic, the chi-square χ^2, is based upon the frequency distributions for observed and predicted populations. These are calculated by grouping the data into K categories, each category having frequency f_k and f_k^*. Then

$$\chi^2 = \sum_{k=1}^{K} \frac{(f_k^* - f_k)^2}{f_k}.$$

Optimum values for these statistics occur when $r = 1$, and $|\sigma - \sigma^*| = 0$, $\zeta = 0$ and $\chi^2 = 0$. Therefore the calibration problem can be seen as one in which optimum values for λ_1 and λ_2 are found by maximising r, and minimising $|\sigma - \sigma^*|$, ζ and χ^2.

The traditional method of calibrating this kind of model is by trial and error. It is assumed that the optimum exists within a predetermined range of parameter values, and the goodness of fit of the model is evaluated at selected points within this range. The interval of search can be narrowed sequentially and there exist highly efficient methods for achieving this to be outlined later in Chapters 6–8. In the case of a model with two parameters λ_1 and λ_2, a grid of possible values for the parameters is established within the predetermined ranges and the fit is evaluated for each combination of values, gradually homing in upon the best combination. This method will be illustrated in some detail in the next chapter.

Perhaps the most important statistics in spatial interaction modelling reflect the amount or cost of interaction in any urban system. In particular, the means of the trip length or cost distributions have been widely used in transport modelling (Wagon and Hawkins, 1970), and these key statistics can be defined in their most general form as

$$\bar{C}(\lambda_1, \lambda_2) = \frac{\sum_i \sum_j T_{ij} F^1(c_{ij})}{\sum_i \sum_j T_{ij}}, \tag{4.1}$$

$$\bar{S}(\lambda_1, \lambda_2) = \frac{\sum_i \sum_j S_{ij} F^2(c_{ij})}{\sum_i \sum_j S_{ij}}, \tag{4.2}$$

where $\bar{C}(\lambda_1, \lambda_2)$ is the mean trip cost in the residential-workplace subsystem and $\bar{S}(\lambda_1, \lambda_2)$ is the mean trip cost in the service subsystem. $F^1(c_{ij})$ and $F^2(c_{ij})$ are functions of generalised travel cost whose particular form depends upon statistical considerations oulined in Chapter 7. However, in this particular application, these functions are defined as

$$\left. \begin{array}{l} F^1(c_{ij}) \\ F^2(c_{ij}) \end{array} \right\} = \ln d_{ij}.$$

The rationale for this definition is given later; readers who wish to anticipate these considerations are referred to the paper by Hyman (1969) for a brief but cogent summary.

Performance of the model

The model took about five months to calibrate although much of this time was concerned with continual refinement of the data and the allocation functions. Part of the process consisted in testing the sensitivity of the model to variation in the parameters and in the time–distance measures.

From the statistical tests performed to optimise the fit, the model was extremely insensitive when the parameters were varied although the allocation of employment and population changed substantially over a range of parameter values. The most sensitive aspect of the model involved the values given to the intra-zonal time–distances. Estimation of these time–distances was made by taking the average time–distance from the centre of gravity of the population distribution of an area to the periphery of the distribution, and this was modified by relating the speed of travel to the density of population. It is easy to see why these distances are most sensitive in the model, for in a large town a slight variation in this value could mean a large addition or subtraction of the amount of non-basic employment or resident population located in that area. The same procedure used by the Haydock study was adopted in that the intra-zonal travel times were varied proportionately over a specified range and the best resulting fit was taken (McLoughlin, Nix and Foot, 1966). The re-measurement of these values does not detract from the validity of the model but it is a fundamental measurement problem which is looked at again in Chapter 9.

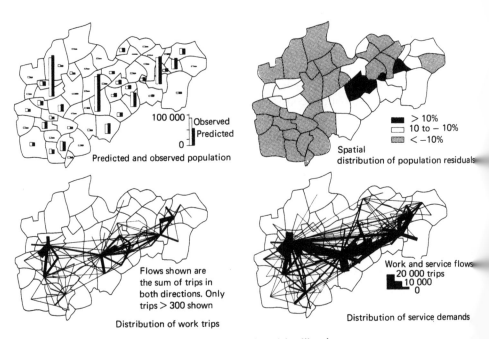

Fig. 4.3. A summary of model calibration.

Two sets of observed data – population and total employment – were used to optimise the fit for 1965 and statistical hypothesis testing based on the previously defined statistics was employed to evaluate the validity of the output. Eventually the distance exponents were fixed at 2.4 for trips to workplaces and 1.7 for trips to the service-shopping centres. The results of the calibration are shown statistically in Table 4.2 and for a selection of zones in Table 4.3. A diagrammatic assessment of the model's performance is given in Figure 4.3. The nature of the high correlation between the observed values and the model's output can only be appreciated when the actual results are scanned, for the statistics used give an almost complete fit whereas the actual results show that there are slight deviations from observed values which are significant in terms of the allocation rules used.

TABLE 4.2. *Goodness of fit of the model*

Residential parameter λ_1	2.4000	Service centre parameter λ_2	1.7000
$\bar{C}(\lambda_1, \lambda_2)$ observed	1.3564	$\bar{C}(\lambda_1, \lambda_2)$ predicted	1.5771
$\bar{S}(\lambda_1, \lambda_2)$ observed	Not available	$\bar{S}(\lambda_1, \lambda_2)$ predicted	1.9161
r^2 for $\{\ln (P_i)\}$	0.9683	ζ for $\{P_i\}$	2073
r^2 for $\{\ln (E_i)\}$	0.9915	ζ for $\{E_i\}$	976
r^2 for $\{\alpha_{ij}\}, i = j$	0.6421	ζ for $\{\alpha_{ij}\}, i = j$	0.6233
r^2 for $\{\beta_{ij}\}, i = j$	0.7678	ζ for $\{\beta_{ij}\}, i = j$	0.0249

TABLE 4.3. *Performance of the model for a selected sample of zones*

Zone number	Name	Observed values 1965		Calibration values 1965	
		Population	Service employment	Population	Service employment
1	Preston	116339	38840	121528	34104
2	Fulwood	16649	1561	16073	1432
5	Walton-le-Dale	20295	3909	21479	4151
14	Leyland	20642	2414	21361	1971
19	Chorley	32195	5681	31203	5824
29	Blackburn	108351	20304	118815	24756
30	Rishton	5520	292	8029	442
31	Oswaldtwistle	12211	1725	12603	2056
35	Accrington	45874	7263	44828	8262
42	Burnley	82346	17994	84631	19014
49	Nelson	32733	4405	33200	5443
50	Colne	20942	2947	20176	3181

The main point arising from the calibration concerns the fact that the populations of the major urban centres are overreading a little. This seems to be due to the nature of the allocation functions which are operated uniformly over the system with no differentiation between rural and urban areas. The excess population in the larger urban centres can be mainly accounted for from the agricultural zones which are underreading; too many trips are being generated from the agricultural areas to the urban centres and this result seems consistent with the fact that different areas generate different types of trips which need to be described by different allocation rules. This reveals an aspect of the model which must be treated with care especially in projection where it is assumed that the agricultural zones will not change very much. Density constraints on the zones have not been needed in calibrating the model, for the size of the zones seems to mesh well with the general structure of the model. Garin's formulation is neatly adapted to model-building at this scale of spatial planning, although in some instances it is quite possible that density constraints would have to be invoked when the repercussions of large increases in basic employment are projected.

In conclusion to this section on system design and calibration, another variant of the model will be mentioned. The model as calibrated describes a closed system since movements across the subregional boundary are not treated. A version which tried to describe this movement was programmed and eight very large 'dummy' zones were placed around the edge of the subregion to account for the trips. Although the dummy zones had similar data requirements to the other 51 zones, movement between them was forbidden. A few runs of this model were made but it soon became apparent that the task of 'tuning up' a partially open system would be long and expensive. The dummy zones were too large for the problem and the total population and employment of the subregion varied with changes in parameter values. This approach, however, is useful and realistic for it is obvious that in the areas outside the subregion, the impact of the new town may be as great as in North East Lancashire. Consequently the model in its present form may overestimate the impact in the valley towns of Blackburn, Accrington, Burnley, Nelson and Colne. More feasible formulations of the problem of relating the spatial system to its environment using dummy zones are presented in Chapters 8 and 9.

Predictive modelling and recursive forecasting

In using any static model in a predictive and necessarily dynamic context, there is a logical inconsistency in that the model has been calibrated to reflect some average spatial history of the system whereas it is being used predictively to allocate marginal change. This is a problem which affects many of the models in this book, inevitably reducing their predictive power. The dynamic modelling of Chapters 11 and 12 presents the only way to resolve this inconsistency and thus the reader must bear in mind these limitations on the predictive analysis which is presented in subsequent sections. In this study, two types of projection have been made – one-shot projections direct to 1990, the horizon year, and recursive projections based on five-yearly intervals to this date. At one extreme, the one-shot projection deals with change over the whole forecast period of the plan. Intervening outputs are not computed, thus the continuous change towards this final date cannot be measured but the purpose of this projection is to establish a single locational equilibrium. Inevitably the approach suffers from the application of distribution rules which are unchanging over the projection period. At the other extreme, recursive projections are based upon a stepwise progression in which the solution at 1990 is based upon a continuous redistribution of activity to that date. In this recursive process, output of an intermediate projection provides input to the next projection, and the process continues in this way until the solution date is reached. Obviously each of these intermediate outputs is an equilibrium in itself, and this involves the question of lagged variables within the system.

How quickly does the spatial distribution of population and non-basic employment respond to a change in basic employment? Is there a simultaneous response or does the system respond after five years or twenty-five years or longer? Do different activities react uniformly to such a change? These are some of the questions which have to be borne in mind when evaluating the different projections. The method of one-shot projection means that certain variables which determine the allocation rules such as population or employment in any zone, operate on a twenty-five year lag. Much less lag is involved in the recursive projections for there is an immediate response to changed transportation patterns, and a response after five years to the new allocation of population and service employment. For both one-shot and recursive projections, the restructuring of the spatial organisation of the system operates equally over all activities, existing activity following the same response to change as the new activity. A variant which can be adopted for both sets of projections is based on an incremental approach. Using this method, new activity is 'layered' on top of the existing pattern which is assumed to be unresponsive throughout the period of the plan, possibly accounting for some of the locational inertia of existing investments.

These different types of projection represent the real world condition only partially and it is impossible at the present time to structure the model to simulate completely realistic conditions for there has been no extensive research focusing directly upon the response of activity to change and the varying lengths of time necessary to determine changes in the pattern of land use. Thus, at best, the projections described here can only be *suggestive* of change and the specific results produced by each projection can only be seen in the light of the assumptions embodied within them.

Rather than describing a recursive form for the whole system of equations given in (3.28)–(3.49), the method of recursive forecasting will be outlined only in relation to the residential and service centre location models. In the following equations, the notation is the same as that used previously, and the postscripts (t) and $(t+1)$ define the appropriate forecast interval used in projections with the model. Note also that the iterative notation of the model is suppressed in the following presentation. Then for the residential location model given in equations (3.28) and (3.29)

$$T_{ij}(t+1) = A_i(t+1) \, B_j(t+1) \, E_i(t+1) f^1(D_j(t), c_{ij}(t)), \qquad (4.3)$$

$$A_i(t+1) = \frac{1}{\sum_j B_j(t+1) f^1(D_j(t), c_{ij}(t))}. \qquad (4.4)$$

The parameter value λ_1 associated with $f^1(D_j(t), c_{ij}(t))$ in (4.3) and (4.4) is altered at each forecast interval to account for assumed changes in the amount expended on transportation in the subregion. The travel times on the network c_{ij} are lagged over the forecast interval on the assumption that changes in network do not affect the distribution of trips or the location of population immediately. The constraints on residential location in Z_2 and Z_4 are also changed at each forecast interval; the attractions of residential locations D_j are lagged over the forecast interval on the assumption that changes in these attractions do not immediately affect residential location.

In the service centre location model given in equations (3.32) and (3.33), the parameter λ_2 is altered at each forecast interval and the attractions of service centres to the location of service employment D_i and the travel times on the network are lagged over the forecast interval

$$S_{ij}(t+1) = R_j(t+1) \, H_j(t+1) \, Q_i(t+1) f^2(D_i(t), c_{ij}(t)), \qquad (4.5)$$

$$R_j(t+1) = \frac{1}{\sum_i Q_i(t+1) f^2(D_i(t), c_{ij}(t))}. \qquad (4.6)$$

As pointed out previously, there is an inconsistency between the time-oriented projection system and the calibration. When the model is calibrated, no lags are built into the system. This inconsistency was consciously accepted in this modelling venture because of the difficulty in projecting the future attractions of residential and service centre locations and the consequent need to use the outputs of population and service employment from one time period as indices of locational attraction in the following time period. Furthermore, the use of this model is not in accurate forecasts of the future system, but in forecasting a range of possible futures for the system. As long as each forecast is based upon a consistent projection system, the different futures predicted by the model can be compared.

There are several trajectories which can be charted from the model's predictions. The work trip and service trip distributions can be analysed, and changes in population and service employment can be plotted

$$P_j(t+1) = \alpha(t+1) \sum T_{ij}(t+1), \tag{4.7}$$

$$S_i(t+1) = \sum_j S_{ij}(t+1). \tag{4.8}$$

This model also provides an interesting mechanism for forecasting migration. Changes in the input variables such as basic employment and the travel times lead to a series of repercussions within the spatial system and it is the changes through time in the directions and strength of these repercussions which create migration. People leaving one zone will reduce their demand for services in other zones; these people associated with service trades will in turn reduce their demand for services in other zones and so on until the process works itself out. Rather than using any explicit submodel of migration within the general framework, the model produces a changed distribution of population and service employment in which migration is treated implicitly. Three types of migration can be derived from this model:

1. Migration which is external to the subregion: changes in basic employment will result in persons entering or leaving the area, these changes being projected independently of the model.
2. Migration which is due to the internal redistribution of basic employment in the subregion.
3. Migration which is caused by the changed potential of the subregion.

This last category needs further explanation. The gravity models which predict the residential locations of workers are based upon the distribution of population and spatial measures of cost impedance, in this case average travel times between the zones. Changes in the distribution of population and changes in the transportation network will generate different residential locations for the same distribution of employment. This leads to a changed distribution of population which is treated implicitly as the response of population to the changing locational attractiveness of each zone. If a zone becomes more attractive in relation to all other zones, the model will predict that the zone in question will attract a greater quantity of population than it originally had, the excess coming from the other zones in the subregion. This flow can be called migration due to the changed potential of the subregion and it represents the most important variable to be used in the projections of the space-economy.

Total net migration of population in any zone j between t and $t+1$, called ΔP_j can be calculated from

$$\Delta P_j = \alpha(t+1) \left[\sum_i T_{ij}(t+1) - \sum_i T_{ij}(t) \right]. \tag{4.9}$$

Here the inverse activity rate α is normalised to $t+1$ so that changes in population due to natural increase or decrease do not obscure changes in population due to increases and decreases in basic employment. One component of total net migration is migration which is caused by the changing attractions of residential locations through time. This net migration called ΔM_j can be calculated by removing the change in population caused by the change in employment ΔE_i from (4.9). Then

$$\Delta M_j = \Delta P_j - \alpha(t+1) \sum_i A_i(t+1) B_j(t+1) \Delta E_i f^1(D_i(t), c_{ij}(t)). \tag{4.10}$$

Summing (4.10) over j and substituting for ΔP_j from (4.9) gives

$$\sum_j \Delta M_j = \alpha(t+1) \left[\sum_i \sum_j T_{ij}(t+1) - \sum_i \sum_j T_{ij}(t) - \sum_i \Delta E_i \right]. \tag{4.11}$$

Now noting that $E_i(t+1) = E_i(t) + \Delta E_i$ in (4.3) and substituting (4.3) into (4.11), it is clear that

$$\sum_j \Delta M_j = \alpha(t+1) \left[\sum_i (E_i(t) + \Delta E_i) - \sum_i E_i(t) - \sum_i \Delta E_i \right] = 0. \tag{4.12}$$

Examining the set of constrained zones Z_2, Z_3, Z_4 and the unconstrained set Z_1, then

$$\sum_{j \in Z_1} \Delta M_j + \sum_{j \in Z_2, Z_3, Z_4} \Delta M_j = 0, \tag{4.13}$$

and

$$\sum_{j \in Z_1} \Delta M_j = - \sum_{j \in Z_2, Z_3, Z_4} \Delta M_j. \tag{4.14}$$

Equation (4.14) shows that a net migration flow between the constrained and unconstrained locations can be calculated. In fact, the net migration across any partition of the system into two mutually exclusive sets of zones can be found, and this is an extremely useful output for assessing the sensitivity of the model. The system of equations in (4.3)–(4.14) is now illustrated with regard to the impact analysis described in the following sections.

A brief history of the subregional space-economy

Central and North East Lancashire is extremely suitable for the application of land-use modelling techniques since the area is physically and economically well defined and interaction with other settlements across the subregional boundary is negligible. The subregion can be divided into two parts – North East Lancashire centred on the Blackburn–Burnley complex and Central Lancashire on the Preston–Chorley area. North East Lancashire has experienced a long period of decline in population and employment due to the contraction of the textile industry around which the area developed, and although there has been considerable diversification in the local economy in recent years, the area is still characterised by a high rate of outward migration. The settlement pattern of the Blackburn–Burnley area has not changed substantially since the turn of the century and the obsolete environment and poor accessibility to major metropolitan markets are important factors discouraging the economic revival of this area.

Central Lancashire has fared a little better than its close neighbour for this area is astride the main north–south communications network in North West England. There has been some industrial expansion in the area in the last ten years, for example at Leyland, but the rate of growth has been well below the national average. The Preston area has a more amenable climate and environment than North East Lancashire, but nevertheless suffers from the legacy left by the Industrial Revolution, especially where its housing stock is concerned. Since 1951, population has declined in North East Lancashire at a rate of approximately 0.3 per cent per annum whereas in Central Lancashire, the population has increased slightly at about 0.4 per cent per annum.

The most striking characteristic of the subregion is the lack of change in the spatial distribution of activities in the last twenty years. There is very little journey to work between the main settlements of Preston, Blackburn and Burnley, and recent industrial surveys have revealed that since the decline of the cotton industry, there are few interdependencies within the industrial structure of the area. In North East Lancashire, decline in basic industries, low *per capita* income, obsolete environment, poor climate, and the ageing population structure all contribute to continuing economic decline. In Central Lancashire, however, there is a little more prosperity, for this area is beginning to feel the advantages of economic decentralisation from the two conurbations of Merseyside and Greater Manchester to the south.

In future years, the space-economy of the subregion is likely to be dominated by the location of a new town, centred on the Preston area, which is to be fed by overspill population from South Lancashire (MHLG, 1967). Therefore, the projections of the space-economy discussed here largely concern the impact which this new town will have upon the settlement pattern in North East Lancashire. It is quite possible that the scale of development proposed in Central Lancashire could lead to severe economic decline in North East Lancashire, for the economy of this area is already depressed, and unless there are positive proposals for its revival, the decline in employment may continue. How can the local economy benefit from the creation of such massive economic potential virtually on its doorstep? What sort of decisions are needed to revive the economy of this area, and what would be the likely spatial distortions to the settlement pattern if proposals for its future are not made? These are some of the questions which this modelling study will attempt to answer, but before the results of projection are described, a recent projection of the space-economy by consultant economists will be outlined, for this provides a useful yardstick against which to compare the forecasts made by the model (MHLG, 1968).

A recent forecast of the space-economy

The framework adopted by the consultants concentrates primarily upon the assessment of the future industrial prospects for North East Lancashire and upon the migration of population into and out of this area. Forecasts of future population and employment levels involve the projection of migration and population independently of employment, and by a method of successive approximation, consistency between these distributions is secured. The mechanics of this study have been well thought out, and recognition of migration as the most important flow involved in impact analysis means that the results of this work are partially comparable with the migration data produced by the model. Although the state of the art sets a limit on the techniques which any study can apply, it would have been better for the problem to have been set within a more rigorous framework in which the independent projections of migration and population, manufacturing and service employment and the journey to work could have been more closely integrated. This method of successive approximation is a useful tool but it has no analogy in the events of the real world. It is therefore impossible to state with complete confidence that the actual impact of the new town will follow the conclusions reached by this study.

A sample survey of the motivations and destinations of migrants who left the area between mid-1965 and mid-1967 provides the data for the analysis of the present migration pattern. This reveals that migrants within different occupational groups have different priorities in the decision to move. Data on the destination of migrants show that of the total out-migration from North East Lancashire, only 6.6 per cent move to Central Lancashire, and the major attraction of the area seems to be due to better housing and a more temperate climate rather than better employment opportunities. The analysis is supplemented by a projection of industrial activity in North East Lancashire which shows that manufacturing employment will continue to fall during the next twenty-five years. The journey to work analysis is confined to an interpretation of the existing pattern of movement in relation to earnings differentials in the subregion, but the results of this section are too vague to constitute the basis for a projection of future changes in the distribution of trips.

The impact of the new town

Impact is defined by the study as the difference in population between projections made for the area without the new town and projections with the new town. The consultants conclude that the new town will attract between 30000 and 40000 people from North East Lancashire over the next twenty-five years, and this compares with a movement of 13000 people which would result if the new town were not developed. The spatial intensity of impact would approximately vary inversely with distance from the new town, but the scale of the impact tends to be obscured by rising population in the subregion due to changes in the activity rates and population-serving ratios. It seems that these conclusions are too optimistic about the future of North East Lancashire, for the projections of change have been modified by consideration of the role of this area as a specialist industrial and residential subsystem of the new town. There is no evidence that North East Lancashire will adapt in this way; it may remain quite separate and the existing differences between the two areas may become even more marked.

Yet despite these shortcomings, the study is a useful contribution to the understanding of impact and although the conclusions are based upon fairly tentative assumptions, the results are probably in the right direction. The involvement with migration streams and differentials, and the implicit treatment of the multiplier effect in migration show that the study has been conceived on a sound theoretical base. Projections with the model mean that migration, population, employment, and the work and service trips are rigorously related, and it becomes possible to measure the change in any one of these variables relative to changes in the others. Projections are made at five-yearly intervals from 1965 to 1990, and during this period 40000 basic jobs are located in the Central Lancashire new town, whose form is shown in Figure 4.4. As the projection reveals that the effect on population and employment is much more critical than the conclusions of the study reviewed above, this analysis must be qualified by some comments on the limitations of the model in simulating change in activities.

The impact may be less serious than it appears at first, for the model is operated within a closed spatial system; without this assumption, a more even distribution of impact in the surrounding areas is likely. Areas not simulated by the model will be affected by the new town, and this may reduce the impact upon North East Lancashire. But on the other hand, it is assumed that basic employment in North East Lancashire does not change during the period of the analysis. This is optimistic in the light of the decline predicted by the consultants' study, and contributes to some reduction in the effect of the new town on the economic base of this area. The most important assumption which helps to confirm that the results to be reported here are reasonably accurate is the fact that the natural increase in the population of the subregion is not treated by the model. Only 40000 employees in basic industry are projected for the new town; this is definitely an underestimate, for more basic industry will be needed on which to base the natural increase in population. Voluntary migration of employment and population into the Preston area will probably occur when the new town becomes large enough to become its own generator of growth, and this is not considered in the following analysis.

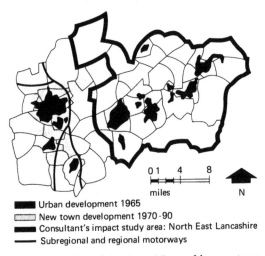

Fig. 4.4. Location of the Central Lancashire new town.

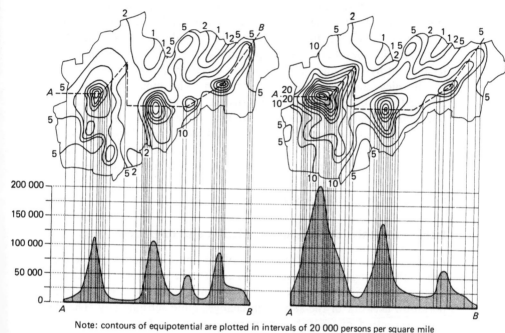

Note: contours of equipotential are plotted in intervals of 20 000 persons per square mile

Fig. 4.5. The impact of the new town on a profile of population potentials, 1965–90.

A general indicator of impact

The word 'potential' has already been used in this chapter as an index for the general locational attractiveness of any area. There is however, a more precise measure of potential which can be computed for every component of the spatial system; this is a measure of the aggregate accessibility of any zone relative to every other zone. By utilising such an index, it is possible to show how the distribution of potential changes over time. When a large change is made to one part of the area, the relative potentials of all the zones in the system change, and it is possible to use this change as an indicator of impact. The conventional population potential formula of Stewart referred to earlier in (2.54) is used to compute this index (Stewart, 1947)

$$V_i = \sum_j P_j \, d_{ij}^{-\lambda_1}.$$

V_i is the population potential at i, and P_j, d_{ij}, and λ_1 are as defined previously. The potential field of a subregion can be summarised by contours of equipotential (Knos, 1968), and Figure 4.5 illustrates a cross-sectional change in potential through time from 1965, without the new town, to 1990, by which time the new town has been developed. From the 1965 situation in which the three focal points of the subregion Preston, Blackburn and Burnley have similar potentials, Preston becomes the major focal point by 1990 and the distribution of potential within the Accrington–Burnley complex becomes more even. The most interesting fact arising from this comparison concerns the potential of Blackburn. This potential increases significantly although there is no physical fusion of development within the Preston–Blackburn area. Does Blackburn benefit from the development of Preston–Leyland–Chorley? To answer this question and to provide a more detailed discussion of the future space-economy, it is now necessary to turn to the detailed population and migration results, predictions made by the model.

Impact analysis: changes in population and migration

In this section, a recursive projection of the space-economy is described, and evaluated against the forecasts made by the consultant economists. Apart from the increase in basic employment in the new town, the transportation network of the subregion changes quite substantially. The new town is centred on an urban motorway system in Central Lancashire, and a motorway linking the new town with Blackburn, Accrington and Burnley is located along the Calder Valley. Changes in population are shown in Figure 4.6 for the larger urban settlements within the subregion. A pointer to the future of this area is the decline in population and total employment within the Accrington–Burnley–Nelson complex. Such extreme change suggests that the economic attractiveness of North East Lancashire is substantially reduced with the expansion of the new town. But these changes must be interpreted spatially, for the increasing population in the suburban zones of Padiham, Clayton-Le-Moors and Brierfield accounts for some of the decline in Accrington and Burnley. Within Central Lancashire, there are some large increases in population within suburban zones such as Fulwood and Walton, and the population of Preston itself increases substantially. The model is able to simulate a decentralisation of activity quite successfully and by 1985, Preston begins to decline in population. As mentioned in the last section, Blackburn thrives with the growth of the new town. It has a growth curve similar to Preston's, eventually losing a small amount of population to suburban areas. The growth of Blackburn can only be discussed implicitly; its location within the subregion and its present population potential mean that a proportion of the service employment generated by the new town is diverted from Preston to Blackburn which is more accessible to some parts of the new

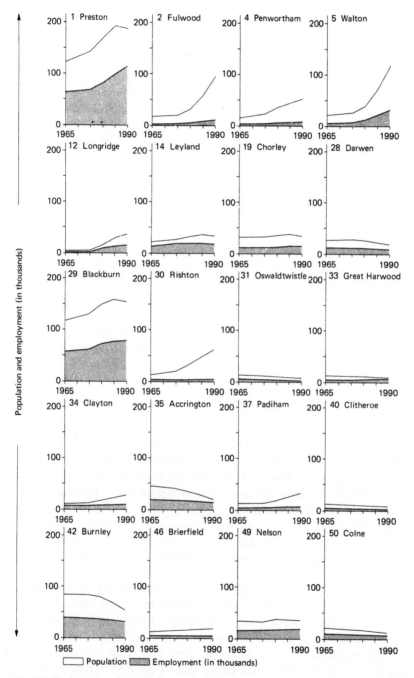

Fig. 4.6. Trajectories of population and employment in the larger urban areas, 1965–90.

town than to Preston. This service employment in turn generates further population and service employment in the Blackburn area.

The cumulative decline of North East Lancashire due to the increasing unattractiveness of the area to locators can be analysed more accurately with reference to internal migration within the subregion. Internal migration was defined earlier in this chapter as that migration which is caused by the changed potential of the zones of the subregion. The particular advantage of using this type of migration measure is that the trend in migration can be isolated and any change in the trend identified. It is possible to find out whether the system is tending towards stability or instability. The migration–time curves for selected urban areas in the subregion are shown in Figure 4.7. This is probably the most useful output from the study; the migration statistics give a crude dynamic orientation to the model but are nevertheless true indicators of change. Besides showing the trajectory or line of behaviour for each component in the spatial system, migration neatly points up the structural deficiencies in the model. The fact that only 7 zones out of 51 have a positive net internal migration between 1965 and 1990 indicates that the model is too sensitive to changes in potential. Perhaps if growth in the system were constrained by physical restrictions on development or by a more realistic formulation of the recursive process, then the model might produce a more dispersed distribution of growth.

Yet this is only a localised problem. It does not detract from the general results which the model forecasts for the subregion. The migration–time curves show how the model can simulate decentralisation. Note for example, the curves of Blackburn and Preston in Figure 4.7. The migration results endorse the population changes in the sense that the large urban centres of North East Lancashire experience heavy out-migration and the suburban areas of the new town become the main residential attractors for the subregion. There are some interesting trends in migration; the shifting centre of development within the new town is revealed by initial net in-migration at Leyland and out-migration at Longridge. When the development moves towards Longridge in the latter years of the plan, Leyland experiences a small net out-migration and Longridge a net in-migration.

Most of these migration results reflect the trend shown in population change; but the change in Nelson is interesting for at one interval within the forecast period, there is a net in-migration of population. At previous and later intervals, there is net out-migration. This curious result seems partly due to the fact that at this time, there is a slight improvement in transportation in this area, and partly due to the overlapping potential fields of Burnley and Colne. As Lowry (1964) has pointed out, if two potential fields overlap in this way, then there is a build-up of population in the area of overlap. In Figure 4.8, the process of migration is spatially

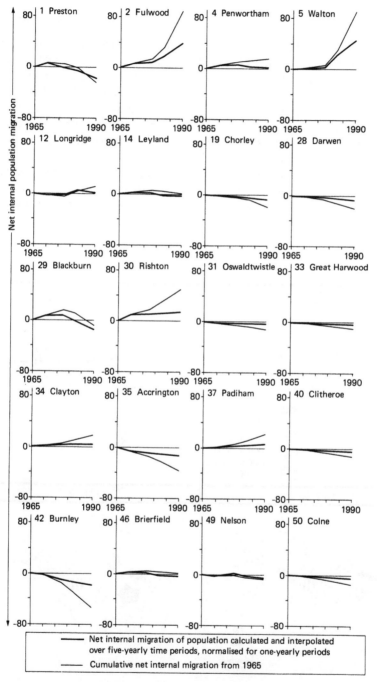

Fig. 4.7. Trajectories of net internal migration in the larger urban areas, 1965–90.

summarised by a diagram showing the critical changes in each forecast
interval. The model has not been used to extract data on inter-zonal migration, but as the sum of the internal migrations is equal to zero by equation
(4.12), what is lost by any one part of the system is gained by the other
part. Flows can thus be interpreted by dividing the system into two parts.
The division which suggests itself is into Central Lancashire and North
East Lancashire, and in Figure 4.9, the flows between these areas are
shown in each forecast interval of the analysis.

Migration into Central Lancashire, although increasing at each forecast
interval, begins to stabilise by 1985. It is easy to speculate on the future
stability of the area in these terms but it is difficult to interpret the eventual
outcome of such a process. One of the reasons why the system has not

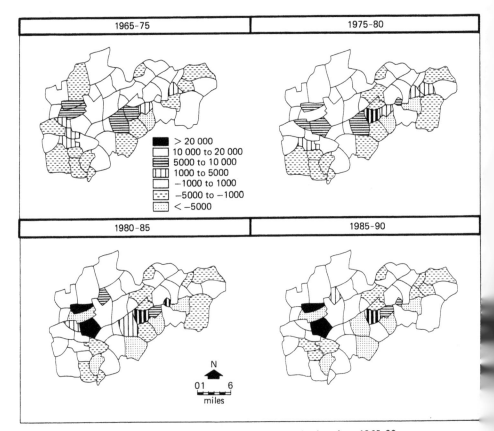

Fig. 4.8. The spatial pattern of net internal migration, 1965–90.

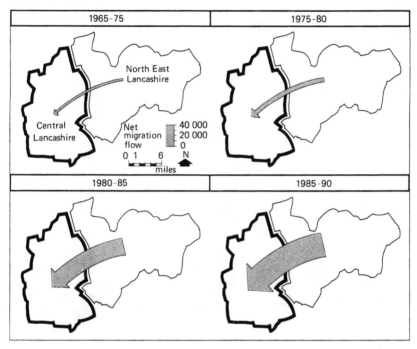

Fig. 4.9. Migration flow between Central and North East Lancashire,
1965–90.

been projected further than 1990 to show the emerging spatial structure
of the subregion, is that forecasting after this period is mere speculation
and examining the rates of change in each zone of the subregion, parts of
the system could well degenerate upon further projection. Another feature
of change involves service employment. This tends to follow a similar
pattern to population although there is no decentralisation of service
employment from the large urban centres of Preston and Blackburn to
the suburban areas. With such radical restructuring of the settlement
pattern, it is likely that basic employment will be affected by the internal
migration of population. This is an aspect of change which the model
cannot predict, for the system is operated on the assumption that changes
in basic employment are completely independent of non-basic employment and population. In general terms, basic employment does not generate
population but when basic employment is changing at different rates in the
system, migration is created which may force a decline in the less
prosperous basic industries.

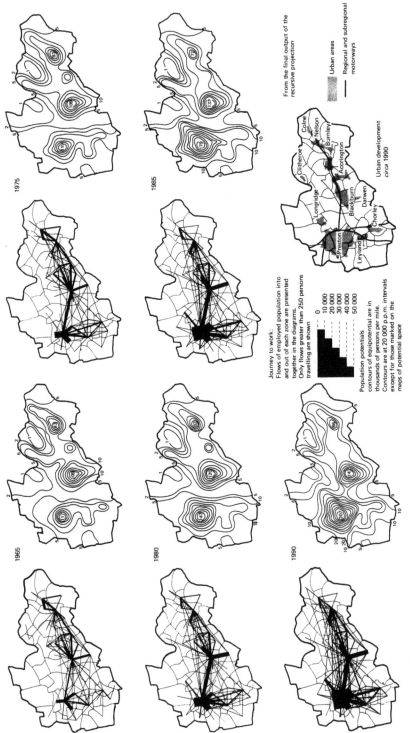

1965

1975

1980

1985

1990

From the final output of the recursive projection

▓ Urban areas

— Regional and subregional motorways

Clitheroe · Colne · Nelson · Burnley · Accrington · Longridge · Blackburn · Darwen · Preston · Leyland · Chorley

Urban development *circa* 1990

Journey to work:
Flows of employed population into and out of each zone are presented together in the diagrams.
Only flows greater than 250 persons travelling are shown

Population potentials
contours of equipotential are in thousands of persons per mile.
Contours are at 20 000 p.p.m. intervals except for those marked on the maps of potential space

0
10 000
20 000
30 000
40 000
50 000

Fig. 4 10. Journey to work and population potential, 1965–90.

The flow of population from North East Lancashire to the new town is double that predicted by the consultants, but just as their study must be interpreted on its assumptions, so must the results given here. They are indicators rather than accurate forecasts: in the same way the diagram in Figure 4.10 provides an indication of the increasing dominance of Central over North East Lancashire, rather than any definitive forecast.

The future of Central and North East Lancashire

If some of these problems are to be solved, then there are two ways to manipulate the future of this subregion; both will involve titanic efforts on the parts of government and planners. First and foremost, employment must be injected into the base of North East Lancashire. But if economic decline is accepted for locational reasons, a second method would be to make the area so attractive as a residential location that people working in the new town would demand housing in North East Lancashire. The first strategy is the most realistic and the easiest to achieve but any proposal will involve an integration of growth in Central and North East Lancashire. Intricate manipulations are needed to sort out the mechanics of such a revival and a subregional strategy is the only way to achieve balance in

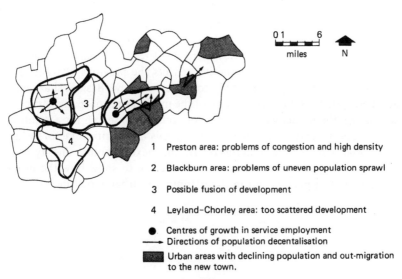

1 Preston area: problems of congestion and high density

2 Blackburn area: problems of uneven population sprawl

3 Possible fusion of development

4 Leyland–Chorley area: too scattered development

● Centres of growth in service employment
——▶ Directions of population decentalisation
▓ Urban areas with declining population and out-migration to the new town.

Fig. 4.11. Future problems concerning the growth and distribution of activity in Central and North East Lancashire.

the economy. Projections of alternative growth patterns for the new town show possible ways in which these goals may be achieved. A more even distribution of basic industry within the subregion realises such objectives, and this model can be used to show how the impact on the subregion can be minimised using different growth locations.

Figure 4.11 suggests a diagrammatic interpretation of the various problems which the subregion will face if the new town is developed. Although there is much work to be done on refining the mathematical and theoretical structure of this model – which is tackled in subsequent chapters – these conclusions do seem to be reasonable indications of the future. If they are, then North East Lancashire is likely to experience an intensification of its present decline. But it is not too late to think again about the future growth of this subregion. By a comprehensive location policy, these trends can be reversed and the area steered back to a state of economic balance.

This chapter has attempted to illustrate the real potential which urban models have in helping to aid the planner in predicting and inventing the future and in this instance, in circumventing undesirable effects of planning policy. The real advantage of such a model in forecasting is that it can produce a very large range of answers to any problem and by doing this, it can define the boundaries of the solution space to that problem. It is these extremes of prediction that planners find very hard to produce, for in a completely intuitive process, there is a continual feedback of information about the problem which results in a series of compromises leading to a single solution; no matter how hard one tries to produce an objective range of alternatives, each alternative reflects the previous alternative in some way, and the range tends to become very narrow. Besides sharpening one's perceptions and understanding of the mechanisms of spatial structure and change, the model widens one's horizons in the search for a solution, and by isolating extremes, it helps one to focus upon critical factors which might otherwise remain unnoticed. In the next chapter, this type of model will be made more realistic in an attempt to show how the model can be used as a positive aid in the planning of urban structure.

5. Calibration and prediction with activity allocation models

In this chapter, the activity allocation model presented formally in Chapter 3 and operationally in Chapter 4 is applied to a more complex problem of subregional modelling. This discussion is organised into three major sections, the first dealing with problems of model calibration, the second with issues affecting the use of the model in evaluating alternative urban structure plans, and the third with a comparative analysis of the problems raised in this and the previous chapter. The model which is applied to the Nottinghamshire–Derbyshire subregion, referred to hereafter as the Notts.–Derbys. subregion, was based upon the system of equations (3.28)–(3.49); however, unlike the Central Lancashire model, locational constraints in the residential population sector were required in the Notts.–Derbys. model and thus the equation system used was specifically based upon equations (3.28)–(3.41) together with (3.42), (3.43), (3.46) and (3.48). No constraints were invoked with regard to location in the service or non-basic sector. A more complex calibration procedure was designed for this model but before this is described, it is worth while outlining some of the factors involved in making this model operational in Notts.–Derbys.

Zoning and information systems

Although the factors affecting the number and size of zones, and the data describing activities within zones are closely intertwined, as was illustrated in the previous chapter, Broadbent (1969a) has suggested a fundamental theoretical principle governing the choice of zone size. When designing spatial interaction models, Broadbent argues that it is important to have a 'sufficient' number of interactions between zones in order that the model describes trip behaviour in an accurate way. In other words, the smaller the ratio of inter-zonal to intra-zonal interaction, the less need there is for a model describing spatial interaction. As a general rule, Broadbent suggests that the average radius of a zone should be less than the mean trip length; a more detailed presentation of this idea is given in Chapter 8. Although this principle is basic to zone definition, it must be

111

tempered against other factors. If possible, zone geometry should be fairly regular for this can ensure that as many zones as possible are packed into the system. The smaller and more regular the zone, the more accurate is the location of the zone centroid, although zone centroids should be placed on or near the main transport network used in measuring the travel times between zones. The spatial distribution of activities within zones should be as homogeneous as possible, especially in the types of model discussed here in which the variables are not disaggregated. The zoning

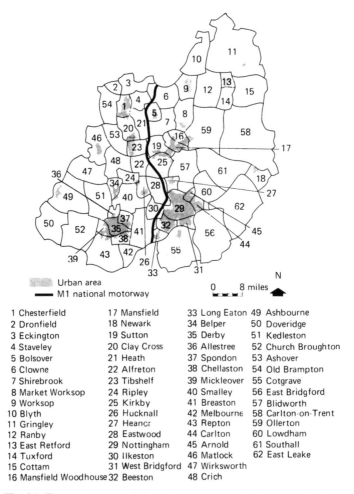

1 Chesterfield	17 Mansfield	33 Long Eaton	49 Ashbourne
2 Dronfield	18 Newark	34 Belper	50 Doveridge
3 Eckington	19 Sutton	35 Derby	51 Kedleston
4 Staveley	20 Clay Cross	36 Allestree	52 Church Broughton
5 Bolsover	21 Heath	37 Spondon	53 Ashover
6 Clowne	22 Alfreton	38 Chellaston	54 Old Brampton
7 Shirebrook	23 Tibshelf	39 Mickleover	55 Cotgrave
8 Market Worksop	24 Ripley	40 Smalley	56 East Bridgford
9 Worksop	25 Kirkby	41 Breaston	57 Blidworth
10 Blyth	26 Hucknall	42 Melbourne	58 Carlton-on-Trent
11 Gringley	27 Heanor	43 Repton	59 Ollerton
12 Ranby	28 Eastwood	44 Carlton	60 Lowdham
13 East Retford	29 Nottingham	45 Arnold	61 Southall
14 Tuxford	30 Ilkeston	46 Matlock	62 East Leake
15 Cottam	31 West Bridgford	47 Wirksworth	
16 Mansfield Woodhouse	32 Beeston	48 Crich	

Fig. 5.1. Zone geometry and the settlement pattern in the Notts.–Derbys. subregion.

system should also follow topographical barriers as far as possible. The zoning system used in Notts.–Derbys. is shown in Figure 5.1, and in Table 5.1, the major characteristics of the subregion are presented.

The choice of zoning system has not only been made with regard to the factors mentioned above; the areal units for which data are available were another critical factor in these decisions. The development of this model was undertaken under a strict limit on the supply of data for no special surveys could be commissioned to collect new data. This is reflected in the fact that the model is designed to operate with only data available from

TABLE 5.1. *Major characteristics of the Notts.–Derbys. subregion*

Total number of zones	62
Total land area in square miles	1456
Average land area per zone in square miles	23.8064
Total population	1 701 050
Average population per zone	27 436
Population density in persons per square mile	1168.303
Basic employment	438 830
Total employment	751 260
Ratio of basic to total employment	0.5841
Ratio of inter-zonal to intra-zonal work trips	0.9073

published sources. The Census of Population 1966 provided the main data source for the model. Population was available for enumeration districts from the Ward and Parish Library, and this provided a fine zoning system which was later aggregated to form larger zones. Total employment data for Local Authorities (aggregations of enumeration districts) were used as a control total, and a detailed classification of the location and size of firms employing over five persons was available from the Employment Exchange Record. The classification of these firms was by Minimum List Headings of the S.I.C. and this was used as a basis for the division of employment into basic and service sectors. The maximum density constraints on each zone were calculated using the inventory of land uses compiled by the Local Planning Authorities.

Data on the spatial distribution of work trips were available from the Census of Population. A special tabulation of work trips had already been carried out by the Census of Population for this area, and furthermore, a cordon survey around the main towns in the subregion was available. As in the Central Lancashire model, no data were available for the trips made between home and service centre, but from other studies in the subregion, mean service trip lengths were available. It was therefore decided to calibrate the model against a range of mean service trip lengths before one particular service trip length was adopted. The constructed variables such as activity and population-serving ratios were calculated from the data. A particularly good data bank had been assembled by the Notts.–Derbys. Subregional Planning Unit and all data were stored in this bank. The zoning system was redesigned several times, taking account of the principles outlined above, and the final design shown in Figure 5.1 is the result of this lengthy process. Before the results of applying the model are presented, it is necessary to look in more detail at some of the issues involved in sectoring employment and in choosing the variables measuring locational attraction.

Detailed decisions in model design

It was stated earlier in both Chapters 3 and 4 that the division of employment into basic and service reflects a weak assumption in this model. The weakness of this assumption is largely due to the practical difficulties involved in dividing employment into these two sectors. Although methods such as the minimum-requirements approach (Ullman and Dacey, 1962) have been suggested to overcome some of these difficulties such methods break down when applied to the local scale. As data were available on the location of each firm and its classification by Minimum List Heading, the division into basic and service employment was carried out by examining each firm from these files and deciding whether or not the firm belonged to the basic or service sectors. As a general rule, the primary and manufacturing sectors constituted basic employment. But there were exceptions to this. For example certain publishing establishments classified under manufacturing were shifted to the service sector; some military and government establishments were transferred from the service to the basic sector on account of their functions and site requirements. An attempt was also made to restrict the amount of employment in the basic sector, for as the ratio of basic to total employment approaches 1, all employment is exogenous to the model, and the service centre location model is redundant. If this ratio is large, then the performance of the model may be biased towards a good fit, especially if fit is measured in terms of the total distribution of population and employment. In this case, the ratio was 0.58 and this was judged to be low enough to ensure that the model's fit would not be biased.

The measurement of locational attraction is one of the most important problems in model design, and as discussed in the previous chapter, this problem has never been resolved satisfactorily. In this model, as in the Central Lancashire model, population is used to measure the attraction of residential areas, and service employment to measure the attraction of service centres; negative exponential functions of time-distance d_{ij} are used in representing the deterrence functions. Then

$$f^1(D_j, c_{ij}) = P_j^* \exp(-\lambda_1 d_{ij}),$$

$$f^2(D_i, c_{ij}) = S_i^* \exp(-\lambda_2 d_{ij}).$$

Set against the tautological implications of the above equations are two arguments which are worthy of note. First, as the models are equilibrium models summarising the whole history of spatial structure by simple equations at one point in time, it is logical to use variables which describe the history of locational attraction. Population and service employment are variables which achieve this description. Second, in the case of residential location, other variables which summarise attraction such as the number of houses or households tend to be highly correlated with population. The same high correlations are found between service employment, and variables such as floorspace and sales in the service centre location model. These problems seem to be a feature of equilibrium models, and can only be resolved in a dynamic context when such variables as site rent, and amenities such as accessibility to schools, recreational resources etc. are used to provide more realistic measures of locational attraction. Such extensions are attempted in Chapter 12.

There are, however, two mechanisms in the activity allocation model which change the measures of locational attraction. The first is the constraints procedure which determines weights on residential and service centre attraction, and the second is the procedure used by Lowry to establish consistency between the input and output variables in the model. Although these procedures have only an operational, not theoretical, meaning, they act as a brake on the model's simulation process and ensure that the model's predictions fall within reasonable limits. The measurements of generalised travel cost within and between zones were based on the travel times along the shortest routes in the subregional road network. The travel times were computed from average driving speeds by car, which varied over the network according to the density of population. The higher the density of population in areas adjacent to the route, the lower the average driving speed. The travel times were also weighted by parking times at each end of the trip

$$d_{ij} = t_i + t_{ij} + t_j,$$

where d_{ij} is the total average travel time between i and j, t_i and t_j are terminal times necessary for parking at i and j, and t_{ij} is the average travel time on the shortest route between i and j. The shortest routes in the network were calculated as in the Central Lancashire model using a minimum path algorithm based on the Murchland's cascade method developed by Foot (1965).

Calibration procedures

The first stage in operating this model is to find values of the parameters λ_1 and λ_2 for the residential and service centre location models, which produce the best correspondence between the model's predictions, and the observed situation at the base date, in this case 1966. This correspondence between predictions and observations, called here the goodness of fit, is measured by the various statistics such as the correlation coefficient outlined in Chapter 4. Research into this model, shows that it is possible to achieve reasonably good approximations to the best parameter values of λ_1 and λ_2 independently of each other. Changes in the value of λ_2 do not substantially affect the fit of the residential location model and changes in λ_1 do not affect the fit of the service centre location model. If the values of λ_1 and λ_2 are first found independently, then this reduces the cost of developing the model and the amount of computer time used. The calibration procedure developed for the Notts.–Derbys. model relies heavily upon these results. A two-stage procedure has been developed which first finds the best parameter values when the model is run without constraints on residential location, and second, modifies these values when the model is run under residential constraint. The elements of this process are summarised in the following argument.

In the first stage, the method finds the values of each parameter independently using iteration. These values are then used as first approximations and a gradient search procedure is used to test the uniqueness of these values. If the fit improves, then the gradient search is initiated once again, and the process stops when the fit does not improve. The method can be described in different stages with a residential parameter λ_1 and a service centre parameter λ_2.

1. As a first approximation, the best values λ_1^k and λ_2^k are found independently by running the model through a range of values for each parameter.
2. Two narrow ranges of values $\lambda_1^k \pm \Delta\lambda_1$ and $\lambda_2^k \pm \Delta\lambda_2$ are fixed.
3. The model is then run through all combinations of values at intervals in the ranges $\lambda_1^k \pm \Delta\lambda_1$ and $\lambda_2^k \pm \Delta\lambda_2$.
4. If the fit does not improve, λ_1^k and λ_2^k are the best parameter values. If the fit does improve, then new parameter values λ_1^{k+1} and λ_2^{k+1} are selected.

5. λ_1^{k+1} and λ_2^{k+1} are substituted for λ_1^k and λ_2^k respectively in 2 above.
6. Stages 2–5 are repeated until there is no further improvement in the model's fit. The best parameter values λ_1^{k+n} and λ_2^{k+n} are then selected. In the case of a tie between two or more best values at any stage, the above procedure is applied to those two or more values.

The second stage of the calibration procedure can now be started. First, the overall fit of the model is assessed and if residential constraints need be incorporated into the model on *a priori* grounds, or on the results of the first-stage calibration, the model is run until such constraints are satisfied. Then a process of testing the fit under small changes in the best parameter values, similar to the test in the first stage, is begun, and this procedure stops when the best fit cannot be improved. The essential elements in this two-stage process are illustrated in Figure 5.2. This process has been developed empirically and by measuring the goodness of fit with statistics which are sensitive to small variations in the parameter values, this process provides a sensible search routine for homing in on the optimum fit of the model to reality. This two-stage procedure will now be applied to the Notts.–Derbys. model, thus providing both a demonstration of its efficacy in model design and a pertinent evaluation of the model's performance.

First-stage calibration

The values of λ_1 and λ_2 were first fitted independently and their goodness of fit was primarily assessed using the mean trip length statistics whose functional form is given in (4.1) and (4.2). The particular form adopted here was specified as

$$\left. \begin{array}{l} F^1(c_{ij}) \\ F^2(c_{ij}) \end{array} \right\} = d_{ij},$$

which is compatible with the maximum-likelihood estimates of the negative exponential deterrence functions (Hyman, 1969). Although these statistics were the most important in calibrating the model, log-transformed versions of the r^2 and ζ root mean square error statistics were used to measure the fit of the locational distributions of population and employment. These statistics were based on log-transforms due to the log-normal distribution of population and employment in the subregion, as is demonstrated later. Earlier it was stated that the two parameter values λ_1 and λ_2 were fairly independent of each other in the model, and to test this proposition, the model was run under several combinations of λ_1 and λ_2. Variation in the values of the statistics measuring the goodness of fit relative to variations in these parameter values is illustrated using isometric forms

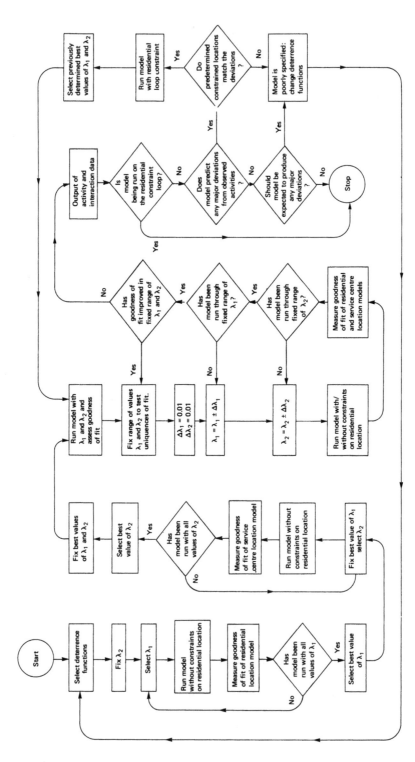

Fig. 5.2. The two-stage calibration procedure.

for population, employment, and the work and service trip distributions in Figure 5.3. Besides confirming the relative independence of λ_1 and λ_2, Figure 5.3 also highlights the ambiguities caused by the use of r^2 and ζ in measuring the fit of the activity distributions.

The values of λ_1 and λ_2 were found independently and no changes in these values were needed when the full model was run. The values of the predicted and observed mean work trip lengths are very close with λ_1 at 0.23. Because no data were available for the service trip distribution, a value for the mean service trip length was assumed and λ_2 was iterated towards this assumed value. Table 5.2 summarises this fit, and indicates the performance of the model in terms of its activity distributions, measured by the log-transformed version of r^2, and the ζ statistics. Figures 5.4 and 5.5 provide a diagrammatic interpretation of the model's fit showing the correspondence between the predicted and observed distributions of population, employment, activity rates and population-serving ratios.

TABLE 5.2. *Best fits at calibration with no*
constraints on residential locations

Residential parameter λ_1	0.2300	Service centre parameter λ_2	0.1600
$\bar{C}(\lambda_1, \lambda_2)$ observed	6.9766	$\bar{C}(\lambda_1, \lambda_2)$ predicted	0.4748
$\bar{S}(\lambda_1, \lambda_2)$ assumed	8.0000	$\bar{S}(\lambda_1, \lambda_2)$ predicted	8.5207
r^2 for $\{\ln (P_i)\}$	0.9364	ζ for $\{P_i\}$	21 296
r^2 for $\{\ln (E_i)\}$	0.9764	ζ for $\{E_i\}$	3052
r^2 for $\{\alpha_{ij}\}$, $i = j$	0.8746	ζ for $\{\alpha_{ij}\}$, $i = j$	1.3224
r^2 for $\{\beta_{ij}\}$, $i = j$	0.5709	ζ for $\{\beta_{ij}\}$, $i = j$	0.0712

At this point, it was necessary to find out whether the model should be run with constraints on residential location. In the Notts.–Derbys. model, this represented a situation of imperfect information or uncertainty for before the model was run, it was difficult to know on *a priori* grounds whether or not the residential location model would provide a sufficiently good explanation of reality. If it did not provide good enough predictions in certain areas of the system, then it would be necessary to run the model with the location of residential activity constrained to the observed situation, in those areas. This is really a process in which the model-builder ascertains the predictive power of the model in certain areas of the system, and if this predictive power is poor, then those areas are constrained by the model and the location of activity is assumed to be based on decisions exogenous to the model's simulation process. In the Notts.–Derbys. subregion, the location of residential development is particularly com-

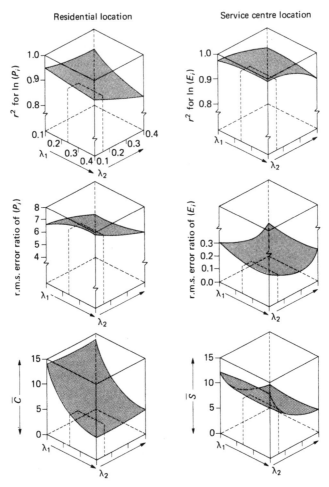

Residential location

Service centre location

A diagrammatic example of the calibration procedure on r^2 of (T_{ij}).

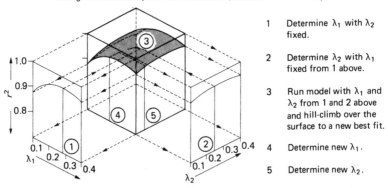

1 Determine λ_1 with λ_2 fixed.

2 Determine λ_2 with λ_1 fixed from 1 above.

3 Run model with λ_1 and λ_2 from 1 and 2 above and hill-climb over the surface to a new best fit.

4 Determine new λ_1.

5 Determine new λ_2.

Fig. 5.3. Analysis of the goodness of fit under simultaneous variation in the parameter values λ_1 and λ_2.

plex in the Chesterfield, Mansfield, Derby and Nottingham urban areas, and before the model was run, it was expected that the simulation of residential activity would be poor in these areas. Several of the zones in these urban areas have reached their holding capacity in accommodating residential land use, and it is unlikely that any gravity model without constraints on residential location could effect a good simulation in such a situation.

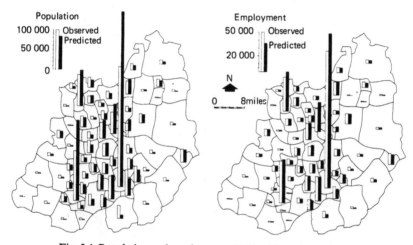

Fig. 5.4. Population and employment, 1966, with no constraints on residential locations.

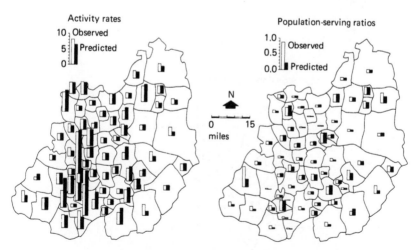

Fig. 5.5. Activity rates and population-serving ratios, 1966, with no constraints on residential locations.

A comparison of the deviations in the model's predictions expected on *a priori* grounds, and the actual deviations in the predictions is illustrated in Figure 5.6. Several of the major urban centres such as Chesterfield, Derby, Mansfield and Nottingham were attracting too much residential activity and the suburban areas were attracting too little; a simple test was designed in the hope that any systematic bias could be revealed. The test was based on a comparison of two variables, the first describing the model's predictions of population, the second describing the proportion of land not yet developed in each zone. The ratio of predicted to observed population was used for the dependent variable

$$Y_j = \sum_m P_j(m,1)/P_j^*,$$

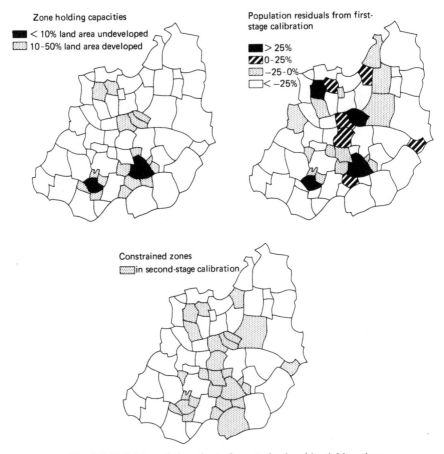

Fig. 5.6. Definition of the subset of constrained residential locations.

and the proportion of land not yet developed in each zone was used for the independent variable

$$X_j = [L_j - (L_j^u + L_j^r + L_j^h)]/L_j.$$

The coefficient of determination r^2 between Y_j and X_j is 0.7459, revealing a highly significant relationship. A regression of Y_j against X_j yielded the following equation in which the slope coefficient is significantly different from zero at the 0.05 per cent level using a t-test. Then

$$Y_j = 1.8062 - 2.0659 X_j.$$

This equation shows that as the proportion of available land in any zone decreases, the ratio of predicted to observed population rises. This relationship supports the use of capacity constraints on the location of population, and on this basis, it was decided to constrain residential development in the main urban areas of the system; 27 out of 62 zones were constrained, as is illustrated in Figure 5.6. Although this decision definitely lowers the predictive capability of the model in forecasting, it is an eminently more sensible procedure than making arbitrary changes to the distances or to other variables in an effort to get a good fit.

Second-stage calibration

With the best parameter values determined at the first stage, the model, as set out in (3.28)–(3.43), (3.46) and (3.48), was run until constraint equation (3.48) was satisfied. The movement to equilibrium is extremely slow with this formulation of the model, and Figure 5.7 illustrates the movement towards equilibrium for some of the zones whose residential activity is constrained. The process of iterating equations (3.28)–(3.41) was stopped after twenty cycles and at this point, all the constrained locations were within 2 per cent of their constraint values. It might be possible in certain instances to speed up this convergence by replacing the relevant part of equation (3.46) with

$$B_j(n+1) = B_j(n) \left[\frac{\delta_j L_j^h}{P_j(n)} \right]^{\psi}, \quad j \in Z_2, Z_4,$$

where ψ is a constant greater than unity. The effect of ψ would be to magnify the change in $B_j(n)$ to $B_j(n+1)$, producing a greater scaling up or down effect, thus hopefully helping the process to converge at a faster rate. Some success has been had with such a technique in the Northampton model discussed in Chapter 8. The performance of the model obviously improves substantially in terms of the residential sector, but the fit of the

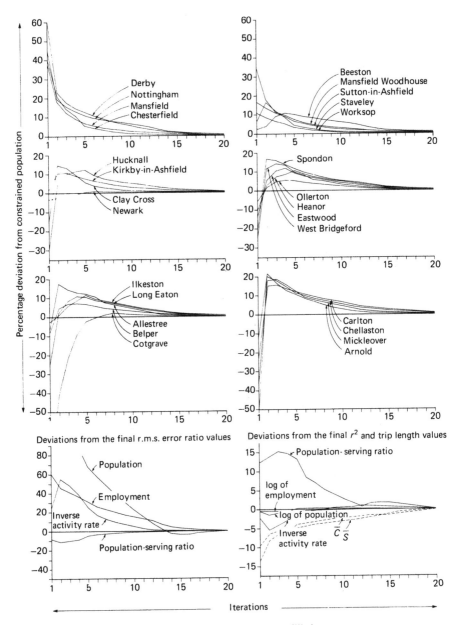

Fig. 5.7. Convergence to equilibrium.

employment sector also improves. This is encouraging for it suggests that service employment is oriented towards the location of population, and it goes some way in showing that the original definition of service employment is substantially correct. The improvement in the model's performance measured by the log-transformed version of the r^2 statistics

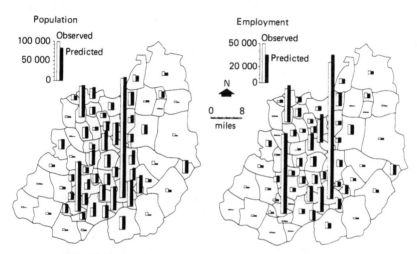

Fig. 5.8. Population and employment, 1966, with constraints on a subset of residential locations.

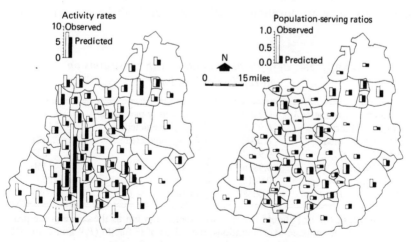

Fig. 5.9. Activity rates and population-serving ratios, 1966, with constraints on a subset of residential locations.

for population and employment is also shown in Figure 5.7. To steer the model towards a best fit, it was necessary to alter only the value of λ_2, and Table 5.3 presents these best fits, and the statistics measuring the overall performance of the model. Figures 5.8 and 5.9 provide a diagrammatic interpretation of the goodness of fit. As a research exercise, the model has also been run with all zones in the residential sector constrained. The fits are not very different from those in Table 5.3 and these new fits are

TABLE 5.3. *Best fits at calibration with constraints on a subset of residential locations*

Residential parameter λ_1	0.2400	Service centre parameter λ_2	0.1600
$\bar{C}(\lambda_1, \lambda_2)$ observed	6.9766	$\bar{C}(\lambda_1, \lambda_2)$ predicted	6.5132
$\bar{S}(\lambda_1, \lambda_2)$ assumed	8.0000	$\bar{S}(\lambda_1, \lambda_2)$ predicted	8.2917
r^2 for $\{\ln (P_i)\}$	0.9402	ζ for $\{P_i\}$	3326
r^2 for $\{\ln (E_i)\}$	0.9802	ζ for $\{E_i\}$	1898
r^2 for $\{\alpha_{ij}\}, \quad i = j$	0.8982	ζ for $\{\alpha_{ij}\}, \quad i = j$	1.0588
r^2 for $\{\beta_{ij}\}, \quad i = j$	0.5083	ζ for $\{\beta_{ij}\}, \quad i = j$	0.0779

presented in Table 5.4. When the residential location model is totally constrained in this fashion, the lengthy system of equations given in (3.28)–(3.49) can be simplified for as the distribution of population is exogenous to the model, the system is simply made up of a traffic distribution model and a service centre location model which can both be run separately.

TABLE 5.4. *Best fits at calibration with constraints on all residential locations**

Residential parameter λ_1	0.2400	Service centre parameter λ_2	0.1700
$\bar{C}(\lambda_1, \lambda_2)$ observed	6.9766	$\bar{C}(\lambda_1, \lambda_2)$ predicted	7.1329
$\bar{S}(\lambda_1, \lambda_2)$ assumed	8.0000	$\bar{S}(\lambda_1, \lambda_2)$ predicted	8.2321
r^2 for $\{\ln (P_i)\}$	0.9992	ζ for $\{P_i\}$	637
r^2 for $\{\ln (E_i)\}$	0.9856	ζ for $\{E_i\}$	1750
r^2 for $\{\alpha_{ij}\}, \quad i = j$	0.9415	ζ for $\{\alpha_{ij}\}, \quad i = j$	0.9543
r^2 for $\{\beta_{ij}\}, \quad i = j$	0.5068	ζ for $\{\beta_{ij}\}, \quad i = j$	0.0799

* A perfect fit for $\{P_i\}$ should occur in this application but as the convergence procedure has been terminated at 20 iterations, the values of r^2 for $\{\ln (P_i)\}$ and ζ for $\{P_i\}$ are not quite equal to their optimum values of 1 and 0 respectively.

This brings up a fairly important problem concerning the degree of constraint on the residential or service sector which the model-builder can accept. As the ratio of constrained to unconstrained activity in the model increases, the purpose to which the model can be applied in planning begins to change; this seems to be an important research problem which is worthy of further study.

A general critique of the model and its performance

The model attempts to simulate a system whose components adjust themselves immediately to some static equilibrium. This highly idealised interpretation of an urban or subregional system is in some ways unrealistic for the structure of the model does not involve the processes of change characteristic of such systems, and the model only simulates an average behaviour at one point in time. This does not mean that such a model is irrelevant to the problems of spatial planning; it does mean, however, that the model can only be used for conditional projection and impact analysis which involves interpreting the equilibrium state of the system resulting from given changes in activity (Lowry, 1965). With these points in mind, the suitability of each location model can be assessed. The service centre location model produces a fairly good simulation of the location of service employment in Notts.–Derbys. The service sector probably responds fairly quickly to changes in the demand for service employment, and this model provides a reasonable tool in simulating the development of service centres (Cordey-Hayes, 1968). On the other hand, the residential location model produces a relatively poor simulation. The complexity of locational decisions in the residential sector, especially in the main urban areas, means that constraints have to be built into the model to effect a reasonable simulation. It seems that this type of elementary model is not suited to the residential sector in Notts.–Derbys., and Wilson (1969*b*) has suggested that considerable disaggregation of such models is necessary before they become feasible tools for simulation. Table 5.5 provides a numerical demonstration of the model's performance under no constraint and partial constraint for a selected sample of zones.

At least 90 per cent of the population in Notts.–Derbys. is concentrated in the main urban settlements, and therefore the parameters of the model are strongly biased towards the location of urban activities. This is evident from the predictions shown in Figures 5.4, 5.5, 5.8 and 5.9. The model produces poor predictions of the residential and service activities in rural areas, and there is a tendency for the urban areas to pull too much activity

away from the rural areas. One way of overcoming this which has not
been tried in this model but has been developed by Cripps and Foot

TABLE 5.5. *Predicted population and service employment for
a sample of zones*

Zone number	Name	Observed values 1966		Calibration without constraints 1966		Calibration with constraints 1966	
		Population	Service employment	Population	Service employment	Population	Service employment
1	Chesterfield	79080	22080	111298	27956	79175*	26334
3	Eckington	27510	1850	18879	1736	28103	2221
5	Bolsover	11070	430	8703	360	12103	455
9	Worksop	33010	8740	36591	8540	33047*	8797
11	Gringley	11450	1220	6786	656	7059	703
16	Woodhouse	22640	2470	30249	3350	22712*	3349
17	Mansfield	55610	18050	77194	24778	55799*	24313
19	Sutton	40840	4200	47445	5201	40985	5227
22	Alfreton	32050	3410	21297	2715	37035	3583
26	Heanor	24130	3410	21607	3242	24297	3771
29	Nottingham	305050	81410	439397	102293	307930*	92904
31	West Bridgeford	65130	10600	43283	7600	65731*	8470
33	Long Eaton	31090	5090	23068	3704	31339*	4485
35	Derby	125900	49340	202644	50940	126782*	48403
37	Spondon	30430	200	24190	163	32642	191
39	Mickleover	22010	3620	13475	1840	23158	2077
41	Breaston	21900	2510	12579	1612	35463	2246
45	Arnold	29840	4130	25735	3697	30113*	3463
47	Wirksworth	8160	1060	5064	475	6225	579
52	Broughton	6620	930	1858	225	5083	293
57	Blidworth	21880	2160	13828	1733	35363	2773
59	Ollerton	23830	1730	22519	1343	23013	1415
62	East Leake	8540	2170	2698	406	5854	577

* Shows zones in which the maximum density constraint on population is necessary.

(1969*b*) in their model of Bedfordshire, is to vary the parameters affecting
intra-zonal location, on the assumption that persons working in settlements
of different sizes have different behaviours with regard to living within
those settlements. Some comments have been made already on the model's
performance, although performance as measured by the goodness of fit
is too narrow a guide to evaluation. A comprehensive evaluation of the

model can only be made if the variables and parameters are subjected to sensitivity-testing. The calibration procedure revealed that the measures of spatial interaction were most sensitive to parameter variation. Small changes in the intra-zonal travel times lead to large differences between the predictions, and this suggests that the ratio of inter- to intra-zonal interaction is too low. Only by reducing the zone size and by packing more zones into the subregion can this problem be overcome. If a variable such as intra-zonal distance is too sensitive, then this means that the use of the model in prediction is suspect if large changes in intra-zonal distances occur. In any redesign of the model, this would be one of the most important problems to tackle.

Another feature of the model revealed by the calibration involves the use of system-wide parameters in residential and service centre location. The model tends to over-allocate population and service employment in urban areas and under-allocate these activities in rural areas. This suggests that the locational parameters should be higher in rural than in urban areas to account for the greater resistance to travel. The constraints procedure partly obscures this problem for the maximum-density constraint ensures that urban areas do not attract too much activity. However, those areas which are not rural and which are not constrained tend to attract too much activity from rural areas. One way of overcoming this is to use Goldner's (1968) method of disaggregating the parameters spatially. Disaggregation of employment and population would probably help to alleviate this problem. Because of the model's structure and its limitations in simulating locational behaviour, the model can only be used for certain types of spatial forecasting. Although the model does not involve an explicit time dimension, projections with the model are explicitly based on different time intervals. This gives rise again to the theoretical inconsistency between calibration and projection already discussed and before the types of projection are outlined, the precise use of the model in forecasting activities in the Notts.–Derbys. subregion must be outlined.

The use of the model in spatial forecasting

The model has been used both in plan design and in plan evaluation. A set of thirteen alternative future strategies for the location of basic employment and transportation was tested by the model and on these results the first set of strategies was revised and reduced to six. These new strategies were then tested by the model, and eventually three strategies were chosen for further development (Thorburn *et al.*, 1969). In this sort of planning process, it is difficult to draw the line between plan design and plan evaluation. Although the model was used to test the first set of strategies, the model's forecasts were then used in the design of the second set. As the differences between the strategies in the second set were much less than the differences between those in the first set, the model was primarily used as an evaluation tool in testing this second set.

Projections made by the model are based upon the recursive system of forecasting outlined in (4.3)–(4.14) using a ten-yearly forecast interval. As in the Central Lancashire model, population and service employment predicted by the model at, for example, 1975 becomes input data to the location models, used in predicting these same variables at 1985. As well as accounting for change in the system between the base and horizon years, a ten-year lag between the change in activity and its impact on the system is also built into such projections. Although it is generally accepted that such a lag exists, there is little information on the length of the lag and the technique is thus open to criticism on this account. Using the technique of recursive forecasting, the trajectories of the critical variables such as population, employment and the work trip and service trip distributions can be charted and analysed. This provides useful information for the planner seeking to control the system and can also lead to some insight into how the system is behaving, thus having some implications for the design or redesign of the subregional system.

Rather than demonstrating all the strategies tested by the model, one particular strategy has been chosen for more detailed exposition and discussion. In this forecast, the general strategy for the subregion is to channel growth from the Greater Nottingham area to the Erewash Valley which in recent years has suffered from a declining economic base and net out-migration of population. As part of this strategy, two goals are explicitly formulated and the forecasts are to be tested against these goals.

1. The need to control the growth of Greater Nottingham and Derby due to the extreme pressures on land for residential development, rising land values and severe traffic congestion.
2. The need to generate a more balanced and prosperous industrial base in the Erewash Valley towns of Mansfield, Sutton, Alfreton and Ilkeston.

A realistic strategy for the subregion could not be implemented and would have no major impact on the structure of activities until 1976, and the forecasts from 1966 to 1976 are based on a projection of existing trends in the subregion. The major growth in basic employment in this period occurs in Chesterfield, Nottingham, Derby, Spondon and Matlock. Basic employment declines in Clay Cross and Heath, in the towns of Ripley, Kirkby, Heanor and Hucknall, in Ilkeston and in Breaston. In this period, improvements in the transportation system of the subregion, for example the opening of the M1 Motorway, are likely to affect the structure of activities, especially in the Erewash Valley. The strategy for 1976–96 proposes growth in basic employment in the Erewash Valley. The largest growth is proposed for Alfreton and smaller but still substantial growth is forecast for Kirkby, Heanor, Hucknall, Eastwood and Smalley. The major declines in basic employment occur in Nottingham, Spondon and Derby. These policies for change are backed up by comprehensive proposals for the subregional transportation system, and major improvements to the transportation network are made in the Erewash Valley and in the Derby–Nottingham area. These changes in basic employment and transportation, from 1976 to 1996, are designed to achieve the two goals stated previously. The model's predictions in terms of population and employment can now be analysed in the light of these changes in the exogenous variables.

Population, employment and migration analysis

Between 1965 and 1976, growth and decline in population mirrors the change in basic employment. Existing constraints on residential development are relaxed to account for possible increases in the density of population. The major increase in population occurs in the Nottingham–Breaston–Derby area and this is counter to the major goals of the strategy. Pressures on agricultural land for conversion to urban uses and traffic congestion are likely to increase during this period. There are few major declines in population except for Ilkeston which loses a large proportion of its basic employment during these years. After 1976, major growth in population is centred on the Heath, Alfreton, Ripley, Hucknall and Breaston areas; this growth is partly due to the increased attractiveness of these areas due to changed transportation facilities. During the projection period, the trajectory of change in population and employment can be plotted and this is illustrated in Figure 5.10. Apart from some rural areas, the major decline in population takes place in Derby where declines in basic industry and some decentralisation of population to suburban areas account for this change.

In Figure 5.11, the net internal migration of population from equation (4.10) is plotted in each forecast interval. This shows that a significant proportion of the growth in population in Heath, Alfreton, Ripley, Hucknall, Spondon and Breaston is accounted for by net inward migration from other parts of the system. Major out-migrations take place in the large centres of Chesterfield, Nottingham, Mansfield and Derby. Like the recursive projections carried out with the Central Lancashire model, this shows that the recursive system of forecasting is quite sensitive to the changes which cause the decentralisation of activity, and in this

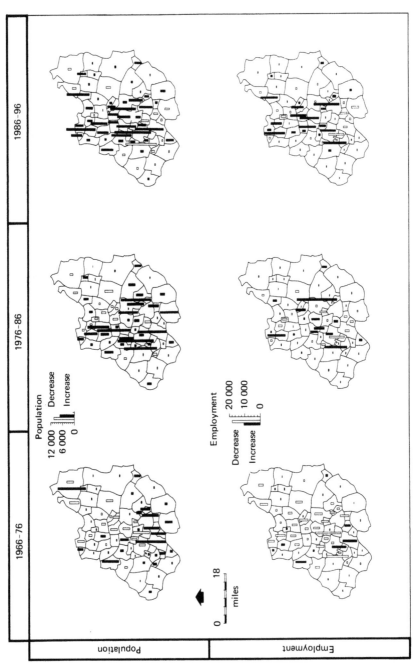

Fig. 5.10. Population and employment change, 1966–96.

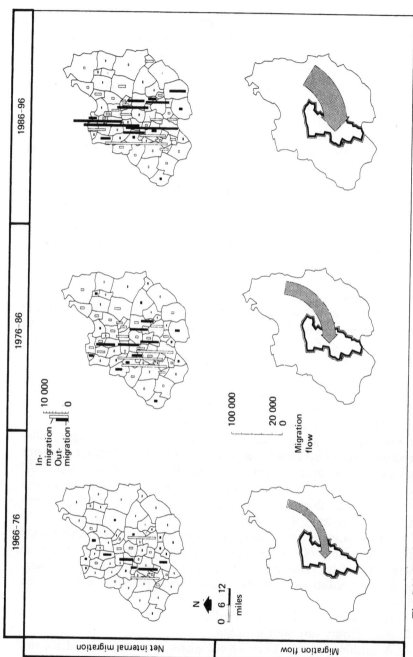

Fig. 5.11. Net internal migration and migration flow between the Erewash Valley and the rest of the system, 1966–96.

respect, the model produces successful simulations. Although it is possible to find actual average movement of population between zones using this model from the elements of (4.9), these are rather complex to display diagrammatically and thus the analysis is restricted to the text. The Spondon–Breaston area gains much of its increase in population from persons moving out of Derby and Nottingham. Such decentralisation is largely due to better transportation facilities in these areas. The growth in Hucknall is due to out-migration from Nottingham and population growth in Heath is due to out-migration from Chesterfield and Mansfield. Net migration to Alfreton poses the most interesting case for migration analysis. Alfreton is equidistant from the four largest towns in the subregion – Chesterfield, Derby, Mansfield and Nottingham, and therefore it is clear that Alfreton gains population from each of these towns. Furthermore, the greatest change in locational attraction for residential development occurs in Alfreton during the projection period; this is largely due to its central location in the subregion, its large growth in basic employment and its increased accessibility due to improvements in the transportation network in this area.

To test the impact of the various changes in basic employment and transportation on the distribution of population, an analysis can be made of the migration flows across any partition of the system into two subsets of zones as in (4.14). As one of the goals of this strategy is to generate growth in the Erewash Valley by improving its overall locational attraction, one subset of zones comprised this area (zones 16, 17, 19, 22, 23, 24, 25, 26, 27, 28, 30, 37, 40, 41); the other subset consists of all other zones. The flow of population between these areas is shown in Figure 5.11 for the three forecast intervals. Net migration into the Erewash Valley increases at each forecast interval and this demonstrates that the projected strategy for the area positively encourages industrial and residential growth in this area. Net migration between any other partition of this system into two subsets can be analysed, and this leads to further insights into how the system is behaving. To demonstrate how these flows can be of use, cumulative net migration over the projection period between eight different partitions of the system is illustrated in Figure 5.12. These net migration analyses provide eight different interpretations of how population is being redistributed in the system. These partitions are described below.

1. An arbitrary north–south partition.
2. An arbitrary east–west partition.
3. A partition into the Derby–Nottingham urban region, and the rest of the system.

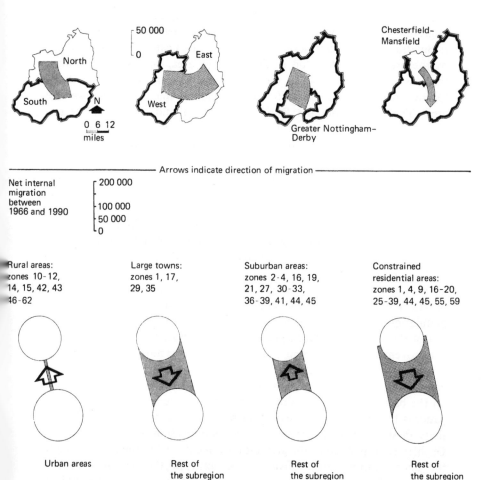

Fig. 5.12. An analysis of cumulative migration flow between 1966 and 1996,
across eight different partitions of the subregional system.

4. A partition into the Chesterfield–Mansfield area, and the rest of the
   system.
5. A rural–urban partition.
6. A partition into zones with population greater than 50000, and zones
   with less than 50000 population in 1966.
7. A suburban area – rest of the system partition.
8. A partition into constrained and unconstrained residential locations
   based on the 1966 definition of these subsets.

6

The first four partitions are into spatially adjacent sets and the net migration flow is shown between each of these partitions. The net loss of population from the northern to the southern area can largely be explained by the presence of Alfreton in the southern area. In a similar manner, the loss of population from the eastern to western areas is accounted for by growth in the Erewash Valley which is mainly in the western area. The losses from the Derby–Nottingham and from the Chesterfield–Mansfield complexes is also due to the decentralisation of population from these areas into the Erewash Valley. Each of these movements is a small percentage of the total number of net moves between 1966 and 1996 and these analyses, unlike the previous analysis of movements between the Erewash Valley and the rest of the system, do not reveal any major impacts.

Partitions 5–8 are more significant. These are essentially topological or non-planar partitions of the system based on different functional relations. The partition into rural and urban areas is especially interesting. The rural areas gain very slightly from the urban areas and this is probably due to advancing urbanisation of the urban–rural fringe, and to the availability of residential land in these areas. Partitions into zones over 50 000 population and the rest of the system, and into suburban areas, and the rest of the system, produce significant migration flows. 50 per cent of the net movement in the system is accounted for by moves from the large towns over 50 000 population to the rest of the system. The suburban areas gain 35 per cent of the net movement from the rest of the system. Again on the basis of the results already presented, these are fairly predictable patterns but they provide useful evidence of the model's ability and sensitivity in simulating the processes of decentralisation at the macro-scale. Of these eight partitions, the greatest movement is from the constrained to the unconstrained zones. Over 50 per cent of the net movement is accounted for but this again is predictable for many of the constrained residential locations have reached their holding capacity and this movement is largely due to the increasing severity of the constraints on residential location in the constrained subset. These eight partitions provide a fairly full analysis of net internal migration in the system. It is also reassuring to note that each one of these eight migration patterns does not indicate as strong an impact on the system as the partition into the Erewash Valley and the rest of the system. Thus, it is fair to conclude that the goals of the plan to steer growth from the Nottingham area to the Erewash Valley will be satisfied under this strategy.

Problems associated with the residential and service centre location models have already been described and these problems apply to projections with the model. The analysis of net internal migration, however, shows how sensitive the model is to changes in its exogenous variables. Net migration between time t and $t+1$ expressed as a percentage of $P_j(t)$ is not stable during the projection period; nor is the change in net internal migration stable during this projection. There is little evidence to suggest that these rates of change should be constant but the tendency for these rates to increase during each forecast interval suggests that the system is overreacting to change. This is a difficult subject to broach because so few data are available on such movements, and furthermore the component of migration treated here which is caused by changes in the distribution of population but not employment, has not been studied in previous research.

In fact, the right amount of net internal migration may be generated by the model, but its distribution is probably suspect. If this is so then it is part of the range of problems associated wih the residential location model. In the results discussed here, the model seems to favour a very small number of locations; it seems that there should be a more even spread of the population which is redistributing itself, and this problem can only be solved by the design of more realistic location models. Rather than assuming that the whole stock of activity moves into a new equilibrium at each forecast interval, it might be assumed that a proportion of the existing stock would move. The modification of the Lowry model due to Crecine (1964) was designed to treat such a proportion, and in any further development of the kind of model presented here, it would be sensible to take account of such behaviour. In Chapter 11, Crecine's model is presented and many of these mover problems are then discussed in the formal context of dynamic modelling.

A comparative analysis of subregional models: the bogus calibration problem

The last theme developed in this chapter involves an analysis of the various problems revealed in calibrating both the Central Lancashire and Notts.–Derbys. models, and these problems form the basis of the explorations of the next three chapters. So far the method of calibrating activity allocation models has been developed heuristically with little emphasis upon either the use of efficient technique or best statistics. In this and the following sections, an attempt will be made to evaluate the worth of these various statistics and some pointers will be given to ways in which such concepts can be improved. However, before this is done, it is worth while outlining one of the most pervasive and wicked of all modelling problems which frequently occurs in developing models of spatial interaction. This is the problem labelled by Cordey-Hayes (1968) as the problem of *bogus calibra-*

tion, and it was first formally demonstrated in the inter-regional freight flow model used in the Portbury study (MOT, 1966).

When the parameter controlling the effect of spatial deterrence in such models tends to zero, this deterrent effect no longer influences the distribution of activity. In such a case, activity is then allocated in proportion to locational attraction, and it is intuitively obvious that a perfect distribution of activity will occur if that activity is allocated in proportion to a measure of attraction based on the same variable which is being allocated. Such a 'bogus' fit could occur in the models of this and the previous chapter where the locational attraction is measured by population in the residential sector and service employment in the non-basic sector. This peculiar result can be demonstrated formally in the following way. Taking as an example the residential location model in (3.28) and (3.29), suppressing the iteration postscripts and substituting the Notts.–Derbys. attraction-deterrence function, this model can be written as

$$T_{ij} = A_i B_j E_i P_j^* \exp(-\lambda_1 d_{ij}), \quad i \in Z, \quad j \in Z_1, Z_3, \quad (5.1)$$

$$A_i = \frac{1}{\sum\limits_{j \in Z} B_j P_j^* \exp(-\lambda_1 d_{ij})}, \quad i \in Z. \quad (5.2)$$

Note here that (5.1) is only applicable to the unconstrained subsets Z_1 and Z_3 for these are the subsets where it is required to predict the location of population. Then in (5.1), $B_j = 1, j \in Z_1, Z_3$. Summing (5.1) over i and scaling by the inverse activity rate α in analogy to (3.30) gives

$$P_j = \alpha \sum_{i \in Z} T_{ij} = \alpha B_j P_j^* \sum_{i \in Z} A_i E_i \exp(-\lambda_1 d_{ij}), \quad j \in Z_1, Z_3. \quad (5.3)$$

If $\lambda_1 = 0$ and $B_j = 1$, (5.3) can be simplified to

$$P_j = \alpha P_j^* \frac{\sum\limits_{i \in Z} E_i}{\sum\limits_{j \in Z} P_j^*}, \quad j \in Z_1, Z_3. \quad (5.4)$$

Note also that $B_j = 1, j \in Z_2, Z_4$ when $\lambda_1 = 0$, a fact which can be deduced by manipulating (5.1). Now as the sum of employment scaled by the inverse activity rate is equal to the total population in the system, (5.4) can be further simplified to

$$P_j = P_j^*, \quad j \in Z_1, Z_3, \quad (5.5)$$

which demonstrates the formal condition characterising bogus calibration.

The same analysis can be undertaken for the service centre model and this argument suggests that statistics such as r^2, ζ and χ^2 will tend to 1, 0 and 0 respectively for these activity distributions as $\lambda_1 \to 0$. This is theoretical evidence suggesting that these statistics are most inappropriate although statistics which measure characteristics of the trip length distributions are not biased in this fashion. For example, the mean work trip length $\bar{C}(\lambda_1, \lambda_2)$ computed from (5.1) with $\lambda_1 = 0$ can be written as

$$\bar{C}(\lambda_1, \lambda_2) = \frac{\sum\limits_{j \in Z} P_j^* \sum\limits_{i \in Z} d_{ij}}{\sum\limits_{j \in Z} P_j^*},$$

thus demonstrating that this is no bogus fit. In the following sections, some empirical evidence of the inappropriateness of traditional statistics measuring the fit of activity distribution will be introduced, thus implying the importance of calibrating these models against trip length statistics.

Sensitivity testing and parameter variation

In the Central Lancashire model, both parameter values λ_1 and λ_2 were varied between 1.0 and 4.0 in steps of 0.5; the parameter values in the Notts.–Derbys. model were varied in steps of 0.05 between 0.1 and 0.4. Within these ranges, the largest and smallest values of the statistics give an approximate indication of their sensitivity. For population, r^2 varied between 0.9538 and 0.9958 in Central Lancashire, and between 0.9493 and 0.9899 in Notts.–Derbys. A similar range of variation occurred for employment in both models. For activity rates and population-serving ratios, r^2 was much more sensitive, and Table 5.6 summarises the range

TABLE 5.6. *Maximum and minimum values of r^2*

Range of parameter variation	Central Lancashire 1.0 → 4.0		Notts.–Derbys. 0.1 → 0.4	
	Maximum	Minimum	Maximum	Minimum
Population $\{P_i\}$	0.9958	0.9538	0.9899	0.9493
Employment $\{E_i\}$	0.9995	0.9363	0.9992	0.9932
Population-serving ratios $\{\beta_{ij}\}$, $i = j$	0.9770	0.0219	0.8721	0.4098
Activity rates $\{\alpha_{ij}\}$, $i = j$	0.9627	0.3719	0.9241	0.8277

of variation for r^2 from the four distributions of activity predicted in the two applications of the model. For population and employment which are the major variables predicted by the model, the insensitivity of r^2 is disturbing, for this is the most common statistic used in measuring the performance of this type of model. Furthermore, it is clear that the range of variation is dominated by bogus calibration which occurs when the parameter values tend to zero.

On comparing the largest and smallest values of the χ^2, σ and ζ statistics, it was found that these are a little more sensitive for all distributions. The results are also consistent in both applications of the model: for example, in the Notts.–Derbys. application, χ^2 varied between 8.9070 and 17.0440, and σ between 53298 and 62154 for population, and these statistics produced a similar range of variation in the Central Lancashire model. The ζ is a fairly sensitive statistic and, in Central Lancashire, it varied between 2072 and 5821 for population. Like r^2, these statistics are biased by the possibility of bogus calibration, and this suggests empirically that calibration against activities is an undesirable way of assessing the goodness of fit.

Another result which is of some interest in investigating calibration concerns the relationship between the two parameter values in each location model. If the parameter in the residential location model is held constant, there is little change in the value of any statistic summarising the population fit when the parameter value in the service centre location model is varied. For example in Central Lancashire with $\lambda_1 = 1.0$ and λ_2 varying between 1.0 and 4.0, r^2 varies between 0.9958 and 0.9955; a similar result occurs in the Notts.–Derbys. model. With the parameter value in the service centre location model held constant and the parameter value in the residential location model being varied, statistics describing the employment fit do not vary very much. This suggests that the parameter value determining residential location is relatively independent of the parameter value determining service centre location, and it also goes some way in showing that values for the parameters in any one location model may be approximated without reference to the parameter value in the other location model. This fact has already been used in designing the two-stage calibration procedure for the Notts.–Derbys. model outlined earlier in this chapter.

A more comprehensive sensitivity analysis of the effects of parameter variation on the statistics summarising population and employment fit in both models is illustrated in Figure 5.13. These diagrams take account of the relative independence between the residential and service centre subsystems; the analysis assumes that the parameter value in one subsystem is constant while the other parameter value varies. These graphs are equivalent to cross-sections of the isometrics in Figure 5.3. The values of each statistic obtained by varying this parameter value are plotted as percentage deviations from the parameter value giving the best overall fit. In general terms, the analysis is consistent for both population and em-

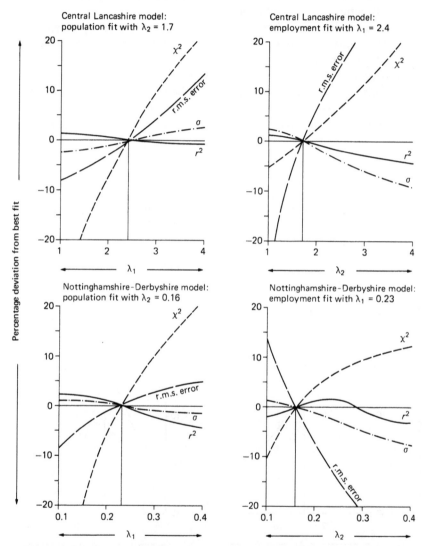

Fig. 5.13. Sensitivity of statistics measuring the goodness of fit of the employment and population distributions.

ployment in each application of the model. The graphs in Figure 5.13 do however reveal minor differences between the sensitivity of equivalent statistics applied to different distributions of activity and different sub-regions. Such differences may be misleading in interpreting the sensitivity of the statistics, but these are probably accounted for by the particular spatial structure of each subregion.

In both models, the distributions of activity predicted by varying the parameter values were remarkably similar, and it seems that the structure of this type of model is a much stronger determinant of the distribution of activity than the parameter values. Statistical tests against the activities are too insensitive and too biased towards bogus calibration to reveal the true effects of parameter variation, and even if such tests are used to measure performance, they must be interpreted with considerable care.

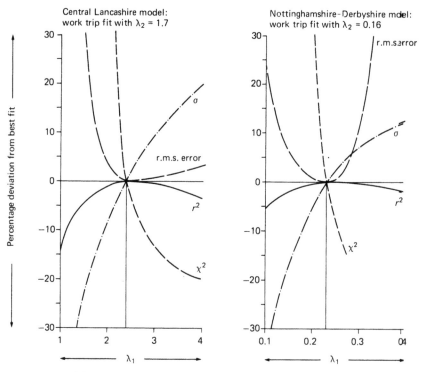

Fig. 5.14. Sensitivity of statistics measuring the goodness of fit of the work trip distributions.

All statistics summarising the work trip distributions were much more sensitive to parameter variation than the statistics summarising the activities. Using the previously given ranges of parameter values for both applications of the model, r^2 varied between 0.8721 and 0.9646 in Notts–

Derbys. and between 0.8432 and 0.9787 in Central Lancashire. The χ^2, σ and ζ also vary significantly, and the smallest and largest values of these statistics are given in Table 5.7. The variations in the values of these statistics also show that the residential location model is highly independent of the service centre location model. In the Central Lancashire model with $\lambda_1 = 1.0$ and λ_2 varying between 1.0 and 4.0, the r^2 for work trips varies between 0.9515 and 0.9751. The r^2 for work trips predicted by the Notts.–Derbys. model shows a similar range of sensitivity. A comprehensive sensitivity analysis of r^2, χ^2, σ, and ζ for the work trip distribution is illustrated in Figure 5.14. As with the activities, the parameter in the

TABLE 5.7. *Maximum and minimum values of r^2, χ^2, σ, and ζ for the work trip distribution*

Range of parameter variation	Central Lancashire $1.0 \rightarrow 4.0$		Notts.–Derbys. $0.1 \rightarrow 0.4$	
	Maximum	Minimum	Maximum	Minimum
r^2	0.9787	0.8432	0.9546	0.8721
χ^2	29.0173	13.4460	32.6370	9.9152
σ	1709	570	2985	1880
ζ	1530	611	961	612

service centre location model is held constant, and the value of each statistic is plotted against different values of the parameter in the residential location model. The statistics are quite sensitive in both applications of the model; r^2 and ζ are not biased towards bogus calibration, and of all the tests outlined up to now, these two statistics applied to the work trip distribution provide the best criteria for judging the goodness of fit.

From this discussion of the relative merits of various statistical tests used in calibrating the activity allocation model, two conclusions can be drawn. First, calibration against distributions of activity such as population and employment does not lead to an accurate assessment of the goodness of fit. Statistics describing the fit are insensitive to parameter variation, and are dominated by a tendency towards bogus calibration. Second, calibration against trip distributions provides quite sensitive tests of the goodness of fit especially for r^2, ζ and the mean trip length statistics. The mean trip length seems to be the best estimate of fit, for besides being sensitive to parameter variation, it is a good summary measure of the amount of travel generated by the model. This supports the theoretical derivation proposed by Wilson (1970a) discussed in Chapter 2 and the statistical work of Hyman (1969) referred to earlier in this chapter.

Assumptions concerning the statistical tests

This chapter has described several statistical tests without inquiring too deeply into the assumptions behind the application of each statistic. Apart from the trip length statistics which have been shown by Hyman (1969) to be best estimators, the use of the other statistics is based upon the assumption that the distributions to which they are applied, are normal. In other words, these statistics are only unbiased, consistent and efficient estimators if the variables which they measure are normally distributed. Zonal activity rates and population-serving ratios seem to be normally distributed in both models but the distributions of population and employment are highly skewed having a reversed-J shape. The purpose of this section is to test the normality of the population and employment distributions in both models, and to find out whether a transform of these distributions might lead to more sensitive statistical tests.

Theory suggests that variables such as population and employment are log-normally distributed and empirical investigation has confirmed this (Simon, 1955; Berry, 1961). Frequency distributions were drawn for population and employment in both subregions and this revealed that the distributions are positively skewed with modes close to their origins. In Central Lancashire, the distributions are highly skewed with Pearsonian coefficients of skewness of 1.1346 for employment and 1.0862 for population. In Notts.–Derbys. the distributions are less skewed with a coefficient of 0.7073 for employment and of 0.6472 for population. The distributions were then plotted on log-probability paper, thus providing a graphical test for log-normality. If the distributions can be closely approximated by straight lines on the graph, then this will be usually sufficient to establish log-normality (Aitchison and Brown, 1957). This test which is shown in Figure 5.15 for population and employment, does indeed reveal that these distributions are near log-normal in both subregions.

On the assumption that these distributions are log-normal, the sensitivity of r^2 has been examined under different parameter values. Log transforms of each distribution were taken and these transformed variables were used in the r^2 statistic. Within the ranges of parameter values used for this investigation, r^2 for population varied between 0.8335 and 0.9273 in Notts.–Derbys. and between 0.9619 and 0.9941 in Central Lancashire. The r^2 for employment was much less sensitive varying from 0.9680 to

0.9804 in Notts.–Derbys. and from 0.9852 to 0.9989 in Central Lancashire. Although r^2 was more sensitive for the normalised distributions, this statistic is heavily biased by the possibility of bogus calibration and this limits its use during the process of calibration. However as a general

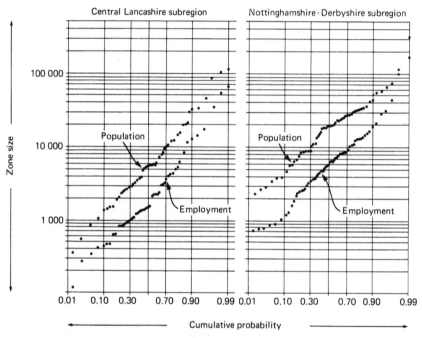

Fig. 5.15. A graphical test for log-normality.

assessment of the goodness of fit of the model in terms of population and employment, r^2 based on the normalised variables is a sound guide to the performance of the model.

The problems revealed by this comparative analysis are taken up, developed and hopefully resolved in the following chapters. In Chapter 6, the calibration problem is explored in the simplest possible terms using a one-parameter partial model of the retail sector. This simple analysis is made more complex in Chapter 7 when partial models with many parameters are calibrated. In Chapter 8, these threads are drawn together and a fast efficient calibration procedure for the activity allocation models of this and the previous chapter is developed. This endeavour to find efficient procedures is not solely concerned with notions of speed and cost of computation for in the process of calibrating such models, essential insights into their form and structure are generated, thus helping to judge their longer-term relevance to planning and urban research.

6. *Exploratory calibration: search by golden section*

During the first decade of urban modelling research, progress in developing suitable methods of parameter estimation or calibration has been slow. There are many reasons for this state of affairs but perhaps the most important is due to the fact that many of the urban models proposed and constructed, such as those reviewed briefly in Chapter 1, are formulated as systems of non-linear equations, and the intractabilities of dealing with non-linear relationships are well known. Yet the process of calibration is perhaps the most fundamental stage of model design, for during calibration the model-builder can develop a basic understanding of the model through exploring its structure and the sensitivity of its variables. Furthermore, these insights which are gained during calibration often provide the tests for evaluating the relevance and limitations of the model to research or to application in planning practice.

Thus, the search for appropriate calibration techniques has only just begun, and it is the purpose of this and the next two chapters to present a variety of techniques for calibrating urban models of the kind described in earlier chapters. In this chapter, these techniques will be explored and demonstrated using as an example a retail location model constructed from data pertaining to the Kristiansand region of southern Norway. As a first step in this investigation, the general form of the model is outlined and some analysis is made of the model's properties. A review and test of simple techniques for calibration based on interpolation follows, and this leads to an outline of more general methods based upon the theory of search. Such methods are first demonstrated in this chapter using a version of the retail model with one parameter, and then the methods are used to explore retail models with two parameters in this and the following chapter.

It is worth while making the logic of these next three chapters quite explicit so that the reader is able to anticipate and relate various calibration techniques. In the spirit of this book in which ideas are developed from the simple to the more complex, it is useful to approach calibration by first developing techniques for the simplest of urban models. In this chapter, techniques for calibrating simple one-parameter and then two-parameter models are presented. In the next chapter, these techniques are extended to deal with simple models with many parameters, and this serves as an important prerequisite to the study of calibration involving more complex models with many parameters, a study which forms the essence of Chapter 8. In short, these three chapters are concerned with developing a calibration methodology suitable for the activity allocation models of the previous chapters. Yet there are some shorter-term problems which are also to be resolved in this chapter dealing with the feasibility of calibrating two-parameter retail models; there is a feeling that with models employing two or more parameters, there may be no unique set of parameters which optimise the model's goodness of fit. As no systematic exploration of these problems has ever been attempted to the author's knowledge, the time seems ripe for a preliminary investigation. Although the choice of urban model has been restricted to the retail sector, the techniques presented here are of much wider relevance to the whole family of spatial interaction and activity allocation models. Before calibration techniques are described in detail, an outline of the model and its relation to other models is a necessary prerequisite to the analysis, and this is presented below.

Retail location models

The model to be developed and tested here is based upon the production-constrained spatial interaction model presented in equations (2.62) and (2.63) of Chapter 2 (Cordey-Hayes and Wilson, 1971). The specific form of the model is given in (2.79)–(2.82); the model allocates consumer expenditures on various commodities to different retail centres in the spatial system. Such a model has its origins in early research into consumer behaviour and marketing in the retail sector (Berry, 1967). The model was first derived by Huff (1963, 1964) using probabilistic notions, and the first major application was made by Lakshmanan and Hansen (1965) to the Baltimore region. The model is restated here in the following terms

$$S_{ij} = A_i c_i P_i W_j^{\lambda_1} d_{ij}^{-\lambda_2}, \tag{6.1}$$

$$A_i = \frac{1}{\sum_j W_j^{\lambda_1} d_{ij}^{-\lambda_2}}. \tag{6.2}$$

S_{ij} is the flow of consumer expenditure between residence in i and shopping centre in j, P_i is the population in i, c_i is the expenditure *per capita* in i, W_j is a measure of locational attraction of the shopping centre at j, such as floorspace, d_{ij} is the distance between i and j, and λ_1 and λ_2 are parameters of the model. This model is the same as the model given in (2.80) and (2.81) and is subject to the following constraint on consumer expenditure

$$\sum_j S_{ij} = c_i P_i. \tag{6.3}$$

Sales in centre j, S_j, can be calculated by summing (6.1) over i

$$S_j = \sum_i S_{ij}, \tag{6.4}$$

and it is obvious that total consumer expenditure in the system must equal total sales in shopping centres. In other words

$$\sum_i \sum_j S_{ij} = \sum_j S_j = \sum_i c_i P_i.$$

Various forms of the retail location model given in (6.1) and (6.2) have been applied in Britain in recent years, and as a first step in investigating the relevance of this model, a comparison of these applications can be attempted. Although some researchers consider that such comparisons are impossible because the measurements of the model's variables may be so different in each study, some comparison is possible in certain applications if it is assumed that different measures are linearly related. For example, two models, one using floorspace for W_j, the other using sales, can be compared if it is assumed that floorspace is some linear function of sales or vice versa. In such cases, the model is scale-invariant and direct comparisons can be made. In support of this assumption, Davies (1970) has shown that many different measures of attraction and deterrence are highly correlated. However, in models where different functional forms for shopping centre attraction or spatial impedance are used, direct comparisons cannot be made.

The best comparison between different applications is in terms of the values of λ_1 and λ_2 which are usually chosen to optimise some criterion summarising the goodness of fit of the model to the real situation. For example, in many of the applications, values of λ_1 and λ_2 have been found which maximise the coefficient of correlation between predicted and observed sales. A comparison of several applications is given in Table 6.1 in terms of parameters and particular variable measurements although it is difficult to compare the Haydock and Oxford models with the others because of differences in their functional form. Excluding these two models, it appears that there is a tendency for the parameter value of λ_1 to cluster around 1, whereas the range for λ_2 is considerably larger. However, in examining the reports of each of these applications, it is clear that there is a lack of thorough exploration and sensitivity-testing of these models apart from the Haydock and Oxford models. This lack of information on the calibration process is important, for one of the main criticisms of this

TABLE 6.1. *A comparison of some shopping models*

Area or region	Attraction parameter (λ_1)	Deterrence parameter (λ_2)	Attraction measure (W_j)	Deterrence measure (d_{ij})	Reference
Haydock	3.0000	2.6000	Composite index measuring variety	Travel time	McLoughlin *et al.* (1966)
Leicestershire	1.6000	0.9500	Floorspace	Airline distance	McLoughlin *et al.* (1969)
Lewisham*	1.0000	1.1000	Sales	Airline distance	Rhodes and Whitaker (1967)
Notts.–Derbys.	1.3000	2.4000	Sales	Travel time	Murray and Kennedy (1971)
Oxford	0.9500	0.2000	Sales	Airline distance	Black (1966)
Severnside	0.9200	0.9100	Sales	Airline distance	Turner (1970*b*)
South Bedfordshire*	1.0000	1.3000	Floorspace	Travel time	NEDO (1970)
Teesside	1.3800	2.3600	Floorspace	Airline distance	NEDO (1970)

* Models with no parameter λ_1 on W_j, that is, an implied value of $\lambda_1 = 1.00$.

type of model lies in the possibility of multiple solutions to the calibration in terms of the values of λ_1 and λ_2. Indeed, Black (1966) in her classic paper on the Oxford model, and Turner (1970*b*) in his work on the Severnside model, have both pointed out this possibility, but the existence of many solutions has never been formally investigated. If there are different values of λ_1 and λ_2 which give an equally good fit in terms of the particular statistic used, then the calibration effort put into several of these models may be suspect. It is particularly useful to illustrate calibration methodologies using this model because of the model's popularity and fairly widespread usage. Before this is done, however, some theoretical analysis of the properties of the model forms an essential background to a thorough exploration of the model's structure.

Prior analysis of the model

In this chapter, analysis will be restricted to this two-parameter retail location model, and some insight into the model's structure can be gained if an analysis is first made of the model's behaviour under extreme values of the parameters. As defined previously, origin zones are subscripted in the range $1 \leqslant i \leqslant I$ and destination zones in the range $1 \leqslant j \leqslant J$. An additional destination zone l is also introduced to help the analysis. Variation of the parameter values λ_1 and λ_2 between 0 and ∞ gives four extreme cases which are identified by the table below.

	Parameter value of λ_1	
	0	∞
Parameter value of λ_2 $\begin{cases} 0 \\ \infty \end{cases}$	Case 1 / Case 3	Case 2 / Case 4

These four cases can be dealt with briefly and in turn. In case 1, when both λ_1 and λ_2 are equal to zero, (6.1) transforms to

$$S_{ij} = \frac{c_i P_i}{J}. \tag{6.5}$$

Equation (6.5) shows that consumer expenditure in each zone of residence i is distributed evenly between all shopping centres j. In other words, $S_{i1} = S_{i2} = \ldots = S_{ij} = \ldots = S_{iJ}$. Sales in each shopping centre are found by summing (6.5) over i

$$S_j = \sum_i S_{ij} = \frac{\sum\limits_i c_i P_i}{J}, \tag{6.6}$$

and from (6.6) it follows that total consumer expenditure in the system is distributed evenly among the shopping centres so that

$$S_1 = S_2 = \ldots = S_j = \ldots = S_J.$$

This is an interesting case which can be derived using Wilson's entropy-maximising method, discussed in Chapter 2, if the constraint equation on travel cost and benefits is omitted. In effect, such a case arises when neither the cost of travel nor the benefits of location are relevant to the locational decision.

In case 2, the analysis is a little more complex; if it is assumed that one shopping centre, say centre l, is more attractive than any other centre, then the analysis is helped. When $\lambda_1 = \infty$ and $\lambda_2 = 0$, then

$$W_l^\infty \simeq \sum_j W_j^\infty.$$

In this case (6.1) transforms to

$$\begin{rcases} S_{il} = c_i P_i, \\ S_{ij} = 0, \quad j \neq l. \end{rcases} \tag{6.7}$$

From (6.7), it is obvious that all consumer expenditure flows to centre l, and this can be shown by summing (6.7) over i

$$S_l = \sum_i S_{il} = \sum_i c_i P_i. \tag{6.8}$$

In cases where two or more centres tie with the largest measures of locational attraction, the total expenditure in the system is distributed evenly among these centres.

Case 3 is similar to case 2 in that an assumption has to be made to help the analysis. If it is assumed that from each zone i there is a minimum distance or travel cost to some zone j, then it is reasonable to suppose that this minimum is the intra-zonal distance d_{ii}. Therefore, when $\lambda_1 = 0$, and $\lambda_2 = \infty$, then

$$\frac{1}{d_{ii}^{\infty}} \simeq \frac{1}{\sum_j (d_{ij})^{\infty}}.$$

Equation (6.1) now transforms to

$$\begin{aligned}
S_{ij} &= c_i P_i, \quad i = j, \\
S_{ij} &= 0, \quad i \neq j.
\end{aligned} \right\} \tag{6.9}$$

In this case, the effect of distance is so powerful on behaviour that no expenditure flows to shopping centres in zones different from the origin zone. By summing (6.9) over i, sales in each centre j are calculated as

$$S_j = \sum_i S_{ij} = c_j P_j. \tag{6.10}$$

If the minimum distances from each zone i are not the intra-zonal distances and if two or more distances are minimum, no general analysis of this case can be made.

Finally, in case 4, the analysis is complicated and considerably less general than the first three cases. As in cases 2 and 3, an assumption has to be made; from each origin zone i to all other zones j, it is assumed that there is one ratio (W_l/d_{il}) which is a maximum. If $\lambda_1 = \infty$ and $\lambda_2 = \infty$, then

$$\left(\frac{W_l}{d_{il}}\right)^{\infty} \simeq \sum_j \left(\frac{W_j}{d_{ij}}\right)^{\infty}.$$

In this case, all that can be said is that consumers living in any zone i allocate all their expenditure to some shopping centre l, although l may be different for each i. In fact, in most applications, it is likely that the set of shopping centres can be divided into two subsets – those with positive sales and those with zero sales. For example, in the Kristiansand model developed here for large values of λ_1 and λ_2, positive sales occur in only twelve out of the thirty shopping centres.

One special case still needs to be dealt with and this occurs when $\lambda_1 = 1$ and $\lambda_2 = 0$. This is the case which was described in Chapter 5 in equations (5.1)–(5.5) and which was termed 'bogus' calibration by Cordey-Hayes (1968). In this case, (6.1) transforms to

$$S_{ij} = c_i P_i \frac{W_j}{\sum\limits_j W_j}, \tag{6.11}$$

and sales in j are calculated by summing (6.11) over i

$$S_j = \sum_i S_{ij} = W_j \frac{\sum\limits_i c_i P_i}{\sum\limits_j W_j}. \tag{6.12}$$

If $\sum\limits_i c_i P_i / \sum\limits_j W_j$ is called η, then (6.12) becomes

$$S_j = \eta W_j, \tag{6.13}$$

and it is clear that sales can be derived as a simple linear function of locational attraction. If, for example, W_j is measured by floorspace, then η is the system ratio of sales per unit of floorspace. However, in many applications of this form of model, suitable measures of W_j have been difficult to obtain and often observed sales have been substituted for W_j. In such cases, η is equal to 1 if total observed sales in the system equal total expenditure. It is obvious that if observed sales are used to measure W_j, then predicted sales will co-vary with observed sales from (6.12), and a perfect and 'bogus' fit occurs. Moreover, as has already been pointed out, many proxies for W_j such as floorspace tend to co-vary with observed sales, and in such cases there is always a danger of bogus calibration.

Several versions of this retail location model have used observed sales as a measure for locational attraction (Black, 1966; Turner, 1970b), and despite the perennial problem of the implied tautology in such usage, an attempt can be made to resolve this problem by iterating the model in the following fashion. Using n as an index denoting iterations, (6.1) and (6.2) become

$$S_{ij}(n+1) = A_i(n) c_i P_i S_j^{\lambda_1}(n) d_{ij}^{-\lambda_2}, \tag{6.14}$$

$$A_i(n) = \frac{1}{\sum\limits_j S_j^{\lambda_1}(n) d_{ij}^{-\lambda_2}}. \tag{6.15}$$

Sales in j on iteration $(n+1)$ are found by summing (6.14) over i, and these sales are then substituted for the previous values of S_j into (6.14) and (6.15). This process is continued until convergence between the input and output values of sales is obtained. In the quest to explore whether or not this procedure will converge, Eilon, Tilley and Fowkes (1969) have provided some useful theorems which reveal that in most simple cases, convergence is assured.

Non-linearity and calibration

As the prime purpose of this chapter is to elaborate on techniques of model calibration, little emphasis need be placed on the detailed application of the model to the Kristiansand region. Yet a brief introduction to the specific form of model and its data base is warranted. The Kristiansand region has been divided into 30 zones which are aggregations of Local Authority units. An effort was made to define the zoning system to minimise the ratio of intra-zonal expenditure to inter-zonal expenditure, following the argument posed by Broadbent (1969a) and mentioned previously. The two-parameter version of the retail model has been applied using floorspace (in square metres) as a measure of locational attraction, and distance (in kilometres) on the major road network as a proxy for travel cost. No attempt has been made to refine this model by disaggregating sales into durable and consumer, or by accounting for expenditures flowing across the regional boundary.

The process of calibrating an urban model of this kind involves the use of techniques to find parameter values which optimise some criterion measuring the goodness of fit of the model's predictions to the real situation. For example, it may be decided that by minimising the sum of the squared deviations between predictions and observations, the best parameter values can be found. Thus in some models it is possible to use analytic methods such as regression analysis. Whether or not an analytic method of calibration can be used depends upon the form of the model. Generally, analytic methods can be used to fit models which are linear in their parameters. Non-linear forms of model are more difficult to fit and Draper and Smith (1966) make an essential distinction between two kinds of non-linear model. Some non-linear models can be linearised by transformation, and in such cases, analytic methods of calibration such as regression analysis can be used despite certain reservations (Seidman, 1969). Such models are called by Draper and Smith *intrinsically linear*. The other set of non-linear models cannot be transformed and these are referred to as *intrinsically non-linear*. Examination of equations (6.1) and (6.2) reveals that the model dealt with here is intrinsically non-linear and attempts to transform the model to a linear form will lead to biased estimates of the parameters. However, it is useful to compare such models with intrinsically linear systems such as that given in (2.51) which can be linearised by a simple transformation as in (2.52). As a slight digression, it is interesting that this distinction between linearity and non-linearity also coincides with the distinction between the traditional geographer's approach to modelling with its inductive bias and the deductive style advocated here.

The trial and error method of searching for best-parameter values by running the model exhaustively through a range of parameter values or combinations thereof represents a somewhat blunt approach to model calibration. There is a need for techniques which are well adapted to the problem and this chapter attempts to introduce some such techniques. Moreover, as each run of the model can be expensive or take a large amount of computer time, few applications have attempted to find systematically the optimum parameter values, and this is seen nowhere more clearly than in the comparative study recently produced by NEDO (1970) where the parameters and fits of several retail location models are compared. Clearly, then, there is a need for the introduction of methods suitable for calibrating intrinsically non-linear models of spatial interaction.

So far the argument has concentrated upon calibration techniques but there are difficulties involved in choosing meaningful statistics measuring the goodness of fit of spatial interaction models. It has been shown that statistics measuring the goodness of fit of the interaction variables are far more sensitive to variation in the parameters of such models than statistics measuring the fit of the distributions of activity. Furthermore, the simpler statistics such as the sum of squared deviations appear to be more sensitive to parameter change than the more complex statistics such as the coefficient of determination as was evidenced in the previous chapter. The theoretical work of Hyman (1969), Evans (1971) and Wilson (1970a) also supports the use of statistics based on interaction such as the mean trip length. Although generalised schemes for calibrating spatial interaction models have been suggested by Wilson, Hawkins, Hill and Wagon (1969), in relation to the SELNEC transport model, specific procedures for evaluating the deterrence parameter of such models have been proposed by Hyman (1969). Although the model dealt with here embodies two parameters, as a first step in exploring this model it was decided to test Hyman's procedures using a one-parameter version of the model. The rationale for Hyman's choice of the mean trip length as a best calibration statistic will be examined in the next chapter, for here interest will centre around techniques for homing-in on parameter values associated with the best statistic.

Hyman's formulae: the rule of false position

The importance of Hyman's work lies in the fact that it represents the first attempt to provide a systematic procedure and statistic for calibrating spatial interaction models. Hyman shows that the mean trip length is the best statistic to use in calibration. This mean trip length, called $\bar{S}$, is defined in this application using a one-parameter version of equation (6.1) given as

$$S_{ij} = A_i c_i P_i W_j d_{ij}^{-\lambda}, \tag{6.16}$$

$$A_i = \frac{1}{\sum_j W_j d_{ij}^{-\lambda}}. \tag{6.17}$$

The mean trip length given in (4.2) is defined as

$$\bar{S} = \frac{\sum_i \sum_j S_{ij} \ln d_{ij}}{\sum_i \sum_j S_{ij}}. \tag{6.18}$$

In fact, in the application described here, $\bar{S}$ is approximately equal to 8 km and for purposes of exploration throughout the rest of this chapter, the observed survey value of $\bar{S}$, called $\bar{S}*$ is set equal to 8 km. By converting the spatial interaction model in (6.16) to a continuous form, and by assuming a negative exponential deterrence function, Hyman argues that the parameter λ is some monotonically decreasing function of $\bar{S}$. In other words that

$$\lambda \bar{S} = \Phi, \tag{6.19}$$

where Φ is a constant with a probable value between 1 and 2. Equation (6.19) could be used to give a first approximation to λ and Hyman has suggested two procedures for computing accurate values of λ. First, a new value for λ, say λ^{n+1} could be calculated from the previous value of the parameter λ_n and the mean trip length $\bar{S}^n$ by

$$\lambda^{n+1} = \frac{\lambda^n \bar{S}^n}{\bar{S}*}. \tag{6.20}$$

Hyman suggests a second procedure based on linear interpolation-extrapolation which converges faster than the process implied by (6.20); this method is known as the 'rule of false position'. For this procedure, two previous values of λ and their associated mean trip lengths need to be known and a new value of λ is calculated from

$$\lambda^{n+1} = \lambda^{n-1} \frac{\bar{S}^n - \bar{S}*}{\bar{S}^n - \bar{S}^{n-1}} + \lambda^n \frac{\bar{S}* - \bar{S}^{n-1}}{\bar{S}^n - \bar{S}^{n-1}}. \tag{6.21}$$

Both these procedures will be demonstrated using the retail location model given in (6.16) and (6.17). Because the deterrence function in the model is a power function (6.19) has not been used to give a first approximation in this case. The two procedures have been used starting with λ equal to 2.0 and 5.0, and in the case of the linear method, the second value

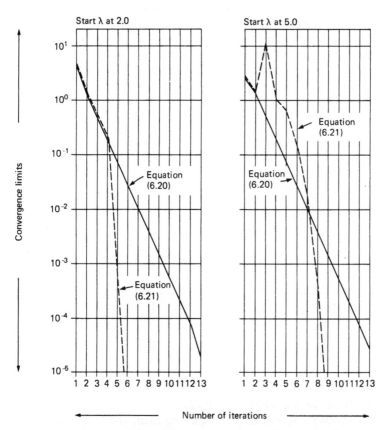

Fig. 6.1. A comparison of Hyman's formulae for model calibration.

of λ was calculated from (6.20). Figure 6.1 compares these two procedures graphically, and Table 6.2 summarises the number of iterations for each procedure required to converge to within specified limits of $\bar{S}^*$. From Table 6.2, it appears that the speed of convergence for (6.20) is independent of its starting point, and in the case of (6.21), the convergence takes longer, as the displacement of the starting point from the final value of the parameter increases. The most interesting result from Table 6.2, however, concerns the number of iterations required to converge to within specific limits. Both procedures take approximately the same number of iterations to converge to within 10^{-1} of $\bar{S}^*$, but to converge to within 10^{-5}, the linear technique procedure is, as Hyman implied, considerably faster.

There are a number of variations in the linear interpolation–extrapolation formula given in (6.21) which are worthy of mention. In particular, the method can be speeded up if on the fourth and subsequent iterations, the two-parameter values which produce values of $\bar{S}$ closest to $\bar{S}^*$ so far are chosen. Karlquist and Marksjo (1971) demonstrate the use of this option which is sometimes called the secant method. Baxter and Williams

TABLE 6.2. *Number of iterations required to come within specified limits of $\bar{S}^*$*

Specified limits	Convergence based on (6.20)		Convergence based on (6.21)	
	Start $(\lambda = 2.0)$	Start $(\lambda = 5.0)$	Start $(\lambda = 2.0)$	Start $(\lambda = 5.0)$
10^{-1}	5	5	5	7
10^{-3}	10	10	6	8
10^{-5}	15	15	7	9

(1973) also give alternatives to (6.21) which are more efficient computationally. Of interest is the case when $\bar{S}^*$ is zero, as in cases where it is required to minimise or maximise some function. Then equation (6.21) can be simplified to

$$\lambda^{n+1} = \lambda^{n-1} - \frac{(\lambda^n - \lambda^{n-1})\bar{S}^{n-1}}{\bar{S}^n - \bar{S}^{n-1}}. \tag{6.22}$$

Dixon (1972) also presents certain procedures for speeding up convergence based on formulae such as (6.21) and (6.22).

Although Hyman's formulae are highly efficient, they are limited in several ways. First, there are difficulties in extending these methods to handle models with two or more parameters and in such cases, search procedures such as gradient search tend to be more useful. Second, use of the methods in (6.20) and (6.21) above required some information concerning the optimum fit of the model, in this case $\bar{S}^*$. In many instances, the researcher may wish to optimise the value of a statistic summarising the goodness of fit, and this value will usually not be known in advance. Such is the case when calibrating a model using statistics which compare variance in predicted and observed distributions. What is required is a more general optimisation procedure which can also be extended to explore models with two or more parameters, and to this end, a brief introduction to the theory of search is now presented.

The theory of search

An informal discussion of the theory of search is sufficient for the purposes of this chapter and in this section, some pertinent definitions will be introduced. For a more formal discussion, the interested reader is referred to Wilde (1964). Search procedures form part of a wider class of problems coming under the general heading of optimisation. The particular characteristic of such problems refers to the need to find the optimum or best value of some function, and this class of problems can be divided into those which are subject to certain constraints and those which are not. Constrained optimisation problems are dealt with either by the calculus or by the methods of mathematical programming such as linear or quadratic programming. The problem of calibration dealt with here, however, is essentially a problem in unconstrained optimisation. The function to be optimised by its very nature cannot be handled analytically, and therefore numerical methods of search are appropriate.

An initial distinction must be made between univariate search in which the optimum value of one variable is required, and multivariate search in which the optimal values of many variables are required. The process of search in which two or more variables must be optimised is often likened to a form of hill climbing, in which the researcher is attempting to reach the summit by some route which he does not know in advance. The geometrical analogue is obvious and the hill is referred to as the *response surface* (Wilde, 1964). In this book, the area within which the search is to take place is referred to as the *parameter space*. Perhaps the most important assumption of all search procedures is that the response surface has the property of unimodality. In other words, that the surface has only one optimum – the global optimum. Following the hill-climbing analogy, surfaces may have saddle points and ridges and in cases where the surface is multimodal, there may be several local optima. A formal definition of unimodality is given in Wilde (1964). It is important to note that most search procedures cannot get over the problems caused by multimodality, and this applies to the search procedures outlined below.

Optimum univariate search procedures have been suggested but no optimum multivariate procedure has been proved. Usually the method of multivariate search involves some method of assessing the gradient of the response surface and proceeding along the line of steepest ascent or descent. In the context of calibrating the two-parameter retail location model, given in (6.1) and (6.2), Turner (1970*b*) has used a gradient search procedure based on a method devised by Marquardt (1963), but he reports that the process always converged to a local optimum. As the parameter space of such models remains largely unexplored, it seems that the development of a multivariate technique such as gradient search, which will only work on unimodal surfaces, is rather premature at this stage. Thus as a preliminary attack on the problem, the procedure suggested below is based on univariate search and this can be easily extended to explore the form of the multivariate response surface.

Fibonacci search

Consider a function such as the one illustrated in Figure 6.2. For purposes of demonstration, it might be assumed that this function represents

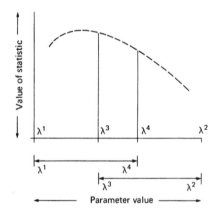

Fig. 6.2. Optimum point in the interval of search.

the value of the coefficient of correlation for different values of the parameter λ in (6.16) and (6.17). The Fibonacci search procedure is an optimum method for finding the maximum or minimum of a function such as the one in Figure 6.2, where information about the shape of the function has to be generated sequentially. This presentation of the method follows the description given by Spang (1962) and Box, Davies and Swann (1969). The method has been proven optimum by several researchers and good accounts of the proof are given by Wilde (1964), Avriel and Wilde (1966) and Bellman (1957).

In Figure 6.2, it is assumed that the maximum lies in the interval $\{\lambda^2 - \lambda^1\}$ and two further function evaluations are chosen such that

$$\lambda^1 < \lambda^3 < \lambda^4 < \lambda^2.$$

Then if $f(\lambda^3) \geqslant f(\lambda^4)$, the maximum lies in the interval $\{\lambda^4 - \lambda^1\}$ and if $f(\lambda^3) \leqslant f(\lambda^4)$, the maximum lies in the interval $\{\lambda^2 - \lambda^3\}$. Further function evaluations in the reduced interval will obviously narrow the interval of search. An optimum strategy for choosing the locations of λ^3 and λ^4 is based upon a series of positive integers called the Fibonacci numbers, so called after their discovery by the Italian mathematician of the thirteenth century. These numbers are defined by the sequence

$$\left.\begin{aligned} u_0 = u_1 &= 1, \\ u_n = u_{n-1} + u_{n-2}, \quad n &\geqslant 2. \end{aligned}\right\} \tag{6.23}$$

Given a total number of function evaluations, say N, then on the kth iteration, the range of parameters has been narrowed to $\{\lambda^{2,k} - \lambda^{1,k}\}$ and two further parameters $\lambda^{3,k}$ and $\lambda^{4,k}$ are chosen as follows

$$\lambda^{3,k} = \frac{u_{N-1-k}}{u_{N+1-k}} (\lambda^{2,k} - \lambda^{1,k}) + \lambda^{1,k}, \tag{6.24}$$

$$\lambda^{4,k} = \frac{u_{N-k}}{u_{N+1-k}} (\lambda^{2,k} - \lambda^{1,k}) + \lambda^{1,k}. \tag{6.25}$$

Using (6.24) and (6.25), the final function evaluations given by $\lambda^{3,N-1}$ and $\lambda^{4,N-1}$ coincide at the mid-point in the interval $\{\lambda^{2,N-1} - \lambda^{1,N-1}\}$. Therefore one of the new parameters, say $\lambda^{3,N-1}$ is displaced from $\lambda^{4,N-1}$ by a small number ϵ. Then

$$\lambda^{3,N-1} = (\tfrac{1}{2} + \epsilon)(\lambda^{2,N-1} - \lambda^{1,N-1}) + \lambda^{1,N-1}, \tag{6.26}$$

$$\lambda^{4,N-1} = \tfrac{1}{2}(\lambda^{2,N-1} - \lambda^{1,N-1}) + \lambda^{1,N-1}. \tag{6.27}$$

After N function evaluations the remaining interval ξ^N is at most

$$\xi^N = \frac{1}{u_N}(\lambda^{2,1} - \lambda^{1,1}) + \epsilon, \tag{6.28}$$

and therefore for any reduction in the interval of search, u_N can be determined from a Fibonacci table.

As in the linear interpolation–extrapolation in (6.21), two function evaluations are needed to start the process, but after this only one additional evaluation is needed at each iteration. For example if as in Figure 6.2 the maximum lies in the interval $\{\lambda^{4,k} - \lambda^{3,k}\}$ on the kth iteration, then on the next iteration

$$\lambda^{4,k+1} = \frac{u_{N-(k+1)}}{u_{N+1-(k+1)}} (\lambda^{4,k} - \lambda^{1,k}) + \lambda^{1,k}. \tag{6.29}$$

Substituting for $\lambda^{4,k}$ in (6.29) from (6.25), then

$$\lambda^{4,k+1} = \frac{u_{N-(k+1)}}{u_{N+1-(k+1)}}\left[\frac{u_{N-k}}{u_{N+1-k}}(\lambda^{2,k}-\lambda^{1,k})+\lambda^{1,k}-\lambda^{1,k}\right]+\lambda^{1,k},$$

$$= \frac{u_{N-1-k}}{u_{N+1-k}}(\lambda^{2,k}-\lambda^{1,k})+\lambda^{1,k} = \lambda^{3,k}. \tag{6.30}$$

Equation (6.30) is obvious from the symmetrical properties of the method (Wilde, 1964). However, one problem remains – in many cases N cannot be found because the final interval required may not be known. For example, the process of search could be terminated when the difference between the values of the goodness of fit on successive iterations falls within a certain limit. To deal with such cases, a generalisation of the Fibonacci search, known as search by golden section, can be used.

Generalisation to search by golden section

Hoggatt (1969) shows that the Fibonacci numbers can be calculated using an equation due to the French mathematician Binet. This equation is

$$u_n = \frac{1}{\sqrt{5}}\left[\left(\frac{1+\sqrt{5}}{2}\right)n-\left(\frac{1-\sqrt{5}}{2}\right)n\right]. \tag{6.31}$$

By substituting (6.31) into the ratios of the Fibonacci numbers given in (6.24) and (6.25) above, then for very large n, these ratios are approximately constant. Noting that $\phi = (1+\sqrt{5})/2$, these ratios are given as

$$\frac{u_{n-1}}{u_{n+1}} \simeq \frac{1}{\phi^2} = \frac{\phi-1}{\phi}, \tag{6.32}$$

$$\frac{u_n}{u_{n+1}} \simeq \frac{1}{\phi}. \tag{6.33}$$

The properties of (6.32) and (6.33) are quite intriguing for these equations imply an approximate calculation scheme for the Fibonacci numbers. The number ϕ is itself of some interest due to the fact that it satisfies the so-called Fibonacci quadratic $\phi^2 = \phi+1$. Manipulation of ϕ can be carried out endlessly, thus justifying the fact that Fibonacci numbers provide a major topic in recreational mathematics. Equation (6.32) is approximately equal to 0.382 and (6.33) approximately equal to 0.618. When N is not known, (6.24) and (6.25) become

$$\lambda^{3,k} = 0.382(\lambda^{2,k}-\lambda^{1,k})+\lambda^{1,k}, \tag{6.34}$$

$$\lambda^{4,k} = 0.618(\lambda^{2,k}-\lambda^{1,k})+\lambda^{1,k}. \tag{6.35}$$

The computational scheme implied by (6.34) and (6.35) is known as *search by golden section* because of the properties of ϕ which is known as the golden section number. The golden section is a proportion which was much used in Greek art and architecture, and is derived by dividing a line segment into two unequal parts so that the ratio of the whole line to the larger part is equal to the ratio of the larger part to the smaller part (March and Steadman, 1971). This can be demonstrated using the interval of search shown in Figure 6.2 and dividing this interval so that

$$\frac{\lambda^{2,k}-\lambda^{1,k}}{\lambda^{4,k}-\lambda^{1,k}} = \frac{\lambda^{4,k}-\lambda^{1,k}}{\lambda^{2,k}-\lambda^{4,k}} = \phi. \tag{6.36}$$

Equation (6.36) can easily be verified by making the correct substitutions from (6.32) to (6.35). Furthermore, Mischke (1968) provides an alternative derivation of search by golden section by dividing the original interval according to (6.36).

The golden section search is approximately 13 per cent slower than the Fibonacci search, although in practice, the method is slightly easier to program, and this could well cancel out the prior advantage of Fibonacci search. For experimental purposes, the golden section search is more flexible for the number of function evaluations can be found in advance if this is required. Then, after k iterations, the interval of search is narrowed by the golden section method to

$$\lambda^{2,k+1}-\lambda^{1,k+1} = (0.618)^k(\lambda^{1,2}-\lambda^{1,1}). \tag{6.37}$$

If it is required to reduce the interval to a particular value then it is necessary to find k. This is achieved by transforming (6.37) to

$$k = \ln\left(\frac{\lambda^{2,k+1}-\lambda^{1,k+1}}{\lambda^{2,1}-\lambda^{1,1}}\right)\bigg/\ln(0.618). \tag{6.38}$$

For example, in the computer program used here, the interval was reduced to 0.0004 of its original size, and using (6.38) this means that about 16 iterations are needed. In fact, 17 function evaluations need to be performed because two evaluations are needed in the first iteration. If the time or cost, called ψ, of each function evaluation is known, the total time or cost Υ is

$$\Upsilon = \psi(k+1).$$

In the case of the Kristiansand model, each evaluation or run of the model takes approximately 7.7 seconds on the Elliot 4130 computer, and therefore the total time taken to narrow the interval of search to 0.0004 of the original interval is about 2 minutes 11 seconds. An example of the use of golden section search in finding the optimum value of one parameter is shown graphically in Figure 6.3, in relation to a maximisation problem. In Table 6.3, the results of Figure 6.3 are tabulated and this shows the degree to which the interval of search can be reduced using this method. It is now necessary to show how the method can be adapted to a problem of multivariate search, and used to explore different kinds of response surface. This is attempted in the following section.

Sequential linear search: exploration of the parameter space

Krolak and Cooper (1963) have proposed a simple extension of the golden section search and its Fibonacci equivalent to multivariate problems. This extension consists in nesting a series of univariate searches within one another and a similar method is outlined by Box *et al.* (1969); however, there is a more direct method of multivariate search and this method based on applying golden section search, called sequential linear search, will be presented here. The essence of this method involves the use of series of golden section searches in such a way that the optimum value of a function is successively improved by optimising on each variable in turn. The method can be best illustrated by an example. Imagine a response surface for a function of two variables; such a surface could be presented geo-metrically in three dimensions, but a more efficient visual presentation can be made in two dimensions by plotting contours of equal response. Such a surface taken from the Notts.–Derbys. model in Chapter 5 is illustrated in Figure 6.4 and a sequence of linear searches is traced on this

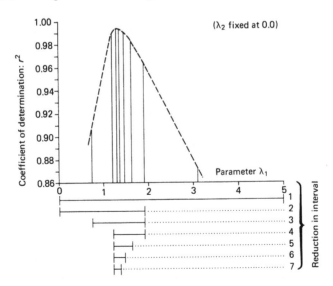

Fig. 6.3. Search by golden section.

graph. It is intuitively obvious that on surfaces which are strongly unimodal, that is concave or convex down (Wilde, 1964), the sequence of searches will eventually reach the global optimum. It is also obvious that if the surface is not strongly unimodal, then the search could end at a saddle point, a ridge, or some other local optimum. Therefore, this method is a useful tool for exploring response surfaces.

The rest of this chapter is concerned with the response surfaces derived from the retail location model in (6.1) and (6.2). An example of the method is given in Figure 6.5 where both parameters of the model λ_1 and λ_2 have been varied sequentially until the goodness of fit was optimum in the sense that further improvement in the fit could not be achieved using this method. The computational procedure is as follows: λ_1 is fixed and an optimum fit is found by varying λ_2. Then the value of λ_2 associated with this optimum is fixed, and λ_1 is varied in an effort to improve on the previous fit of the model. This sequence is reiterated until no further improvement is gained within a predetermined limit. In applying the model in this way, three statistics have been used to measure the goodness of fit. First, the

TABLE 6.3. *Reduction of the interval of search using search by golden section*

Iteration number	Variation of parameter value (λ_1)	Coefficient of correlation (r)	Coefficient of determination (r^2)
1	1.9098	0.9819	0.9642
1	3.0902	0.9371	0.8782
2	1.1804	0.9951	0.9903
3	0.7295	0.9512	0.9049
4	1.4590	0.9961	0.9923
5	1.6312	0.9920	0.9841
6	1.3526	0.9972	0.9944
7	1.2868	0.9970	0.9941
8	1.3932	0.9969	0.9940
9	1.3274	0.9972	0.9945
10	1.3119	0.9972	0.9944
11	1.3370	0.9972	0.9945
12	1.3430	0.9972	0.9945
13	1.3334	0.9973	0.9945
14	1.3311	0.9972	0.9945
15	1.3348	0.9972	0.9945
16	1.3325	0.9972	0.9945

NOTE: Deterrence parameter λ_2 fixed at 0.0.

coefficient of determination r^2 has been calculated based on the predicted distribution of sales S_j and the observed distribution S_j^*. The form
of the r^2 statistic has been given previously in Chapter 4. The second
statistic calculated is based on the sum of the absolute deviations between
predicted and observed sales, and in this case, the model is run to find the
minimum value which is zero of

$$\sum_j |S_j - S_j^*|.$$

The third and final statistic is based upon the mean trip-length. In this
case, it is required to find the minimum of the absolute difference between
the predicted $\bar{S}$ and observed $\bar{S}^*$ mean trip lengths. This value is at a
minimum when equal to zero which implies that $\bar{S} = \bar{S}^*$. This statistic
has the form
$$|\bar{S} - \bar{S}^*|.$$

The three optimisation problems associated with these three statistics
can each be handled by the golden section search, thus illustrating the
power and generality of the method.

In any application of a search procedure, it is essential to have some

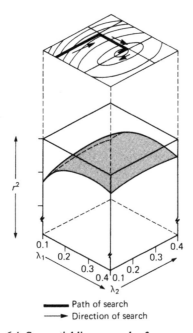

Fig. 6.4. Sequential linear search of a response surface.

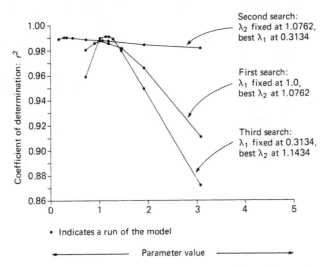

Fig. 6.5. Sequential linear search based on search by golden section.

initial idea of the form of the response surfaces associated with each measure of fit. As a first step in the exploration, the retail location model was run through a series of combinations of the parameter values λ_1 and λ_2 in the range 0–5. A general rule for finding the total number of function evaluations is n^x, where x is the number of variables or parameters and n is the number of evaluations in the range. In this case, evaluations were taken at intervals of 0.5 between 0 and 5, and at 0.5 between 0.25 and 4.75, and, in total, the model was run 222 times. The three response surfaces are presented in Figure 6.6 and contours of equal response have been interpolated visually from the grid of function evaluations also shown in Figure 6.6. In general terms, these surfaces seem to be far from unimodal; only the r^2 surface has a global optimum and this is an extreme value of the range, thus reflecting the problem of bogus calibration. On the other two surfaces, there appear to be an infinity of combinations of λ_1 and λ_2 which give a best fit, and this implies that one of these parameters is redundant. Therefore, the fears expressed earlier, that previous applications of the two-parameter retail location model might be suspect in this regard, seem well founded. However, the construction of these response surfaces is far too crude to make definitive statements about their precise form, and it is therefore necessary to explore these surfaces in greater detail using the search by golden section.

For each surface, the sequential linear search has been started from six different points, that is from $\lambda_2 = 0, 1, ..., 5$. In Figures 6.7–6.9, the

7

sequence of searches from each of the different starting points is illustrated for each surface. In almost every case, convergence to an optimal fit yields different sets of parameter values λ_1 and λ_2. In Figure 6.7, which illustrates the r^2 surface, the search always converges to the ridge which cuts across the surface. In Figure 6.6, this surface appears to have a high plateau but the golden section search reveals that this is in fact a ridge. In Figures 6.8 and 6.9, the searches converge to the valleys which are the major features of these surfaces, and in these cases, this provides a good demonstration that the optimum value always depends upon the starting points. In using such search procedures, care must be taken in fixing convergence limits. If, for example, the search moves onto slowly rising ground, then the exploration may terminate if the gradient is seemingly too small to improve the fit above a certain limit. Such an instance may have occurred in

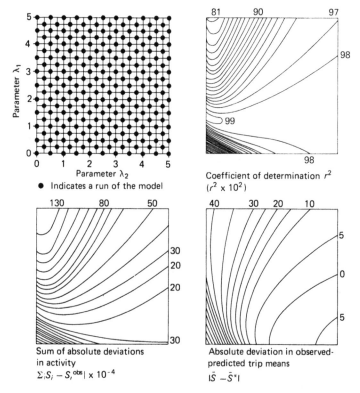

Fig. 6.6. An evaluation of the statistical response surfaces.

the searches illustrated in Figure 6.7, thus preventing the search ever reaching the global optimum. In Table 6.4, a summary of the start and end points for each of these examples is given, and this table illustrates the difficulties of finding the truly best fit.

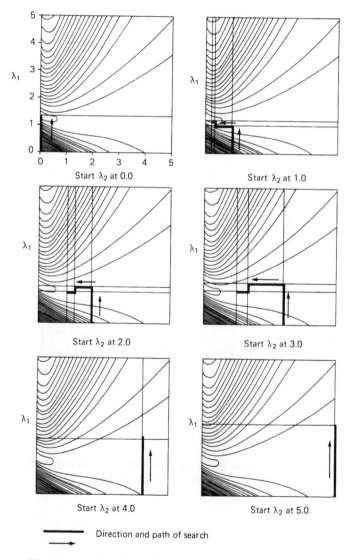

Start λ_2 at 0.0   Start λ_2 at 1.0

Start λ_2 at 2.0   Start λ_2 at 3.0

Start λ_2 at 4.0   Start λ_2 at 5.0

Direction and path of search

Fig. 6.7. Sequential linear search from different start points across the r^2 surface.

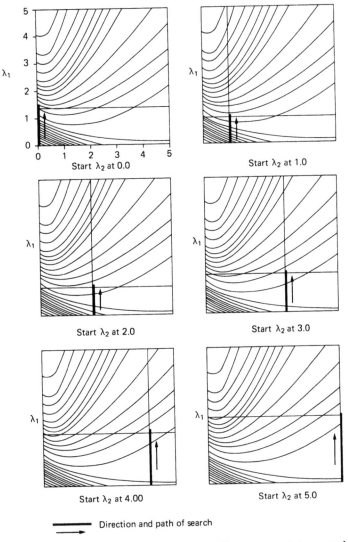

Direction and path of search

Fig. 6.8. Sequential linear search from different start points across the
surface based on the absolute deviations.

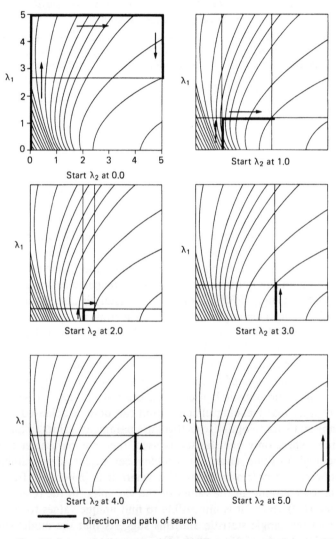

Fig. 6.9. Sequential linear search from different start points across the surface based on the mean trip lengths.

TABLE 6.4. *Start and end points for each response surface using sequential linear search*

Starting value	Coefficient of determination (r)		Sum of absolute deviations		Absolute deviation of predicted from observed ($\bar{S}$)	
	λ_1	λ_2	λ_1	λ_2	λ_1	λ_2
0.0	1.3334	0.0000	1.2964	0.0000	2.6800	4.9985
1.0	1.1434	0.2024	0.9173	1.0000	1.2329	2 8920
2.0	1.1790	1.0703	1.0164	2.0000	0.4427	2.3762
3.0	1.2713	1.2261	1.4567	3.0000	1.3288	3.0000
4.0	2.0163	4.0000	1.9607	4.0000	2.0547	4.0000
5.0	2.6156	5.0000	2.4708	5.0000	2.6814	5.0000

This analysis is disturbing news for analysts using the two-parameter version of the retail location model, and these results surely apply to other spatial interaction models such as residential location models. Yet the problems of finding an optimum fit have been anticipated in previous work (NEDO, 1970; Turner, 1970*b*). Moreover, the analysis also highlights the problem of finding meaningful statistics measuring the goodness of fit. Perhaps the most definite conclusion which can be drawn from these experiments is concerned with the use of two parameters in such models. Although there may be good theoretical reasons why such models should have two parameters, one of these parameters must be fixed *a priori* to get a best fit if only one statistic is used in calibration. In fact, it is shown in the next chapter that meaningful calibration can only be achieved if there are as many statistics to optimise as there are parameter values to find. Yet in situations where only one statistic is used, then one-parameter models should be used. In some senses, this problem can be considered similar to the identification problem in economics where it is impossible from the given data to determine all the values of the variables. In the retail model in (6.1) and (6.2) above, it is impossible to find unique values for both λ_1 and λ_2 from one single statistic and this suggests that the model should be reformulated as in (6.16) and (6.17).

Alternative univariate search procedures

Although the golden section search and its Fibonacci equivalent are the proven optimum methods for univariate search, there may be other methods which are faster in practice. Although not applied to the retail model discussed here, two such methods which are used extensively in the next two chapters, are stated here in terms of the simple case. First, the technique known as the Newton–Raphson method which forms one of the most popular methods of numerical analysis is presented. It is well known that the value of any function, say $\bar{S}(\lambda+\epsilon)$, can be found by expanding the function around some point λ using Taylor's theorem (Stephenson, 1961). Then expanding $\bar{S}(\lambda)$ in this fashion gives

$$\bar{S}(\lambda+\epsilon) = \bar{S}(\lambda)+\epsilon\frac{\mathrm{d}\bar{S}(\lambda)}{\mathrm{d}\lambda}+\frac{\epsilon^2}{2!}\frac{\mathrm{d}^2\bar{S}(\lambda)}{\mathrm{d}\lambda^2}+\ldots+\frac{\epsilon^r}{r!}\frac{\mathrm{d}^r\bar{S}(\lambda)}{\mathrm{d}\lambda^r}+\ldots$$

(6.39)

Now an approximation to $\bar{S}(\lambda+\epsilon)$ can be found by truncating (6.39) after a given number of terms. The Newton–Raphson technique is based on truncation of (6.39) after the first-order term, thus giving

$$\bar{S}(\lambda+\epsilon) \simeq \bar{S}(\lambda)+\epsilon\frac{\mathrm{d}\bar{S}(\lambda)}{\mathrm{d}\lambda}.$$

(6.40)

An iterative scheme based on (6.40) forms the essence of the Newton–Raphson technique in which a new parameter value λ^{k+1} on iteration $k+1$ is computed from

$$\lambda^{k+1} = \lambda^k+\epsilon^k = \lambda^k+\{\bar{S}(\lambda+\epsilon)-\bar{S}(\lambda^k)\}\bigg/\frac{\mathrm{d}\bar{S}(\lambda^k)}{\mathrm{d}(\lambda^k)}.$$

(6.41)

Equation (6.41) is derived from (6.40) noting that the value of the function $\bar{S}(\lambda+\epsilon)$ represents the optimum value which is sought. Extension of this technique to the mean trip length problem treated earlier is obvious in terms of the notation used.

Second, a family of methods based upon the fit of a quadratic to the parameter space has been widely used in problems of unconstrained optimisation. Dixon (1972) presents a useful summary of the general method but a particularly appealing example which is simple to use has been suggested by Box *et al.* (1969). This method is an iterative quadratic interpolation procedure in which the minimum of a quadratic is found analytically based on three equally-spaced parameter evaluations at λ^{k-1}, λ^k and λ^{k+1}. A new value of the parameter λ^{k+2} can be found from

$$\lambda^{k+2} = \lambda^k+\frac{\Delta\lambda(\bar{S}^{k-1}-\bar{S}^{k+1})}{2(\bar{S}^{k-1}-2\bar{S}^k+\bar{S}^{k+1})}.$$

(6.42)

Note that in (6.42), $\Delta\lambda$ is the interval between each of the parameters λ^{k-1}, λ^k and λ^{k+1} and the variables $\bar{S}^{k-1}$, $\bar{S}^k$ and $\bar{S}^{k+1}$ are those associated with these parameters. An interpretation of (6.42) in terms of the mean trip length problem is again obvious.

The message of this chapter is quite straightforward in that the calibration of urban models appears to be well suited to the use of unconstrained non-linear optimisation methods, at least for simple cases. In the next chapter, these techniques, particularly those outlined in the previous two paragraphs, will be extended to many-parameter urban models. Yet the problem of calibration cannot be dealt with summarily for the choice of calibration procedure remains a largely intuitive affair to be guided by a feel for the problem in hand. Usually, it is necessary for the model-builder to have some idea of the shape of the response surface in the parameter space, and in this respect, it is unlikely that only one technique of calibration can be universally applied, for each application can be quite different. The calibration problem is many-faceted like a diamond, each facet highlighting some aspect of the model's structure which can lead to revealing insights, the richness of which are further demonstrated in the next chapter.

7. Calibration as non-linear optimisation

The choice of appropriate statistical tests for urban models has not yet been dealt with in this book in any depth although certain conventional statistics measuring model performance have been used in the previous three chapters. In the last chapter, the emphasis was largely upon methods for finding parameters producing the best value of some statistic, rather than upon the choice of the statistic itself, and although this chapter will be concerned with extending such procedures, it is also devoted to establishing a theoretically acceptable method for deriving statistical tests. This method has already been anticipated in previous chapters in brief reference to the work of Hyman (1969), and in this chapter, the method will be explored and applied in the context of the Kristiansand retail location model described in Chapter 6 and a trip distribution model of the Reading subregion.

In introducing statistical testing of urban models, a brief review of existing calibration techniques which are mainly proposals rather than applications, sets a useful perspective for the statistical maximum-likelihood analysis which is first developed using the Kristiansand model. Five techniques for solving the maximum-likelihood equations to which the calibration problem is reduced, are then outlined and contrasted in terms of their efficiency. These methods are based upon the numerical search procedures outlined in Chapter 6. The maximum-likelihood method is then extended to the trip-distribution modelling problem and further comparisons of the savings in cost and computer time posed by the use of these techniques, help in assessing their relevance to urban modelling. First, however, it is worth while reviewing existing proposals for solving the calibration problem.

Existing methods of calibration

The most popular scheme for calibrating spatial interaction models especially in the field of locational geography (Chisholm and O'Sullivan, 1973), is based upon transformation of the model equations to linear form. The unconstrained spatial interaction model given in (2.51) is intrinsically linear and therefore linear regression analysis can be used to estimate the parameters. Equation (2.51) is rewritten below as a one-parameter model with an inverse power function of travel cost. Note that $\{T_{ij}^*\}$ is the observed trip distribution and the statistical problem is to find the parameter λ associated with this distribution. Then

$$T_{ij} = GO_i D_j c_{ij}^{-\lambda}. \tag{7.1}$$

By manipulating (7.1) and using a logarithmic transformation, an equation linear in its parameters is derived.

$$\ln\left(\frac{T_{ij}^*}{O_i D_j}\right) = \ln G - \lambda \ln c_{ij} + \xi_{ij}, \tag{7.2}$$

where ξ_{ij} is an error term. In (7.2), $\ln G$ and λ can be estimated using bivariate linear regression analysis, and the full range of linear statistics can be used to measure the goodness of fit (King, 1969). Equation (7.1) and its transformation in (7.2) have been widely used in geographic analysis to describe interaction phenomena. Indeed, Olsson (1965) remarks that 'much of the misunderstanding connected with the gravity model would probably disappear if it were more frequently treated as a type of regression analysis'. The use of regression analysis in estimating one or more parameters of intrinsically linear equations such as (7.1) above does have the disadvantage that the largest values of $\{T_{ij}^*\}$ have the smallest weight in the regression. Seidman (1969) has recognised this disadvantage and suggests that analysts should be exceedingly wary of using such transformations.

Apart from the unconstrained model, all other models in the family of spatial interaction models have equations which are intrinsically non-linear. These equations are complicated by the balancing factors which involve summations of the model's parameters, and therefore cannot be transformed as in (7.2). However, it is still possible to use the method of least squares to estimate the parameters, although the assumptions of the linear model no longer hold. It is necessary to minimise

$$\Phi = \sum_i \sum_j (T_{ij}^* - T_{ij})^2. \tag{7.3}$$

If, for example, there are K parameters λ_k, $k = 1, 2, ..., K$, minimisation of (7.3) yields K normal equations of the following form

$$\sum_i \sum_j (T_{ij}^* - T_{ij}) \frac{\partial T_{ij}}{\partial \lambda_k} = 0, \quad k = 1, 2, ..., K. \tag{7.4}$$

This method of least squares has been tested by Tanner (1961) for a production-attraction constrained trip-distribution model. Tanner reports that the normal equations had to be solved iteratively and the complex form of such equations usually means that the partial derivatives in (7.4) must be evaluated numerically. Kirby (1974) also provides conditions for the calibration of trip-distribution models according to the method of least squares.

An alternative to the least squares method involves a linearisation of the interaction model using Taylor's theorem. From first approximations to the parameters, called λ_k^m, the interaction equation can be expanded to terms of the first order as follows. Terms of the second and higher order are disregarded on the assumption that they contribute little to the expansion, and it is obvious that this assumption is only valid if λ_k^m is a good approximation to the unknown best value λ_k

$$T_{ij}^* \simeq T_{ij}(m) + \sum_{k=1}^{K} \frac{\partial T_{ij}(m)}{\partial \lambda_k^m} (\lambda_k - \lambda_k^m). \tag{7.5}$$

To clarify the presentation, the variables in (7.5) can be redefined in the following way

$$Y_{ij}(m) = T_{ij}^* - T_{ij}(m),$$

$$X_{ij}^k(m) = \frac{\partial T_{ij}(m)}{\partial \lambda_k^m},$$

$$a_k(m) = \lambda_k - \lambda_k^m.$$

It is easily seen that (7.5) has a linear form if substitutions are made according to the definitions above and (7.5) is rearranged as

$$Y_{ij}(m) = \sum_k a_k(m) X_{ij}(m) + \xi_{ij}. \tag{7.6}$$

ξ_{ij} is an error term which is assumed to be randomly distributed. The parameters $a_k(m)$ of (7.6) can now be estimated using least squares and new values for λ_k are calculated from

$$\lambda_k^{m+1} = \lambda_k^m + a_k(m). \tag{7.7}$$

λ_k^{m+1} is substituted for λ_k^m in equation (7.5) and the procedure is reiterated until a convergence limit is reached. This method, which is outlined in Draper and Smith (1966) and in Watt (1968), has been used by Broadbent (1968) in calibrating production-attraction constrained trip-distribution models, although it appears that convergence of the procedure can be extremely slow. However, this method has been applied to three different spatial interaction models in the Reading subregion and although in two cases the procedures diverged, in one case the procedure converged to within 10^{-3} of the best parameter value in three iterations. Despite this success, the method is too unreliable for general use. Seidman (1969) has also used this procedure in calibrating non-linear models as part of the

Activities Allocation model for the Delaware Valley Regional Planning Commission.

Hyman's work has already been referred to in Chapter 6 and will be further detailed in the next section, and it is of interest to note that Evans (1971) has produced similar results to Hyman. However, in contrast to the interpolation–extrapolation method suggested by Hyman for finding the parameter λ of a one-parameter trip-distribution model, Evans has shown that the derivatives of such a model are relatively simple to calculate where λ is equal to zero. By expanding the interaction equation around the point where λ equals zero using Maclaurin's theorem, the best value of λ is calculated from

$$\bar{C}* = \sum_{r=0}^{\infty} \left(\frac{\lambda^r}{r!} \frac{d^r \bar{C}}{d\lambda^r}\right)_{\lambda=0}, \tag{7.8}$$

where $\bar{C}*$ is the observed mean trip length and $\bar{C}$ the predicted mean trip length based on (4.1) with $F^1(c_{ij}) = c_{ij}$. Evans has given methods for calculating the derivatives and suggests that any standard method such as Newton's method can be used to solve the polynomial in (7.8). Baxter and Williams (1972) have succeeded in deriving a more general form for Evans' method which they have tested on a trip-distribution model of the town of Reading. The statistical methods proposed by Hyman and Evans will now be discussed further in terms of a methodology for deriving best statistics.

Introduction to statistical estimation in urban models

In the next sections of this chapter, several of the methods and applications introduced will be illustrated using the production-constrained retail location model of Kristiansand. Although the methods will be specific to this model, generalisations to other models in the family and to models with different parameter structures will be indicated. The main advantage in using this retail model to demonstrate a variety of techniques lies in the ease with which results can be compared, and efficient methods selected. To introduce the principle of maximum-likelihood as a tool for estimating relevant statistics for interaction models, it is necessary to convert the retail model given in (6.1) and (6.2) to a probabilistic form. Noting the following definitions,

$$C_i = c_i P_i$$

and

$$C = \sum_i C_i,$$

the model in (6.1) can be written as

$$S_{ij} = C p_{ij}. \tag{7.9}$$

To keep the reader informed, it is worth while redefining these terms. S_{ij} is the expenditure on goods made by the population living at i and shopping at j, C is the total amount of expenditure on goods in the system, C_i is the expenditure available in each zone i, and p_{ij} is the probability that a person living at i will shop for goods at j. This is defined as

$$p_{ij} = p_i A_i W_j^{\lambda_1} d_{ij}^{-\lambda_2}, \qquad (7.10)$$

$$A_i = \frac{1}{\sum_j W_j^{\lambda_1} d_{ij}^{-\lambda_2}}, \qquad (7.11)$$

$$p_i = \frac{C_i}{\sum_i C_i}. \qquad (7.12)$$

W_j is a measure of shopping centre attraction at j and d_{ij} is the distance or travel time between i and j. λ_1 and λ_2 are parameters of the model to be estimated by calibration. By substituting (7.10), (7.11) and (7.12) into (7.9) it is easily seen that (7.9) has an identical form to (6.1), the production-constrained retail location model.

The interaction probability p_{ij} can also be expressed as the product of the conditional probability $p(j|i)$ and the marginal probability $p(i)$

$$p_{ij} = p(j|i)\, p(i). \qquad (7.13)$$

The conditional probability $p(j|i)$ is the probability that a person will shop at j given that he lives at i, and the marginal probability $p(i)$ is the probability that the shopper lives at i. Referring to (7.10), it is hypothesised that these probabilities take the following form

$$p(j|i) = A_i W_j^{\lambda_1} d_{ij}^{-\lambda_2}, \qquad (7.14)$$

$$p(i) = p_i. \qquad (7.15)$$

The proportion of i, j events or trips that have been observed is defined as

$$s_{ij} = \frac{S_{ij}^*}{\sum_i \sum_j S_{ij}^*} = \frac{S_{ij}^*}{S}. \qquad (7.16)$$

Note here that $S = C$. The principle of maximum-likelihood can be used to derive relevant estimators of the parameters in the hypothesised formulation of $\{p_{ij}\}$ from the observed frequency proportions $\{s_{ij}\}$. This principle has been used to estimate the parameters of a production-attraction constrained model by Evans (1971) and is related to the Bayes estimators and contingency table approach used by Hyman (1969). Mackie (1971) has taken the principle of maximum-likelihood further by explicitly relating it to decision theory, and Wilson (1970a) has shown how these estimators are closely connected and complementary to the entropy-maximising methodology. Kirby (1974) has produced an important paper in which the maximum-likelihood is generalised for a variety of frequency distributions governing the sampling of interactions.

The principle of maximum-likelihood

The likelihood function L for the S_{ij}^* independent observations is proportional to the multinomial distribution

$$L = \prod_i \prod_j p_{ij}^{S_{ij}^*}. \tag{7.17}$$

Then according to the maximum-likelihood principle, the value of the parameters of the p_{ij}'s which maximise L or equivalently $\ln L$ subject to any constraints, are their best estimates. Note that in this form, $\ln L$ is proportional to the entropy used in statistical mechanics, and thus the problem is similar to entropy-maximisation (Tribus, 1969; Batty, 1973). However, it is necessary to ensure when finding these optimum parameters that $p(j|i)$ and $p(i)$ still obey the probability laws which are stated in the following equations

$$\sum_j p(j|i) = 1, \tag{7.18}$$

$$\sum_i p(i) = 1. \tag{7.19}$$

These constraints can be built in by maximising the following Lagrangian form

$$L^* = \ln L - \sum_i \mu_i [\sum_j p(j|i) - 1] - \gamma [\sum_i p(i) - 1], \tag{7.20}$$

where μ_i, $i = 1, 2, ..., I$, and γ are Lagrange multipliers. Using (7.13), (7.14), and (7.15), equation (7.20) can be written out fully as

$$L^* = \sum_i \sum_j S_{ij}^* (\ln A_i + \lambda_1 \ln W_j - \lambda_2 \ln d_{ij} + \ln p_i)$$

$$- \sum_i \mu_i [\sum_j (A_i W_j^{\lambda_1} d_{ij}^{-\lambda_2}) - 1] - \gamma (\sum_i p_i - 1). \tag{7.21}$$

Then to find the maximum of L^* with respect to A_i, p_i, λ_1 and λ_2, it is necessary to solve the following equations which are obtained by differentiating (7.21) and setting the partial derivatives equal to zero. These differential equations are given as

$$\frac{\partial L^*}{\partial A_i} = \frac{\sum_j S_{ij}^*}{A_i} - \mu_i \sum_j W_j^{\lambda_1} d_{ij}^{-\lambda_2} = 0, \tag{7.22}$$

$$\frac{\partial L^*}{\partial \lambda_1} = \sum_i \sum_j S_{ij}^* \ln W_j - \sum_i \mu_i (\sum_j A_i W_j^{\lambda_1} d_{ij}^{-\lambda_2} \ln W_j) = 0, \qquad (7.23)$$

$$\frac{\partial L^*}{\partial \lambda_2} = -\sum_i \sum_j S_{ij}^* \ln d_{ij} + \sum_i \mu_i (\sum_j A_i W_j^{\lambda_1} d_{ij}^{-\lambda_2} \ln d_{ij}) = 0, \qquad (7.24)$$

$$\frac{\partial L^*}{\partial p_i} = \frac{\sum_j S_{ij}^*}{p_i} - \gamma = 0, \qquad (7.25)$$

$$\frac{\partial L^*}{\partial \mu_i} = \sum_j A_i W_j^{\lambda_1} d_{ij}^{-\lambda_2} - 1 = 0 \qquad (7.26)$$

and

$$\frac{\partial L^*}{\partial \gamma} = \sum_i p_i - 1 = 0. \qquad (7.27)$$

Rearranging (7.26) and substituting into (7.22), the Lagrange multipliers μ_i are calculated as

$$\mu_i = \sum_j S_{ij}^*, \qquad (7.28)$$

and from (7.26)

$$A_i = \frac{1}{\sum_j W_j^{\lambda_1} d_{ij}^{-\lambda_2}}. \qquad (7.29)$$

Equations (7.25) and (7.27) can be rearranged to give

$$\gamma = \sum_i \sum_j S_{ij}^* = S, \qquad (7.30)$$

and therefore

$$p_i = \frac{\sum_j S_{ij}^*}{\sum_i \sum_j S_{ij}^*} = \sum_j s_{ij}. \qquad (7.31)$$

Then (7.28) and (7.31) give

$$\mu_i = p_i \sum_i \sum_j S_{ij}^* = p_i S. \qquad (7.32)$$

Substituting (7.32) into (7.24) and rearranging gives

$$(\sum_i \sum_j p_i A_i W_j^{\lambda_1} d_{ij}^{-\lambda_2} \ln d_{ij}) \sum_i \sum_j S_{ij}^* = \sum_i \sum_j S_{ij}^* \ln d_{ij}. \qquad (7.33)$$

In a similar fashion, substituting (7.32) into (7.23) gives

$$(\sum_i \sum_j p_i A_i W_j^{\lambda_1} d_{ij}^{-\lambda_2} \ln W_j) \sum_i \sum_j S_{ij}^* = \sum_i \sum_j S_{ij}^* \ln W_j. \qquad (7.34)$$

The four relevant equations from this analysis associated with λ_1, λ_2, A_i and p_i can now be brought together. Equations (7.33) and (7.34) are

reinterpreted below and (7.29) and (7.31) are restated. The best estimates
of the model's parameters can therefore be found by solving

$$\sum_i \sum_j p_{ij} \ln d_{ij} = \sum_i \sum_j s_{ij} \ln d_{ij}, \tag{7.35}$$

$$\sum_i \sum_j p_{ij} \ln W_j = \sum_i \sum_j s_{ij} \ln W_j, \tag{7.36}$$

$$A_i = \frac{1}{\sum_j W_j^{\lambda_1} d_{ij}^{-\lambda_2}}, \tag{[(7.29)]}$$

and

$$p_i = \sum_j s_{ij}. \tag{[(7.31)]}$$

Evans (1971) has pursued a similar analysis for a production-attraction
constrained model with a negative exponential function of travel cost, and
this method could easily be applied to the unconstrained model given in
(7.1) above. Furthermore, the equations for the estimators depend upon
the particular set of parameters embedded in the model, and different
parameter structures would yield different equations. Such extensions to
the principle are quite straightforward and could be tackled by the reader.

At this point, it is worth while stating a fundamental principle of urban
model calibration based on the method of maximum-likelihood. In the
above analysis, it is clear that each of the parameters λ_1 and λ_2 is associated
with a particular equation, in this case with equations (7.36) and (7.35)
respectively. Then in general, the calibration problem can be reduced to a
problem involving the solution of as many equations as there are unknowns.
Thus, it is stated without proof that urban model calibration can only be
achieved if there are as many statistics to be optimised as there are parameters to be found: the following sections are devoted to elaborating and
demonstrating this principle.

Solution of the maximum-likelihood equations

Of the four estimating equations given above, (7.29) and (7.31) can be
calculated directly from exogenous data and any set of parameter values.
The solution of (7.35) and (7.36), however, depends upon finding the
values of λ_1 and λ_2 which satisfy these equations, and the rest of this
chapter is concerned with methods of searching for these parameter values.
Equations (7.35) and (7.36) are rewritten below in a form more suitable to
the methods described in later sections

$$\min F_1(\lambda_1, \lambda_2) = \min \left| \sum_i \sum_j p_{ij} \ln d_{ij} - \sum_i \sum_j s_{ij} \ln d_{ij} \right| = 0, \tag{7.37}$$

$$\min F_2(\lambda_1, \lambda_2) = \min \left| \sum_i \sum_j p_{ij} \ln W_j - \sum_i \sum_j s_{ij} \ln W_j \right| = 0. \quad (7.38)$$

Some of the methods for finding λ_1 and λ_2 use a statistic based on a combination of (7.37) and (7.38)

$$\min \Lambda(\lambda_1, \lambda_2) = \min [F_1(\lambda_1, \lambda_2) + F_2(\lambda_1, \lambda_2)] = 0. \quad (7.39)$$

Equation (7.37) refers to the mean trip-cost equation in (7.35) whereas (7.38) refers to (7.36) which can be called the mean trip-benefit equation. The global minimum values of (7.37) and (7.38) and therefore (7.39) only occur when the predicted mean trip cost and benefit are equal to their observed values.

Equations (7.37)–(7.39) are intrinsically non-linear and methods for their solution can be divided into two classes: *numerical* methods and *search* procedures. There are several standard numerical methods which can be used to solve systems of non-linear equations, and two methods, one based on simple iteration, the other based on the Newton–Raphson method will be outlined. Search procedures deal essentially with problems of unconstrained optimisation, and a distinction is usually made between *direct search*, the subject of the last chapter, and *gradient search*. Direct searches do not involve any evaluation of the derivatives of the objective function whereas in gradient search, the derivatives are used to guide the direction of search. In this chapter like the last, only the methods of direct search will be introduced for it appears that the direct search is generally more efficient than gradient search when, as in this case, derivatives are usually found by numerical methods and not analytically. Box *et al.* (1969) divide direct search procedures into tabulation, sequential and quadratic methods, and examples of each of these three methods will be presented. Tabulation methods, as described in earlier chapters, deal with progressive reduction of the region of search; a method based on the sequence of Fibonacci/golden section numbers, outlined in Chapter 6, will be described further. Sequential methods investigate the objective function using factorial designs which are expanded or contracted as the search progresses; an example of this class of search – the Simplex method – will be demonstrated. Finally, quadratic methods depend on a process for finding the minimum of a quadratic in a specified number of iterations; a method devised by Powell (1964) will be outlined.

As a guide to the efficiency of the numerical and search procedures, the response surfaces formed by evaluating (7.37)–(7.39) with respect to the Kristiansand model, are plotted in Figure 7.1. Figure 7.1(a) shows the points within the parameter space which relate to the parameter values of λ_1 and λ_2 under which the objective functions have been evaluated.

Figures 7.1 (*b*) and 7.1 (*c*) show the response surfaces formed from (7.37) and (7.38); in Figure 7.1 (*d*), these surfaces are overlaid and the minimum values of (7.37) and (7.38) are plotted in Figure 7.1 (*e*). Finally, in Figure 7.1 (*f*), a composite surface from (7.39) is plotted. A mean trip length of 1.75 and a mean trip benefit of 5.25 were judged to be good approxima-

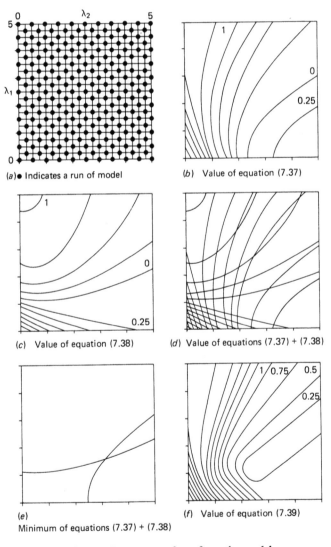

Fig. 7.1. Response surfaces from the model.

tions to the observed values of these statistics, and Figure 7.1 is based on these values. In the following sections, first the numerical methods, and then the search procedures, will be described, and a comparison of the relative performance of each method will ultimately be made.

Numerical methods: first-order iteration and the Newton–Raphson method

A first-order process based on simple iteration was used in the attempt to solve (7.37) and (7.38). At each iteration m, the mean trip benefit $\overline{W}^m$ and mean trip cost $\overline{C}^m$ were computed from λ_1^m and λ_2^m respectively.

$$\overline{W}^m = \sum_i \sum_j p_{ij}(m) \ln W_j, \qquad (7.40)$$

$$\overline{C}^m = \sum_i \sum_j p_{ij}(m) \ln d_{ij}. \qquad (7.41)$$

New values of the parameters λ_1^{m+1} and λ_2^{m+1} were computed by weighting the previous values of these parameters according to the ratios given in the following equations. Hyman (1969) has suggested a similar procedure mentioned in Chapter 6 for a one-parameter production-attraction constrained model

$$\lambda_1^{m+1} = \lambda_1^m \frac{\overline{W}^*}{\overline{W}^m}, \qquad (7.42)$$

$$\lambda_2^{m+1} = \lambda_2^m \frac{\overline{C}^m}{\overline{C}^*}. \qquad (7.43)$$

Equations (7.40) and (7.41) were then recomputed using λ_1^{m+1} and λ_2^{m+1} and the process is continued in this way until some convergence limit is

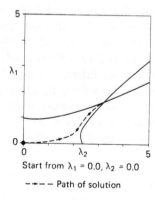
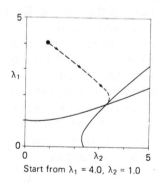

Start from $\lambda_1 = 0.0$, $\lambda_2 = 0.0$

Start from $\lambda_1 = 4.0$, $\lambda_2 = 1.0$

– · – · – Path of solution

Fig. 7.2. Solutions using first-order iteration.

reached. This method was tried from two different sets of starting points for λ_1 and λ_2; the convergence is described in Table 7.1 and the solution paths are illustrated in Figure 7.2. It is obvious from these results that the process has extremely slow convergence and is therefore too expensive to apply generally. However, it is possible that the method could be used to provide good first approximations to λ_1 and λ_2 for some other method, for the convergence can be fast at the outset of the process.

TABLE 7.1. *Convergence of the first-order iterative process*

Iterations or runs of model	λ_1	Value of equation (7.38)	λ_2	Value of equation (7.37)
Start from $\lambda_1, \lambda_2 = 0.0001$				
10	0.0039	1.6756	0.7046	2.2926
20	0.0174	0.4047	2.2323	0.0002
30	0.0418	0.3954	2.2200	0.0014
40	0.0897	0.3764	2.1949	0.0274
50	0.1700	0.3493	2.1526	0.0097
Start from $\lambda_1 = 4.0, \lambda_2 = 1.0$				
10	2.0215	0.1404	3.4153	0.0231
20	1.6187	0.1009	2.9098	0.0252
30	1.3686	0.0739	2.5843	0.0154
40	1.2165	0.0487	2.4130	0.0084
50	1.1281	0.0299	2.3264	0.0044

The second numerical method used to solve (7.37) and (7.38) is based on an extension of the Newton–Raphson method given in (6.39)–(6.41) to systems of equations with two or more unknowns. This method can be found in most books on numerical analysis (Milne, 1949; Redish, 1961), and is similar to the method of scoring proposed by Rao (1952) for solving maximum-likelihood equations. It is also of some interest to note that Ginsberg (1972) has suggested a related technique for solving the likelihood equations associated with a migration model based on spatial interaction. The method will be detailed here for a two-parameter model. From good first approximations to the parameter values, called λ_1^m and λ_2^m, the best values can be computed as

$$\lambda_1 = \lambda_1^m + \epsilon_1, \tag{7.44}$$

$$\lambda_2 = \lambda_2^m + \epsilon_2, \tag{7.45}$$

where ϵ_1 and ϵ_2 are differences between the best and approximated values. To find ϵ_1 and ϵ_2, it is possible to expand functions such as those given in (7.37) and (7.38) around the values of λ_1^m and λ_2^m using Taylor's theorem. For example, taking the function in (7.37) the expansion is

$$F_1(\lambda_1+\epsilon_1, \lambda_2+\epsilon_2) = \sum_{r=0}^{\infty} \frac{1}{r!} *D^r F_1(\lambda_1^m, \lambda_2^m), \qquad (7.46)$$

$$*D^r = \left(\epsilon_1 \frac{\partial}{\partial \lambda_1} + \epsilon_2 \frac{\partial}{\partial \lambda_2}\right)^r_{\lambda_k=\lambda_k^m}. \qquad (7.47)$$

Note that equation (7.46) is the two-parameter version of (6.39).

If the terms ϵ_1 and ϵ_2 in (7.47) are fairly small, thus implying that λ_1^m and λ_2^m are good first approximations, then approximate values of the function can be obtained by truncating (7.46) at terms of the first order. This is similar to the process of linearisation used by Broadbent (1968), which was described earlier. Expanding and truncating (7.37) and (7.38) around the points λ_1^m and λ_2^m in this way gives

$$F_1(\lambda_1^m+\epsilon_1, \lambda_2^m+\epsilon_2) \simeq F_1(\lambda_1^m, \lambda_2^m)$$
$$+\epsilon_1 \frac{\partial F_1(\lambda_1^m, \lambda_2^m)}{\partial \lambda_1^m} + \epsilon_2 \frac{\partial F_1(\lambda_1^m, \lambda_2^m)}{\partial \lambda_2^m}, \qquad (7.48)$$

$$F_2(\lambda_1^m+\epsilon_1, \lambda_2^m+\epsilon_2) \simeq F_2(\lambda_1^m, \lambda_2^m)$$
$$+\epsilon_1 \frac{\partial F_2(\lambda_1^m, \lambda_2^m)}{\partial \lambda_1^m} + \epsilon_2 \frac{\partial F_2(\lambda_1^m, \lambda_2^m)}{\partial \lambda_2^m}. \qquad (7.49)$$

Rearranging (7.48) and (7.49) gives two linear equations in two unknowns which can be solved by any of the standard solution methods. The structure of this system of equations is clarified using explicit matrix notation

$$-\begin{bmatrix} F_1(\lambda_1^m, \lambda_2^m) \\ F_2(\lambda_1^m, \lambda_2^m) \end{bmatrix} = \begin{bmatrix} \dfrac{\partial F_1(\lambda_1^m, \lambda_2^m)}{\partial \lambda_1^m} & \dfrac{\partial F_1(\lambda_1^m, \lambda_2^m)}{\partial \lambda_2^m} \\ \dfrac{\partial F_2(\lambda_1^m, \lambda_2^m)}{\partial \lambda_1^m} & \dfrac{\partial F_2(\lambda_1^m, \lambda_2^m)}{\partial \lambda_2^m} \end{bmatrix} \begin{bmatrix} \epsilon_1 \\ \epsilon_2 \end{bmatrix}. \qquad (7.50)$$

Matrix equation (7.50) can be written generally for the case of K parameters as

$$-\mathbf{F} = \mathbf{\Delta}\boldsymbol{\epsilon}, \qquad (7.51)$$

where $\mathbf{F}$ and $\boldsymbol{\epsilon}$ are $1 \times K$ column vectors and $\mathbf{\Delta}$ is a $K \times K$ matrix. Under most conditions a solution to (7.51) will be given by

$$\boldsymbol{\epsilon} = -\mathbf{\Delta}^{-1}\mathbf{F}. \qquad (7.52)$$

New values for the parameters can be found as follows

$$\lambda_1^{m+1} = \lambda_1^m + \epsilon_1, \qquad (7.53)$$

$$\lambda_2^{m+1} = \lambda_2^m + \epsilon_2. \qquad (7.54)$$

These values are now used to compute new values in (7.51) and equations (7.51)–(7.54) are reiterated until some convergence limit is reached.

In Table 7.2 and Figure 7.3, the use of this method is shown from two different sets of starting points. It is clear that the method is considerably more efficient than the first-order process by at least a factor of 10 although there are two limitations which must be mentioned. First, good approximations to λ_1 and λ_2 are needed to achieve convergence. On some runs of the method which were started from poor approximations, the process diverged to such an extent that certain values predicted by the model exceeded the permissible limit of the computer. Second, as the partial derivatives in (7.50) are evaluated numerically in the programme used here, the step size used to approximate $\partial \lambda_1$ and $\partial \lambda_2$ affected the convergence. For large step sizes (> 0.01), the process tended to oscillate around the best values of λ_1 and λ_2. Therefore, in applying this method, some initial sensitivity-testing of the process may be necessary.

Direct search using the Fibonacci/golden section numbers

The search procedure based on the series of positive integers called the Fibonacci numbers has already been stated in Chapter 6 as the optimal method for locating the maximum or minimum value of a univariate unimodal function. The method was first proven to be optimal by Kiefer (1953) and interested readers are again referred to the proof given in Wilde (1964). To introduce this search procedure in multivariate terms, assume that it is required to find the minimum of a function

$$f(\lambda_1, \lambda_2, ..., \lambda_k, ..., \lambda_K)$$

by varying λ_k and holding all other parameters constant. The Fibonacci numbers are first restated as

$$\left. \begin{array}{l} u_0 = u_1 = 1, \\ u_n = u_{n-1} + u_{n-2}, \quad n \geqslant 2. \end{array} \right\} \qquad [(6.23)]$$

The Fibonacci numbers u_n are defined from Binet's equation in (6.31) or another formula for u_n can be derived by solving the second-order difference equation in (6.23) with respect to its initial conditions (Goldberg, 1958).

TABLE 7.2. *Convergence of the Newton–Raphson method*

Iterations or runs of model*	λ_1	Value of equation (7.38)	λ_2	Value of equation (7.37)
		Start from $\lambda_1, \lambda_2 = 0.0$		
3	0.0000	0.7718	0.0000	2.5343
6	0.6486	0.2029	3.1132	0.1600
9	1.2762	0.2927	0.9138	0.8732
12	0.8410	0.0122	1.7475	0.2123
15	0.9459	0.0125	2.1376	0.0167
18	1.0148	0.0014	2.2441	0.0032
21	1.0117	0.0000	2.2284	0.0006
24	1.0131	0.0000	2.2320	0.0001
25	1.0128	NC	2.2312	NC
		Start from $\lambda_1, \lambda_2 = 1.0$		
3	1.0000	0.0897	1.0000	0.7930
6	0.8447	0.0197	1.8458	0.1142
9	0.9982	0.0095	2.2512	0.0020
12	1.0112	0.0003	2.2253	0.0014
15	1.0140	0.0000	2.2343	0.0006
18	1.0123	0.0000	2.2298	0.0003
21	1.0132	0.0000	2.2321	0.0002
24	1.0127	0.0000	2.2309	0.0000
25	1.0130	NC	2.2316	NC

NC means that the value has not been computed.

* The derivatives are evaluated numerically in the programme and therefore each stage of the method is in multiples of 3.

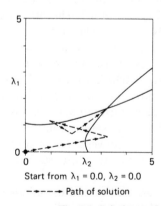

Start from $\lambda_1 = 0.0$, $\lambda_2 = 0.0$

–•–•–• Path of solution

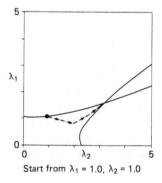

Start from $\lambda_1 = 1.0$, $\lambda_2 = 1.0$

Fig. 7.3. Solutions using the Newton–Raphson method.

With a total of N function evaluations, and on the mth iteration when the interval of search has been narrowed to $\{\lambda_k^{2,m} - \lambda_k^{1,m}\}$, the next two parameter values $\lambda_k^{3,m}$ and $\lambda_k^{4,m}$ are selected as

$$\lambda_k^{3,m} = \frac{u_{N-1-m}}{u_{N+1-m}}(\lambda_k^{2,m} - \lambda_k^{1,m}) + \lambda_k^{1,m}, \tag{7.55}$$

$$\lambda_k^{4,m} = \frac{u_{N-m}}{u_{N+1-m}}(\lambda_k^{2,m} - \lambda_k^{1,m}) + \lambda_k^{1,m}. \tag{7.56}$$

Note that (7.55) and (7.56) are equivalent to (6.24) and (6.25) but with k now indicating the parameter to be optimised and m the iteration number. This change in notation is important for it can lead to confusion if not made explicit. The generalisation to search by golden section has already been demonstrated in Chapter 6 and it consists of replacing the Fibonacci ratios in (7.55) and (7.56) by the fractions 0.382 and 0.618 respectively (Vorobev, 1961). The method of extending the Fibonacci search to a two-parameter model is based on the sequential linear search defined in the last chapter although this procedure is illustrated with respect to the minimisation of (7.37) and (7.38) in an alternating fashion. A set of outer iterations corresponding to each linear search is indexed by m' and, at each m', a univariate Fibonacci search is carried out using (7.55) and (7.56) above. Then

$$F_1(\lambda_1^{m'}, \lambda_2^{m'+1}) = \min_{\lambda_2^m} F_1(\lambda_2^m | \lambda_1^{m'}), \tag{7.57}$$

$$F_2(\lambda_1^{m'+2}, \lambda_2^{m'+1}) = \min_{\lambda_1^m} F_2(\lambda_1^m | \lambda_2^{m'+1}). \tag{7.58}$$

On iteration $m'+1$, the optimum value of λ_2^m is found with respect to the function $F_1(\lambda_1, \lambda_2)$ as in (7.57) by holding λ_1 at the value found on iteration m'. In (7.58), a new value for λ_1 is found on iteration $m'+2$ with respect to $F_2(\lambda_1, \lambda_2)$ holding λ_2 at the value found on $m'+1$. This procedure is continued until some convergence limit is reached. This procedure has been applied to estimating the parameters of the Kristiansand model, and it has been made more accurate and efficient by increasing the value of N in (7.55) and (7.56) as the minimum is approached. In Table 7.3 and Figure 7.4, the convergence and search directions using multivariate Fibonacci search are shown from two different starting points; although the search procedures show a reasonably efficient convergence in this case, there is no guarantee that the process will always converge for such linear searches depend upon the precise shape of the response surfaces in Figure 7.1.

Multivariate Fibonacci search has also been used to find the minimum of the combined function given in (7.39). The process is similar to (7.57) and (7.58) in which one parameter is varied at each iteration.

TABLE 7.3. *Convergence of the multivariate Fibonacci search*

		Start from $\lambda_1 = 0.0$		
Iterations or runs of model	λ_1	Value of equation (7.38)	λ_2	Value of equation (7.37)
9	0.0000	NC	2.2542	0.0044
18	1.0081	0.0059	2.2542	NC
27	1.0081	NC	2.1884	0.0047
36	0.9674	0.0050	2.1884	NC
45	0.9674	NC	2.1884	0.0047
54⎫ 63⎬ 72⎭	The procedure repeats itself in all following iterations for the search is not fine enough to achieve a better convergence			

		Start from $\lambda_1 = 4.0$		
Iterations or runs of model*	λ_1	Value of equation (7.38)	λ_2	Value of equation (7.37)
3	4.0000	NC	3.8196	0.2055
7	1.9098	0.0247	3.8196	NC
13	1.9098	NC	3.0901	0.0044
20	1.4589	0.0057	3.0901	NC
29	1.4589	NC	2.5986	0.0005
39	1.1803	0.0017	2.5986	NC
50	1.1803	NC	2.3606	0.0028
62	1.0739	0.0016	2.3606	NC

NC means that the value has not been computed.
* In each linear search, the convergence limit is computed as limit $(N+1) =$ limit $(N)/2.0$ where limit $(0) = 1.0$.

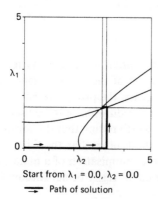

Start from $\lambda_1 = 0.0$, $\lambda_2 = 0.0$
⇌ Path of solution

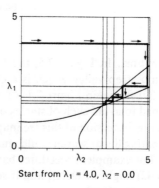

Start from $\lambda_1 = 4.0$, $\lambda_2 = 0.0$

Fig. 7.4. Solutions using Fibonacci search.

$$\Lambda(\lambda_1^{m'}, \lambda_2^{m'+1}) = \min_{\lambda_2^m} \, [F_1(\lambda_2^m|\lambda_1^{m'}) + F_2(\lambda_2^m|\lambda_1^{m'})], \qquad (7.59)$$

$$\Lambda(\lambda_1^{m'+2}, \lambda_2^{m'+1}) = \min_{\lambda_1^m} \, [F_1(\lambda_1^m|\lambda_2^{m'+1}) + F_2(\lambda_1^m|\lambda_2^{m'+1})]. \qquad (7.60)$$

The use of (7.59) and (7.60) however illustrates some of the problems which can occur with search procedures. As all search procedures assume not only that the response surface is unimodal but that the surface is concave or convex down (Wilde, 1964), surfaces which have ridges, saddle points and valleys can be difficult to handle. Such irregularities on the surface act as obstacles to the search and quite often the search procedure can terminate at such points for they have some of the features which characterise the

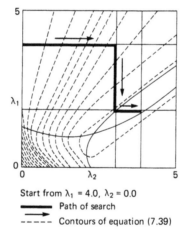

Start from $\lambda_1 = 4.0$, $\lambda_2 = 0.0$

▬▬▬ Path of search

→

- - - - Contours of equation (7.39)

Fig. 7.5. Oscillating solution for variable
Fibonacci search based on minimisation
of equation (7.39).

global optima. In Figure 7.5, the Fibonacci search procedure has terminated in a steep valley which is a characteristic of the surface associated with (7.39) shown in Figure 7.1 (f). In such cases, the procedure has to be redesigned to avoid such obstacles or other procedures have to be used. In concluding discussion of this technique, it is worth noting that this strategy of alternating linear search could employ methods other than the Fibonacci search. For example, procedures based on the optimisation of a quadratic as in (6.42) might be faster, and if so, these could easily be substituted for the Fibonacci search.

Sequential search using the Simplex method

The Simplex method which was first introduced by Spendley, Hext and Himsworth (1962), involves the evaluation of the objective function at $K+1$ points in K-parameter space. These points are regularly spaced and form the vertices of a regular simplex. The method works by changing one point of the simplex at each iteration in such a way that the optimum value of the function is approached. A modification of the Simplex method, proposed by Nelder and Mead (1965), is developed here for this method gives greater flexibility in the construction of the simplex.

For a problem with K parameter values λ_k, $k = 1, 2, ..., K$, the simplex is formed by evaluating the objective function at $K+1$ points, called $\pi_1, ..., \pi_{K+1}$, the co-ordinates of these points being parameter values. The values of the function of each of these points are called $\Lambda_1, ..., \Lambda_{K+1}$, and the superscripts h, v and l relate to the highest, second-highest, and lowest values of the function. The method will be described for a typical iteration for the case of two parameters λ_1 and λ_2 using an explicit matrix notation when the search is for a *minimum* function value. From the existing simplex, the centroid of all the vertices, called $\bar{\lambda}$, is first calculated. Then the highest value of the function λ^h is chosen and this point is reflected through $\bar{\lambda}$ to form a new point λ^*. This reflection operation is described by

$$\begin{bmatrix} \lambda_1^* \\ \lambda_2^* \end{bmatrix} = \begin{bmatrix} 1+\omega & 0 \\ 0 & 1+\omega \end{bmatrix} \begin{bmatrix} \bar{\lambda}_1 \\ \bar{\lambda}_2 \end{bmatrix} - \begin{bmatrix} \omega & 0 \\ 0 & \omega \end{bmatrix} \begin{bmatrix} \lambda_1^h \\ \lambda_2^h \end{bmatrix}. \tag{7.61}$$

ω is a constant called the coefficient of reflection. If $\Lambda_k^v \geqslant \Lambda_k^* \geqslant \Lambda_k^l$, then λ^* replaces λ^h as the new point in the simplex and a new reflection is carried out on the next iteration. If, however, $\Lambda_k^* < \Lambda_k^l$, then the new direction in which the reflection is made appears promising and a new point λ^{**} is found by expansion

$$\begin{bmatrix} \lambda_1^{**} \\ \lambda_2^{**} \end{bmatrix} = \begin{bmatrix} 1-\rho & 0 \\ 0 & 1-\rho \end{bmatrix} \begin{bmatrix} \bar{\lambda}_1 \\ \bar{\lambda}_2 \end{bmatrix} + \begin{bmatrix} \rho & 0 \\ 0 & \rho \end{bmatrix} \begin{bmatrix} \lambda_1^* \\ \lambda_2^* \end{bmatrix}. \tag{7.62}$$

ρ is a constant called the coefficient of expansion. If $\Lambda_k^{**} < \Lambda_k^l$, then λ^{**} replaces λ^h; otherwise λ^* replaces λ^h and a new reflection is carried out on the next iteration.

In the case where $\Lambda_k^* > \Lambda_k^v$, then λ^h is replaced by λ^* if $\Lambda_k^* < \Lambda_k^v$. Then a contraction operation is necessary where λ^h is contracted to

$$\begin{bmatrix} \lambda_1^{**} \\ \lambda_2^{**} \end{bmatrix} = \begin{bmatrix} 1-\kappa & 0 \\ 0 & 1-\kappa \end{bmatrix} \begin{bmatrix} \bar{\lambda}_1 \\ \bar{\lambda}_2 \end{bmatrix} + \begin{bmatrix} \kappa & 0 \\ 0 & \kappa \end{bmatrix} \begin{bmatrix} \lambda_1^h \\ \lambda_2^h \end{bmatrix}. \tag{7.63}$$

κ is the coefficient of contraction. λ^h is then replaced by λ^{**} unless $\Lambda_k^{**} > \min(\Lambda_k^{*}, \Lambda_k^h)$ when all points π are replaced by $(\pi_k + \pi_l)/2$. The method appears to have the useful property that it is able to traverse the parameter space efficiently in its search for the optimum. Because of the three exploratory operations – reflection, expansion and contraction, the method is more able to avoid local optima than other search methods, and Mackie (1971) reports that tests of the method show that it converges to the same position from several different starting points.

An application of the method is shown in Figure 7.6 and Table 7.4 and the coefficients used were based on those suggested by Nelder and Mead (1965); values for these constants were $\omega = 1$, $\rho = 2$ and $\kappa = 0.5$, thus giving a simple reflection, a doubling of length when expanding and halving when contracting. The method is much more efficient than the Fibonacci search although slightly less efficient than the Newton–Raphson method. The main advantage of the method seems to be its generality and ability to converge to the global optima from extreme starting values.

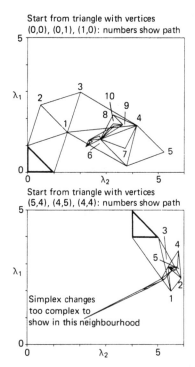

Fig. 7.6. Solutions using the Nelder–Mead Simplex method.

TABLE 7.4. *Convergence of the Nelder–Mead Simplex method**

Iterations or runs of model†	λ_1	Value of equation (7.38)	λ_2	Value of equation (7.37)
		Start from $\lambda_1, \lambda_2 = 0.0$		
4	1.5000	0.3424	1.5000	0.3945
14	1.8046	0.0905	3.2890	0.0479
24	1.0359	0.0030	2.2679	0.0060
34	1.0138	0.0000	2.2331	0.0003
44	1.0128	0.0000	2.2311	0.0000
54	1.0129	0.0000	2.2313	0.0000
		Start from $\lambda_1, \lambda_2 = 4.0$		
4	2.0000	0.1667	5.5000	0.2084
14	2.7762	0.0041	5.5694	0.1255
24	2.4210	0.0006	4.9180	0.1236
34	1.0596	0.0058	2.3063	0.0120
44	1.0193	0.0022	2.2336	0.0004
54	1.0135	0.0002	2.2312	0.0001

* Step sizes for the construction of the initial simplex are $+1.0$ in both cases.
† As three vertices are required for the initial simplex, the fourth point is the first iteration endogenous to the search procedure.

Quadratic search using conjugate directions

Quadratic search procedures, like Fibonacci search, are based on the optimisation of a univariate unimodal function. Such optimisation involves fitting a quadratic to three points and finding the maximum or minimum of the fitted function. The procedure can then be reiterated until some convergence limit is reached. Taking the case of the function in (7.39) and holding $K-1$ parameters constant, the optimum value of λ_k in direction η_k is calculated from

$$\lambda_k = \frac{1}{2} \frac{[(\lambda_k^2)^2 - (\lambda_k^3)^2]\Lambda_k^1 + [(\lambda_k^2)^2 - (\lambda_k^1)^2]\Lambda_k^2 + [(\lambda_k^1)^2 - (\lambda_k^2)^2]\Lambda_k^3}{(\lambda_k^2 - \lambda_k^3)\Lambda_k^1 + (\lambda_k^3 - \lambda_k^1)\Lambda_k^2 + (\lambda_k^1 - \lambda_k^2)\Lambda_k^3}. \tag{7.64}$$

The three lowest values of the function defined from λ_k, λ_k^1, λ_k^2 and λ_k^3 form the basis for a new minimum which can be progressively improved by repeated application of (7.64). It is possible to design a search procedure similar to multivariate Fibonacci search but using (7.64) instead of (7.55) and (7.56) in the scheme implied by (7.59) and (7.60). Quadratic search based on conjugate directions is more efficient, however, for it makes use of the concept of quadratic convergence.

Methods which have the property of quadratic convergence, ensure that a quadratic function can be minimised in a given number of iterations. Several researchers have shown that if the directions of search called η_k, $k = 1, 2, \ldots, K$, where η_k is a $1 \times K$ direction vector, are chosen to be conjugate to each other, then it is possible to find the minimum of a quadratic by only searching once along each direction η_k. More rigorous definitions of conjugacy are given by Box et al. (1969) and by Powell (1964). Most methods, however, start with the co-ordinate directions as in sequential linear search, and gradually replace these co-ordinates with conjugate directions. The method can be best illustrated in relation to the search for the minimum of the two-parameter function in (7.39). On the mth iteration, the search begins along the two linearly-independent directions called η_1^m, η_2^m. Starting from the preceding approximation to the minimum π_0, the minimum of (7.39) is found sequentially in each of these directions, and the amount of total progress θ is calculated from

$$\theta = \pi_2 - \pi_0. \tag{7.65}$$

A search is then made along θ and a new minimum π_0 is found. A new set of direction vectors for iteration $m+1$ is then set up as

$$\eta_1^{m+1} = \eta_2^m, \quad \eta_2^{m+1} = \theta. \tag{7.66}$$

The method of search implied in (7.65) and (7.66) has been refined considerably by Powell (1964) who has introduced a procedure into the scheme for avoiding linearly-dependent direction vectors which can result

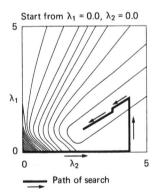

Fig. 7.7. Solutions using Powell's method of quadratic convergence based on conjugate directions.

if no progress is made between iterations. The specific details of Powell's algorithm are too lengthy to present here, and the reader is referred to the article by Powell (1964) which contains proofs of the efficiency of the search and its quadratic convergence. Powell's method has been used to find the minimum of (7.39) and in Figure 7.7, and Table 7.5 the sequence of search is presented. Although the method is efficient from reasonable starting points, it converges slowly from poor first approximations and may tend to converge to a local optimum from more extreme starting points. There are several local optima in the response surface of (7.39) which are merely slight depressions in the surface. Unlike Nelder and Mead's Simplex method which tends to skim over such local optima, Powell's method sometimes converges to these 'false' positions.

TABLE 7.5. *Convergence of Powell's quadratic search procedure*

Iterations or runs of model*	Start from $\lambda_1 = 0.0$		
	λ_1	λ_2	Value of equation (7.39)
8	0.0000	4.1469	0.4870
15	2.1029	4.1469	0.1302
66	1.8008	3.5511	0.1228
77	1.6930	3.5511	0.1060
106	1.0232	2.2302	0.0066
115	1.0116	2.2302	0.0004
123	1.0120	0.2309	0.0003
129	1.0129	2.2309	0.0002
134	1.0132	2.2316	0.0001

* The number of iterations is dependent upon the number of local explorations needed to determine conjugate directions.

The five methods outlined above for solving the maximum-likelihood equations of the retail gravity model have various advantages and limitations. In the following section, a short synthesis of these methods will be attempted by a comparison of their relative efficiency in terms of their abilities to locate the global optima and their speed of convergence.

A comparison of solution methods

A comparison can be made between these methods in terms of their convergence from starting points where the parameters are zero. In Table

7.6, the time of convergence to within specified limits is recorded for each method in terms of the real time used in computation. The cumulative number of runs of the model is also presented in Table 7.6, and this indicates the variation of the real time per run in each of the methods. It is clear from this table that the Newton–Raphson method is the most efficient within the limit 10^{-3} and that the Simplex method is the second most efficient. The first-order method and Powell's algorithm are the least efficient although Table 7.6 does not completely reveal the relative advantages of each method. In Figure 7.8 the time of convergence is plotted against the convergence limits thus showing that the rate of convergence varies widely between methods and also within different limits for each method. For example, up to 10^{-1} and 10^{-2}, the Newton–Raphson and Fibonacci methods are most efficient and below 10^{-2}, the Newton–Raphson method has the greatest efficiency.

As no one method dominates, it is apparent that a best search strategy can only be evolved by combining particular methods for use over different sequences of the search. The search could start using a first-order or Fibonacci scheme until convergence to 10^{-1} had been reached; the scheme could then be switched to the Newton–Raphson method until the limit 10^{-4} had been reached and the search could be concluded using Powell's algorithm or the Simplex method. Several hybrid strategies can be mixed from the available search procedures, and such strategies could be usefully tested in future research.

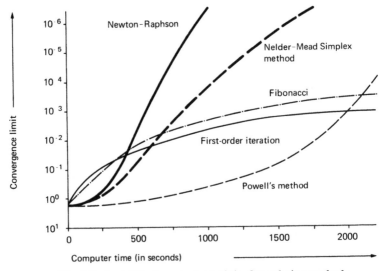

Fig. 7.8. A graphical comparison of the five solution methods.

TABLE 7.6. *A comparison of convergence times for the five methods**

Convergence limit for equation (7.39)†	First-order	Newton–Raphson	Fibonacci	Simplex	Quadratic
$\leqslant 10^{-1}$	182 (13)	390 (15)	270 (18)	432 (16)	1696 (106)
$\leqslant 10^{-2}$	$\gg 700$ (50)	468 (18)	540 (36)	621 (23)	1696 (106)
$\leqslant 10^{-3}$	NC	546 (21)	> 1350 (90)	864 (32)	1840 (115)
$\leqslant 10^{-4}$	NC	702 (27)	NC	1107 (41)	2144 (134)
$\leqslant 10^{-5}$	NC	NC	NC	1296 (48)	NC
Average time per iteration	14 s	26 s	15 s	27 s	16 s

* The convergence times are in seconds and the number of iterations associated with each time is given in brackets. All the computation times reported here have been taken from runs of these models on the Reading University Elliott 4130 computer. In the author's experience, this machine is about 10 times slower than the Reading University ICL 1904S, and about 80 times slower than the London University CDC 7600.

† In cases where (7.39) has not been computed explicitly, (7.37) and (7.38) have been summed to give an index of overall convergence.

There are other limitations of each method which must be taken into account when designing a hybrid search strategy. The first-order process is inefficient from starting points with low parameter values (1.0) and there is no guarantee that the Fibonacci method will converge, for convergence is dependent upon the interaction of the two surfaces (7.37) and (7.38). The Newton–Raphson method and Powell's algorithm both diverge from poor starting values. The Simplex method has none of these disadvantages and therefore this method could be used as an alternative if any of the above procedures begin to diverge or converge at too slow a rate. In conclusion, it appears that the Newton–Raphson method is probably the most efficient single method, and therefore, it is worth while describing its application in the calibration of other models of spatial interaction. In the following section, the Newton–Raphson and Simplex methods are again illustrated in the context of a two-parameter trip-distribution model of the Reading subregion.

Trip distribution modelling

The various search routines already introduced can be easily extended to trip-distribution models based on production-attraction constrained models of spatial interaction. Indeed, virtually all the statistical work produced in

8

this field so far was originally demonstrated in relation to these models by researchers such as Hyman (1969), Evans (1971), Kirby (1974) and Cesario (1973). The importance of the trip-distribution model and its widespread use in traffic modelling is probably responsible for this interest by researchers, although the model is perhaps the most mathematically interesting of all the models in the family of spatial interaction models discussed in Chapter 2. In this section and the next, maximum-likelihood estimates will be presented for an example of such a distribution model.

It is worth while restating formally the model given in Chapter 2 and this is done as follows. The model is subject to the usual origin and destination constraints

$$\sum_j T_{ij} = O_i, \qquad\qquad [(2.57)]$$

$$\sum_i T_{ij} = D_j. \qquad\qquad [(2.58)]$$

The form of the model with a generalised travel-cost function $f(c_{ij})$ is

$$T_{ij} = A_i O_i B_j D_j f(c_{ij}), \qquad\qquad [(2.59)]$$

where the balancing factors A_i and B_j ensuring that (2.57) and (2.58) are met, are given as

$$A_i = \frac{1}{\sum_j B_j D_j f(c_{ij})}, \qquad\qquad [(2.60)]$$

$$B_j = \frac{1}{\sum_i A_i O_i f(c_{ij})}. \qquad\qquad [(2.61)]$$

The usual method for calculating the A_i's and B_j's is based on iteration and as Evans (1970) has shown, convergence to a unique value for $A_i B_j$ is guaranteed from any non-trivial set of starting values. In the results to be reported here, the B_j's were first set to 1 in this iterative procedure and a coarse limit of 10^{-3} was set for convergence. Alternative but complementary iterative procedures are suggested by Edens (1970) and the Bureau of Public Roads (1968). Another possible procedure for setting an initial value for one of the balancing factors could be taken from the approximations given by Kirby (1970, 1972). For example, A_i could be calculated from

$$A_i = \frac{\sum_j T_{ij}^*/f(c_{ij})}{O_i},$$

and then B_j calculated as usual from (2.61), although these procedures have not been tested and Kirby's suggestion in this regard is mainly of analytical rather than practical import.

As the calibration methods discussed here are based on iteration, it is possible to devise various short-cuts which reduce the need for the A_i's and B_j's to be calculated each time the model is run. It is possible, for example, to hold B_j constant and to calculate A_i analytically over ranges where the parameter value is only marginally altered, thus reducing computation time as in the SELNEC Study (Wagon and Hawkins, 1970). To be certain about the use of these sorts of methods, it is necessary to experiment, and in a study by Mackie (1971), it was found that for the level of accuracy required in calibration, such short-cuts lengthened rather than shortened the overall computation time. Therefore, such approximations are not used in the model discussed here, but in certain circumstances they may be appropriate.

To pursue the maximum-likelihood method of deriving appropriate statistical tests for trip-distribution models, it is necessary to rewrite (2.59) in a probabilistic form. Then,

$$T_{ij} = Tp_{ij}, \qquad (7.67)$$

where p_{ij} is the probability of working in i and living in j defined from

$$p_{ij} = a_i b_j o_i d_j f(c_{ij}). \qquad (7.68)$$

The model in (7.68) is subject to the following constraints; note that a_i, b_j, o_i and d_j are clearly related to the non-probabilistic trip-distribution model variables A_i, O_i, B_j and D_j. The model is constrained so that

$$\sum_i \sum_j p_{ij} = 1, \qquad (7.69)$$

$$\sum_j p_{ij} = o_i, \qquad (7.70)$$

$$\sum_i p_{ij} = d_j. \qquad (7.71)$$

It is clear from (7.70) and (7.71) that o_i and d_j are marginal probabilities whose values are computed from $\sum_j T_{ij}^*/T$ and $\sum_i T_{ij}^*/T$ respectively.

Maximum-likelihood estimates

The particular form of trip-distribution model examined here is based upon the deterrence function first suggested by Tanner (1961). This two-parameter function has a similar form to a gamma function although constraints on its values are less rigid than in the pure gamma case. The function is

$$f(c_{ij}) = \exp(-\lambda_1 d_{ij}) \, d_{ij}^{-\lambda_2}. \qquad (7.72)$$

Maximising log-likelihood $\ln L$ defined in (7.17) subject to (7.69)–(7.71), the following maximum-likelihood equations are derived. The intermediate working is lengthy and is thus omitted for it contributes nothing to the argument. Furthermore, it also follows the working in (7.20)–(7.34). Then the model must satisfy

$$a_i = \frac{1}{\sum_j b_j d_j \exp\left(-\lambda_1 d_{ij}\right) d_{ij}^{-\lambda_2}},\qquad(7.73)$$

$$b_j = \frac{1}{\sum_i a_i o_i \exp\left(-\lambda_1 d_{ij}\right) d_{ij}^{-\lambda_2}},\qquad(7.74)$$

$$\sum_i \sum_j p_{ij} d_{ij} = \sum_i \sum_j t_{ij} d_{ij},\qquad(7.75)$$

and

$$\sum_i \sum_j p_{ij} \ln d_{ij} = \sum_i \sum_j t_{ij} \ln d_{ij}.\qquad(7.76)$$

Note that in (7.75) and (7.76), t_{ij} is the observed trip proportion calculated from T_{ij}^*/T. Equations governing the calculation of o_i and d_j from data are obvious and have been omitted.

The functions to be minimised by the calibration procedure are derived from (7.75) and (7.76) and can be stated as

$$\min F_1(\lambda_1, \lambda_2) = \min \left| \sum_i \sum_j p_{ij} d_{ij} - \sum_i \sum_j t_{ij} d_{ij} \right| = 0,\qquad(7.77)$$

$$\min F_2(\lambda_1, \lambda_2) = \min \left| \sum_i \sum_j p_{ij} \ln d_{ij} - \sum_i \sum_j t_{ij} \ln d_{ij} \right| = 0.\qquad(7.78)$$

A composite function $\Lambda(\lambda_1, \lambda_2)$ has also been constructed by summing (7.77) and (7.78) and this is used in the Simplex procedure, whereas (7.77) and (7.78) are used in the Newton–Raphson method. These applications are now described.

Application of the Newton–Raphson and Simplex methods

The model to be tested here uses data from a 23 zone subdivision of the Reading subregion. The data base for this area has been produced by the Population Census Office from the 1966 Transport Tables and a full trip matrix of observations disaggregated by mode, housing type, occupation order and industry is available. These data have been aggregated across all these classes for this work although a variety of disaggregated residential location models are hypothesised and tested using this data base in Chapter 10. In calibrating the trip-distribution model using the Newton–Raphson method, the procedure was initially started from $\lambda_1, \lambda_2 = 0$

although from this position, it quickly diverged to extreme values. This is due to the peculiar response surface generated by this Tanner model in which the optimum point lies in a steep valley cutting across the surface. In such cases, fairly close first approximations to λ_1, λ_2 are needed and from previous experience with Tanner's function reported later in Chapter 10, the correct order of magnitude for λ_1 and λ_2 appears to be in the regions 0.1 and 1.0 respectively. The procedure was then started from these points and converged to within 10^{-5} in five iterations of the Newton-Raphson method. Because each iteration of the procedure involves calculating two sets of partial derivatives which are found numerically, three runs of the model are needed on each iteration. These results are presented in Table 7.7.

TABLE 7.7. *Calibration of Tanner's function by the Newton–Raphson method*

Iterations or runs of model	Start from $\lambda_1 = 0.1$, $\lambda_2 = 1.0$			
	λ_1	Value of equation (7.77)	λ_2	Value of equation (7.78)
3	0.0822	0.2763	1.0228	0.0346
6	0.0861	0.0317	1.0047	0.0038
9	0.0857	0.0034	1.0062	0.0002
12	0.0858	0.0003	1.0061	0.0001
15	0.0858	0.0000	1.0061	0.0000

In the case of the Simplex method, the procedure was started with an initial simplex located at points (0.0, 0.0), (0.0, 0.5), and (0.5, 0.0) but the method takes many iterations to determine that the optimum lies in a narrow valley which cuts across the response surface. The procedure was restarted in the valley from points (0.10, 0.50), (0.10, 0.55) and (0.15, 0.50) and Figure 7.9 shows the convergence along this valley. In Table 7.8, the convergence of the process is presented from the restart points. In this case, it is clear that both methods find it difficult to negotiate the response surface in advance and a certain amount of 'eyeballing' is necessary to get the procedures onto the right tracks. This illustrates that the calibration problem can never be totally mechanised, at least not in these terms, and thus the role of intuition can still be fairly large in this particular context.

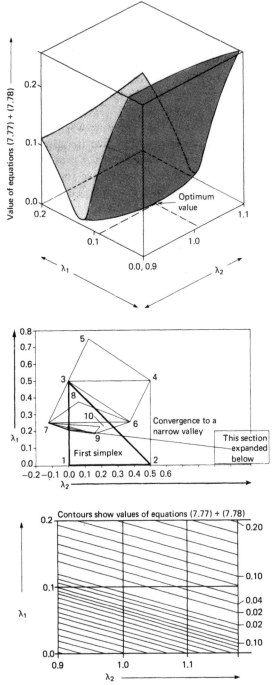

Fig. 7.9. Convergence of the Nelder–Mead Simplex method on
Tanner's function.

TABLE 7.8. *Calibration of Tanner's function
using the Nelder–Mead Simplex Method*

Iterations or runs of model	Start from $\lambda_1, \lambda_2 = 0.1$		
	λ_1	λ_2	Value of equations $[(7.77)+(7.78)]$
5	0.1500	0.5000	0.0232
25	0.1500	0.5000	0.0232
51	0.1104	0.8082	0.0154
75	0.0875	0.9936	0.0022
101	0.0859	1.0055	0.0000

Comparisons and hybrid strategies

Comparisons between the two methods are extremely difficult because of the badly behaved nature of the Tanner function. The Newton–Raphson method appears to be much faster than the Simplex method by about a factor of 6; however, the Newton–Raphson method can only be started from *good* approximations to the final parameter values, whereas the Simplex method can be started from any position. This suggests the need for a hybrid strategy in which the order of magnitude of the parameters is established by the Simplex method and then the optimum is determined from these points by the Newton–Raphson method. Yet in comparison with the traditional methods of calibration by trial and error iteration, these procedures are far superior. For example, calibration using the most inefficient method of tabulation based on evaluating the function at Δ_k equal subintervals in the given range for K parameters requires

$$\prod_{k=1}^{K} (\Delta_k + 1)$$

evaluations. Taking the Tanner function, to use this tabulation method to find the parameter values to within a limit of say 10^{-2}, over the ranges $\lambda_1 = (0.0, 1.0)$ and $\lambda_2 = (0.0, 5.0)$, would require over 50 000 runs of the model. This quite formidable number of runs can probably be reduced to about 200 using systematic search procedures such as multivariate Fibonacci search. The Newton–Raphson method which requires about 10 runs from the *best* starting value and the Simplex method requiring about 100 runs from the *worst* starting values, both compare favourably with these other methods.

TABLE 7.9. *Relative calibration times in terms of the*
number of zones and degree of accuracy*

Number of zones	Limit of accuracy of the Newton–Raphson method†					10 runs of the Simplex method	Data input time
	10^{-1}	10^{-2}	10^{-3}	10^{-4}	10^{-5}		
20	3	6	9	12	15	10	0
40	12	23	35	47	58	39	0
60	26	52	78	104	130	87	1
80	46	92	138	185	231	154	1
100	72	144	216	288	360	140	2
200	286	572	859	1145	1431	954	8
300	643	1286	1929	2572	3215	2143	17
400	1142	2284	3426	4569	5711	3807	31
500	1784	3567	5351	7135	8918	5946	48

* One run of the model is based on $33 + 10I + 15J + 25IJ$ FORTRAN equations where I is the number of origin zones and J is the number of destination zones.

† The limit of accuracy is in terms of the $\Lambda(\lambda_1, \lambda_2)$ statistic.

It is worth while stressing the importance of these speeds relative to existing methods and, in Table 7.9, an attempt has been made to judge these speeds for the Newton–Raphson and Simplex methods for different sizes of problem. It is important to describe how this table has been constructed; all the times reported in the table are expressed as a proportion of the time taken to run a 20 zone trip-distribution model once, and these times are normalised to a base index of 1. Thus, the times are relative and independent of the particular computer installation used. An example of how the table is to be used will suffice. Imagine the analyst is designing a trip distribution model for 20 zones. Then if the time taken in seconds to run this model once, is multiplied by all values in the table, this will give the actual computer time needed for a range of accuracy required for a model of any number of zones. If however the analyst knows the time taken to run a model with a particular number of zones rather than 20 zones, then multiplication of this time by the first row of the table will yield the calibration time. The limits of accuracy on the table are given in terms of the Newton–Raphson method; if the Simplex method is required prior to this method, then column 6, based on an average of 10 runs, should be added to columns 1–5.

Some fairly dramatic techniques have been introduced in this chapter in the quest to explore models and to speed up their operation, but the research embodied here has only just begun. This chapter of the book is least likely to stand the passage of time for already there are new ideas of calibration on the horizon, many of which take the mathematics into realms way beyond the level of expertise in this book. But the techniques here will probably always form the rudiments of any non-linear calibration process and thus they are unlikely to be drastically modified conceptually. The extension of all the techniques to K parameters is obvious but, in the next chapter, the calibration problem will be complicated slightly by the notion of using such techniques to calibrate sets of interrelated submodels where the parameters of each submodel depend upon one another. Yet the focus adopted in the approach to the last two chapters will change in the next, where the notion of spatial system design as well as calibration becomes a basic modelling problem. Thus, although calibration will still be an essential focus in the subsequent chapters, it is now necessary to extend the scope of urban modelling by reference to other related problems.

8. *Spatial system design and fast calibration of activity allocation models*

Development of the urban models presented in Chapters 2 and 3 can be carried out in several ways but substantive improvements seem to focus mainly upon two central issues: the problem of *disaggregation* of the model's variables in the quest to achieve a better description of the variety in the real world, and the problem of *dynamics*, essentially concerned with incorporating an explicit time dimension into such models. These two themes are to be dealt with at some length in Chapters 10–12 where a synthesis of many of the ideas in this book will be tentatively attempted. Yet there are several characteristics of model design, particularly those dealing with design of the spatial zoning system, still to be explored before these more ambitious developments are demonstrated.

Questions of model design involving variable definition, measurement and zoning have received far less attention than the problems of calibration reviewed in the last two chapters. But sound model design may make the difference between the success or failure of a modelling project in practice. The success of the Pittsburgh model (Lowry, 1964) and its subsequent modification and widespread application to many modelling problems in Britain (Goldner, 1971; Batty, 1972a) must be largely due to the careful way in which the model was originally formulated and applied. The hybrid simulation model of Detroit at present under construction at the National Bureau of Economic Research by Ingram *et al.* (1972) provides another example of the principle that good model design is essential in producing a model which is robust enough to withstand the inevitable inconsistencies and gaps in the data set yet sensitive enough to provide useful insights into planning problems.

However, in a small number of modelling projects, there have been certain tentative investigations into these more detailed questions of model design involving such problems as spatial system design and zone size, problems of calibration and problems of data management. In the model built by the Centre for Environmental Studies for Cheshire County Planning Department (Barras *et al.*, 1971), a fairly substantial amount of time was spent in exploring questions of zone size and the design of hierarchical zoning systems (Broadbent, 1970a, 1971) as well as problems of variable definition and measurement (Massey, 1973) and information systems (Willis, 1972). As part of the research undertaken at the Centre for Land Use and Built Form Studies into townscale models, problems of spatial aggregation have also been studied and a cordon model, similar to the hierarchical model mentioned above, has been developed (Baxter, 1971). Many of these model design techniques are diffuse and one of the central purposes of this chapter is to pull some of these techniques together and to demonstrate their application to an activity allocation model of the Northampton region.

The Northampton model was designed using data supplied by the East Midlands Technical Plan Unit and thus, the process of model design was essentially orientated towards problems of calibration and zoning other than those involving detailed study of the data base. This exercise is of further interest for the work reported in this chapter was completed in an intensive six-week project, including the writing of computer programs, thus demonstrating the speed at which such projects can be carried out under favourable conditions. Three main problems of model design are explored in this chapter. First, the internal design of the spatial system is explored in terms of questions concerning zone size and the number of zones, together with empirical work on the change in model performance and output at different levels of spatial aggregation. Second, the fast calibration techniques, originally applied and tested on single spatial interaction models and presented in Chapter 7, are extended to activity allocation models and finally, questions concerning the external design of the spatial system in terms of dummy zones are investigated. Although the structural logic of the model has been extensively dealt with in Chapter 3, it is worth while refreshing the reader's memory by listing the model equations here, thus avoiding the need to turn back continually to the relevant section in Chapter 3.

The structural logic of the model

To summarise the structure briefly once again, the model has two primary functions, the first dealing with the *derivation* of activities from certain exogenously specified activities, and the second dealing with the *allocation* of these derived activities to the zones of a bounded region. The derivation of activities is based upon the economic base mechanism in which service (non-basic) employment and population can be derived from basic employment using the appropriate multipliers. The allocation of derived activities is based upon spatial interaction models which locate activity at 'destinations' in accordance with the amount of activity in different 'origins'. These mechanisms involving derivation and allocation are stitched together

using the expanded form of the economic base multiplier in which increments of population and service employment are derived and allocated
sequentially. These two mechanisms are further strengthened by the constraints procedure which is invoked if and when residential population
exceeds given density limits. Note that in the Northampton model, no
constraints on the minimum size of service centres are included.

The system of equations used by the model is given in (3.28)–(3.43) with
(3.46) and (3.48). The inner iteration m controls the generation of activities
through the expanded form of the economic base mechanism, whereas the
outer iteration n controls the residential density constraints. Then on any
inner iteration m, the increment of persons working in i and living in j,
called $T_{ij}(m, n)$ is calculated from

$$T_{ij}(m, n) = A_i(n) B_j(n) E_i(m, n) f^1(D_j, c_{ij}, \lambda_1), \qquad (8.1)$$

$$A_i(n) = \frac{1}{\sum_j B_j(n) f^1(D_j, c_{ij}, \lambda_1)}. \qquad (8.2)$$

Equations (8.1) and (8.2) are equivalent to (3.28) and (3.29). $E_i(m, n)$ is the
increment in workers employed at i, $B_j(n)$ is a weight on residential
attraction D_j, which is less than unity if the density constraint has been
violated on any previous outer iteration, c_{ij} is the generalised travel cost
between i and j, and λ_1 is a parameter of the travel-cost function. The
functional form of the residential attraction and deterrence in (8.1) need
not be precisely specified yet, in order that the flexibility of the model can
be appreciated. Next, population $P_j(m, n)$ is derived from

$$P_j(m, n) = \alpha \sum_i T_{ij}(m, n), \qquad (8.3)$$

and the demand for services by the population in j called $H_j(m, n)$ is
calculated as
$$H_j(m, n) = \beta P_j(m, n). \qquad (8.4)$$

Equations (8.3) and (8.4) are equivalent to (3.30) and (3.31); α and β are
the inverse activity rate and population-serving ratio appropriately defined.
The location of service employment at different centres i is derived from

$$S_{ij}(m, n) = R_j(n) H_j(m, n) f^2(D_i, c_{ij}, \lambda_2), \qquad (8.5)$$

$$R_j(n) = \frac{1}{\sum_i f^2(D_i, c_{ij}, \lambda_2)}. \qquad (8.6)$$

Note that (8.5) and (8.6) differ from (3.32) and (3.33) in that no weight on
D_i has been incorporated. $S_{ij}(m, n)$ is the number of service employees
demanded at j and working in i and λ_2 is a parameter of the service travel-

cost function. Service employees at i are calculated by summing (8.5) over j. Thus

$$S_i(m, n) = \sum_j S_{ij}(m, n).\tag{8.7}$$

At this point, the next increment of employment $E_i(m+1, n)$ is set as

$$E_i(m+1, n) = S_i(m, n),\tag{8.8}$$

if $\sum_i E_i(m, n) > \xi_e$, where ξ_e is a convergence limit. Then, $E_i(m+1, n)$ is substituted into (8.1), and (8.1)–(8.8) are reiterated until the limit is reached. These iterations will ensure that the total service employment and population generated will converge to their respective regional totals if $0 < \alpha\beta < 1$ which must be the case for non-trivial solutions. It may however take many iterations for the process to converge to an acceptable limit and in such cases, the process can be speeded up by applying the following approximation taken from Chapter 2 or by formulating and solving the model in the matrix algebra given in Chapter 3. From (2.37), the proportion of activity, population or employment generated up to any iteration m is given as

$$\Psi = 1 - \alpha\beta^{m+1}.\tag{8.9}$$

From (8.9), it is clear that total employment generated so far can be derived from

$$\sum_i \sum_{k=1}^{m} E_i(k, n) = \sum_i E_i(1 - \alpha\beta^{m+1}).\tag{8.10}$$

Making the assumption that the final amount of activity in any zone i can be approximated from the amount so far located there, then $E_i(n)$ can be found by manipulating (8.10) and dropping the summation over i,

$$E_i(n) = \sum_{k=1}^{m} E_i(k, n)\,(1 - \alpha\beta^{m+1})^{-1}.\tag{8.11}$$

Total population $P_j(n)$ can be approximated in a similar way,

$$P_j(n) = \sum_{k=1}^{m} P_j(k, n)\,(1 - \alpha\beta^{m+1})^{-1}.\tag{8.12}$$

All the usual totals of activity and interaction can be calculated from equations similar to (8.11) and (8.12) and for details, the reader is referred back to Chapter 3.

To demonstrate the application of the density constraint, if $P_j(n) > \delta_j L_j^h$, where $\delta_j L_j^h$ is the maximum population limit of zone j, then the value $B_j(n+1)$ is computed as

$$B_j(n+1) = B_j(n)\frac{\delta_j L_j^h}{P_j(n)}.\tag{8.13}$$

$B_j(n+1)$ is now substituted into (8.1), and (8.1)–(8.13) are reiterated until the population density limits are met. The convergence of this process can only occur if

$$\sum_j P_j(n) \geqslant \sum_j \delta_j L_j^h,$$

and experience suggests that faster convergence occurs when the zones contiguous to any constrained zone have enough capacity to accept any surplus population reallocated from the constrained zones. This completes the statement of the model and at this point, the first problem of model design can be introduced.

Broadbent's rule as a basis for the design of zoning systems

The design of a zoning system appropriate to a particular model application is perhaps the most important, yet the most poorly explored and least understood question in model design. The zoning system determines the level of spatial description and in interaction models this system also determines the amount of interaction detectable in the system. At one extreme, the zoning system may be so aggregated that no interaction occurs across zone boundaries, thus negating the whole purpose of model-building based on spatial interaction. Broadbent (1969a, 1969b), whose work on zoning systems has already been hinted at in earlier chapters, was the first to explore such questions; the rule attributed to him suggests that the first major problem the model-builder must examine and resolve in developing a spatial interaction model is in designing a zoning system which detects a *sufficient* amount of interaction for the model to be meaningful. At first sight, this rule may appear somewhat naïve but it is surprising how low the ratio of inter-zonal to total interaction has been in many previous modelling applications, thus implying that the design of the zoning system is far less than optimum. For example, in the Central Lancashire model in Chapter 4, this ratio is 0.5059 and in the Bedfordshire model (Cripps and Foot, 1969a) it is 0.5791; these values are really too low, thus implying that there is very little inter-zonal interaction to be modelled. Broadbent (1969b) has also made a preliminary investigation of a zoning system suitable for a one-dimensional probability location model in which employment is concentrated at the origin. This type of analysis, although highly theoretical, can easily be extended to a two-dimensional system in the quest to gain insights about zoning systems for spatial interaction models.

Consider a highly idealised city in which travel is equally likely in any direction from the origin to the periphery and in which all employment is located at the origin or centre. Residential location in such a monocentric radially symmetric city can be described by a population density cone, and an appropriate location probability density can be written as

$$p(r, \theta) = G \exp(-\lambda r). \tag{8.14}$$

$p(r, \theta)$ is the probability of locating at distance r from the centre of the city and θ represents the angular variation about the centre or pole. λ is a parameter of the function and G is a normalising constant defined to ensure that

$$\int_0^{2\pi} \int_0^{\infty} p(r, \theta) \, r \, d\theta \, dr = 1. \tag{8.15}$$

G is evaluated from (8.15) as

$$G = \frac{\lambda^2}{2\pi}. \tag{8.16}$$

Note that, in the following discussion, the limit of the periphery of the city is taken as ∞ thus simplifying the ensuing algebra and analysis. In fact, this approximation to reality makes little difference to the subsequent analysis.

Broadbent's rule implies that the ratio of intra-zonal to total interaction should be as small as possible and he states that an acceptable value for this ratio might be 0.1. The cumulative probability function defined from (8.14) gives the radius R from the central origin zone for any value of this ratio. Then from (8.14)

$$\int_0^{2\pi} \int_0^R G \exp(-\lambda r) \, r \, d\theta \, dr = 0.1, \tag{8.17}$$

and evaluating (8.17) gives

$$1 - (1 + \lambda R) \exp(-\lambda R) = 0.1. \tag{8.18}$$

This ratio of 0.1 is arbitrary and an optimal value for this ratio is likely to vary between different applications. For example, if (8.17) or (8.18) is very sensitive to changes in R around the value 0.1, it may be worth while accepting a larger value for this ratio if this leads to a much smaller value for R. Thus, the analyst is trading-off zone size against the amount of interaction.

For any parameter λ, the value of R can be found by iteration on (8.18). In fact, the value of the parameter can also be calculated from the formula for the mean travel time-distance $\overline{R}$ which is

$$\bar{R} = \int\limits_{0}^{2\pi} \int\limits_{0}^{\infty} G \exp(-\lambda r) r^2 \, d\theta \, dr, \qquad (8.19)$$

and (8.19) is evaluated as

$$\bar{R} = \frac{2}{\lambda}. \qquad (8.20)$$

To demonstrate the application of this kind of analysis, the cumulative probability distribution in (8.17) is plotted in Figure 8.1 for different values of λ or $\bar{R}$. This graph can be used in the following way: given the mean trip-length, the radius R can be found for different proportions of interaction retained within that radius. For example, if the mean trip-length were 10.0 minutes travel time, the zone radius retaining 10 per cent of the total interaction would be about 2.2 minutes in contrast to a radius of 8.4 minutes for a zone retaining 50 per cent of the total interaction. A similar analysis can be made for problems involving the regional boundary. Broadbent suggests that the proportion of interaction within the region should be at least 90 per cent although this value is arbitrary and subject to the same kind of trade-off mentioned above. Using Figure 8.1, with a

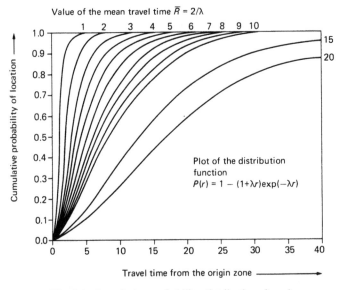

Value of the mean travel time $\bar{R} = 2/\lambda$

Plot of the distribution function
$P(r) = 1 - (1 + \lambda r) \exp(-\lambda r)$

Cumulative probability of location

Travel time from the origin zone ⟶

Fig. 8.1. Cumulative probability distributions based on mean trip lengths.

mean trip length of 10.0 minutes, the regional boundary would be at a minimum radius of 19.6 minutes from the origin. Although this analysis is highly theoretical, it must be possible to extend this method to a spatial system with many competing centres, thus generalising these results; at present, some research is in progress to achieve this generalisation (Batty, 1973, 1974).

The problem of locational attraction

In static models which attempt to simulate urban systems whose structure has evolved slowly through time, there are unavoidable problems involving variable definition and measurement. The most intractable of these problems seems to involve the measurement of locational attraction, in the residential rather than service sector, and the critical nature of this problem has already been revealed in Chapters 4 and 5. The choice of one variable which summarises the relative change in residential attraction through time is difficult and several researchers have been forced to use proxies such as existing population or housing stock. These problems are only likely to be satisfactorily resolved in a dynamic context, yet there are certain considerations which can be outlined in the choice of attraction measures for static models (Batty, 1971). A more fundamental attack on this problem is pursued in Chapter 12.

An important consideration involves the effect of the zoning system on the measurements of locational attraction. Broadbent (1970 a) following Seidman (1969) suggests that the variables in spatial models can be divided into two types – extensive and intensive. Extensive variables change by an order of magnitude as the zoning system is altered whereas intensive variables do not change thus. For example, the absolute amount of spatial interaction changes as zone boundaries change whereas the measure of locational attraction is only altered in relative terms. In several activity allocation models, extensive variables such as population have been predicted using measures of locational attraction based on intensive variables; in such cases where the zoning system is irregular, bias is being introduced into the model. There are two ways around this problem, both involving the principle that extensive and intensive variables should not be mixed within the same model equations. For example, in many applications of residential location models, extensive variables such as population have been predicted using intensive variables as measures of residential attraction. In these cases, it is possible to use the model as a predictor of population density or to change the intensive attractor variable to an extensive variable based on zone size, in predicting population.

The weighting of such models by variables reflecting spatial magnitude is an intuitively obvious conclusion, yet these results can also be derived by more formal methods. The method of entropy-maximising as used by Wilson (1970a) in deriving spatial interaction models treats space implicitly by assuming that spatial partition is regular, or that all appropriate variables are extensive. However it is possible to incorporate spatial magnitude explicitly into this kind of analysis. Only a brief synopsis of this modification to Wilson's method will be indicated here for this subject is explored elsewhere in some depth (Batty, 1974) and is really outside the scope of this book. The task is to define a discrete approximation to continuous entropy, thus introducing the idea of space explicitly. Consider a model in which p_{ij} gives the probability of working in i and living in j. Such a probability model would be subject to the usual constraints on origins and on total travel cost in the system. Instead of maximising discrete entropy, maximise the discrete form of continuous entropy called *spatial entropy* defined as

$$H = -\sum_i \sum_j p_{ij} \ln\left(\frac{p_{ij}}{L_j}\right), \tag{8.21}$$

subject to the usual constraints. Note that L_j is a measure of space in j and that p_{ij}/L_j is a kind of spatial probability density. The resulting model determines the probability density of location,

$$\frac{p_{ij}}{L_j} = \frac{\exp(-\lambda c_{ij})}{\sum_j L_j \exp(-\lambda c_{ij})}, \tag{8.22}$$

and (8.22) can be rewritten as

$$p_{ij} = \frac{L_j \exp(-\lambda c_{ij})}{\sum_j L_j \exp(-\lambda c_{ij})}. \tag{8.23}$$

Equation (8.23) clearly demonstrates how spatial interaction-allocation models can be weighted to incorporate space. Note also that if

$$L_1 = L_2 = \ldots = L_N,$$

which is the case where the zones are based on a square grid, the L_j's cancel from the equations.

The preceding analysis suggests that residential location models which are constructed on irregular spatial systems should be weighted to account for such irregularities. For example, the residential location submodel of the Northampton model has been specified in this way. Defining the functional form in (8.1) and (8.2) and suppressing the iteration indices (m) and (n) introduced earlier as part of the complete equation system, the model is written as

$$T_{ij} = E_i \frac{L_j B_j D_j \exp{(\lambda_1 d_{ij})}}{\sum\limits_j L_j B_j D_j \exp{(-\lambda_1 d_{ij})}}. \tag{8.24}$$

Note that D_j is a measure of the existing population in j. Substituting (8.24) into (8.3) and rearranging gives

$$\frac{P_j}{L_j} = \alpha \sum_i E_i \frac{B_j D_j \exp{(-\lambda_1 d_{ij})}}{\sum\limits_j L_j B_j D_j \exp{(-\lambda_1 d_{ij})}}, \tag{8.25}$$

which explicitly demonstrates the role of intensive and extensive variables in such models. In (8.25), the term $B_j D_j$ is an intensive variable used in the prediction of population density, also an intensive variable, in contrast to (8.24) where $L_j B_j D_j$ is an extensive variable used to predict population. To conclude this section, it is worth while specifying the service centre location model in (8.5) and (8.6). This model is written as

$$S_{ij} = H_j \frac{F_i \exp{(-\lambda_2 d_{ij})}}{\sum\limits_i F_i \exp{(-\lambda_2 d_{ij})}}, \tag{8.26}$$

where F_i is floorspace in i. In (8.26), no spatial weight need be incorporated for both F_i and S_{ij} are intensive variables and thus the model has no inbuilt spatial bias.

Spatial aggregation and calibration by the Newton–Raphson method

The theoretical results which were briefly discussed in the two previous sections have been used along with other criteria in the design of the zoning system for the Northampton model. The basic data units on which all data were provided comprised 130 parishes and local authorities in the County of Northamptonshire, and this fixed an upper bound on the potential number of zones. Figure 8.2 presents the geometry of the basic data units, but it was decided at an early stage that these units would be aggregated to 50 zones so that the model could be run quickly and efficiently several times a day. This restriction imposed by computer capacity and access was taken with the knowledge that the theoretical analysis of zone size suggests that between 80 and 100 zones will meet the criteria set down by Broadbent (1969 a). Other considerations involving homogeneity of zonal activities, natural and artificial physical barriers, the nodal structure of the region with regard to main transport routes and the placement of zone centroids were also taken account of when zoning the region.

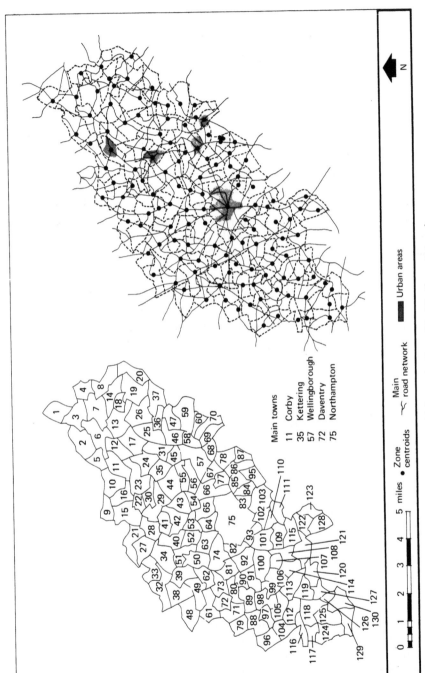

Main towns

11   Corby
35   Kettering
57   Wellingborough
72   Daventry
75   Northampton

• Zone centroids   Main road network   ▬ Urban areas

0   1   2   3   4   5 miles

N

Fig. 8.2. Spatial organisation of the Northampton region.

As one of the purposes of this project was to assess the effect of different zonal aggregations on model performance, three additional zoning systems based on 41, 26, and 23 zones were also constructed and, in Figure 8.3,

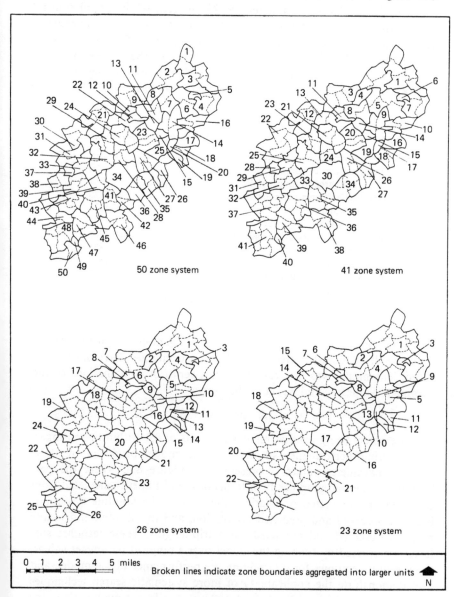

Fig. 8.3. Alternative zoning systems defined from the
original data units.

these zoning systems are presented with the 50 zone system. The design of these zoning systems is based on the simple idea that spatial aggregation must take into account the differences in the density of different activity locations. In the Northampton region, 73 per cent of the population is resident in 15 of the 50 zones. Therefore it was decided to aggregate systematically the least urbanised zones, retaining the 15 urban zones in each of the 3 additional zoning systems. In this way, the greatest possible differentiation within the region is contained by these zoning systems. Table 8.1 presents the major characteristics of the Northampton sub-region.

TABLE 8.1. *Major characteristics of the Northampton subregion*

Total number of zones	50
Total land area in square miles	914
Average land area per zone in square miles	18.2820
Total population	429075
Average population per zone	8581
Population density in persons per square mile	469.3961
Basic employment	83831
Total employment	153562
Ratio of basic to total employment	0.5459
Ratio of inter-zonal to intra-zonal work trips	0.5073

The differences between the performance of the model on these different systems will be assessed after the calibration techniques have been introduced. The model was first run through a series of combinations of the parameter values λ_1 and λ_2 set in the ranges

$$0 \leqslant \lambda_1 \leqslant 1.2 \quad \text{and} \quad 0 \leqslant \lambda_2 \leqslant 1.2,$$

the parameters being fixed at regular intervals of 0.1 within these ranges. The differing performance of the 50 zone model produced by these different parameter values is presented in Figure 8.4, where the performance is plotted graphically in terms of the r^2 statistic calculated from observed and predicted population, the sum of the absolute deviations between observed and predicted population, and the absolute differences between observed and predicted mean trip-lengths. These response surfaces constructed by running the model over a range of parameter values, are useful mnemonics for interpreting the performance of the model, and also demonstrate the applicability of more systematic search techniques which build on their regularity and pattern. A relevant methodology for deriving best statistics by the technique of maximum-likelihood has already been suggested in Chapter 7 and this technique is of obvious relevance to the calibration problem discussed here. From the principle of maximum-likelihood comes the general rule for calibrating interaction models stated previously which suggests that a unique set of parameter values can only be derived if each parameter value is related to a particular

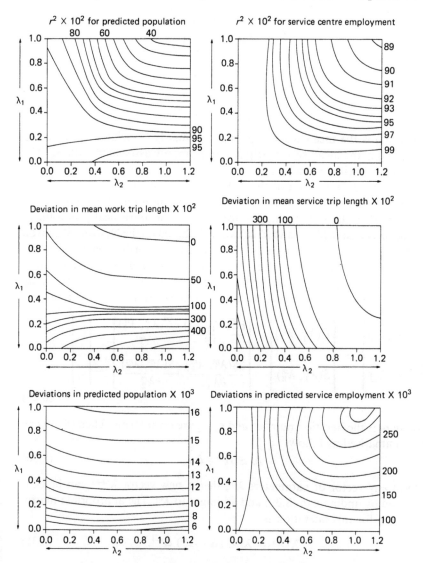

Fig. 8.4. Response surfaces for the 50 zone model constructed by systematic variation of the parameter values.

calibration statistic. In short, the calibration problem can be seen as a problem of solving a set of K equations – derived from K statistics, in K unknowns – the K parameters. In the Northampton model, the two parameters λ_1 and λ_2 which are related through the model equations are associated with two statistics derived as

$$\bar{C}(\lambda_1, \lambda_2) = \frac{\sum_i \sum_j T_{ij} d_{ij}}{\sum_i \sum_j T_{ij}}, \tag{8.27}$$

$$\bar{S}(\lambda_1, \lambda_2) = \frac{\sum_i \sum_j S_{ij} d_{ij}}{\sum_i \sum_j S_{ij}}. \tag{8.28}$$

$\bar{C}(\lambda_1, \lambda_2)$ is the mean work trip length primarily associated with λ_1 and $\bar{S}(\lambda_1, \lambda_2)$ is the mean service trip length primarily associated with λ_2. The maximum-likelihood technique is not detailed here; interested readers will find a related description of the technique in Chapter 7.

From the experience with non-linear optimisation in Chapter 7, it appears that the best technique for solving the intrinsically non-linear equations given in (8.27) and (8.28) would be based on the Newton–Raphson method. This method given in (7.44)–(7.54) is worth repeating in this context, thus highlighting the essence of calibrating activity allocation models. An approximation to (8.27) and (8.28) can be derived using Taylor's theorem and in matrix terms, this approximation is written

$$\begin{bmatrix} \bar{C}(\lambda_1, \lambda_2) \\ \bar{S}(\lambda_1, \lambda_2) \end{bmatrix} \simeq \begin{bmatrix} \bar{C}(\lambda_1^m, \lambda_2^m) \\ \bar{S}(\lambda_1^m, \lambda_2^m) \end{bmatrix} + \begin{bmatrix} \dfrac{\partial \bar{C}(\lambda_1^m, \lambda_2^m)}{\partial \lambda_1^m} & \dfrac{\partial \bar{C}(\lambda_1^m, \lambda_2^m)}{\partial \lambda_2^m} \\ \dfrac{\partial \bar{S}(\lambda_1^m, \lambda_2^m)}{\partial \lambda_1^m} & \dfrac{\partial \bar{S}(\lambda_1^m, \lambda_2^m)}{\partial \lambda_2^m} \end{bmatrix} \begin{bmatrix} \epsilon_1 \\ \epsilon_2 \end{bmatrix}, \tag{8.29}$$

where m is the iteration number and ϵ_1, ϵ_2 are error terms. Then (8.29) can be summarised as follows

$$\Lambda \simeq \Lambda^m + \Delta\epsilon. \tag{8.30}$$

Given any vector of parameters λ^m, then a new vector λ^{m+1} can be constructed by finding ϵ in (8.30) and adding it to λ^m. The appropriate matrix equation for this operation is

$$\lambda^{m+1} = \lambda^m + (\Lambda - \Lambda^m)\, \Delta^{-1}. \tag{8.31}$$

Note that in (8.31) if Λ is a zero vector, as would be the case if the required function values were first derivatives at zero indicating a maximum or minimum, then (8.31) would collapse to the standard Newton–Raphson equation given in most books on numerical analysis (Dixon, 1972).

Good first approximations to λ_1 and λ_2 are always useful in any method involving iteration. In a previous section, it was shown that good first approximations for λ_1 and λ_2 can be taken as $2/\bar{C}(\lambda_1, \lambda_2)$ and $2/\bar{S}(\lambda_1, \lambda_2)$ respectively. There are however other approximations which are worth computing. For example, Schneider (1959) has suggested that the parameter values can be approximated from the known medians. In terms of the probability location model of the monocentric radially symmetric city outlined earlier, the parameter λ can be found from

$$\int_0^{2\pi} \int_0^{R_m} G \exp\left(-\lambda r\right) r\,d\theta\,dr = \tfrac{1}{2}, \tag{8.32}$$

where R_m is the known median value. Evaluating (8.32) leads to

$$\lambda = \frac{\ln 2 + \ln\left(1 + \lambda R_m\right)}{R_m}. \tag{8.33}$$

The parameter λ can be found by iteration on (8.33). Another possibility for a first approximation to λ is to relate the parameter to the known modal value R_0. Using the probability distribution $P(r)$ defined as

$$P(r) = \lambda^2 \exp\left(-\lambda r\right) r = \int_0^{2\pi} G \exp\left(-\lambda r\right) r\,d\theta, \tag{8.34}$$

and differentiating (8.34) to find the maximum value, then

$$\frac{dP(r)}{dr} = \lambda^2 \exp\left(-\lambda r\right)\left(1 - \lambda r\right) = 0. \tag{8.35}$$

Evaluating (8.35) leads to the result

$$\lambda = \frac{1}{R_0}. \tag{8.36}$$

A fourth approximation to λ can be found from the variance statistic and to demonstrate this, it is necessary to show that $P(r)$ defined in (8.34) is a gamma function. This function has some interesting recurrence properties and it is usually stated as

$$\Gamma(\alpha+1) = \int_0^\infty r^\alpha \exp\left(-r\right) dr$$

$$= \alpha\Gamma(\alpha) = \alpha(\alpha-1)\,\Gamma(\alpha-1) = \ldots = \alpha!. \tag{8.37}$$

Note now that α has been redefined as a parameter of the gamma distribution to make the analysis consistent with conventional statistical usage. Then, from (8.37) it is easily seen that (8.34) is also a gamma function with the following form

$$P(r) = \frac{\lambda^{\alpha+1}r^\alpha \exp(-\lambda r)}{\Gamma(\alpha+1)} = \frac{\lambda^{\alpha+1}r^\alpha \exp(-\lambda r)}{\alpha!}. \tag{8.38}$$

It is well known that the variance σ^2 of a gamma function has a simple form (Mood and Graybill, 1963) given as

$$\sigma^2 = \frac{\alpha+1}{\lambda^2}, \tag{8.39}$$

and where $\alpha = 1$ as in the model presented above, λ can be calculated from

$$\lambda = \frac{\sqrt{2}}{\sigma}. \tag{8.40}$$

These four approximations have not been tested in the Northampton region but in the Reading region, they have been used as first approximations to the parameters used in the trip-distribution model described in Chapter 7. In fact these approximations are so similar to one another, that it is worth showing these values. Table 8.2 presents these results for the Reading subregion as well as a composite approximation which is a simple average of (8.20), (8.32), (8.36) and (8.40).

TABLE 8.2. *Approximations to the parameter value λ from trip length statistics in the Reading subregion*

Statistic	Value of statistic	Parameter value λ
Mean trip length $\bar{R}$	7.2232	0.2768
Modal trip length R_0	3.6721	0.2723
Median trip length R_m	5.6698	0.2960
Variance σ^2	26.3778	0.2753
Approximation as a simple average of the four statistics		0.2801

In the Northampton model, only the approximation given by (8.20) was used and it was argued that the limits of λ_1 and λ_2 would fall within the ranges $1/\bar{C}(\lambda_1, \lambda_2) \leqslant \lambda_1 \leqslant 2/\bar{C}(\lambda_1, \lambda_2)$ and $1/\bar{S}(\lambda_1, \lambda_2) \leqslant \lambda_2 \leqslant 2/\bar{S}(\lambda_1, \lambda_2)$. The lower bounds represent the values of the parameters for a one-dimensional system (Broadbent, 1969*a*) whereas the upper bounds reflect the parameter values of a two-dimensional system. It would be interesting to find out how the values of $\lambda_1 \bar{C}(\lambda_1, \lambda_2)$ and $\lambda_2 \bar{S}(\lambda_1, \lambda_2)$ change as the level of zonal aggregation changes in the system for this might produce a useful index of spatial aggregation. As a tentative speculation, it seems that the value of such an index would fall as the level of aggregation increased

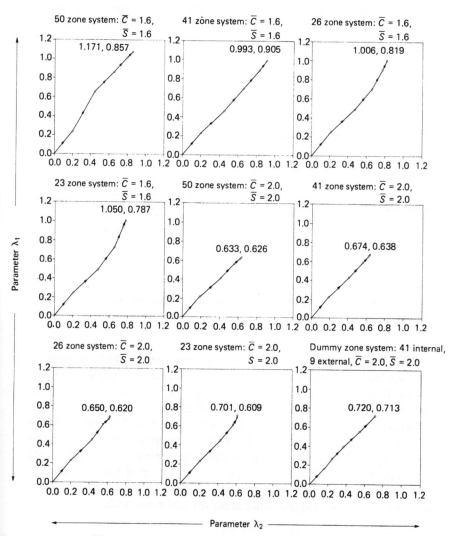

Fig. 8.5. Calibration of the alternative models using the
Newton–Raphson method.

and the zones become more coarse but as yet, there is no evidence to support such a speculation, thus suggesting an interesting area for some future research.

In Figure 8.5, the final parameter values determined by an application of the Newton–Raphson method are shown graphically for each of the 4 zoning systems with the observed values of $\bar{C}(\lambda_1, \lambda_2)$ and $\bar{S}(\lambda_1, \lambda_2)$ set first at 1.6 and then at 2.0. The rather peculiar values of these trip lengths are due to the fact that the set of travel times $\{c_{ij}\}$ has been measured in arbitrary units. Such arbitrariness in no way affects the working of these models and if it is required to relate the trip lengths or the parameters to conventional travel times, the trip lengths should be multiplied by and the parameters divided by a factor of 5. The performance of the model on each of the 4 zoning systems is presented in Table 8.3. As the zones become

TABLE 8.3. *Performance of the model at different levels of spatial aggregation*

Number of zones	50	41	26	23
Parameter λ_1	0.8715	0.9935	1.0086	1.0680
Parameter λ_2	0.8575	0.9056	0.8193	0.7871
r^2 population	0.9476	0.9430	0.9147	0.8990
r^2 service employment	0.9067	0.9033	0.9107	0.9109
Absolute deviations in population	158627	173781	217932	230837
Absolute deviations in service employment	25716	25947	26229	26698

NOTE: The mean trip lengths for $\bar{C}(\lambda_1, \lambda_2)$ and $\bar{S}(\lambda_1, \lambda_2)$ are taken as 1.6 (8.0 minutes of travel time).

coarser, the performance of the model worsens quite markedly in terms of the location of population, less so in terms of service employment. In some senses these results accord with intuition although it is possible that some threshold might exist above and below which performance worsens. Unfortunately, this hypothesis cannot be tested in this model for the maximum number of zones is fixed at 50. Moreover, there are problems in assessing the change in performance between different zoning systems due to the fact that there are difficulties in aggregating the set of travel times $\{c_{ij}\}$ which have an unknown effect on the change in parameter values. These questions, however, suggest other areas for useful research.

Dummy zones and the problem of closure

The problem of defining the regional boundary in spatial interaction modelling has been handled by several researchers in terms of a set of dummy zones. Frequently, other considerations might make it impossible to minimise the amount of interaction crossing the regional boundary in either direction, and in such cases, the role of the dummy zones is to act as a filter or buffer between the system and its environment. In general, dummy zones are likely to be larger than the zones within the region itself, and in certain cases, there may be different bands of dummy zones layered around the region, each band having a different role. For example, in the Oxford shopping model designed by Black (1966), an inner set of dummy zones was defined to predict flows between zones immediately adjacent to the region and zones within the region, and an outer set of dummy zones was designed to ensure that the relative attraction between the inner set of zones and the region itself was of the right order. Several different types of dummy zones can be designed and readers interested in the general implications of this approach are referred to Wilson (1970a). The hierarchical model (Broadbent, 1971) and the cordon model (Baxter, 1971) mentioned earlier are also relevant in this particular context.

The problem in the Northampton region was to design a set of dummy zones around the region to represent centres having a significant effect on the region at the present or in the near future. Furthermore, the set of dummy zones involving interaction into the region need not be equivalent to the set of dummy zones involving interaction out of the region, although in the Northampton model, these two sets were equivalent. The two sets of origin and destination zones inside the region are referred to by subscripts i and j respectively; the set of dummy origin zones are referred to by k and the dummy destination zones by l. Using this notation and noting that the links between the dummy zones are irrelevant to the analysis, the matrix of travel times $\{c_{ij}\}$ can be partitioned in the following way. Note that the subscripts i and j refer to the I origin zones and J destination zones inside the region and that the subscripts k and l refer to the K dummy origin zones and the L dummy destination zones outside the region. Note also that L has been redefined from its previous notation as land.

In applying this idea of dummy zones to the singly-constrained residential model given in (8.1) and (8.2), two types of system can be designed. In the first system, the origin constraints within I zones inside the region are met, and the model is also constrained to predict the total net interaction across the regional boundary. The origin constraint is written as

$$E_i = \sum_j T_{ij} + \sum_l T_{il}. \tag{8.41}$$

The flow out of the region is called T^L and the flow into the region T^K. The model is constrained to meet

$$T^L = \sum_i \sum_l T_{il}, \tag{8.42}$$

$$T^K = \sum_k \sum_j T_{kj}. \tag{8.43}$$

The model satisfying (8.11)–(8.43) can now be written as follows.

$$T_{ij} = a_i E_i D_j f(c_{ij}), \tag{8.44}$$

$$T_{il} = Q^L a_i E_i D_l f(c_{il}), \tag{8.45}$$

$$T_{kj} = Q^K E_k D_j f(c_{kj}). \tag{8.46}$$

Note that Q has been now redefined from its earlier context in Chapter 3. The quantities a_i, Q^L and Q^K refer to the constraint equations (8.41)–(8.43) in that order and can be evaluated by summing (8.44)–(8.46) over the appropriate subscripts. These normalising factors are evaluated as

$$a_i = \frac{1}{\sum_j D_j f(c_{ij}) + Q^L \sum_l D_l f(c_{il})}, \tag{8.47}$$

$$Q^L = \frac{T^L}{\sum_i \sum_l a_i E_i D_l f(c_{ij})}, \tag{8.48}$$

$$Q^K = \frac{T^K}{\sum_k \sum_j E_k D_j f(c_{kj})}. \tag{8.49}$$

Equations (8.47) and (8.48) must be solved by iteration and the whole scheme can then be built into the comprehensive modelling framework outlined at the beginning of the chapter or indeed any of the modelling frameworks presented in this book.

The second type of system considered in the Northampton model was constrained to a greater degree than the system outlined above. The constraints in (8.42) and (8.43) can be replaced by origin and destination constraints which turn the submodel dealing with interaction between the regional and dummy zones into a type of production-attraction constrained interaction model. These equations are written as

$$D_l = \sum_i T_{il}, \tag{8.50}$$

$$E_k = \sum_j T_{kj}. \tag{8.51}$$

Note that D_l and E_k are now the activity totals forming the interaction between the dummies and the region. For the intra-regional case, the model has the same form as (8.44) and the models consistent with (8.50) and (8.51) are written as

$$T_{il} = a_i b_l E_i D_l f(c_{il}), \tag{8.52}$$

$$T_{kj} = a_k E_k D_j f(c_{kj}). \tag{8.53}$$

The quantities a_i, b_l and a_k are evaluated as

$$a_i = \frac{1}{\sum_j D_j f(c_{ij}) + \sum_l b_l D_l f(c_{il})}, \tag{8.54}$$

$$b_l = \frac{1}{\sum_i a_i E_i f(c_{il})}, \tag{8.55}$$

$$a_k = \frac{1}{\sum_j D_j f(c_{kj})}. \tag{8.56}$$

Equations (8.54) and (8.55) are solved by iteration. The scheme outlined in (8.41) and (8.50)–(8.56) is the one which was chosen for the Northampton model. The way in which the dummy zone system was connected to each submodel of the activity interaction-allocation model outlined earlier was complicated by the population density constraint; the algebra is somewhat lengthy and contributes little to what has been already discussed, and is therefore omitted.

Figure 8.6 presents a 41 zone system with 9 external dummy zones and the network connecting those zones. The travel times between the dummies were arbitrarily set at exp(79), the largest number the Reading University Elliott 4130 computer could take. In Figure 8.7, the constrained flows between the dummies and the zones inside the region are mapped, thus demonstrating the magnitudes of the flows across the regional boundary. In proportional terms, these flows are small, at present, 4 per cent of the working population living in the region working outside it, and 2 per cent living outside the region working within it. The performance of the 41 zone model with these dummies is not quite as good as the original 50 zone system although the performance is acceptable and the model has a greater relevance if used in a predictive context. In fact, the East Midlands

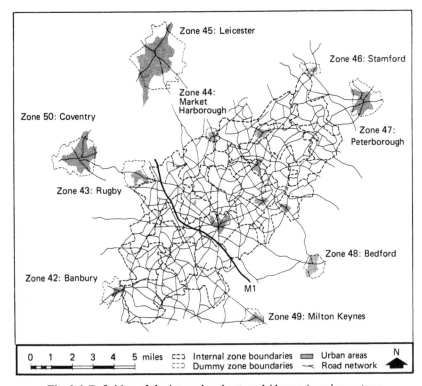

Fig. 8.6. Definition of the internal and external (dummy) zoning systems.

Technical Plan Unit were especially interested in the effects that changes in the large towns and cities outside the region would have on the location of activities inside the region, and this model was designed with such predictions in mind. These predictions are not included here but the use of the model in such a context is worthy of mention, and followed the ideas presented in Chapters 4 and 5.

Zoning systems: the fundamental problem of model design

Several questions of model design have been broached in this chapter and it seems that this area of urban modelling provides a potentially rich field for further research. In particular, the Northampton modelling project demonstrates that techniques are now available for speedy and efficient design and calibration of activity interaction-allocation models, and such

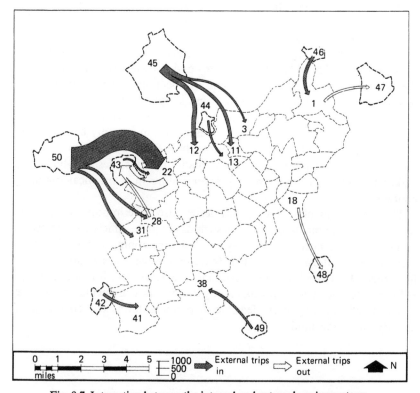

Fig. 8.7. Interaction between the internal and external zoning systems.

techniques are of fundamental importance to applications where fast model design is critical. But perhaps the most important issues raised in this chapter concern the definition and design of zoning systems. Although the theoretical work reported here suggests that a large number of zones is necessary for sound urban modelling, it is often impossible to meet such criteria. However, the model-builder must be continually aware that in any application, he is always operating at the limits of practical feasibility and theoretical acceptability. Such a compromise between theory and practice inevitably imposes strict limits on what the model can and cannot be used for.

The problem of zoning also suggests that the work of theoretical geographers on regionalization and map geometry might be linked in some way to these modelling issues, thus tapping a field of research which hitherto has largely not been used in a practical context (Tobler, 1963). Indeed, the problem of optimum zoning might even be considered as the problem of geography. Most work in this field so far has been descriptive with little emphasis upon optimum zoning appropriate to particular spatial processes. It is in this area that the greatest research is needed; there are, however, signs that some progress is being made along these lines (Batty, 1972b, 1974; Masser, Batey and Brown, 1973). Furthermore, the whole question of measurement of locational attraction and the relationship between the demand for and supply of different locations is of prime importance, and is likely to provide another fruitful area for further research. Although many of these issues might only be ultimately resolved in terms of model structure, there still remain many, useful improvements and innovations to be made in model design which may make the difference between success or failure in a practical planning context.

These problems of spatial system design also have important repercussions on more immediate problems such as computer efficiency and representation. In the next chapter, ways of designing zoning systems in which their inherent information content is traded-off against size are explored in terms of hierarchies, and methods are suggested for speeding-up, reducing storage space, approximating certain measurements of distance and generally making more feasible in practical terms the operation of activity allocation models.

9. *Hierarchical modelling*

This chapter, like the last, is primarily concerned with elaborating and exploring, in a somewhat less direct way, the intractable and pervasive influence of space on the design and calibration of numerical models. Previous chapters have shown that calibration problems and issues concerned with the numerical analysis and operation of models have yielded fairly readily to the application of standardised techniques but questions of space, particularly those dealing with the design of optimum zoning systems, have not yet been handled in a sufficiently rigorous way for these problems to have been explored in depth. Most of the research groups working in urban modelling have looked at this problem in various ways but the usual emphasis has been on techniques for speeding-up computation or cutting down computer storage, as for example in the hierarchical interaction model designed by Broadbent (1971), and the cordon model applied by Baxter (1971). Yet there is an urgent need for further exploration of theoretical and practical criteria for defining zone size and shape, and although certain studies have tentatively broached these problems (Broadbent, 1970a; Batty, 1972b; Masser et al., 1973) such matters are far from being resolved. The description of space is the central problem of theoretical geography (Bunge, 1966), and although investigation of such problems has only just begun, significant progress is seemingly being made (Cliff and Ord, 1973).

This concern for space provides a focus for the problems of spatial decomposition in urban modelling to be discussed here. In particular, the idea of building efficient urban models on spatial systems organised hierarchically continues the problems of system closure and dummy zoning discussed in Chapter 8. Yet there is another focus, equally important, but perhaps of conceptual rather than technical import. Urban models should be capable of generating insights into the functioning of spatial systems as well as providing a means for simulating urban phenomena. Thus modelling should be able to contribute to theory in this way rather than being solely concerned with the operational description of theory. However, it is not easy, in the social sciences, to point to work in which real insight has occurred. This is partly due to the nature of the

9-2

subject matter and its presentation but it is also due to the rather ill-defined nature of social and economic systems. Where insights have flourished, however, dramatic progress has been made and new interpretations of the subject matter have helped benefit the task of research in the field. That such insights can be of immense significance has been cogently illustrated by de Bono (1967) in his concept of lateral thinking and by Koestler (1964) in his analysis of the creative act. The work of Alexander (1964), for example, in which he identifies the current dilemma in architecture as being due to man's inability to handle complexity reveals immense insight and his work has been widely acclaimed in the design sciences. The analysis of planning as problem-solving by Rittel and Webber (1972) who suggest in Macluhian fashion that 'the problem is the solution: the solution is the problem' provides another example of real insight where such insight originates from turning a problem on its head and/or inside out in the quest to capture its essential significance.

Returning to the field of urban modelling, there is a beautiful example demonstrating such insight to be found in an article in *Nature* by Tobler and Wineburg (1971). These authors have inverted a gravity model for use in an archaeological problem in a most ingenious way. From data concerning the movements of merchant caravans in Central Turkey in the pre-Hittite age, taken from the famous Cappadocian tablets, Tobler and Wineburg have used the gravity model, not to predict these flows but to predict the associated distances between origins and destinations in an effort to find the relative locations of the sites. In formal terms, the inverted gravity model can be written

$$d_{ij} = \left(\frac{GO_i D_j}{T_{ij}^*}\right)^{1/\lambda},$$

where O_i and D_j are measures of the origin and destination activity respectively, T_{ij}^* is the observed number of merchant transactions between i and j, G is a scaling constant, d_{ij} is the distance from i to j and λ is a parameter. From the predicted distances, Tobler and Wineburg have used a multidimensional scaling programme to find the actual co-ordinates of the various sites in terms of three known sites, thus providing the archaeologists with alternative results on 'where to dig'. The use of a gravity model in this fashion is not new and, despite the obvious limitations of such analysis, the appropriateness of this application is beyond dispute. Indeed, the techniques to be described in this chapter, some of which involve such inversions, flow directly from this idea of using models to predict structures which are normally taken as given but which are often poorly specified in terms of available data. It is hoped to demonstrate the practical advantages of such an approach both in terms of speeding-up models, cutting down computer storage, and improving model accuracy.

The various short-cuts and tricks which can be applied in model design when spatial systems are decomposed or partitioned into hierarchies or sets where different criteria apply, are described using a trip-distribution production-attraction constrained model as example. By way of introduction, various measures of hierarchical decomposition due to Theil (1972) set the context to an examination of three different models in which a mixture of analytic and iterative solution is used to speed-up their running. A further problem concerns the use of inverted models in finding unknown or difficult-to-measure information such as distances across bridges, intra-zonal distances and measures of locational attraction, and these lead quite naturally to possible interpretations in terms of the geography of perception. These models and their short-cuts are illustrated using a 29 zone model of Merseyside, decomposed into two sets, the 21 zone Liverpool set and the 8 zone Wirral set. The performance of these models on this system is then presented and this provides a comparison of increased speeds, storage and accuracy. But first, certain notions concerning spatial decomposition will be introduced.

Measures of spatial decomposition

One of the traditional concerns of theoretical geography relates to ways in which regions can be aggregated or disaggregated to meet certain measurement criteria such as those involving homogeneity. For example, it may be necessary to study certain areas in more detail than others for practical or theoretical purposes; such is the case in urban modelling where it is necessary to take account of a spatial system in its wider environment using dummy zones where the modelling of urban phenomena is at a coarser level than in the spatial system itself. The Oxford shopping model described briefly in Chapter 8, is a case in point (Black, 1966) in which an inner ring of dummy zones accounting for flows between the system and its immediate environment is used, and which in turn is surrounded by an outer ring of zones designed to balance the competition on the inner set of dummies with the competition on the system itself. This kind of logic is similar to that used by Wilson (1970a) in his study of missing information and entropy-maximising and also relates to the arguments of Broadbent (1971) and Baxter (1971). To introduce measures of decomposition, consider a spatial system which is partitioned into K origin regions called Z_k, $k = 1, 2, ..., K$, and L destination regions, Z_l, $l = 1, 2, ..., L$. In each set Z_k, there are I_k origin zones i, $i = 1, 2, ..., I_k$, and in each set Z_l, there are J_l destination zones j, $j = 1, 2, ..., J_l$. In the following presentation, the summations are over all origin and destination sets and/or zones unless otherwise explicitly stated. First define a probability of interaction p_{ij} from the known trips T_{ij}^* on each i–j pair

$$p_{ij} = T_{ij}^* \Big/ \sum_i \sum_j T_{ij}^* = T_{ij}^*/T. \tag{9.1}$$

The total within-system interaction probability P^w can be defined as

$$P^w = \sum_k \sum_l \sum_{i \in Z_k} \sum_{j \in Z_l} p_{ij}, \quad k = l, \tag{9.2}$$

and the between-system probability P^b is calculated from

$$P^b = \sum_k \sum_l \sum_{i \in Z_k} \sum_{j \in Z_l} p_{ij}, \quad k \neq l. \tag{9.3}$$

If it is required to model within-system interaction in a fine manner in contrast to between-system interaction which is to be modelled in a coarse manner, then it is necessary to choose a decomposition which maximises (9.2), which in turn implies minimisation of (9.3). To express this idea, the ratio P^w/P^b which is a crude measure of the density of interaction should be maximised.

A more sophisticated decomposition statistic is based on the notion of entropy first defined in an information-theoretic sense by Shannon (1948) and widely used in econometric decomposition analysis by Theil (1972). Information or entropy H is defined from

$$H = -\sum_i \sum_j p_{ij} \ln p_{ij}, \tag{9.4}$$

where the probabilities sum to 1. Define P_{kl} as the probability of interaction between set k and set l calculated from

$$P_{kl} = \sum_{i \in Z_k} \sum_{j \in Z_l} p_{ij}. \tag{9.5}$$

Then entropy H can be expressed as the sum of a *between-set* entropy and a series of weighted *within-set* entropies defined by the entropy decomposition principle (Theil, 1972) as

$$H = -\sum_k \sum_l P_{kl} \ln P_{kl} - \sum_k \sum_l P_{kl} \sum_{i \in Z_k} \sum_{j \in Z_l} \frac{p_{ij}}{P_{kl}} \ln \frac{p_{ij}}{P_{kl}}. \tag{9.6}$$

Taking each term in (9.6) and tracing its implications for disaggregation, consider first within-set entropies. A choice of zoning system which maximises within-set entropy for $i, j \in Z_k$ and minimises this entropy for $i \in Z_k$, $j \in Z_l$, $k \neq l$, is required. With regard to between-set entropy, the entropy $P_{kl} \ln P_{kl}$ for $k = l$ must be maximised and for $k \neq l$, this entropy must be minimised. In formal terms, this problem is equivalent to maximising the ratio of (9.6) with $k = l$ to (9.6) with $k \neq 1$. A demonstration of these ideas will be given later in relation to the Merseyside region. Given that the zoning system and its hierarchy have been chosen to minimise information loss, then the various short-cuts and inversions described in the following sections are likely to be of relevance.

Doubly-constrained models based on fast analytic-iterative solution

The doubly-constrained trip-distribution model referred to as the production-attraction constrained model in the family of interaction models (Cordey-Hayes and Wilson, 1971) satisfies constraints on the activities O_i and D_j located respectively at origin zones i and destination zones j. Formally, these constraints are stated in (2.57) and (2.58) and are restated here

$$\sum_j T_{ij} = O_i \qquad\qquad [(2.57)]$$

and

$$\sum_i T_{ij} = D_j. \qquad\qquad [(2.58)]$$

The model satisfying these constraints can be of the type used by Furness (1965) or of the more conventional gravity-type given in (2.59) and redefined here as

$$T_{ij} = a_i O_i b_j D_j \exp\left(-\lambda c_{ij}\right), \qquad (9.7)$$

where c_{ij} is the travel cost between i and j, often measured in proportion to time or distance, λ is a parameter of the negative exponential distribution and a_i and b_j are balancing or normalising factors ensuring that the constraints in (2.57) and (2.58) are satisfied. These factors are evaluated as

$$a_i = \frac{1}{\sum_j b_j D_j \exp\left(-\lambda c_{ij}\right)}, \qquad (9.8)$$

$$b_j = \frac{1}{\sum_i a_i O_i \exp\left(-\lambda c_{ij}\right)}. \qquad (9.9)$$

a_i and b_j can be found by iteration. As Evans (1970) has demonstrated, their product $a_i b_j$ is unique although the values of a_i and b_j will depend upon their starting points and any other constants in the gravity model equations. Note that the results in this and the following sections can be easily generalised to singly-constrained interaction models.

One of the central themes in this chapter revolves around the idea that it is worth while modelling different parts of a spatial system in different degrees of detail, for example by modelling fine and coarse interactions or by modelling interactions with fine and coarse models. To relate this idea to distribution models, write constraint equations (2.57) and (2.58) as

$$\sum_{j \in Z_k} T_{ij} + \sum_l \sum_{j \in Z_l} T_{ij} = O_i, \quad i \in Z_k, \quad k \neq l, \tag{9.10}$$

$$\sum_{i \in Z_k} T_{ij} + \sum_l \sum_{i \in Z_l} T_{ij} = D_j, \quad j \in Z_k, \quad k \neq l. \tag{9.11}$$

Assume that the first terms on the left-hand sides of (9.10) and (9.11) are to be modelled using a fine model and the second terms using a coarser model. As the interactions $\{T_{ij}\}$ are known, then it is possible to find a set of additional travel costs $\{c_{ij}^*\}$ which gives a perfect fit for any interaction on an i–j link. In such cases it is possible to express the interactions between the decomposed sets of the system as

$$T_{ij} = O_i D_j \exp\left[-\lambda(c_{ij} + c_{ij}^*)\right],$$
$$= O_i D_j \exp\left(-\lambda c_{ij}\right) \exp\left(-\lambda c_{ij}^*\right), \quad i \in Z_k, \quad j \in Z_l, \quad k \neq l. \tag{9.12}$$

As T_{ij} is known from data, now called T_{ij}^*, c_{ij}^* can be found analytically from

$$c_{ij}^* = \frac{\ln O_i}{\lambda} + \frac{\ln D_j}{\lambda} - \frac{\ln T_{ij}^*}{\lambda} - c_{ij}, \quad i \in Z_k, \quad j \in Z_l, \quad k \neq l, \tag{9.13}$$

or a new total travel cost C_{ij} is found from

$$C_{ij} = c_{ij} + c_{ij}^* = \lambda^{-1} \ln\left(\frac{O_i D_j}{T_{ij}^*}\right), \quad i \in Z_k, \quad j \in Z_l, \quad k \neq l. \tag{9.14}$$

Therefore, (9.12) is used to predict inter-system trips and an equation similar to (9.7) is used to predict intra-system flows

$$T_{ij} = A_i O_i B_j D_j \exp\left(-\lambda c_{ij}\right), \quad i \in Z_k, \quad j \in Z_l, \quad k = l, \tag{9.15}$$

where A_i and B_j are normalising factors similar to a_i and b_j in (9.8) and (9.9).

The evaluation of these normalising factors provides the most interesting aspect of this development. Substituting (9.12) and (9.15) into (9.10) gives

$$A_i O_i \sum_{j \in Z_k} B_j D_j \exp\left(-\lambda c_{ij}\right) + O_i \sum_l \sum_{j \in Z_l} D_j$$
$$\times \exp\left(-\lambda c_{ij}\right) \exp\left(-\lambda c_{ij}^*\right) = O_i, \quad i \in Z_k, \quad k \neq l, \tag{9.16}$$

in which the O_i's can be cancelled and the form for A_i found as

$$A_i = \frac{1 - \sum_l \sum_{j \in Z_l} D_j \exp\left(-\lambda c_{ij}\right) \exp\left(-\lambda c_{ij}^*\right)}{\sum_{j \in Z_k} B_j D_j \exp\left(-\lambda c_{ij}\right)}, \quad i \in Z_k, \quad k \neq l. \tag{9.17}$$

In a similar fashion, (9.12) and (9.15) are substituted into (9.11) giving

$$B_j D_j \sum_{i \in Z_k} A_i O_i \exp(-\lambda c_{ij}) + D_j \sum_l \sum_{i \in Z_l} O_i$$

$$\times \exp(-\lambda c_{ij}) \exp(-\lambda c_{ij}^*) = O_i, \quad i \in Z_k, \quad k \neq l, \qquad (9.18)$$

which simplifies to

$$B_j = \frac{1 - \sum_l \sum_{i \in Z_l} O_i \exp(-\lambda c_{ij}) \exp(-c_{ij}^*)}{\sum_{i \in Z_k} A_i O_i \exp(-\lambda c_{ij})}, \quad j \in Z_k, \quad k \neq l. \qquad (9.19)$$

Equations (9.17) and (9.19) are balancing factors, modified to take account of the inter-system trips, and these factors will converge to a unique product $A_i B_j$ from any starting point. To develop an alternative interpretation for these factors redefine (9.12) in probabilistic terms as

$$T_{ij} = O_i p_{ij}, \quad i \in Z_k, \quad j \in Z_l, \quad k \neq l, \qquad (9.20)$$

where p_{ij} is calculated as

$$p_{ij} = D_j \exp(-\lambda c_{ij}) \exp(-\lambda c_{ij}^*), \quad i \in Z_l, \quad k \neq l. \qquad (9.21)$$

Substituting (9.21) into constraint (9.16) and (9.18) yields the balancing factors

$$A_i = \frac{1 - \sum_l \sum_{j \in Z_l} p_{ij}}{\sum_{j \in Z_k} B_j D_j \exp(-\lambda c_{ij})}, \quad i \in Z_k, \quad k \neq l, \qquad (9.22)$$

and

$$B_j = \frac{1 - \sum_l \sum_{i \in Z_l} p_{ij}}{\sum_{i \in Z_k} A_i O_i \exp(-\lambda c_{ij})}, \quad j \in Z_k, \quad k \neq l. \qquad (9.23)$$

Comparing (9.22) and (9.23) with (9.8) and (9.9), it is clear that these equations are related by

$$A_i = a_i \left(1 - \sum_l \sum_{j \in Z_l} p_{ij}\right), \quad i \in Z_k, \quad k \neq l, \qquad (9.24)$$

$$B_j = b_j \left(1 - \sum_l \sum_{i \in Z_l} p_{ij}\right), \quad j \in Z_k, \quad k \neq l. \qquad (9.25)$$

Then the model (9.15) can be written as

$$T_{ij} = A_i O_i B_j D_j \exp(-\lambda c_{ij}),$$

$$= a_i \left(1 - \sum_l \sum_{j \in Z_l} p_{ij}\right) O_i b_j \left(1 - \sum_l \sum_{i \in Z_l} p_{ij}\right) D_j \exp(-\lambda c_{ij}),$$

$$= a_i O_i^* b_j D_j^* \exp(-\lambda c_{ij}), \quad i \in Z_k, \quad j \in Z_l, \quad k = l. \qquad (9.26)$$

From (9.26), instead of weighting the A_i's and B_j's, the origin and destination totals O_i and D_j are weighted to account only for activity within the spatial system. New origin and destination totals are defined from

$$O_i^* = O_i\left(1-\sum_l \sum_{j \in Z_l} p_{ij}\right), \quad i \in Z_k, \quad k = l, \tag{9.27}$$

$$D_j^* = D_j\left(1-\sum_l \sum_{i \in Z_l} p_{ij}\right), \quad j \in Z_k, \quad k = l. \tag{9.28}$$

Using the model whose development is outlined in (9.10)–(9.28) in preference to the model in (9.7)–(9.9), a model involving the iteration of $(I_1+I_2+...+I_K)(J_1+J_2+...+J_L)$ equations has been transformed to one involving $I_1J_1+I_2J_2+...+I_KJ_L$ iterations ($K = L$) and

$$I_1(J_2+J_3+...+J_L)+I_2(I_1+J_3+...+J_L)+...+I_K(J_1+J_2+...+J_L)$$
$$(K \neq L)$$

analytic solutions. In the case where there are K origin and destination sets and I_K origin and destination zones in each set, the reduction in computation time for this model is in the region of $1/K$ which is substantial if the system is divided into several regions. Moreover, the model predicts exactly the inter-system trips $T_{ij}, i \in Z_k, j \in Z_l, k \neq l$, although, as in many of these kinds of problems, zero entries in the trip matrix have to be ignored or new estimates included by some sort of smoothing procedure (Chilton and Poet, 1973). The advantages of using such a coarse model in a predictive sense are only realised when this type of model is examined in a forecasting context: as in more refined models, changes in activity at the origins and/or destinations and changes in inter-zonal distances can be reflected in these coarse models, although such models cannot be subject to origin or destination constraints. However, as in any modelling venture, the use of these procedures is a matter of judgement reached by weighing information loss and weaker predictive power against improved accuracy and computer feasibility.

Hierarchical interaction models soluble by iteration

In contrast to the previous model in which computer time, not storage, is reduced, the hierarchical interaction model due to Broadbent (1971), in which computer storage is conserved, will be outlined in this section, in preparation for its speed-up which is described in the next section. Broadbent's hierarchical model works on the principle of modelling fine zone interaction within any region but coarse zone interaction between a fine zone in any region and all the zones of any other region. The model has similarities to Baxter's cordon model developed for the Cambridge urban model (Baxter, 1971), although Broadbent's notation is more relevant to the approach presented here and is thus used.

The origin and destination constraints given previously in (2.57) and (2.58) and then in (9.10) and (9.11) hold but the inter-system interaction is at a coarser level of aggregation. First define the coarse level interaction T_{il} from any zone i, $i \in Z_k$ to region Z_l, $k \neq l$, and the interaction T_{lj} from any zone j, $j \in Z_k$ to region Z_l, $k \neq l$. Formally,

$$T_{il} = \sum_{j \in Z_l} T_{ij}, \quad i \in Z_k, \quad k \neq l, \tag{9.29}$$

and

$$T_{lj} = \sum_{i \in Z_l} T_{ij}, \quad j \in Z_k, \quad k \neq l. \tag{9.30}$$

Constraint equations (9.10) and (9.11) can now be written using (9.29) and (9.30) as

$$\sum_{j \in Z_k} T_{ij} + \sum_l T_{il} = O_i, \quad i \in Z_k, \quad k \neq l, \tag{9.31}$$

$$\sum_{i \in Z_k} T_{ij} + \sum_l T_{lj} = D_j, \quad j \in Z_k, \quad k \neq l. \tag{9.32}$$

First, for the model predicting the regional trips given in (9.29) and (9.30), appropriate regional distances c_{il} and c_{lj} are required. Using a doubly-constrained distribution model, inter-system trips are computed from

$$\begin{aligned} T_{ij} &= A_i O_i B_j D_j \exp\left[-\lambda(c_{il} + c_{lj})\right], \\ &= A_i O_i B_j D_j \exp\left(-\lambda c_{il}\right) \exp\left(-\lambda c_{lj}\right), \quad i \in Z_k, \quad j \in Z_l, \quad k \neq l. \end{aligned} \tag{9.33}$$

Substituting (9.33) into (9.29) and (9.30) respectively, the coarse-level trips can be predicted from

$$T_{il} = A_i O_i \exp\left(-\lambda c_{il}\right) \sum_{j \in Z_l} B_j D_j \exp\left(-\lambda c_{lj}\right), \quad i \in Z_k, \quad k \neq l, \tag{9.34}$$

$$T_{lj} = B_j D_j \exp\left(-\lambda c_{lj}\right) \sum_{i \in Z_k} A_i O_i \exp\left(-\lambda c_{il}\right), \quad j \in Z_k, \quad k \neq l. \tag{9.35}$$

Equations (9.34) and (9.35) contain the essential logic of the hierarchical model in which flows are predicted from an origin zone $i \in Z_k$ to region Z_l, $k \neq l$, and are then distributed to zone $j \in Z_l$ from the regional to zonal level. Note that this is only made possible by the use of the negative exponential deterrence function which can be split. Broadbent (1971) visualised this process as one in which traffic was distributed between regions on a higher-order network and within regions on a secondary network: this interpretation has not been kept here where trips are distributed directly on a network $c_{il} \rightarrow c_{lj}$ rather than $c_{ik} \rightarrow c_{kl} \rightarrow c_{lj}$ as in Broadbent's model. The balancing factors are easily defined by substituting

(9.34), (9. 35) and (9.15) into (9.31) and (9.32); these factors are evaluated as

$$A_i = \frac{1}{\sum\limits_{j \in Z_k} B_j D_j \exp\left(-\lambda c_{ij}\right) + \sum\limits_{l} \exp\left(-\lambda c_{il}\right) \sum\limits_{j \in Z_l} B_j D_j \exp\left(-\lambda c_{lj}\right)},$$
$$i \in Z_k, \quad k \neq l, \quad (9.36)$$

$$B_j = \frac{1}{\sum\limits_{i \in Z_k} A_i O_i \exp\left(-\lambda c_{ij}\right) + \sum\limits_{l} \exp\left(-\lambda c_{lj}\right) \sum\limits_{i \in Z_l} A_i O_i \exp\left(-\lambda c_{il}\right)},$$
$$j \in Z_k, \quad k \neq l. \quad (9.37)$$

Measurement of the distances c_{il} and c_{lj} is likely to be difficult for there are few guidelines to use. Two possible schemes suggest themselves, the first based on measurement from disaggregated trip data, the second on the basis of disaggregated models. From disaggregated trip data, c_{il} and $c_{lj}, i \in Z_k, j \in Z_l, k \neq l$, can be measured by the following mean trip lengths

$$c_{il} = \frac{\sum\limits_{j \in Z_l} T_{ij} c_{ij}}{\sum\limits_{j \in Z_l} T_{ij}}, \quad i \in Z_k, \quad k \neq l, \quad (9.38)$$

$$c_{lj} = \frac{\sum\limits_{i \in Z_l} T_{ij} c_{ij}}{\sum\limits_{i \in Z_l} T_{ij}}, \quad j \in Z, \quad k \neq l. \quad (9.39)$$

This scheme can be carried out for all regions, although it is likely to lead to estimates for c_{il} and c_{lj} which are biased upwards. In other words, $c_{il} + c_{lj} \geqslant c_{ij}$, for all i and j; although this is only speculation, it has in fact been borne out in practice.

Another scheme for finding aggregate distances in terms of predicted rather than observed trips, has been suggested by Beardwood (1972). If it is required to ensure that the aggregated model predicts trips similar to the disaggregated model, then in terms of, say, (9.34), the trips T_{il} can be predicted from

$$T_{il} = A_i O_i \sum\limits_{j \in Z_l} (B_j D_j) \exp\left(-\lambda c_{il}\right) \exp\left(-\lambda c_{lj}\right), \quad i \in Z_k, \quad k \neq l, \quad (9.40)$$

or from

$$T_{il} = \sum\limits_{j \in Z_l} A_i O_i B_j D_j \exp\left(-\lambda c_{ij}\right), \quad i \in Z_k, \quad k \neq l. \quad (9.41)$$

Comparing (9.40) and (9.41) and rearranging, the aggregated deterrence function can be predicted from

$$\exp\left(-\lambda c_{il}\right) \exp\left(-\lambda c_{lj}\right) = \frac{\sum\limits_{j \in Z_l} B_j D_j \exp\left(-\lambda c_{ij}\right)}{\sum\limits_{j \in Z_l} B_j D_j}, \quad i \in Z_k, \quad k \neq l.$$
$$(9.42)$$

The same kind of analysis can be performed on (9.35) and this gives

$$\exp\left(-\lambda c_{il}\right)\exp\left(-\lambda c_{lj}\right) = \frac{\sum\limits_{i \in Z_k} A_i O_i \exp\left(-\lambda c_{ij}\right)}{\sum\limits_{i \in Z_k} A_i O_i}, \quad j \in Z_l, \quad k \neq l.$$

(9.43)

Values for c_{il} and c_{lj} can thus be chosen from some iterative scheme based on (9.42) and (9.43). In the following applications, these aggregated distances are based upon (9.38) and (9.39), although in future applications, a test of the scheme given in (9.42) and (9.43) would be desirable.

The great advantage of this model is in terms of storage reduction over the doubly-constrained non-hierarchical equivalent. For example, storage of one matrix, say the distance matrix, is reduced from order

$$(I_1 + I_2 + \dots + I_K)(J_1 + J_2 + \dots + J_L)$$

to

$$(I_1 J_1 + I_2 J_2 + \dots + I_K J_L) + 2(I_1 + I_2 + \dots + I_K + J_1 + J_2 + \dots + J_L).$$

When $K = L$ and $I_k = J_l$ for all k and l, and when K is large, storage is reduced to approximately $(1/K)$th the storage needed by the non-hierarchical model, a saving similar to the saving in computer time of the previous model. However, iteration of the A_i's and B_j's is over the whole system of regions and there are no constraints on the actual amounts of interaction originating from or entering a region; in the following section, this model will be modified to account for such constraints.

Faster hierarchical models based on analytic-iterative solutions

The simplest way to speed-up the operation of the hierarchical model is to predict analytically factors c_{il}^* and c_{lj}^* which relate to observed flows T_{il}^* and T_{lj}^*, thus following the same logic as in the speeding-up of the non-hierarchical model outlined in (9.10)–(9.28). The trips T_{il} and T_{lj} are predicted by a coarse model

$$T_{il} = O_i D_l \exp\left(-\lambda c_{il}\right)\exp\left(-\lambda c_{il}^*\right), \quad i \in Z_k, \quad k \neq l, \quad (9.44)$$

$$T_{lj} = O_l D_j \exp\left(-\lambda c_{lj}\right)\exp\left(-\lambda c_{lj}^*\right), \quad j \in Z_k, \quad k \neq l. \quad (9.45)$$

Then the factors c_{il}^* and c_{lj}^* can be predicted analytically from

$$c_{il}^* = \lambda^{-1}\ln\left[\frac{O_i D_l \exp\left(-\lambda c_{il}\right)}{T_{il}^*}\right], \quad i \in Z_k, \quad k \neq l, \quad (9.46)$$

$$c_{lj}^* = \lambda^{-1}\ln\left[\frac{O_l D_j \exp\left(-\lambda c_{lj}\right)}{T_{lj}^*}\right], \quad j \in Z_k, \quad k \neq l. \quad (9.47)$$

Substituting (9.44) and (9.45) into the hierarchical constraint (9.31) and (9.32) and using the doubly-constrained distribution model in (9.15), the balancing factors are derived as

$$A_i = \frac{1 - \sum_l D_l \exp(-\lambda c_{il}) \exp(-\lambda c_{il}^*)}{\sum_{j \in Z_k} B_j D_j \exp(-\lambda c_{ij})}, \quad i \in Z_k, \quad k \neq l, \quad (9.48)$$

$$B_j = \frac{1 - \sum_l O_l \exp(-\lambda c_{lj}) \exp(-\lambda c_{lj}^*)}{\sum_{i \in Z_k} A_i O_i \exp(-\lambda c_{ij})}, \quad j \in Z_k, k \neq l. \quad (9.49)$$

These balancing factors have the same form as the factors in (9.17) and (9.19) although in this case, the model has now been speeded-up by approximately the same order as the non-hierarchical model, and yet retains the storage advantages of the hierarchical model. This is a much cruder approximation to reality for the origin and destination totals in each region are highly aggregated and thus a substantial amount of information has been lost along with a large reduction in the model's predictive power. As this model is so similar to its non-hierarchical equivalent, it has not been used in the application to be outlined in a later section, although in terms of speed and storage it is certainly the most efficient of the models presented here.

The second model presented in this section rests on the idea of designing a model which satisfies exactly the constraints in (9.29) and (9.30). This is accomplished by predicting the distances c_{il}^* and c_{lj}^* by a combination of iterative and analytic solution. Then for inter-system trips, the following model is used

$$T_{ij} = O_i D_j \exp[-\lambda(c_{il}^* + c_{lj}^*)],$$
$$= O_i D_j \exp(-\lambda c_{il}^*) \exp(-\lambda c_{lj}^*), \quad i \in Z_k, \quad j \in Z_l, \quad k \neq l. \quad (9.50)$$

Substituting (9.50) into (9.29) and (9.30) and rearranging gives

$$T_{il} = O_i \exp(-\lambda c_{il}^*) \sum_{j \in Z_l} D_j \exp(-\lambda c_{lj}^*), \quad i \in Z_k, \quad k \neq l, \quad (9.51)$$

$$T_{lj} = D_j \exp(-\lambda c_{lj}^*) \sum_{i \in Z_l} O_i \exp(-\lambda c_{il}^*), \quad j \in Z_k, \quad k \neq l. \quad (9.52)$$

The appropriate distances can be found by solving (9.51) and (9.52) for $i \in Z_k, j \in Z_l, k \neq l$ iteratively and choosing new values for c_{il}^* and c_{lj}^* from

$$c_{il}^* = \lambda^{-1} \ln\left[\frac{O_i \sum_{j \in Z_l} D_j \exp(-\lambda c_{lj}^*)}{T_{il}^*}\right], \quad i \in Z_k, \quad k \neq l, \quad (9.53)$$

and

$$c_{lj}^* = \lambda^{-1} \ln \left[\frac{D_j \sum\limits_{i \in Z_l} O_i \exp{(-\lambda c_{il}^*)}}{T_{lj}^*} \right], \quad j \in Z_l, \quad k \neq l. \quad (9.54)$$

Iteration on (9.51) and (9.52) is similar to the iteration required to find the balancing factors A_i and B_j. These normalising factors can be found by substituting (9.51) and (9.52) together with (9.15) into (9.31) and (9.32) and rearranging. First for trips leaving the origin region Z_k

$$A_i O_i \sum_{j \in Z_k} B_j D_j \exp{(-\lambda c_{ij})} + O_i \sum_l \exp{(-\lambda c_{il}^*)} \sum_{i \in Z_l} D_j \exp{(-\lambda c_{lj}^*)}$$

$$= O_i, \quad i \in Z_k, \quad k \neq l, \quad (9.55)$$

and solving for A_i gives

$$A_i = \frac{1 - \sum\limits_l \exp{(-\lambda c_{il}^*)} \sum\limits_{j \in Z_l} D_j \exp{(-\lambda c_{lj}^*)}}{\sum\limits_{j \in Z_k} B_j D_j \exp{(-\lambda c_{ij})}}, \quad i \in Z_k, \quad k \neq l. \quad (9.56)$$

Then, for trips entering the destination region Z_k

$$B_j D_j \sum_{i \in Z_k} A_i O_i \exp{(-\lambda c_{ij})} + D_j \sum_l \exp{(-\lambda c_{lj}^*)} \sum_{i \in Z_l} O_i \exp{(-\lambda c_{il}^*)}$$

$$= D_j, \quad j \in Z_k, \quad k \neq l, \quad (9.57)$$

and solving for B_j gives

$$B_j = \frac{1 - \sum\limits_l \exp{(-\lambda c_{lj}^*)} \sum\limits_{i \in Z_l} O_i \exp{(-\lambda c_{il}^*)}}{\sum\limits_{i \in Z_k} A_i O_i \exp{(-\lambda c_{ij})}}, \quad j \in Z_k, \quad k \neq l. \quad (9.58)$$

The same probabilistic interpretation can be developed for the two models outlined in this section as in the model presented in (9.10)–(9.28). In the last model, developed in (9.50)–(9.58), the number of iterations required is slightly less than in Broadbent's hierarchical model; the reduction is achieved by breaking up the iterations into main diagonal iterations, of the supermatrix and off-diagonal iterations, whereas Broadbent's iterations are over the whole supermatrix. Thus, Broadbent's model is also likely to converge more slowly than in the model outlined above. To demonstrate this point a little more cogently consider the supermatrix presented below in which the essential nature of the iterative process is displayed: the main diagonal elements denoted by $I_k J_k$ involve the computation of $A_i B_j$ factors as in (9.56) and (9.58) whereas the off-diagonal elements Q_{kl}, $k \neq l$ denote iteration based on (9.51) and (9.52). The reduction in iterations can be formally compared as follows. In Broadbent's hierarchical model, $(I_1 + I_2 + \ldots + I_K)(J_1 + J_2 + \ldots + J_L)$ equations

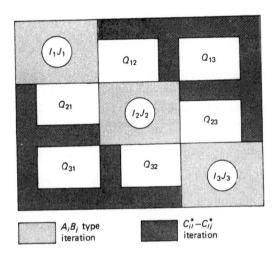

are iterated whereas in the modified model $I_1J_1 + I_2J_2 + \ldots + I_KJ_L$ (where $K = L) + K(I_1 + I_2 + \ldots + I_K) + L(J_1 + J_2 + \ldots + J_L)$ equations are solved by iteration. Apart from the increased accuracy of the modified model, computer time is cut to about $1/K + 2/k$ of Broadbent's model (where there are K origin and destination regions each with k origin and destination zones).

Hierarchical articulation problems: barrier effects

The logic of predicting certain elements of spatial structure using inverse forms of conventional urban models is nowhere more apparent than in cases where structure is almost impossible to measure in any objective sense. Such is the case in systems which are divided by natural barriers such as rivers or mountain ranges where the connecting link, be it a bridge, tunnel or ferry, has an important but unknown effect upon contact-interaction between the two systems. In graph-theoretic terms, such a point of connection is called an 'articulation point' whose removal from the graph separates the two systems into two disconnected subgraphs. In such instances, it is possible to develop a model in which prediction alternates between simulating the interaction between the two systems and deriving an appropriate measure of distance between the two systems. An example of this problem is presented in the transport network of Merseyside illustrated in Figure 9.1 where the articulation point between the two subsystems is clearly marked. Prediction of the relevant inter-system distances can be accomplished using the following equation system where n denotes an iteration of the overall system. First,

$$T_{ij}(n) = A_i(n) \, O_i \, B_j(n) \, D_j \exp\left[-\lambda c_{ij}(n)\right], \quad \text{for all } k \text{ and } l. \quad (9.59)$$

Then new distances $c_{ij}(n+1)$ for the next iteration $n+1$ are calculated from

$$c_{ij}(n+1) = \begin{cases} c_{ij}, & i \in Z_k, \quad j \in Z_l, \quad k = l, \\ c_{ij}(n) + c_{ij}^*(n), & i \in Z_k, \quad j \in Z_l, \quad k \neq l, \end{cases} \tag{9.60}$$

where $c_{ij}^*(n)$ is predicted from

$$c_{ij}^*(n) = \lambda^{-1} \ln \left\{ \frac{A_i(n) \, O_i \, B_j(n) \, D_j \, \exp\left[-\lambda c_{ij}(n)\right]}{T_{ij}(n)} \right\}, \quad i \in Z_k, \quad j \in Z_l, \quad k \neq l. \tag{9.61}$$

This system given in (9.59)–(9.61) can be iterated until $|c_{ij}(n+1) - c_{ij}(n)|$ is less than some limit for $i \in Z_k$, $j \in Z_l$, $k \neq l$.

The average additional distance factor on the link between the two systems Z_k and Z_l can be found by computing the appropriate mean trip lengths. Then

$$\bar{C}_{kl} = \frac{\sum\limits_{i \in Z_k} \sum\limits_{j \in Z_l} T_{ij}(n) \, c_{ij}(n)}{\sum\limits_{i \in Z_k} \sum\limits_{j \in Z_l} T_{ij}(n)}, \quad k \neq l,$$

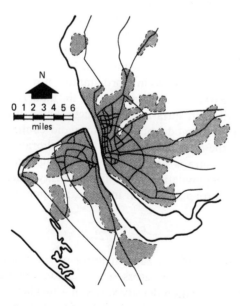

N

0 1 2 3 4 5 6
miles

▦▦▦ Urban area, 1966

——— Major transport network

Fig. 9.1. Transport network and urban area on Merseyside.

and

$$\bar{C}_{lk} = \frac{\sum\limits_{i \in Zl} \sum\limits_{j \in Zk} T_{ij}(n)\, c_{ij}(n)}{\sum\limits_{i \in Z_l} \sum\limits_{j \in Z_k} T_{ij}(n)}, \quad k \neq l.$$

Apart from the additional accuracy imparted to the model by this process, the whole methodology could be helpful in studying the ways in which people perceive distance. The analysis can easily be extended to deal with several links across natural barriers and the use of the model to study perception of distances over the system as a whole could provide an interesting way of tackling the definition of mental maps. Further applications abound: for example, use of the model in predicting locational attractions in proportion to the factors $B_j D_j$ could also be developed along lines already suggested by Masser *et al.* (1973) and Baxter and Williams (1972).

The intra-zonal distance problem

Perhaps the most important measurement problem of all in spatial model design concerns the question of intra-zonal distances. This is a practical rather than theoretical problem for if Broadbent's rule is adhered to in constructing zones, then such distances should be no more difficult to measure than any others. But in practice, a much larger proportion than Broadbent's measure of 10 per cent of the interaction in the system, is often retained within the zones themselves. In Notts.–Derbys., this proportion was 52 per cent whereas in Northampton, it was 66 per cent and in Central Lancashire 67 per cent. In such cases, the model is likely to be most sensitive to variation in intra-zonal distances, and a great deal of willpower is needed if the model-builder is to avoid continual alteration of such distances in the quest to remeasure and recalibrate the model.

The simplest measure is based upon the assumption that the zone is evenly spread with a population at a constant density. Then on the assumption that the zone is roughly circular in shape, an approximation to c_{ii} can be found from

$$c_{ii} = \frac{r_i}{\sqrt{2}},$$

where r_i is the radius of the zone in terms of travel cost, in this case. A slight modification to this gross simplification can be made, if it is assumed that the population density varies in a regular way, and if it can be described by a mathematically tractable function, fitted of course to the particular zone in question. Using the function given in (8.19), and assuming that the population density varies around some pole or centroid in the zone, then c_{ii} can be calculated from

$$c_{ii} = \int_0^{2\pi} \int_0^{r_i} G \exp{(-\lambda r)} r^2 \, d\theta \, dr,$$

$$= \frac{2}{\lambda} - \exp{(-\lambda r_i)} \left(\lambda r_i^2 + \frac{2r_i}{\lambda} + 2 \right), \tag{9.62}$$

where r_i is the radius of the zone. Equation (9.62) is clearly a mean trip length which is affected by the finite boundary of the zone. These two methods are highly approximate and are probably of more analytical than practical interest, but in certain circumstances may be the only methods available. A method of zoning based on (9.62) is presented in a related paper by the author (Batty, 1974).

The most consistent way of defining intra-zonal distances is from trip and distance data disaggregated within each individual zone. The intra-zonal distance problem can be seen as a problem in finding the mean trip length within any zone. If any zone i is divided into x origin zones and y destination zones, then c_{ii} can be found from

$$c_{ii} = \frac{\sum_x \sum_y T_{xy} c_{xy}}{\sum_x \sum_y T_{xy}}, \quad x, y \in i.$$

Measurements of c_{xx} in turn could be made in the same way and so on, thus implying that the problem has the characteristic of a set of Chinese boxes. However data are not usually available for such a process and thus these more elegant methods are often impossible to use. Finally, in the spirit of the methods advocated in this chapter, it is possible to predict c_{ii} using an equation of the form given in (9.61). Then

$$c_{ii}(n+1) = c_{ii}(n) + c_{ii}^*(n), \tag{9.63}$$

where

$$c_{ii}^*(n) = \lambda^{-1} \ln \left\{ \frac{A_i(n) \, O_i(n) \, B_i(n) \, D_i(n) \exp{[-\lambda c_{ii}(n)]}}{T_{ii}(n)} \right\}. \tag{9.64}$$

No suggestion that (9.63) and (9. 64) be used as a basis for the sole measurement of c_{ii} in modelling applications, is implied here for (9.63) and (9.64) represent an exploratory scheme for investigating the influence of space and distance in interaction models. The final choice of c_{ii} must clearly rest on many issues, and might be based on some synthesis of all the methods presented in this section.

Application to a simple hierarchy: Merseyside decomposed

The decomposition of Merseyside into two subsystems – a 21 zone system based on Liverpool and an 8 zone system based on Wirral – is illustrated in Figure 9.2. This decomposition arising from the natural barrier of the river is also a good partition according to the measures of decomposition presented in an earlier section. An examination of the trip matrix for Merseyside reveals dense flows within Liverpool and within Wirral but sparse flows between the two subsystems; these flows are illustrated in Figure 9.3. Equation (9.2) shows that 94 per cent of all flows occur within Wirral and within Liverpool and the ratio of (9.2) to (9.3) is about 15.3, demonstrating that there is 15 times as much interaction within these systems as between them. The ratio of within-system, not set, to between-system entropies from (9.6) is about 12.2 thus confirming the excellence of this natural decomposition in interaction and information loss terms. The values of these various decomposition statistics are presented in Table 9.1.

Six of the models developed in this chapter have been run for Merseyside; by way of a bench mark, the doubly-constrained trip distribution model given in (9.7)–(9.9) can be compared to the five other models – the speeded-up doubly-constrained model in (9.10)–(9.28), Broadbent's hierarchical model in (9.29)–(9.37), the speeded-up hierarchical model in (9.44)–(9.58), the hierarchical articulation model in (9.59)–(9.61) and the

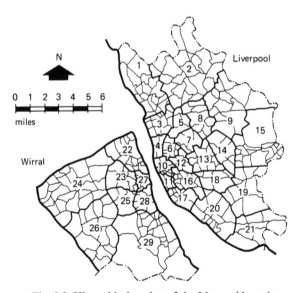

Fig. 9.2. Hierarchical zoning of the Merseyside region.

TABLE 9.1. *Measures of decomposition applied to Merseyside*

Decomposition statistic	Merseyside	Liverpool subsystem	Wirral subsystem	Liverpool → Wirral subsystem	Wirral → Liverpool subsystem
Percentage of trips	1.0000	0.7554	0.1826	0.0104	0.0510
Total entropy and percent of total entropy*	5.5535 (1.0000)	4.1089 (0.7528)	0.9548 (0.1719)	0.0893 (0.0161)	0.3284 (0.0591)
Within-set entropy and per cent of total entropy*	4.8315 (0.8700)	3.9690 (0.7147)	0.6443 (0.1160)	0.0415 (0.0075)	0.1766 (0.0318)
Between-set entropy and per cent of total entropy*	0.7220 (0.1300)	0.2118 (0.0381)	0.3105 (0.0559)	0.0477 (0.0086)	0.1518 (0.0273)

* Figures in brackets are the relevant percentage.

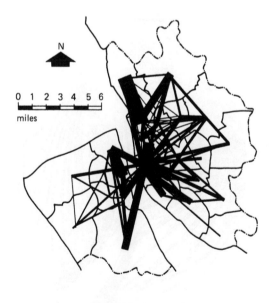

Fig. 9.3. Trip distribution on Merseyside.

intra-zonal distance model in (9.63) and (9.64). For each of these six models, a series of statistics demonstrating goodness of fit to the observed trip distribution $\{T_{ij}^*\}$ has been computed. First the r^2 statistic is calculated and second, a measure of information difference used by Theil (1972) is used. This measure is defined as

$$H^* = \sum_i \sum_j p_{ij} \ln \frac{p_{ij}}{p_{ij}^*}, \tag{9.65}$$

where p_{ij} is the probability of interaction predicted by the model (T_{ij}/T) and p_{ij}^* is the observed probability (T_{ij}^*/T). The minimum value for H^* occurs at zero when $p_{ij} = p_{ij}^*$ for all i and j, otherwise (9.65) is always positive. Two other statistics are based on the intercept w and slope ρ of the regression line relating observed to predicted trips

$$T_{ij} = w + \rho T_{ij}^*. \tag{9.66}$$

In the case of (9.66), a best fit occurs when the intercept w is zero and when the slope ρ is equal to one.

Each of the models has been run with a value for λ calculated for the 29 zone doubly-constrained model. The value for λ has been found by

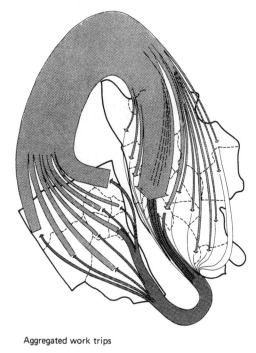

20 000
15 000
10 000
5 000
0
Aggregated work trips

Fig. 9.4. Hierarchical trip distribution on Merseyside.

use of a linear interpolation formula first suggested for calibration by Hyman (1969), and presented previously in (6.21). The value to which λ converges using (6.21) is 0.5281. The goodness of fit statistics are presented in Table 9.2 and it is clear that, in general, the hierarchical models perform less well, but only slightly so, than the non-hierarchical models. Indeed, on all statistics, the speeded-up models have a similar performance to the original models and real differences between them exist in computational rather than performance terms. A diagrammatic presentation of performance is given in Figure 9.4. In the articulation problem, the values of the mean trip lengths from the scheme in (9.60) and (9.61) taking Liverpool as Z_k and Wirral as Z_l, were computed as 0.5004 and -0.0203 respectively. This shows that the perception of persons living in Liverpool but working in the Wirral is on the average about one-half mile greater than the measurable distance whereas the distance perception of those living in Wirral and working in Liverpool is more or less equal to the measurable distance. This is a reasonable result given the relative attraction of Liverpool over Wirral and noting that the mean trip length in the system as a whole is 2.5371 miles.

TABLE 9.2. *Performance of the distribution models*

Type of model	Theil's statistic from (9.65)	Coefficient of determination r^2	Intercept w from (9.66)	Slope ρ from (9.66)
Doubly-constrained in (9.7)–(9.9)	0.1180	0.8477	68.3299	0.8787
Speeded-up doubly-constrained in (9.10)–(9.28)	0.1029	0.8425	37.4701	0.9913
Broadbent's hierarchical model in (9.29)–(9.37)	0.1198	0.8309	48.6654	0.9135
Short-cut hierarchical model in (9.44)–(9.58)	0.1729	0.8362	19.2923	0.9408
Hierarchical articulation model in (9.59)–(9.61)	0.0997	0.8726	47.4060	0.9157
Intra-zonal distance model in (9.63)–(9.64)	0.0015	0.9989	8.2677	0.9849
Optimum value	0.0000	1.0000	0.0000	1.0000

Finally, it is worth while comparing four of these models in terms of the computational time required for their running, and the space necessary for their storage in the computer. With regard to storage space, the doubly-constrained model and its speeded-up version require the storage of matrices equal in dimension to the total number of zones, in contrast to the hierarchical models – Broadbent's model and its speeded-up version – which require substantially less storage. In terms of computational times required, the speeded-up models are faster than their slower equivalents, due to the fact that iteration occurs over decomposed sets of model equations, rather than over the total set. To compare performance, computer time and storage, a crude index has been constructed relating these results. This index V is defined as

$$V = \frac{2r^2}{(e+s)},$$

where r^2 is the coefficient of determination, e is the number of equations solved as a proportion of the doubly-constrained distribution model equations and s is the storage needed as a proportion of storage required for the doubly-constrained distribution model. This index is equal to 1 when the doubly-constrained model gives a perfect fit, and models which are deemed 'more efficient' than the doubly-constrained model score higher values of V. Table 9.3 provides a comparison of the various computer times, storage and efficiency indices for the four models, excluding the hierarchical articulation model which is not comparable. Clearly, the index of efficiency is weighted in favour of the short-cut models, as this index does not consider any criterion measuring information loss and lower predictive power. Nevertheless, the short-cuts presented in this chapter are significant even in the context of a two-system hierarchy and these short-cuts are positively dramatic when systems are partitioned into several subsystems.

Unresolved problems of model design

The logic underlying the decomposition and partition of systems into subsystems to which various fine and coarse models can be applied, can in principle be extended to any modelling venture involving a natural hierarchy. For example, this kind of approach can be extended to input–output modelling as is demonstrated by Theil (1967), and in spatial interaction terms, these ideas seem immensely suitable for migration problems involving intra- and inter-regional movements. Extensions of the framework to handle other problems of missing information such as problems of intra-zonal distance, and locational attraction appear promising but at

TABLE 9.3. *A comparison of computational efficiency for various distribution models applied to Merseyside*

Type of model	Equations solved by iteration	Number of iterations	Equations solved analytically	Total number of equations solved	Storage required in terms of matrices	Index of efficiency
Doubly-constrained in (9.7)–(9.9)	$(I_1+I_2)(J_1+J_2)$	5	—	4205	1682	0.8477
Speeded-up doubly-constrained in (9.10)–(9.28)	$I_1J_1+I_2J_2$	5	$I_1J_2+I_2J_1$	2861	1682	1.0030
Broadbent's hierarchical model in (9.29)–(9.37)	$(I_1+I_2)(J_1+J_2)$	5	—	4205	1126	0.9954
Short-cut hierarchical model in (9.44)–(9.58)	$I_1J_1+I_2J_2$ $2(I_1+J_2+J_1+J_2)$	5 3	$3(I_1+I_2+I_3+I_4)$	3047	1126	1.9980

every step, improvements in specification, accuracy and computational efficiency must be cautiously balanced against theoretical relevance, information loss and lower predictive power.

Another possibility is raised by the applications in this chapter. It might be possible to use such model inversions as crude design tools involving the design of urban structures such as transport networks. Given an idealised trip distribution, it is possible from an already calibrated model, to find the appropriate distances or travel times, thus giving some idea of the form of the relevant transport network. Some sort of iterative design process could be worked out in which these applications would fit. Future research could investigate all the leads mentioned here, but an important piece of work involves the use of these techniques in a wider framework of activity-allocation modelling, in similar fashion to the application of the hierarchical model to the Cheshire region (Barras *et al.*, 1971). In developing faster and more efficient urban models, such applications are essential; coupled with the fast calibration techniques described in Chapters 7 and 8, these techniques can make the difference between infeasibility and feasibility in a practical planning task as well as in research and development. Thus, the techniques described here appear to be of some import and in the quest to make urban modelling a less formidable and more practical proposition in planning practice, such techniques could provide the anchor for the design of relevant models.

The problems of model design addressed in this and the previous chapter are far from being resolved and the dilemmas inherent within these problems suggest that they have a perennial nature. As in the calibration problem, the techniques presented here are likely to be changed beyond recognition in the next decade as such problems begin to be tackled systematically by researchers. Yet there is another dimension of problems concerning substantive rather than methodological issues and in the rest of this book, such problems of disaggregating urban models and making them dynamic will be explored. In this quest, the techniques already described in this book continue to play an essential part.

10. *Disaggregated residential location models*

Any examination of the history of urban modelling during the last decade reveals a curiously strong distinction between theory and practice. There is a class of urban models briefly referred to in Chapter 1 which are based on essentially theoretical statements of urban phenomena and the development of such models has been largely governed by mathematical analysis of their causal structures. In contrast, the model designs already introduced in this book have been constrained by the need to construct operational tools capable of being used in forecasting, and the emphasis here has been on empirical rather than theoretical analysis. Yet the distinction between these two classes of model becomes even sharper when their formulations are contrasted. Theoretical models of urban structure tend to be deeply rooted in the micro-economic theory of both the consumer and the producer and usually their formulation is highly abstract and exceedingly elegant. As these models are stated using continuous mathematics for ease of analysis, the spatial dimension is difficult to handle comprehensively yet such models display a richness of detail which is lacking in their more operational counterparts.

Operational models of urban structure, on the other hand, are usually formulated in discrete mathematics which enables the spatial dimension to be easily incorporated. Although such models imply certain hypotheses concerning micro-economic behaviour, their previous exposition has shown that they tend to be constructed at a level of detail which inhibits empirical verification of such assumptions. Therefore, such models are frequently regarded as statistical descriptions of urban phenomena in which the focus lies on estimating or calibrating the model to fit the data. In the quest to design more relevant urban models, there is a clear need to integrate the best features of both approaches. In particular, this need has been recognised by researchers working with models of urban housing markets and residential location where the distinction between theory and practice is most marked. Already, there have been some notable attempts at building operational models of the housing market based on the classical economic theory of such markets. An early attempt by Kain (1962) using econometric methods is worthy of note and a more recent attempt by Wilson (1969*b*)

257

at linking micro-economic assumptions with spatial interaction and trip-making models has had some success (Cripps and Cater, 1972; Senior and Wilson, 1972). The difficulty of handling the spatial dimension using the classical approach is highlighted in a paper by Papageorgiou and Casetti (1971) who reveal the rather cumbersome nature of any solution procedure designed to generalise the classical model.

What then are required in the design of operational models of the housing market are forms incorporating both the flexible solution procedures characteristic of the operational econometric and spatial interaction models and the assumptions governing the micro-economic behaviour of consumers in these markets. In this chapter, a series of related models labelled collectively disaggregated residential location models, are presented and elaborated. In particular, the classical theory of the housing market provides the key set of assumptions for these models which all reflect, to a greater or lesser degree, the micro-economic theory of such markets. These models have been applied to two different spatial problems based on data from the Reading subregion, and the performance of these models is also explored and evaluated in a similar fashion to the previous modelling applications outlined in this book. However, before these models are stated, it is necessary to introduce and review the classical theory of demand in housing markets which forms the basic assumptions adopted in these residential models.

Classical approaches to modelling the housing market

The demand by individuals for residential space in particular locations in the urban system can be treated as part of the wider theory of consumer behaviour. As space at particular locations commands a price or rent, space can be handled in the same manner as other economic goods which are purchased by consumers. As a preliminary to a statement of the method by which space is allocated and purchased by the individual, it is worth while briefly reviewing the classical theory in general terms. Any consumer confronted by the purchase of a set of goods $x_1, x_2, ..., x_m$ will attempt to maximise the utility U associated with various combinations of these goods. Utility must, however, be maximised subject to the constraint that the consumer spends no more and no less than his income w: this is the so-called *budget constraint*. Formally, utility is expressed as a function of the set of goods x_i

$$U = U(x_1, x_2, ..., x_m), \tag{10.1}$$

and (10.1) is maximised subject to

$$w - \sum_{i=1}^{m} p_i x_i = 0, \tag{10.2}$$

where p_i is the price of good x_i. To maximise (10.1), a Lagrangian L is constructed as follows

$$L = U(x_1, x_2, ..., x_m) + \psi\left(w - \sum_{i=1}^{m} p_i x_i\right), \tag{10.3}$$

where ψ is the undetermined multiplier. Differentiating (10.3) with respect to each x_i and setting the resulting equations equal to zero, leads to the first-order conditions for a maximum

$$\frac{\partial L}{\partial x_i} = U_{x_i} - \psi p_i = 0, \quad i = 1, 2, ..., m, \tag{10.4}$$

where U_{x_i} is the partial differential of U with respect to x_i. By manipulating (10.4), the first-order conditions can be written as

$$\frac{U_{x_i}}{U_{x_j}} = \frac{p_i}{p_j}, \quad i \neq j. \tag{10.5}$$

Equation (10.5) can be interpreted as the well-known result that equilibrium occurs when the ratio of the marginal utilities is equal to the ratio of the prices. Differentiation of (10.3) with respect to ψ leads to the budget constraint in (10.2) being satisfied. The second-order conditions are too complex and lengthy to present here: interested readers are referred to the appropriate section in Henderson and Quandt (1958) for an elaboration of these conditions.

The utility-maximising model presented in (10.1)–(10.5) has formed the starting point for all serious contributions to the theory of the housing market during the last decade. Most authors have formulated their models for the case of a highly idealised city in which housing is distributed symmetrically around a pole which contains the source of employment. Thus the supply side of such models is implicit rather than explicit and equilibrium between the demand for and supply of space has usually been found by determining the margin of development in the city which in turn determines the rent profile in the fashion first introduced by Von Thunen (Hall, 1966). Perhaps the first researcher to develop explicitly the utility-maximising approach to residential location was Alonso (1964) although the approach is implicit in the work of Wingo (1961). The most complete statement, however, is to be found in the writings of Muth (1969) who examines several different utility functions, thus demonstrating the power of this type of analysis in explaining the structure of the housing market. Mills (1972) has also adopted this framework in formulating urban models which include not only housing but other economic markets.

There has recently been a spate of literature devoted to extending this line of research. Among the most important contributions, Beckmann's model (Beckmann, 1969) and its revision by Montesano (1972) are particularly neat statements of the problem which take account of variable incomes in the housing market. Solow (1972) has rigorously built the transportation component into the model, thus reflecting such phenomena as congestion, while Casetti and Papageorgiou (1971) have generalised the Alonso model and derived explicit density and rent profiles from their analysis. Yet in all of this work, the authors find it difficult, although not impossible, to generalise their conclusions to cities with many centres of employment and other imperfections in the real market.

As a demonstration of the pertinent conclusions from this stream of analysis, consider the following statement of utility which is a function of the amount of residential space demanded called q, and a composite of all other goods demanded called z. For an individual in the market, this function can be written as

$$U = z^a q^b, \tag{10.6}$$

where a and b are parameters reflecting the relative importance of z and q. Equation (10.6) must be maximised subject to the budget constraint which is now stated as

$$w - vz - s(r)q - cr = 0. \tag{10.7}$$

In (10.7), v is the price of the composite good z, $s(r)$ is the price or rent of the space q demanded at location r and c is the unit cost of transport. The location r refers to the distance between the location of employment and residence. Maximising (10.6) subject to the budget constraint in (10.7) yields two first-order conditions which are written as follows

$$\frac{aq}{bz} = \frac{v}{s(r)}, \tag{10.8}$$

$$\frac{ds(r)}{dr}q = -c. \tag{10.9}$$

Equation (10.8) has the same role as (10.5) explained previously whereas (10.9) implies that the marginal cost of purchasing space at r must be equal to the marginal savings in transport cost. Explicit demand functions for the quantity of space demanded at any location and the demand for the composite good can be found by expressing q and z in terms of each other in (10.8) and substituting the results into (10.7). Solving for q and z gives

$$q = \frac{\eta(w - cr)}{s(r)}, \tag{10.10}$$

$$z = \frac{(1 - \eta)(w - cr)}{v}, \tag{10.11}$$

where $\eta = b/(a+b)$. Equations (10.10) and (10.11) imply that the total expenditure on space and on the composite good z demanded at any location r are constant proportions of the budget. This completes the statement of the classical model and now it is necessary to examine the spatial implications of this approach.

Spatial analysis of the classical model

The main type of spatial analysis of the classical model concerns the form of the price or rent function $s(r)$ and the spatial demand and supply relationships in an idealised monocentric radially symmetric city bounded at radius R. Analysis of the form of the rent profile $s(r)$ has suggested that as the distance r increases in any direction away from the pole, which is usually taken to be the CBD, the function $s(r)$ is monotonic decreasing. A particularly cogent demonstration of this result is given by Solow (1972) but Mills (1972), Muth (1969), Beckmann (1969) and Casetti and Papageorgiou (1971) all present similar results. Of some interest is the possibility that this function might take a negative exponential form for this would imply that the density function q^{-1} would also be negative exponential. Muth (1969) has shown that this result could occur if the own-price elasticity of demand for space is -1. Indeed, Muth (1969) argues that empirical evidence justifies this value for the elasticity. To demonstrate this result more formally, the demand function in (10.10) can be written as

$$q = \frac{G}{s(r)}, \qquad (10.12)$$

where G is now constant. Substituting for q in (10.9) above gives a differential equation which can be solved for $s(r)$

$$\frac{ds(r)}{dr}\frac{G}{s(r)} = -c. \qquad (10.13)$$

Then solving (10.13), the rent function $s(r)$ is

$$s(r) = Q \exp(-\lambda r), \qquad (10.14)$$

where Q is the rent at the CBD or at the edge of the CBD when there is no housing at the centre. The parameter λ is defined as c/G. A similar analysis for q^{-1} shows that the density function is also negative exponential.

With regard to the demand and supply of space in the idealised city, most researchers have assumed that the supply of space is fixed, and that land is available for housing between $r = 1$ and $r = R$. If at distance r, a fraction $\Phi(r)$ of land is used for housing, then the population $P(r)$ contained within a small ring of width dr is given as

$$P(r) = 2\pi\Phi(r)\,rq^{-1}.$$

Note that this analysis can be easily generalised to other monocentric cities where a pie-slice of $2\pi - \theta$ radians is not available for development (Mills, 1972). Then the total urban population P must satisfy

$$P = \int_1^R P(r)\,dr = 2\pi \int_1^R \Phi(r)\,rq^{-1}\,dr. \qquad (10.15)$$

Generally, (10.15) must be solved iteratively together with (10.9)–(10.11). This approach to the supply side of the housing market is somewhat crude although it has been demonstrated by Muth (1969) that these conclusions are not substantially altered when housing producers are considered explicitly. In the ensuing analysis, the emphasis will be restricted to the demand side of this model and the supply of housing will be taken to be exogenously determined.

The limitations of the classical approach in providing explicit formulations for operational models can be clearly seen in the previous exposition. The assumptions of monocentricity, and uniformity of utility between individuals must be relaxed in designing realistic residential location models. Although there have been empirical tests concerning the form of the density and rent functions on strongly monocentric cities such as Chicago, the classical model can never be operational in the sense in which discrete urban models are operational. Indeed, it can be argued that the purpose of the classical approach is to provide insights into certain basic conditions which must be represented in any operational model if it is to be at all relevant. It is in this spirit that the following series of residential models is presented.

Elementary residential location models

Perhaps the most important spatial relationship suggested by the previous analysis involves the demand function relating the demand for space to its price and to the individual's budget. This relationship which is presented in (10.10) can be rewritten as

$$\overline{qs(r)} = \overline{\psi(w-cr)}, \qquad (10.16)$$

where the horizontal bars denote averaging. Equation (10.16) suggests that, over the whole population, the average price paid for housing is equal to the average expenditure available. Thus, the strong conditions implicit in (10.10) have been relaxed to take account of imperfections in the market caused by land taxes and subsidies, differences in tastes, planning controls, and other factors. Although it is certain that the average price paid for housing co-varies with income, within any income group both price paid and expenditure available are likely, to some extent, to vary independently of each other. Such a conclusion can be derived by considering variation in the parameters a and b in the utility function in (10.6). However, there are many other factors which affect the variance in price and expenditure and such imperfections in the market must be accounted for by any operational model.

To introduce residential location models which attempt to build on these micro-economic assumptions, it is worth while tracing the development of such models from the simplest case. There are two reasons for this: first, several of the models developed in this chapter and applied to the Reading subregion are based on these simpler forms, and second, the rationale for making these models more complex and hopefully more realistic can be presented as it has evolved. The basic residential location model which has been quite widely applied within the context of the more general activity allocation model is well known and has already been presented formally in (2.75)–(2.78). That model is formulated as an attraction-constrained model in Wilson's terms (Wilson, 1969a, 1969b), although in this chapter, all the models have the reverse form which is production-constrained. A simple two-parameter model based on (2.75)–(2.78) is applied here and is given as

$$T_{ij} = A_i E_i H_j^{\lambda_1} c_{ij}^{-\lambda_2}, \tag{10.17}$$

$$A_i = \frac{1}{\sum_j H_j^{\lambda_1} c_{ij}^{-\lambda_2}}. \tag{10.18}$$

All terms are as defined previously but note that H_j is now the amount of housing in zone j. This model is subject to the production constraint

$$\sum_j T_{ij} = E_i. \tag{10.19}$$

The appropriate maximum-likelihood equations used in the solution of (10.17) and (10.18) can be derived from the analysis in Chapter 7 and are stated as

$$\sum_i \sum_j T_{ij} \ln H_j = \sum_i \sum_j T_{ij}^* \ln H_j, \tag{10.20}$$

$$\sum_i \sum_j T_{ij} \ln c_{ij} = \sum_i \sum_j T_{ij}^* \ln c_{ij}. \tag{10.21}$$

Note also that T_{ij}^* are the observed, T_{ij} the predicted trip values.

In developing these models towards the classical theory presented above, disaggregation of variables into discrete classes is essential. As a first step, the model in (10.17) can be disaggregated into income groups. Then T_{ij}^w now represents the numbers of workers living in i and working in j and earning an income in the group w. Other variables can be appropriately notated using w as a superscript. One version of this disaggregated model can be written as

$$T_{ij}^w = A_i^w E_i^w (H_j^w)^{\lambda_1^w} \exp\left(-\lambda_2^w c_{ij}\right), \tag{10.22}$$

$$A_i^w = \frac{1}{\sum_j (H_j^w)^{\lambda_1^w} \exp\left(-\lambda_2^w c_{ij}\right)}. \tag{10.23}$$

This model is subject to the constraint

$$\sum_j T_{ij}^w = E_i^w, \tag{10.24}$$

and the appropriate maximum-likelihood equations can be written as

$$\sum_i \sum_j T_{ij}^w \ln H_j^w = \sum_i \sum_j T_{ij}^{w*} \ln H_j^w, \tag{10.25}$$

$$\sum_i \sum_j T_{ij}^w c_{ij} = \sum_i \sum_j T_{ij}^{w*} c_{ij}. \tag{10.26}$$

Note that the asterisk denotes an observed value and not summation as is used by some authors. A third model which has been developed replaces the two-parameter term in (10.22) by a modified gamma function, or more specifically by the function due to Tanner (1961). This model has the form

$$T_{ij}^w = A_i^w E_i^w c_{ij}^{-\lambda_1^w} \exp\left(-\lambda_2^w c_{ij}\right), \tag{10.27}$$

$$A_i^w = \frac{1}{\sum_j c_{ij}^{-\lambda_1^w} \exp\left(-\lambda_2^w c_{ij}\right)}. \tag{10.28}$$

Equations (10.27) and (10.28) are subject to (10.24) and the maximum-likelihood equations are given by (10.26) and a further equation

$$\sum_i \sum_j T_{ij}^w \ln c_{ij} = \sum_i \sum_j T_{ij}^{w*} \ln c_{ij}. \tag{10.29}$$

In the above description, the maximum-likelihood equations have not been scaled by the total trips in the appropriate system or subsystem but this could easily be achieved, if required.

Residential location models based on simple micro-economic assumptions

The introduction of a micro-economic component into residential location models based on spatial interaction was first suggested in a remarkable paper by Wilson (1969*b*) which is also reproduced in his book (Wilson, 1970*a*). Wilson proposed a production-attraction constrained model in which the focus was upon distributing persons earning income w to housing of type k, rather than allocating persons to housing in a particular zone. The relevant constraints are stated as

$$\sum_i \sum_w T_{ij}^{wk} = H_j^k, \tag{10.30}$$

and

$$\sum_j \sum_k T_{ij}^{wk} = E_i^w. \tag{10.31}$$

The distribution of trips according to the constraint equations (10.30) and (10.31), is also influenced by what Wilson calls the *budget term*; this is a term which suggests that the average person balances his budget with regard to the terms in (10.7) but that there are individuals who expend more or less than their available resources. The distribution around this average is assumed to be normal, and this logic is reflected through an additional constraint equation of the form

$$\sum_i \sum_j \sum_k T_{ij}^{wk} [s_j^k - \psi^w(w - c_{ij}^*)]^2 = \sigma_w^2. \tag{10.32}$$

s_j^k is the price of house-type k in j and c_{ij}^* is the amount expended on travel which can be quite different from c_{ij}. σ_w^2 is a variance term showing the total variation around the mean which in this case is a mean value of zero.

The appropriate model derived by Wilson using the method of entropy-maximising, can also be derived heuristically. The model is written as

$$T_{ij}^{wk} = A_i^w E_i^w B_j^k H_j^k \exp(-\lambda_2^w c_{ij}) \exp\{-\lambda_1^w [s_j^k - \psi^w(w - c_{ij}^*)]^2\}, \tag{10.33}$$

$$A_i^w = \frac{1}{\sum_j \sum_k B_j^k H_j^k \exp(-\lambda_2^w c_{ij}) \exp\{-\lambda_1^w [s_j^k - \psi^w(w - c_{ij}^*)]^2\}}, \tag{10.34}$$

$$B_j^k = \frac{1}{\sum_i \sum_w A_i^w E_i^w \exp(-\lambda_2^w c_{ij}) \exp\{-\lambda_1^w [s_j^k - \psi^w(w - c_{ij}^*)]^2\}}. \tag{10.35}$$

The appropriate maximum-likelihood equations for this model include (10.32) together with

$$\sum_i \sum_j \sum_k T_{ij}^{wk} c_{ij} = \sum_i \sum_j \sum_k T_{ij}^{wk*} c_{ij}. \tag{10.36}$$

In the rest of this section, the budget term is not written out explicitly but is rewritten according to the following substitution

$$y_{ij}^w = s_j^k - \psi^w(w - c_{ij}^*).$$

The budget term in the above equations then becomes

$$\exp\left[-\lambda_1^w(y_{ij}^w)^2\right] = \exp\left\{-\lambda_1^w[s_j^k - \psi^w(w - c_{ij}^*)]^2\right\}.$$

A version of Wilson's model which has been fitted to the Reading sub-region by the author and his colleagues (Cripps and Cater, 1972) is based upon a production-constrained residential location model. This model which is obtained by dropping constraint equation (10.30), can be written

$$T_{ij}^{wk} = A_i^w E_i^w H_j^k \exp\left(-\lambda_2^w c_{ij}\right) \exp\left[-\lambda_1^w(y_{ij}^w)^2\right], \qquad (10.37)$$

$$A_i^w = \frac{1}{\sum_j \sum_k H_j^k \exp\left(-\lambda_2^w c_{ij}\right) \exp\left[-\lambda_1^w(y_{ij}^w)^2\right]}. \qquad (10.38)$$

The maximum-likelihood equations are the same as those mentioned above but the model not only distributes persons between incomes and house types but also locates them in space.

A further version of the model with three parameters, that is an additional parameter on house type H_j^k, has been fitted. This model is a little more consistent than that in (10.37) and (10.38) and can be written as

$$T_{ij}^{wk} = A_i^w E_i^w (H_j^k)^{\lambda_3^w} \exp\left(-\lambda_2^w c_{ij}\right) \exp\left[-\lambda_1^w(y_{ij}^w)^2\right], \qquad (10.39)$$

$$A_i^w = \frac{1}{\sum_j \sum_k (H_j^k)^{\lambda_3^w} \exp\left(-\lambda_2^w c_{ij}\right) \exp\left[-\lambda_1^w(y_{ij}^w)^2\right]}. \qquad (10.40)$$

An additional maximum-likelihood equation related to λ_3^w is now required and this is given by

$$\sum_i \sum_j \sum_k T_{ij}^{wk} \ln H_j^k = \sum_i \sum_j \sum_k T_{ij}^{wk*} \ln H_j^k. \qquad (10.41)$$

Although these models take account of budget considerations, there are immense difficulties in finding an interpretation for λ_1^w, as will be discussed a little later, and to counter such problems, another model based on a somewhat more direct statistical logic has been applied. This model can best be discussed in probabilistic terms and the following section is concerned with the statement of this model.

A probabilistic residential location model

An analysis of the budget balance equation in (10.32) is somewhat difficult if an explicit statistical comparison with conventional variance functions is sought. It appears that σ_w^2 is a type of co-variance, rather than a simple variance statistic, measuring the amount of co-variation between the distribution of rents or prices of housing and the actual expenditure distribution on housing from individual budget allocations. The confusion over interpreting the parameter λ_1^w alluded to above is probably caused by this difference from conventional usage. Therefore a more direct statistical model accounting for both variance and co-variance in these two distributions and based upon the standard bivariate normal distribution has been proposed. It is important to note that this model is no more 'correct' than Wilson's model although the parameters are easier to interpret, and in the event, the model is considerably easier to calibrate.

To introduce this model, a probability p_{ij}^{wk} is defined which gives the proportion of persons working in i and living in a house type k at j for a particular income group w. This probability is defined from

$$p_{ij}^{wk} = \frac{T_{ij}^{wk}}{\sum_i \sum_j \sum_k T_{ij}^{wk}}.$$

These probabilities sum to 1 for each income group w and the model estimating their value is derived according to the following constraint equations reflecting variation within the housing market. Two constraints relating to the variance in the rent-price distribution $\{s_j^k\}$ and the housing expenditure distribution $\{\psi^w(w-c_{ij}^*)\}$ are first presented. The appropriate constraint equations can be stated

$$\sum_i \sum_j \sum_k p_{ij}^{wk}(s_j^k - \mu_1)^2 = \sigma_{w_1}^2, \qquad (10.42)$$

$$\sum_i \sum_j \sum_k p_{ij}^{wk}[\psi^w(w-c_{ij}^*)-\mu_2]^2 = \sigma_{w_2}^2. \qquad (10.43)$$

The constants μ_1 and μ_2 in (10.42) and (10.43) respectively refer to the relevant means of these two distributions. The co-variation can now be written as

$$\sum_i \sum_j \sum_k p_{ij}^{wk}(s_j^k - \mu_1)[\psi^w(w-c_{ij}^*)-\mu_2] = \sigma_w^2. \qquad (10.44)$$

To simplify the following presentation, the price and expenditure distributions are redefined as

$$x_j^k = s_j^k - \mu_1,$$

and

$$y_{ij}^w = \psi(w-c_{ij}^*) - \mu_2.$$

The probability model consistent with (10.42)–(10.44) can now be presented.

The model has three parameters, one relating to each of the three constraint equations and is based on the following standard form

$$p_{ij}^{wk} = \frac{\exp\left[-\lambda_1^w(x_j^k)^2 - \lambda_2^w(y_{ij}^w)^2 - \lambda_3^w(x_j^k)(y_{ij}^w)\right]}{\sum_i \sum_j \sum_k \exp\left[-\lambda_1^w(x_j^k)^2 - \lambda_2^w(y_{ij}^w)^2 - \lambda_3^w(x_j^k)(y_{ij}^w)\right]}. \qquad (10.45)$$

Equation (10.45) is the discrete form of the bivariate normal distribution (Mood and Graybill, 1963) based on an assumption that the partitioning of the continuous density is into equal sized intervals or units. If this is the case, then a good first approximation to the parameters of the model in (10.45) can be taken from

$$\lambda_1^w = \frac{1}{2(1-\rho^2)\,\sigma_{w_1}^2},$$

$$\lambda_2^w = \frac{1}{2(1-\rho^2)\,\sigma_{w_2}^2},$$

and

$$\lambda_3^w = -\frac{\rho}{(1-\rho^2)\,\sigma_{w_1}\sigma_{w_2}}.$$

ρ is the correlation coefficient which can be estimated using bivariate regression analysis and this represents the most appealing feature of the model for it means that the iterative and often time-consuming calibration procedures characteristic of intrinsically non-linear urban models can be avoided. An interpretation for the parameters can also be made at this stage: λ_1^w and λ_2^w help to scale the probabilities so that the expected means and variances are reproduced by the model. Clearly, the values of λ_1^w and λ_2^w will be partly related to the values of $\sigma_{w_1}^2$ and $\sigma_{w_2}^2$. The parameter λ_3^w controls the co-variation between prices and expenditures and the range of ρ is between -1 and $+1$. If there is zero correlation, then the co-variance must also be zero and the bivariate model then becomes the product of two univariate densities. It is difficult to argue what the value of ρ is likely to be on *a priori* grounds for this would anticipate the degree of randomness inherent in any particular housing market. However, on intuitive grounds, ρ is likely to be positive for this would imply that location had a measurable effect on the purchase price of housing.

The means μ_1 and μ_2 can also be set equal to one another according to the budget balance argument contained in (10.16). Then rewriting (10.16) using the notation of this section gives

$$\sum_i\sum_j\sum_k p_{ij}^{wk}s_j^k = \psi(w-\sum_i\sum_j\sum_k p_{ij}^{wk}c_{ij}^*). \tag{10.46}$$

From (10.46), ψ, the proportion of the budget available for housing after transport costs have been deducted, is calculated from

$$\psi = \frac{\sum_i\sum_j\sum_k p_{ij}^{wk}s_j^k}{w-\sum_i\sum_j\sum_k p_{ij}^{wk}c_{ij}^*} = \frac{\sum_i\sum_j\sum_k p_{ij}^{wk}s_j^k}{\sum_i\sum_j\sum_k p_{ij}^{wk}s_j^k+vz}. \tag{10.47}$$

The relationship between the model in (10.45) and the models derived from Wilson's work given in (10.30)–(10.41) can be related and compared formally; furthermore, this model can be derived using the entropy-maximising method (Tribus, 1969) and these extensions are carried out in a related paper by the author (Batty, 1972c) in which a slightly different interpretation and presentation of some of the material in this chapter is given.

The final step in outlining this model is to embed it in the spatial inter-action framework used in making it operational. Two versions of the model both using the probability distribution $\{p_{ij}^{wk}\}$ have been designed and these are stated below. The first model is unconstrained in the sense defined by Cordey-Hayes and Wilson (1971) and described in Chapter 2. For each income group w, the total numbers of workers E^w are allocated to both workplace and residence using the following equation

$$T_{ij}^{wk} = E^w p_{ij}^{wk}. \tag{10.48}$$

Note here that the workers in each income group E^w are calculated by summing (10.31) over i

$$E^w = \sum_i E_i^w = \sum_i \sum_j \sum_k T_{ij}^{wk}. \tag{10.49}$$

The total number of workers purchasing house type k in zone j is

$$P_j^k = \sum_i T_{ij}^{wk} = E^w \sum_i p_{ij}^{wk}, \tag{10.50}$$

and the total number buying all types of housing at j is

$$P_j = \sum_i \sum_k T_{ij}^{wk} = E^w \sum_i \sum_k p_{ij}^{wk}. \tag{10.51}$$

The performance of this probability model can be explicitly compared with the real situation by calibrating the parameters using (10.48)–(10.51) or by comparing predicted to observed probabilities. The second variant of the model is production-constrained and each set of parameters λ_1^w, λ_2^w and λ_3^w relates to the particular production zone i. In other words

$$\sum_i \sum_k p_{ij}^{wk} = 1.$$

The model has a similar form to (10.48)

$$T_{ij}^{wk} = E_i^w p_{ij}^{wk}, \tag{10.52}$$

where it is clear that (10.52) satisfies the production constraint which is verified by summing (10.52) over i and k

$$\sum_i \sum_k T_{ij}^{wk} = E_i^w. \tag{10.53}$$

Several other variants of this probability model could easily be designed according to various accounting systems or by adding explanatory variables measuring locational cost or benefit. In the next section, however, the two models outlined here together with the models described in previous sections will be calibrated to the Reading subregion.

Application to an urban housing market

The probability model has been applied to a subregion centred on the town of Reading which is located in the outer fringe of the London region. In terms of population and employment, the area has grown quickly in the last two decades and the population of the area had reached 260 000 by 1966. Average incomes are among the highest of any urban area in Britain, and the subregion has all the outward signs of economic prosperity such as low, almost negligible unemployment, growth in the so-called 'boom' industries such as electronics and scientific research, extreme pressure on land for housing and industry, and fast inflation in land and house prices. The model has been fitted using data collected for 1966, and as a preliminary to discussing data sources, it is worth while examining certain requirements for disaggregating the spatial system, income distribution and house types into various discrete groups.

There are many requirements relevant to zoning the spatial system but perhaps the most fundamental relates to the arguments presented in Chapter 8 concerning the number of zones necessary to approximate the various spatial distributions to a sufficient level of accuracy. Work by Broadbent (1969 a, 1969 b), already described, and by Angel and Hyman (1971) suggests that, for any area with the dimensions of this subregion, the desirable number far exceeds this possible maximum number of zones available from the data base. Two zoning systems have been defined, the first a prototype based upon a division of the subregion into 23 zones, the second a more complete system based on 64 zones. The use of these two zoning systems reflects the order in which the models presented here were developed, and their geometry is shown in Figure 10.1. Similar arguments apply to the partitioning of the income and house-type distributions, but from practical considerations, only three income groups and five house-types can be defined.

Another consideration involves the size of the various zones or class intervals. The mathematical form of the model depends upon the assumption that each of the class intervals are equal. This is not often the case for boundaries and partitions have to be based on ease of definition, and therefore, if such intervals are of variable size, the model must in some way account for this. By weighting the probability equation by class interval

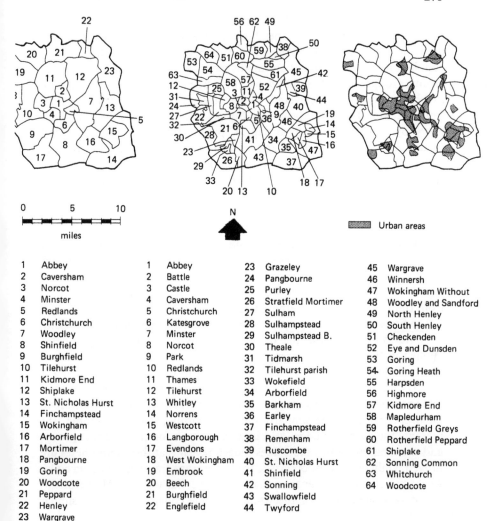

Fig. 10.1. The 23 and 64 zone systems in the Reading subregion.

1	Abbey	1	Abbey
2	Caversham	2	Battle
3	Norcot	3	Castle
4	Minster	4	Caversham
5	Redlands	5	Christchurch
6	Christchurch	6	Katesgrove
7	Woodley	7	Minster
8	Shinfield	8	Norcot
9	Burghfield	9	Park
10	Tilehurst	10	Redlands
11	Kidmore End	11	Thames
12	Shiplake	12	Tilehurst
13	St. Nicholas Hurst	13	Whitley
14	Finchampstead	14	Norrens
15	Wokingham	15	Westcott
16	Arborfield	16	Langborough
17	Mortimer	17	Evendons
18	Pangbourne	18	West Wokingham
19	Goring	19	Embrook
20	Woodcote	20	Beech
21	Peppard	21	Burghfield
22	Henley	22	Englefield
23	Wargrave		

23	Grazeley	45	Wargrave
24	Pangbourne	46	Winnersh
25	Purley	47	Wokingham Without
26	Stratfield Mortimer	48	Woodley and Sandford
27	Sulham	49	North Henley
28	Sulhampstead	50	South Henley
29	Sulhampstead B.	51	Checkenden
30	Theale	52	Eye and Dunsden
31	Tidmarsh	53	Goring
32	Tilehurst parish	54	Goring Heath
33	Wokefield	55	Harpsden
34	Arborfield	56	Highmore
35	Barkham	57	Kidmore End
36	Earley	58	Mapledurham
37	Finchampstead	59	Rotherfield Greys
38	Remenham	60	Rotherfield Peppard
39	Ruscombe	61	Shiplake
40	St. Nicholas Hurst	62	Sonning Common
41	Shinfield	63	Whitchurch
42	Sonning	64	Woodcote
43	Swallowfield		
44	Twyford		

size such problems can be handled, although in the work presented here, this has not yet been done (Batty, 1972*b*). The parameter estimates vary if the model is so weighted, and therefore the results reported here can only be regarded as first approximations, although such approximations are likely to be good.

The data base for this study has been compiled from a variety of sources but mainly from a special analysis of the 1966 Census of Population. As it is not the central purpose of this chapter to discuss the data base in detail, the reader is referred to a paper by Cripps and Cater (1972) where this problem is exhaustively discussed and elaborated. Classification of the population into professional and managerial, white collar and blue collar income groups is based on the 1966 Census whereas information pertaining to the composition of the average budget in each of these groups was taken from the 1966 Family Expenditure Survey. Housing types are classified, firstly by tenure into owner-occupied, private rented and public rented groups, and secondly the owner-occupied group is subdivided into large and small and the private rented group into poor and good condition. This classification is not continuous with regard to the size of house-type but is based on the present structure of recognisable housing-types in the Reading subregion. The rationale for this classification is given by Cripps and Cater (1972). The prices which match these house-types have been compiled from a special survey of estate agents in the subregion, and at this point, it is worth emphasising the doubtful quality of this data and the severe difficulties in discounting back and checking the house-price data for internal consistency. Rent data in the public sector was obtained from the Local Housing Authority records.

The first stage in making operational any model design involves checking the data to ascertain whether or not the many commonsense hypotheses implied in the model are essentially correct. For example, in this model, one hypothesis suggests that average income in the professional group is greater than that in the white collar group which in turn is greater than that in the blue collar group; also that the different items of expenditure in the average budgets are similarly ranked according to income. Table 10.1 presents the average budget and its composition for each income group, and examination of this table does indeed reveal that these hypotheses are proved. Only one exception exists, for the average travel cost of blue collar workers is slightly greater than that of white collar workers. However this is not very significant for the white and blue collar incomes are similar in size.

With regard to the average expenditure on each type of house by different income groups, there is an implicit hypothesis that for any given type of house, professional workers spend more than white collar workers who in turn spend more than blue collar workers. Such differences are accounted for by location, by variations in taste and most of all, by income. There is also an implicit ranking in house prices from owner-occupied large to small to private rented good to poor public rented. Table 10.2 gives average expenditures on each type of housing for each income group and all the hypotheses are proved apart from a deviation in ranking in the public sector. Another interesting feature from the data

TABLE 10.1. *Composition of average budgets according to expenditures*

In £ sterling	Professional and managerial	White collar	Blue collar
Weekly wage	38.6600	27.5900	25.5900
Mean housing expenditure	4.1814	3.1894	2.3224·
Mean travel cost	0.6472	0.5604	0.6174
Mean expenditure on the composite good	33.8313	23.8400	22.6501
Budget ratio ψ	0.1100	0.1180	0.0930
Ratio $(1-\psi)$	0.8900	0.8820	0.9070

concerns the relative similarity between the white and blue collar groups in economic terms. This similarity supports the thesis that real differences between these two groups are social rather than economic although a significant difference between them does exist in terms of average housing expenditure.

TABLE 10.2. *Average housing expenditures*

In £ sterling	Professional and managerial	White collar	Blue collar
Owner-occupied: large	5.2856	4.7483	3.5887
Owner-occupied: small	3.6700	3.3789	2.6763
Private rented: good condition	3.5750	3.4464	2.6534
Private rented: poor condition	1.9201	1.8415	1.4358
Public rented	0.9182	0.9260	0.7287

The joint distribution of prices $\{x_j^k\}$ and expenditures $\{y_{ij}^w\}$ for each income group are diagrammed as three-dimensional solids in Figure 10.2. This mnemonic provides an intuitive grasp of the nature of the bivariate probability model, for in essence, the task in constructing that model is to find parameters which fit (10.48) or its variant to the surfaces contained in Figure 10.2. To analyse the detailed shape of these solids, it is necessary to present them as probability surfaces. A mapping of the solids onto the horizontal plane can be summarised using contours of equal probability.

These surfaces are presented in Figure 10.3 for each income group, and from Figure 10.3, it is immediately apparent that the surfaces are negatively skewed on the y_{ij}^w-axes. The calculation of correlation between the x_i^k's and y_{ij}^w's is left until a later section but from Figure 10.3, the correlation appears to be low. However, the correlation of expenditure with prices over the three income groups is positive and significant. This correlation has been computed as 0.3809 ($r^2 = 0.1451$) which, although low, supports the hypothesis that expenditure on housing co-varies with income. Furthermore, this result is of similar magnitude to the one derived by Anthony (1970) in association with the econometric model of residential location designed by Apps (1970).

Calibration of intrinsically non-linear residential models

The first five residential location models presented in this chapter have been fitted to the 23 zone Reading subregion using calibration methods based on the Newton–Raphson and Simplex techniques outlined in Chapter 7. The two-parameter model described in (10.17) and (10.18) has been calibrated using the Newton–Raphson method to solve the maximum-likelihood equations in (10.20) and (10.21) from starting points of

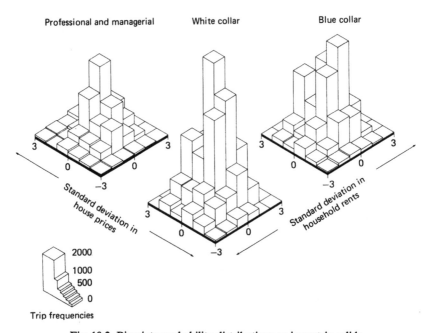

Fig. 10.2. Bivariate probability distributions as isometric solids.

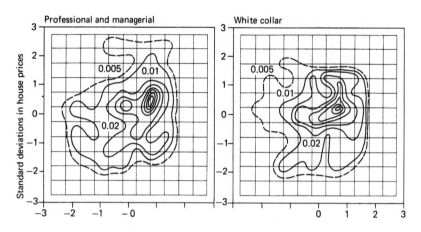

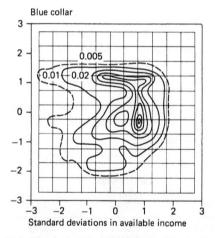

Fig. 10.3. Bivariate probability distributions in the plane.

λ_1, $\lambda_2 = 0.0$. Convergence of the method is fast and the results are presented in Table 10.3. Of particular interest in all the five models described in this section is the fact that their response surfaces measuring the goodness of fit of the trip distributions using the r^2 statistic are fairly classic in form, in that they are concave-down and unimodal. This result is illustrated for the simple model in (10.17) and (10.18) in Figure 10.4, where it is clear that the maximum r^2 is close to the parameters given by solving the maximum-likelihood equations.

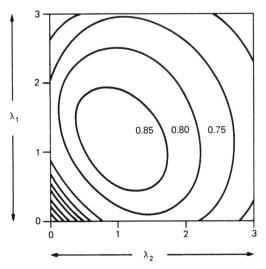

Fig. 10.4. Response surface for the simple residential model
based on the coefficient of determination r^2.

TABLE 10.3. *Convergence of an elementary residential model
using the Newton–Raphson method*

Iterations or runs of model	Start from $\lambda_1 = 0.0$, $\lambda_2 = 0.0$			
	λ_1	Normalised value of (10.20)	λ_2	Normalised value of (10.21)
3	0.2225	0.0631	2.2789	0.3103
6	0.7719	0.0593	1.1954	0.1484
9	0.5747	0.0008	1.5178	0.0011
12	0.5760	0.0000	1.5155	0.0000

The two models disaggregated by income group w but excluding the budget term have also been calibrated using the Newton–Raphson method. The model in (10.22) and (10.23) with maximum-likelihood equations (10.25) and (10.26) and the model based on Tanner's function in (10.27) and (10.28) with maximum-likelihood equations (10.26) and (10.29), converged quickly to their best parameter values. The first of these models is fairly insensitive to starting values and Table 10.4 presents the appropriate

TABLE 10.4. *Calibration of residential location model based on the function* $(H_j^k)^{\lambda_1^w} \exp{(-\lambda_2^w c_{ij})}$

Professional group (w = 1): iterations or runs	λ_2^1	Normalised value of (10.26)	λ_1^1	Normalised value of (10.25)
		Start from $\lambda_1^1, \lambda_2^1 = 0.0000$		
3	0.0000	7.3604	0.0000	0.6363
6	1.1463	0.7449	0.3799	0.1138
9	0.1644	0.0617	0.5698	0.0097
12	0.1663	0.0006	0.5899	0.0000
13	0.1663	0.0000	0.5899	0.0000

White collar group (w = 2): iterations or runs	λ_2^2	Normalised value of (10.26)	λ_1^2	Normalised value of (10.25)
		Start from $\lambda_1^2, \lambda_2^2 = 0.0000$		
3	0.0000	8.2339	0.0000	0.8178
6	0.1800	0.0410	0.2327	0.1580
9	0.2116	0.1340	0.4216	0.0229
12	0.2170	0.0012	0.4626	0.0005
13	0.2170	0.0000	0.4637	0.0000

Blue collar group (w = 3): iterations or runs	λ_2^3	Normalised value of (10.26)	λ_1^3	Normalised value of (10.25)
		Start from $\lambda_1^3, \lambda_2^3 = 0.0000$		
3	0.0000	8.2405	0.0000	0.6395
6	0.1594	1.0961	0.3437	0.1357
9	0.1909	0.1316	0.5427	0.0193
12	0.1960	0.0004	0.5797	0.0003
13	0.1960	0.0000	0.5797	0.0000

results for each income group w. In the case of the model based on Tanner's function, the procedure only converged from starting points where $\lambda_1^w = 1.0$ and $\lambda_2^w = 0.1$. From all other points such as zero, the procedure diverged, thus implying that the global optimum exists in a long narrow valley in the response surface which can only be located from good first approximations. The optimum was located in this case by starting the procedure from several different positions and stopping the process if and when it began to diverge. These results are presented in Table 10.5.

TABLE 10.5. *Calibration of a residential location model based on Tanner's function*

Professional group ($w = 1$): iterations or runs	Start from $\lambda_1^1 = 1.0$, $\lambda_2^1 = 0.1$			
	λ_2^1	Normalised value of (10.26)	λ_1^1	Normalised value of (10.29)
3	0.1000	2.5644	1.0000	0.3449
6	0.0325	0.3230	1.3390	0.0684
9	0.0752	0.0005	0.9079	0.0003
12	0.0747	0.0000	0.9120	0.0000
13	0.0747	0.0000	0.9120	0.0000

White collar group ($w = 2$): iterations or runs	Start from $\lambda_1^2 = 1.0$, $\lambda_2^2 = 0.1$			
	λ_2^2	Normalised value of (10.26)	λ_1^2	Normalised value of (10.29)
3	0.1000	3.7004	1.0000	0.4682
6	0.0187	0.1469	0.8067	0.0602
9	0.1290	0.0615	0.8521	0.0102
12	0.1254	0.0002	0.9012	0.0001
13	0.1254	0.0000	0.9013	0.0000

Blue collar group ($w = 3$): iterations or runs	Start from $\lambda_1^3 = 1.0$, $\lambda_2^3 = 0.1$			
	λ_2^3	Normalised value of (10.26)	λ_1^3	Normalised value of (10.29)
3	0.1000	3.3372	1.0000	0.4059
6	0.0610	0.0904	1.2711	0.0457
9	0.1384	0.0164	0.6085	0.0031
12	0.1400	0.0001	0.6037	0.0000
13	0.1400	0.0000	0.6037	0.0000

The model developed by Cripps and Cater (1972) given in (10.37) and (10.38) was also calibrated using the Newton–Raphson method. The results are presented in Table 10.6 in which several major points of interpretation emerge: convergence is extremely fast from starting values where λ_1^w and λ_2^w are zero and only nine runs of each of the submodels, are needed to find the best values of λ_1^w and λ_2^w to four decimal places. Perhaps the most important finding from the analysis in Table 10.6 concerns the sign of the parameters.

TABLE 10.6. *Calibration of the Cripps–Cater version of*
Wilson's residential location model

Professional group ($w = 1$): iterations or runs	Start from $\lambda_1^1, \lambda_2^1 = 0.0000$			
	λ_2^1	Normalised value of (10.36)	λ_1^1	Normalised value of (10.32)
3	0.0000	4.6400	0.0000	2.4699
6	0.1414	0.4256	−0.0486	2.2479
9	0.1562	0.0167	−0.0338	0.1675
12	0.1568	0.0020	−0.0324	0.0052
13	0.1568	0.0000	−0.0324	0.0002

White collar group ($w = 2$): iterations or runs	Start from $\lambda_1^2, \lambda_2^2 = 0.0000$			
	λ_2^2	Normalised value of (10.36)	λ_1^2	Normalised value of (10.32)
3	0.0000	5.3748	0.0000	0.7430
6	0.1624	0.8827	−0.0046	0.5750
9	0.2045	0.0729	−0.0009	0.0165
12	0.2087	0.0001	−0.0008	0.0009
13	0.2087	0.0000	−0.0008	0.0000

Blue collar group ($w = 3$): iterations or runs	Start from $\lambda_1^3, \lambda_2^3 = 0.0000$			
	λ_2^3	Normalised value of (10.36)	λ_1^3	Normalised value of (10.32)
3	0.0000	0.6202	0.0000	2.9673
6	0.1564	0.8518	0.0066	0.8257
9	0.1925	0.0547	0.0110	0.0192
12	0.1952	0.0003	0.0111	0.0013
13	0.1952	0.0000	0.0111	0.0000

The parameter λ_2^w is positive and the final values are of similar magnitude to the values found in other models of spatial interaction using negative exponential functions of travel cost, for example see Table 6.1. In the case of λ_1^w, however, the sign is the reverse to that hypothesised for professional and white collar wage groups, and in all three cases the value of λ_1^w is near to zero. The budget term was introduced by Wilson (1969b) to ensure that most persons allocated by the model, purchased house-types which they could afford. In two of the submodels here, the negative value of λ_1^w implies that persons are more likely to purchase housing as the difference between available income for housing and house price increases. Such a finding is clearly untenable but little significance can be attached to these results for, in all cases, the parameters are close to zero. In this particular case, the zoning system is probably too coarse to detect the variation in house price requisite to the model formulation in (10.37) and (10.38), and more realistic results would probably be obtained using a finer zoning system. In fact, this was one of the reasons for developing the probability model given in (10.45) which is fitted to the 64 zone version of the subregion in the next section.

The final model to have been fitted to the 23 zone Reading subregion is based on the three-parameter model in (10.39) and (10.40). This model has not been calibrated using the Newton–Raphson method but the Simplex method has been applied. The results are shown diagrammatically in Figures 10.5–10.7 for each income group w. In these diagrams, the contours of equal response are difficult to construct, but the response-solid could be visualised as a doughnut in which the search is attempting to locate its centre. The convergence in this case is quite fast and demonstrates the flexibility of such unconstrained optimisation techniques. A similar presentation in terms of three-dimensional response contours is given in a paper by Cesario (1973).

Calibration and empirical verification of the probability models

In this section, the results of fitting the two probability models given in (10.48) and (10.52) will be presented and discussed, and a simple test of each model's performance as a spatial interaction model will be outlined. The model given in (10.48) will be referred to as the 64 zone model in which the parameters are estimated for the total system of zones, whereas the model given in (10.52) is called the origin zone model for the parameters are estimated for each origin zone in the system. In each of these cases, the parameters λ_1^w, λ_2^w and λ_3^w are taken from parameter estimates for the continuous bivariate normal distribution. The variances and correlation associated with these parameters are calculated using standard methods of statistical analysis for grouped data.

The parameters of the 64 zone model are shown in Table 10.7 and it is immediately clear from the values presented in this table that the magnitude of each parameter is affected by the magnitude of its associated variance statistic. Perhaps the most interesting result displayed here, however, involves the small negative correlations which exist between house prices and expenditures in each income group. This is inconsistent with the hypothesis advanced earlier that these correlations should be positive but

Professional and managerial population

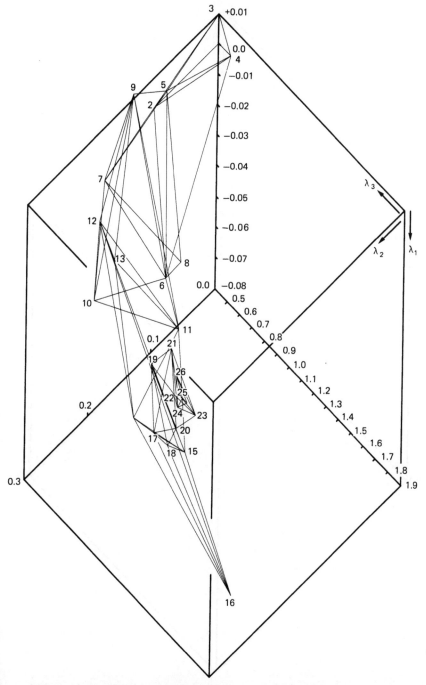

Fig. 10.5. Calibration of 3-parameter professional–managerial model by the
Simplex method.

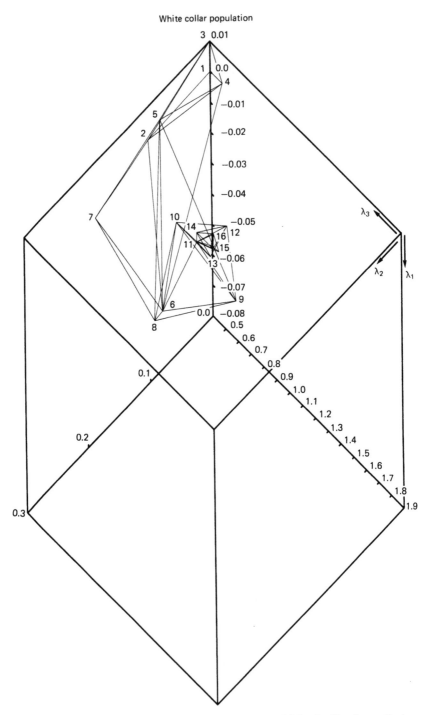

Fig. 10.6. Calibration of 3-parameter white collar model by the Simplex method.

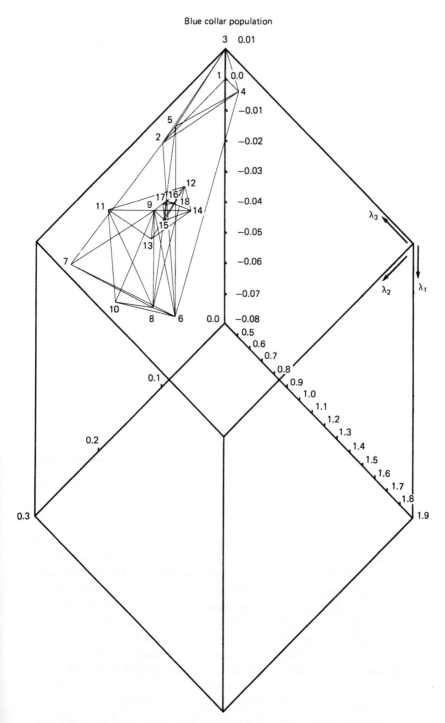

Fig. 10.7. Calibration of 3-parameter blue collar model by the Simplex method.

such anomalies are obviously accounted for by factors which are not included in the classical theory. In fact, this point illustrates the essential difference between the classical approach and the approach adopted here. Although such anomalies cannot be explained by the classical model, this does not discount the value of this model for its purpose is to lay bare certain fundamentals. The probability model, on the other hand, assumes such fundamentals but has enough flexibility to account for other factors which might appear to be random. In one sense, these low correlations reflect the performance of the classical model whereas such statistics are accepted by the probability model as independent variables.

TABLE 10.7. *Parameter estimates for the 64 zone probability model*

	Professional and managerial ($w = 1$)	White collar ($w = 2$)	Blue collar ($w = 3$)
Variance in prices	2.5428	2.7273	1 6025
Parameter λ_1^w	0.2029	0.1845	0.3126
Variance in expenditures	0.0031	0.0026	0.0019
Parameter λ_2^w	162.5684	189.7340	259.7956
Co-variance	−0.0158	−0.0069	−0.0025
Parameter λ_3^w	2.0329	0.9704	0.8357
Correlation ρ	−0.1769	−0.0819	−0.0463

A similar set of parameters has been estimated for each zone of the origin zone model given in (10.52). These parameters vary around the values presented in Table 10.7 for the 64 zone model and the distribution of these values appears to be normal. These distributions are presented in Figure 10.8 for each parameter and each income group. An explicit set of parameter values is shown in Table 10.8 for origin zone 1 – Central Reading, and a comparison with Table 10.7 reveals a strong similarity in the magnitude of these values. The actual performance of these models has not yet been discussed, and as one of the purposes of this probability model is to predict locations by means of interaction, it is necessary to compare the trips predicted by the model with the trips observed.

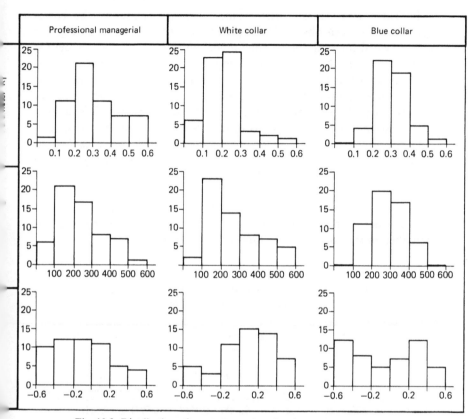

Fig. 10.8. Distribution of parameter values for the origin zone model.

TABLE 10.8. *Parameter estimates for origin zone 1 –*
Central Reading

	Professional and managerial (w = 1)	White collar (w = 2)	Blue collar (w = 3)
Variance in prices	2.7392	2.6424	1.5227
Parameter λ_1^w	0.2106	0.2014	0.3319
Variance in expenditures	0.0017	0.0020	0.0011
Parameter λ_2^w	333.4630	263.6402	429.4071
Co-variance	−0.0251	−0.0179	−0.0044
Parameter λ_3^w	6.1237	3.5886	2.4875
Correlation ρ	−0.3653	−0.2462	−0.1041

In Table 10.9, various performance statistics measuring the correspondence between observed and predicted trips in each income group are presented for both the 64 zone model and the origin zone model for origin zone 1. In the case of the 64 zone model, the performance is relatively poor, whereas when the origin constraint is introduced, as in the case of the origin zone model, the performance is dramatically improved. This is expected for the origin zone model utilises much more information about existing locational patterns in the system than the 64 zone model. The performance of the origin zone model is made more explicit in Figure 10.9 where the flows from zone 1 are mapped, and in Figure 10.10 where these same flows are graphed against travel cost. At this stage, such models are ready for forecasting if they are judged to perform well enough. It is useful, however, to examine the way in which these models could fit into a wider framework of activity allocation such as the one which is described in the concluding section to this chapter.

TABLE 10.9. *Performance of the 64 zone and origin zone probability models*

	64 zone model			Origin zone model‡		
	Professional and managerial	White collar	Blue collar	Professional and managerial	White collar	Blue collar
Correlation coefficient *r* for trips	0.2136	0.2251	0.2557	0.7971	0.8649	0.8055
Coefficient of determination *r*² for trips	0.0456	0.0506	0.0653	0.6353	0.7480	0.6489
Slope *b* of regression line‡	0.0430	0.0458	0.0592	0.5724	0.7241	0.5938
Intercept *a* of regression line‡	3.7711	10.2806	6.8708	26.1241	72.4306	42.3899

† The statistics produced for the origin zone model are for origin zone 1.
‡ The slope *b* and intercept *a* are from the regression of predicted on observed trips $T_{ij}^{wk} = a + bT_{ij}^{wk*}$.

A necessary comment on the efficacy of this model must be made here for it is clear that many variations in the model design could be made. In some senses, this reflects the power of the approach. For example, the probability distributions may not approximate the bivariate normal, and if this is so, then clearly other probability models based on perhaps the

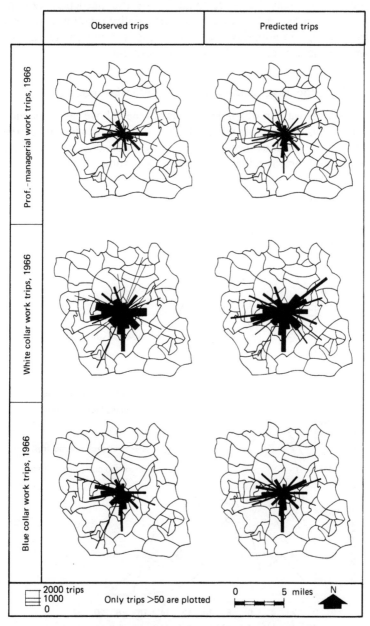

Fig. 10.9. Observed and predicted flows from origin zone 1 –
Central Reading.

bivariate gamma may be more suitable. In the particular examples discussed here, some such change in the probability function is probably required although in adopting such changes, it is important to base new functions on theoretical as well as empirical criteria.

An activity allocation framework for residential models

There are several ways in which the models outlined above can be extended, and as a conclusion, some of the most promising extensions will be briefly mentioned. An ambitious theoretical, possibly intractable but nevertheless important development might consist of a derivation of the budget term models directly from utility theory. Such a derivation might depend upon establishing some explicit relationship between utility-maximising and

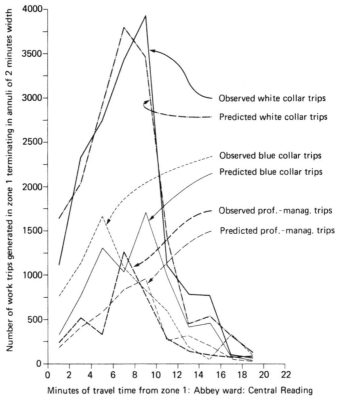

Fig. 10.10. Graphical distribution of flows from origin zone 1 – Central Reading.

entropy-maximising, although in view of recent advances in this area, it is possible that the approach of Golob and Beckmann (1971) could now be used to derive a similar model. It is a fairly straightforward matter to include location explicitly in the utility function but this has not been pursued here as such functions tend, at the present time, to be arbitrarily conceived. A second extension involving a much more straightforward application, might be an attempt to model the distribution of house prices which would then be input to the budget term models. The feasibility of this type of modelling would largely depend upon the quality of house price data which in this application leaves much to be desired.

Perhaps the most exciting development would be to embed these types of model in a more comprehensive approach to modelling the urban system. By including, for example, the retail sector, several economic relationships concerning the distribution of expenditures other than journey to work costs and house prices, might be modelled. Such a model might be based on the following set of equations in which the probabilities of location and interaction are now expressed as absolute frequencies. The budget constraint might take the following form for each income group w with a population P in any group.

$$Pw = \sum_i \sum_j \sum_k T_{ij}^{wk} s_j^k + \sum_i \sum_j \sum_k T_{ij}^{wk} c_{ij}^* + \sum_j \sum_l S_{jl} + \omega \sum_j \sum_l S_{jl} c_{jl}, \quad (10.54)$$

where S_{jl} is the expenditure on other goods by persons living at j and purchasing goods at l. Note that c_{jl} is the transport cost incurred by purchasing the composite good and ω is a trip generation rate. Dividing (10.54) by P would yield the budget equation for the average individual with income w. Furthermore, the average amount spent on the composite good vz is clearly

$$vz = \sum_j \sum_l S_{jl}/P. \quad (10.55)$$

The variation in house prices around the mean μ_1 called x_j^k is the same as that given in a previous section but the variation in expenditure on housing is redefined as

$$y_{ij}^w = w - c_{ij}^* - vz - \sum_l S_{jl} c_{jl}/P_j. \quad (10.56)$$

Equation (10.56) is the first basic equation in the comprehensive activity allocation model.

The proposed framework essentially relates together residential with retail location. The residential model could be based on the probability model in (10.48) which might take the following form

$$T_{ij}^{wk} = P \frac{\exp\left[-\lambda_1^w(x_j^k)^2 - \lambda_2^w(y_{ij}^w)^2 - \lambda_3^w(x_j^k)(y_{ij}^w)\right]}{\sum_i \sum_j \sum_k \exp\left[-\lambda_1^w(x_j^k)^2 - \lambda_2^w(y_{ij}^w)^2 - \lambda_3^w(x_j^k)(y_{ij}^w)\right]}. \quad (10.57)$$

The retail location model could be based on the well-known shopping model first made operational by Lakshmanan and Hansen (1965) and would predict the flow of expenditure S_{jl} from the residential location j to the shopping centre l.

$$S_{jl} = vz\sum_i\sum_k T_{ij}^{wk} \frac{F_l^\tau \exp(-\theta c_{jl})}{\sum_l F_l^\tau \exp(-\theta c_{jl})}. \qquad (10.58)$$

F_l is the attraction of the shopping centre at l and τ and θ are now parameters to be estimated by calibration. Equations (10.57) and (10.58) are interdependent through the location of population, the cost of the journey to work and also the cost of the journey to shop. Clearly, some iterative solution procedure involving (10.56)–(10.58) could be devised to ensure consistency between input and output values. Moreover, a further dependence between (10.57) and (10.58) could be set up if the model involved some economic base relationship such as that used in the Pittsburgh model (Lowry, 1964).

Working population resident in zone j is easily predicted from (10.57)

$$P_j = \sum_i\sum_k T_{ij}^{wk}, \qquad (10.59)$$

and expenditures S_l in each shopping centre l can be predicted from (10.58)

$$S_l = \sum_j S_{jl}. \qquad (10.60)$$

The elements of a workable urban model are contained in (10.54)–(10.60) and these provide a sound basis on which to extend the activity allocation models described in Chapter 3 *et seq*. As a further speculation, it is hoped that eventually this kind of comprehensive model will be able to handle the composite good in a more satisfying way by accounting for varying prices between shopping centres and varying demands for such goods in different residential locations.

In the quest to link urban economic theory more closely to numerical urban models, the approach of this chapter appears promising. Even more important is the possibility that such models may be able to handle or at least provide insights into the thorny problems of resource allocation, taxation and subsidy in housing markets. Data availability inevitably imposes a limit on what is feasible in an operational sense, yet it is often surprising what can be achieved using the most meagre data sources. A major purpose of urban modelling must ultimately involve forecasting in the context of planning and it is to be hoped that the approach presented here might represent some small step towards this goal. An alternative and equally important extension of activity allocation models based on making such models, dynamic in the temporal sense, provides the focus for the final two chapters in this book. Although disaggregation is not formally discussed in a dynamic context, it would be possible to build disaggregated dynamic models, data and other resources permitting, and although such connections between this and the next chapters are not explicitly made, readers might care to speculate on such developments.

11. Urban dynamics

Chorley and Kennedy (1971), in their recent book *Physical Geography: A Systems Approach*, make a comment extremely pertinent to the modelling of urban systems. These authors, in discussing the structure and behaviour of systems in general, state that a major feature of system behaviour is the *relaxation time* or the time taken for the system to respond to external stimuli and to return to a steady state or equilibrium condition. Chorley and Kennedy continue by stating that the areas in which there is greatest conflict in methodology concern systems whose relaxation times are difficult, if not impossible, to observe and they quote the case of urban systems. This difficulty in observing relaxation times or 'lags' in urban systems has meant that model-builders have concentrated their resources on modelling the structure rather than behaviour of such systems and consequently few models exist which attempt to simulate the dynamics of change in urban systems. From a systems viewpoint, such bias reflects an incomplete and only partial approach to modelling, for the basic propositions of systems theory imply that system structure cannot be interpreted without knowledge of system behaviour and vice versa. Indeed, most statements of general systems are framed in terms of system structure and behaviour (Klir and Valach, 1965).

The models introduced so far in this book have avoided explicit consideration of system behaviour and are usually described by a class of analytical method which economists call *comparative statics*. Such models attempt to represent the static structure of urban systems at one cross-section in time without recourse to any explanation of the changes in structure over time which constitute system behaviour. Yet to model urban structure in a static way always involves some implicit measure of the system behaviour for different behaviours lead to different structures.

Perhaps the most important concept involved in any dynamic approach revolves around the idea that urban structure is an inevitable reflection of several complex processes of change in the urban system (Batty, 1971). To understand structure, it is therefore essential to explore the processes, past and present, which have generated that structure. One of the central problems of the static equilibrium approach to modelling echoes this argument over process and structure; of critical importance to static models are variables which attempt to measure locational attraction, and the difficulties of finding suitable indices of attraction reflecting the locational history of the system are paramount. Furthermore, there are severe difficulties of building-in constraints on location into static models, and also in interpreting the real meaning of such constraint procedures. Although Harris (1970) has argued that static equilibrium models are preferable for generating the consequences of long-term forecasts in a planning context, there is an argument for the use of dynamic models in shorter-term forecasting where interest is centred around marginal changes in the distribution of urban activity. From a research viewpoint, however, there is little doubt that a model of urban dynamics adds a new dimension to hypothesis formulation and testing, and provides a considerably richer tool for exploring the structure of urban systems.

The recent history of urban modelling both in Britain and North America reveals that static models are severely limited as practical planning aids in a forecasting and design context. Apart from theoretical criticisms, very few applications have in fact been made in practice and, consequently, there is little experience on which to draw in assessing the difficulties and advantages of such applications. This dearth of practical application is due to many factors; some argue that the organisational and financial problems of implementing models in practice are too severe; some maintain that the technical skill is lacking while others argue that the model-builders themselves have been somewhat reluctant to push untested models onto an unwary profession. Few are willing to admit that the models themselves may fundamentally be limited, for the probable truth is that system structure cannot be modelled separately from system behaviour with any degree of success.

In the quest to design relevant and operational urban models, the simple models introduced in Chapters 2 and 3 have already been modified by variable disaggregation outlined in the previous chapter. In this chapter, the rationale for further modification of such models by explicitly building-in the time dimension will be considered, and the context will be set for the development and application of a large-scale dynamic model presented in the next chapter. In some senses, this chapter and the next represent the intended focus to which this book has been oriented. These developments reach their most complex, and hopefully most realistic, in these chapters, although this should not, in any way, suggest finality. Indeed, the arguments of this book only barely scratch the surface of what could and should be a much larger endeavour involving many disciplines and many viewpoints. In this chapter, the idea of simulation and the peculiarities posed by the temporal dimension set the context to a review of several different ways in which dynamics have been handled in existing urban models. This review attempts to highlight and evaluate certain modelling styles and techniques which are to be used in the design of the dynamic model in Chapter 12. In particular, linear models, activity allocation models, systems dynamics models and macro-economic urban models will be described with a view to establishing the ground rules governing dynamic model design.

Simulation as a medium for dynamic modelling

The term simulation was referred to in Chapter 1 and two definitions were then presented. In popular terms, all mathematical models which involve the use of large-scale computational facilities are referred to as simulation models. Simulation, however, has a more precise meaning in this context than that implied generally, for the distinction is made here, as before, between *analytic* and *simulation* methods of modelling. Analytic methods of modelling involve the use of mathematical analysis to arrive at explicit equations representing the behaviour of the system, whereas simulation methods are used to derive the behaviour of the system when the system is too complex to be modelled using the more direct analytic approach. Elton and Rosenhead (1971) point out the essential characteristic of simulation when they say '...one does not arrive at explicit equations expressing the behaviour of systems of this general type; rather one achieves a number of potential histories of the system, from which the effects of possible modification to the system can be predicted'.

Simulation is almost exclusively used to model the behaviour of systems and this implies that the time dimension is basic to such procedures. Indeed, many authors define simulation as the method of dynamic modelling. For example, Naylor (1971) defines simulation as 'a numerical technique for conducting experiments with certain types of mathematical models which describe the behaviour of a complex system on a digital computer over extended periods of time'. In this case, Naylor associates simulation with computation as well as system behaviour and the time element. A good example of the use of simulation in the social sciences is provided by the work of Orcutt *et al.* (1961); these researchers show that, although deductive solutions to their demographic model are theoretically possible, the practical difficulties of obtaining solutions in this way are so great that simulation is the only feasible method of modelling.

This discussion raises an important point concerning the suitability of the system being modelled to simulation. Although most models of urban development have some part of their solution reached by simulation, the central feature of simulation concerns the repeated application of the model's equations in a sequence leading to a solution. It is immediately apparent why dynamic models are suited to the technique of simulation for the sequential nature of time forms the organising process on which the simulation can be based. Indeed, many of the classic simulation models such as the industrial dynamics models of Forrester (1961) and the household sector models of Orcutt *et al.* (1961) are structured around the temporal dimension. Apart from the fundamental advantages which simulation techniques have in dealing with complexity, the concept of simulation is deeply embedded in the experimental approach to understanding natural and artificial phenomena. In the social sciences, simulation has been identified with computer modelling, and the ease with which different hypotheses can be tested experimentally using computer simulation is obvious. The experimental approach has also been adopted in other applications of urban models such as those presented previously but the techniques of simulation provide a greater flexibility in the design of such experiments.

Perhaps the most important feature of simulation concerns new insights into the behaviour of the system under study which can be gained by experiment. If the structure of the model is difficult to interpret *a priori*, simulation can lead to useful appraisals of the validity of the model, and the process of model design can be much improved using the results of simulation. The value of simulation in handling complexity and revealing solutions and predictions which are impossible to obtain deductively is the main argument adopted by Forrester (1969) who maintains that simulation is the only method of modelling capable of revealing that the behaviour of social systems may in many instances be counter-intuitive. Another important feature of simulation is described by Simon (1969) who argues that simulation is essential in the behavioural sciences for generating new knowledge about how the system works and how it is likely to work under foreseeable conditions. Therefore, with these arguments in mind, the simulation approach to urban research is seen as a fundamental method for setting and testing hypotheses about the workings of the urban system.

Time in urban modelling

The need to build dynamic urban models has already been anticipated in several previous chapters and, in particular, it was suggested that many of the problems associated with static models could only be resolved within a dynamic context. The basic inconsistency between static models and their use in a planning context which is intrinsically dynamic in terms of the future would be sufficient in itself to require dynamic modelling. Cordey-Hayes (1972), for example, demonstrates the need for such models in policy planning by suggesting that most planning is in terms of marginal change and that the phasing of policies through time is often as important as the policy itself. Moreover, the fact that comparative static models attempt to simulate history at one cross-section in time gives rise to a host of measurement problems especially those dealing with locational attraction which are almost impossible to resolve. Attraction can only be measured notionally in any case and if such a measure is not restricted to an observable point in time, the problem is completely confounded.

There are, however, good reasons why the comparative static approach has been widely applied. The status of theory in urban economic and geographic systems with regard to time is almost non-existent. Although many have criticised the economists for their disregard, blatant or otherwise, of space (Isard, 1956), the economists could level the same criticism against urban theorists for their disregard of time. Yet there are severe problems in trying to develop dynamic theory, two of which are worthy of some discussion. Perhaps the major problem concerns the ability to observe or monitor the urban system. Unlike the physical sciences in which the effect of critical variables on the system of interest can be isolated in the laboratory, such a search for cause and effect is practically impossible in social systems. Thus, there are many instances when it is difficult, if not impossible, to disentangle one cause from another in the changing behaviour of such systems. This is a fundamental limitation which is referred to here as the *observational dilemma*. A second problem concerns that hoary perennial – data. As has been demonstrated in previous chapters, data are often difficult to assemble for one cross-section in time, and the collection of time series data is usually a formidable and sometimes infeasible undertaking. Furthermore, such data often become less consistent and sparser as earlier time periods are needed and, frequently, the time periods between points at which data have been collected, are too large to be useful for dynamic modelling.

Despite these problems, dynamic modelling is essential if rather arbitrary allocation mechanisms of existing urban models are to be made more realistic. The limitations to the comparative static approach are spelt out nowhere more clearly than in the prologue to a description of the Detroit model by Ingram *et al.* (1972). These authors say that '...in existing theories of location it is assumed that either cities are destroyed every night and rebuilt the next morning or that households live in house trailers that are relocated daily'. The tendency for static models to relocate all of the stock in whatever forecast interval they are applied to, highlights this limitation. In Chapters 4 and 5, these problems were encountered in projecting with activity allocation models and, in the Notts.–Derbys. example, only the increment or decrement to the existing stock was allocated. This discussion raises the notion of the *mover pool* or pool of activities which are relocating in the city. In fact, these relocators account for a very large proportion of all change in cities, often greater than 70 per cent, and there is thus a strong argument for treating this component explicitly. Several dynamic models attempt to isolate this mover pool from the stayers.

A further component of change in the behaviour of urban systems involves the so-called *distributed lag* in which the values of variables from previous time periods affect the value of variables in the time period under consideration (Paelinck, 1970). In general, an nth order lag in any system can be written

$$x_{t+n} = f(x_{t+n-1}, x_{t+n-2}, ..., x_t),$$

where the lag is distributed over the previous n time periods. Such a lag might be due to perception delays, for example in the case where the locational attraction at time $t+n$ is a function of the change in some activity between $t+n-1$ and $t+n-2$, and so on. Alternatively, the lag could be of a reaction or equilibrium-seeking kind in which activities are readjusting to some new state configuration; in certain models, the lag might be functional in nature such as that involved in the generation or growth in activities caused by other events at earlier points in time, for instance those due to the multiplier.

The emphasis in dynamic models on the concept of the lagged variable raises the question of the equilibrium or disequilibrium inherent in such models. Dynamic models obviously have a greater capability in simulating the disequilibrium which is a feature of the real world but Harris (1970) provides a warning in this regard which he suggests might be a guiding principle for dynamic model design. Harris argues that as urban systems are usually tending to move to equilibrium, '...for well constructed models a set of equilibrium solutions will be available for most inputs of policies and environmental conditions'. This principle suggests that although disequilibrium may be the usual condition of a dynamic model, such a model should always be tending to equilibrium and, in the absence of further stimuli, should reach this state. In this and the next chapter, *Harris's Principle* as this argument has been called, will be used both to evaluate existing dynamic models and to help in the design of the model which is described in Chapter 12.

As a conclusion to this section, it is necessary to introduce briefly the problems concerned with defining the length of time interval appropriate to any dynamic model. This problem is analogous to the zoning or spatial interval problem discussed in Chapter 8, and thus, the work of Broadbent (1969*a*, 1969*b*) is of interest here. Using an argument similar to Broadbent's, it is essential to define a time interval which is small enough to detect the time-varying phenomena of interest. If the time interval is too large, then the dynamic model will become trivial and thus decomposable into a series of comparative static models, one for each time period. At this point, it is convenient to start a review of existing dynamic models in terms of the ideas described above; the simplest of dynamic models based on linear forms will be presented first.

Dynamic linear models

As linear models have not been dealt with in this book, it might appear somewhat curious to include them in a dynamic context. Yet certain useful insights can be generated from a brief review for in these examples, the dynamic component is clearly visible. The first model, although there are many similar to it, is due to Czamanski (1965) who has applied a simple time-oriented economic base model to the Baltimore region. This model is a four-equation second-order model which can be stated as

$$P(t+1) = a_1 + b_1 E(t-1), \tag{11.1}$$

$$S(t+1) = a_2 + b_2 P(t), \tag{11.2}$$

$$E^b(t+1) = a_3 + b_3 X(t+1), \tag{11.3}$$

and
$$E(t+1) = E^b(t+1) + E^l(t+1) + S(t+1). \tag{11.4}$$

The notation is as in previous chapters but to refresh the reader's memory, P is population, S is service employment, E^b is now derived basic employment, X is exogenous basic employment and E^l is locationally-oriented basic employment which includes X. a_1, a_2, a_3 and b_1, b_2, b_3 are parameters to be estimated; the time notation is self evident. The various lags included in (11.1)–(11.4) are quite realistic although Czamanski (1965) has not fitted these equations using any of the simultaneous forms of regression analysis appropriate to such a system. Nevertheless, the model provides a simple approach to generating urban activities although there is no spatial dimension.

In contrast, the EMPIRIC model is based on a system of first-order linear difference equations which refer to different zones i and different activities j. This model was designed by Hill (1965) for the Boston Regional Planning Project and has since been revised through several versions (Irwin and Brand, 1965). In contrast to Czamanski's model, the EMPIRIC model is spatially based; furthermore, the solution method adopted by EMPIRIC recognises the simultaneous nature of urban interrelationships, and formal solution methods, such as those based on two-stage least squares, have been used. The time interval adopted is ten years, and consequently the emphasis upon dynamics is implicit rather than explicit in the model. This model can be stated as follows from the description by Hill *et al.* (1965). First, a difference operator $\Delta Y_{ik}(t)$ which measures the change on activity Y_{ik} in zone i between t and $t+1$, is defined by

$$\Delta Y_{ik}(t) = Y_{ik}(t+1) - Y_{ik}(t).$$

The model has the following form for each activity j and zone i

$$g_j \Delta Y_{ij}(t) = \sum_{\substack{k=1 \\ k \neq j}}^{K} a_{ik} g_k \Delta Y_{ik}(t) + \sum_{l=1}^{m} b_{il} h_l \Delta X_{il}(t)$$

$$+ \sum_{l=m+1}^{M} b_i \left[\frac{1}{I} - q_l X_{il}(t+1) \right]. \quad (11.5)$$

In (11.5), Y_{ik} refers to the endogenous (located) variables produced by the equation system whereas X_{il} refers to exogenous (locator) variables. The constants a_{ik} and b_{il} are parameters to be estimated by the regression, M is the total number of exogenous variables, K is the total number of endogenous variables and I is the total number of zones. Thus there are IK equations in the system. The constants g_k, h_l and q_l are scalars which change the variables into regional shares. These are defined from

$$g_k = \frac{1}{\sum_i \Delta Y_{ik}(t)}, \quad (11.6)$$

$$h_l = \frac{1}{\sum_i \Delta X_{il}(t)}, \quad (11.7)$$

and

$$q_l = \frac{1}{\sum_i X_{il}(t+1)}. \quad (11.8)$$

The EMPIRIC model has been widely applied in North America and a useful application exists in Britain by Masser *et al.* (1971). Foot (1973) has also produced an important comparative study of the EMPIRIC and activity allocation models which demonstrates their relative advantages and limitations. A continuous non-linear equivalent called the POLIMETRIC model was also designed alongside the EMPIRIC; readers can get further details in the paper by Irwin and Brand (1965).

One central problem with these linear models revolves around their rather inductive bias in that the emphasis upon explanation is completely statistical and lacks little of the causal focus of the activity allocation models. Although certain lags are built into the system, their explanation is also largely statistical and, as the dynamic process which these models are attempting to simulate is implicit, there are few guiding principles in the choice of time interval. Furthermore, these models do not attempt to identify the mover pool and their equilibrium properties are unspecified. In short, these models, although acknowledging the importance of time, do little else; it is in the activity allocation models that a more explicit approach has been adopted and first the TOMM model due to Crecine (1964) will be described.

The Time-Oriented Metropolitan Model (TOMM)

The Time-Oriented Metropolitan Model (TOMM) is of interest for two reasons; first, the earliest version of this model was based upon the original Pittsburgh model (Lowry, 1964) and second, in the spirit engendered in this book, it attempted to turn a simple static model into a more complex dynamic model by specific consideration of system behaviour. This model was developed by Crecine (1964) for the Pittsburgh Community Renewal Program, and the first version attempted to model changes in the stock of activity over five-year time intervals using the same mechanisms as in Lowry's model; an important distinction was made in the model between new locators and relocators. The TOMM model has been improved in several ways since the first attempt, and at least three major versions of the model, including the first, now exist. The second version – TOMM II – was developed for the METRO gaming project at the University of Michigan and fitted to data from the town of Lansing (Crecine, 1967). In this second version, a more realistic formulation of the measure of locational attraction, incorporating site rent, amenity and transport cost, was provided although the simulation procedure is still similar to that used in Lowry's model (Crecine, 1968). TOMM III is the model at present under development at Michigan (Crecine, 1969) and it appears that research is centred on questions of dynamics and mover behaviour in the model. A time interval of two years is now being used in the model.

The model can be best presented using the equation system given in (3.9)–(3.27) which refers to the original Lowry model. In this presentation, the iteration postscripts m, n will be suppressed as will be the explicit zonal notation referring to the zonal sets Z_1, Z_2, Z_3 and Z_4. A full system of equations will not be given here but the reader wishing to programme this dynamic model from these equations should have no difficulty if continual reference is made to Chapter 3. The first point to note is that the order in which the activities are handled in TOMM I is the reverse of the Lowry model. In this model, services are allocated before population and thus the appropriate equation system of Chapter 3 is reordered in a revised sequence: (3.17)–(3.26), then (3.9)–(3.16), followed by (3.27). All variables are now postscripted according to particular points in time t, $t+1$. Furthermore, the population is disaggregated into different household types given by P^l and the service sector into different service employments S^k. The inverse activity rates α^l and population-serving ratios β^k are also disaggregated to match population and service employments.

Total land in the system at time $t+1$ is made up from the following components

$$L_j(t+1) = L_j^u(t+1)+L_j^b(t+1)+L_j^r(t+1)+L_j^h(t+1). \qquad (11.9)$$

However, land used for services $L_j^r(t+1)$ and households $L_j^h(t+1)$ are further divided into land which is prejudged to be stable in any given time period and land which can change use. Stable land is derived from total land available in (11.9) by

$$L_j^{r*}(t+1) = a_j(t+1)\,L_j^r(t+1), \qquad (11.10)$$

$$L_j^{h*}(t+1) = b_j(t+1)\,L_j^h(t+1), \qquad (11.11)$$

where the asterisk denotes stable land and $a_j(t+1)$ and $b_j(t+1)$ are the proportions of such land at time $t+1$. Equations (11.10) and (11.11) articulate the mover pool assumption and in fact, the whole model is constrained in terms of land use rather than activity location. Also the total stock is reallocated at each time period by the model but the stable land uses act as a crude constraint on what is able and unable to move. First, services are generated from the economic base equation

$$S^k(t+1) = \beta^k\sum_l P^l(t) = \beta^k\sum_l \alpha^l\sum_i E_i^b(1-\alpha^l\sum_k \beta^k)^{-1}. \qquad (11.12)$$

Equation (11.12) is analogous to (3.17). Then services are allocated to service centres using a potential model similar to that in (3.18)

$$S_i^k(t+1) = S^k\frac{\sum_j\sum_l g^{kl}P_j^l(t)f^2(c_{ij})+q^k E_i(t)}{\sum_i\sum_j\sum_l g^{kl}P_j^l(t)f^2(c_{ij})+q^k\sum_i E_i(t)}. \qquad (11.13)$$

At this point, it is necessary to determine whether or not the minimum size constraint has been met in terms of the allocated services, and thus the procedure in (3.19)–(3.22) is operated. Land required for services is now calculated from

$$L_i^r(t+1) = \sum_k e^k S_i^k(t+1), \qquad (11.14)$$

and then the change in land over the time interval is found,

$$\Delta L_i^r(t) = \sum_k e^k[S_i^k(t+1)-S_i^k(t)]. \qquad (11.15)$$

At this point, the mover pool constraint in terms of stable land use is brought to bear by choosing a final value of $\Delta L_i^r(t)$ which meets the stable land constraint. Then, $\Delta L_i^r(t)$ is the maximum of

$$\Delta L_i^r(t) = \max\left\{\sum_k e^k[S_i^k(t+1)-S_i^k(t)], L_i^{r*}(t+1)-\sum_k e^k S_i^k(t)\right\}, \quad (11.16)$$

and total land for services and employment at $t+1$ are calculated as follows

$$L_i^r(t+1) = L_i^r(t)+\Delta L_i^r(t), \quad (11.17)$$

$$E_i(t+1) = E_i^b(t+1)+\sum_k S_i^k(t+1). \quad (11.18)$$

At this point, the model moves into the population sector and population is first calculated from the appropriate economic base equation

$$P(t+1) = \sum_l \alpha^l \sum_i E_i(t+1). \quad (11.19)$$

This population in (11.19) is now allocated to residential areas using a potential function similar to that in (3.11). Then

$$P_j(t+1) = P(t+1)\frac{\sum_i E_i(t)f^1(c_{ij})}{\sum_i \sum_j E_i(t)f^1(c_{ij})}. \quad (11.20)$$

It is now necessary to test to see if the density constraint on population has been violated. However, because the stable residential land constraint sets a lower limit on the amount of land required in any zone j, the constraint now becomes both a minimum and maximum size limit. If

$$P_j(t+1)\begin{cases} < \delta_j L_j^{h*}(t+1) \\ > \delta_j L_j^h(t+1), \end{cases} \quad (11.21)$$

then the constraint procedure in (3.12)–(3.16) is operated until population falls within the permissible range. The change in population is calculated from

$$\Delta P_j(t) = P_j(t+1)-P_j(t), \quad (11.22)$$

and population in each household-type l is computed from a function

$$\Delta P_j^l(t) = \Phi\left[P_j^l(t), \sum_i E_i(t+1)f^1(c_{ij})\right]. \quad (11.23)$$

Equation (11.23) is normalised so that it sums to (11.22) and then population in l at time $t+1$ is calculated as

$$P_j^l(t+1) = P_j^l(t)+\Delta P_j^l(t). \quad (11.24)$$

The model sketched out in (11.9)–(11.24) can be operated within the wider framework of the original Pittsburgh model in which consistency between input and output variables is achieved. If this is required, then the outputs of (11.24) and (11.18) are fed into (11.13) and (11.20) respectively, and the whole equation system is iterated until some convergence limit is met.

Although this model is organised around the concept of a mover pool, the mechanism designed to ensure this operation is curious to say the least. Apart from the rather inelegant way of achieving some stability or inertia in the existing configuration of land uses, there is no consistency between mobile activities and their relationship through the economic base. New locators and relocators are not separated out, thus the equilibrium properties of the model are difficult to trace. Yet lags are built into the locational attraction indices through the potential function and, although not specified in the above equation system, also through the deterrence functions. As a first attempt, the model was a useful exercise although several obvious ways of improving it are now apparent, and the reader could easily undertake such extensions if required.

A quasi-dynamic activity allocation model

A quasi-dynamic version of the activity allocation model was presented for projection purposes in Chapter 4 and, in this section, this model will be explored a little further. The original equation system for the static model is given in (3.28)–(3.59) and in this presentation, like the last, the iteration postscripts and zonal set notation will be suppressed. The model is operated from the basic employment sector and complete consistency between various activities is secured in this way. In terms of employment, a distinction is made between new locators $\Delta E_i(t)$ and relocators $\pi_i(t+1) E_i(t)$, where $\pi_i(t+1)$ is the mover pool ratio for zone i at $t+1$. Then, for the residential location model, gross changes in trips can be calculated from

$$\Delta^* T_{ij}(t) = A_i(t+1) B_j(t+1) [\Delta E_i(t) + \pi_i(t+1) E_i(t)] f^1(D_j, c_{ij}). \quad (11.25)$$

All terms are as defined previously, $A_i(t+1)$ and $B_j(t+1)$ are the appropriate normalising factors and Δ^* represents a difference operator specifying gross change. Changes due to relocators defined by $^*\Delta$ are computed from

$$^*\Delta T_{ij}(t) = A_i(t) B_j(t) \pi_i(t+1) E_i(t) f^1(D_j, c_{ij}). \quad (11.26)$$

Then the new trip distribution at $t+1$ can be calculated as follows

$$T_{ij}(t+1) = T_{ij}(t) + \Delta^* T_{ij}(t) - {}^*\Delta T_{ij}(t). \quad (11.27)$$

Note here that $f^1(D_j, c_{ij})$ is a lagged function from the previous time interval. If the changes in trips due to relocation are required, then (11.26) needs to be calculated for time $t+1$ as well and a comparison made between t and $t+1$; this gives the internal migration in terms of changes in the trip distribution. The change in population can now be found from

$$\Delta P_j(t) = \alpha(t+1)\left[\sum_i \Delta^* T_{ij}(t) - \sum_i {}^* \Delta T_{ij}(t)\right]. \qquad (11.28)$$

The rest of the equation system in (3.28)–(3.59) can be traced through in an analogous manner and such extensions are so straightforward that there is little point in pursuing them here.

This model represents a fairly clear application of the mover pool principle; lags in terms of changing attraction and deterrence link the time periods to one another and the process of change depends upon both new location and relocation which influence one another between time periods. The ability of the model to compute interval migration provides essential data describing the effect of the mover pool. However, Harris's Principle, in which the equilibrium properties of the model depend upon the idea that the system 'runs down' in the absence of further stimuli, is not embodied in any of the models described so far. In fact, there are two kinds of equilibrium which need to be defined. First, there is the steady state equilibrium which occurs when the system simply reproduces itself from time period to time period. This relative equilibrium is contrasted with a more absolute equilibrium which occurs when the system is cut off from external stimuli. This does not imply that the system stops but that the effect of previous external stimuli gradually disappears in the equilibrium. A good example of the first kind of equilibrium is presented in the next section which deals with Systems Dynamics; this is in contrast to the equilibrium built into the model of the next chapter which is of the second kind.

The Systems Dynamics models

With the recent interest in problems of world population and resources, a set of techniques devised by Forrester (1961) for simulating industrial processes in firms, called collectively *Systems Dynamics*, has been employed in the modelling of hypothetical urban systems and world systems (Forrester, 1969, 1971). The application to urban systems is of prime interest here but the technique is of fairly wide applicability in the sense that all kinds of natural and artificial systems have recently been simulated using these concepts. The technique of Systems Dynamics has its foundations in ideas from control engineering; the concept of system structure and behaviour is conceived in terms of levels of stocks which are progressively altered through time by rates of change which are affected by various positive and negative feedbacks within the system of interest. This type of system description is not new for it forms the basis of that branch of mathematics dealing with the study of change through difference – differential equations. Forrester emphasises the idea of feedback which is essential to change in any case but he goes further in asserting that the behaviour of social systems is counter-intuitive in that their workings are not obvious, and that their appearance is positively misleading. The counter-intuitive argument is separate from the Systems Dynamics technique although Forrester maintains that Systems Dynamics is an appropriate, if not the only method for understanding such complex system behaviour.

Many of these models are based on the notion that a system is fundamentally constrained by some fixed limit on resources which affect the growth of the system through time. Typically, such a system grows explosively or exponentially at first and then as its resource limit is neared, the growth is damped and an equilibrium condition is eventually reached, usually with some oscillation around the steady state. The growth of population which in certain circumstances follows a logistic curve, is based on this kind of argument, as is the diffusion of ideas or information in a relatively isolated social system. In Forrester's hypothetical urban system,

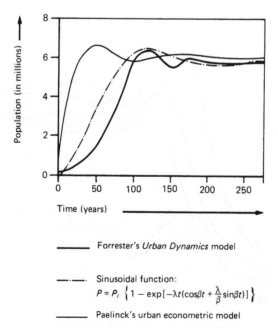

———— Forrester's *Urban Dynamics* model

—·—· Sinusoidal function:
$$P = P_l \left\{ 1 - \exp[-\lambda t(\cos\beta t + \frac{\lambda}{\beta}\sin\beta t)] \right\}$$

———— Paelinck's urban econometric model

Fig. 11.1. Typical dynamic behaviour in fixed resource systems.

the growth of activities such as industry and its labour force and housing is halted as the land available for new activities runs out. This kind of behaviour is also characteristic of physical systems such as servo-mechanisms which hover around some equilibrium value or steady state, and there are well known sinusoidal equations describing such behaviour. Figure 11.1 presents this type of system behaviour in terms of various profiles characterising the Systems Dynamics models and other related representations; their similarity in terms of their implied causal structures is obvious from this diagram.

Forrester's model of the urban system is organised around three sectors: housing, industry and the labour force. Each of these sectors is disaggregated in turn into three subsectors. In terms of the labour force, there are the managerial, labour and underemployed groups who reside in premium, worker and underemployed housing in one–one correspondence. However, varying proportions of the labour force work in the new enterprise, mature business, and declining industry subsectors. Through time, industry and housing age from new business and premium housing through to the poorer quality stock. Also there are rates of migration between the subsectors in the labour market, and the movements into and out of the total system in terms of labour represent the key link between the system and its

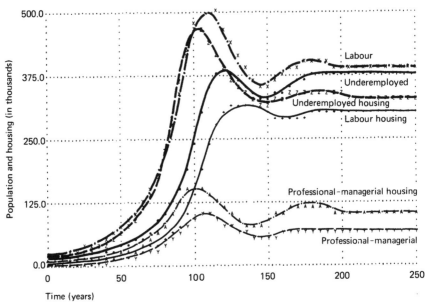

Fig. 11.2. Growth profiles from Forrester's *Urban Dynamics* model.

environment. The system grows exponentially at first but as the land limit is reached, new enterprises fail to be built and the system stagnates to an uneasy equilibrium characterised by large proportions of obsolete industry and housing and high unemployment. This situation is built into the structure of the model through its critical reliance on the wealth sectors – managers, premium housing and new enterprises, and it is not surprising that all policies for improving the system, which are not framed in terms of these wealth sectors, are deemed, by Forrester, to be failures. The growth paths of critical activities in the model simulated over a 250-year time period are presented in Figure 11.2.

Criticisms of this model have matched in scale the enormous popularity which the approach has gained through the popular press and the Systems Dynamics public relations machine. These criticisms are worth briefly sketching here and they are of two main kinds. First, technical criticisms mainly concern the complete disregard shown by Forrester for incorporating well-demonstrated and accepted urban theory into the model. Thus, the failure to deal with the spatial or geographic sector has outraged urban geographers, economists and planners. Furthermore, the hypothetical nature of the model which is based on literally hundreds of unproven and usually untestable hypotheses goes against the grain of work in this field which has been painstakingly slow in validating theoretical relationships. The 250-year time span for the simulation is also arbitrary and the idea that the model simulates a 'typical' twilight or inner area of a 'typical' North American city is completely notional. The model could never be calibrated in the traditional way for it ignores the observational dilemma mentioned earlier. Finally, if the model were made more realistic, it would have to be drastically pruned and would probably approach an activity allocation model in this event.

The second major criticism of the model really revolves around Forrester's philosophy which, to say the least, implies a right-wing view that help only comes to those who help themselves. This somewhat outspoken criticism of present urban policies which attempt to provide housing and jobs for the poor and underprivileged demonstrates his faith in the private enterprise system as a cure for all ills. The model also reflects this view in the way it is constructed, the results that it produces, and the way these results are interpreted by Forrester.

Nevertheless, a large amount of work emanating from the physical rather than social sciences has been stimulated by the Forrester model (Chen, 1972), although much of the work has been in terms of sensitivity-testing. Certain researchers (Kadanoff, 1972; Graham, 1972) have attempted to make the model spatial but this does not seem to have met with much success for the original model appears to be too constraining an influence. An interesting, fruitful and amusing piece of work has been undertaken by Stonebraker (1972) who has simplified the model drastically by reducing the total number of model equations by two-thirds. The results of running the model in this fashion are much the same as Forrester's and this has led Smith and Sage (1973) to propose the use of hierarchical system theory as a tool for simplifying the model.

With regard to application of these models to real situations, only two appear to exist at present. An attempt to apply the model to Harris County, Texas (Porter and Henley, 1972) reveals little if any additional interest but perhaps the most exciting application is to the Venice subregion by Costa and Piasentin (1971). Costa and Piasentin divide Venice into three zones – Centro Urbano, Estuario and Terraferma – and their model simulates the growth in population, employment and housing from 1951 in one-year periods to the present day. Particular emphasis is placed upon migration between the three zones but the appropriateness of this application comes from the fact that the Venice subregion is highly constrained in spatial terms and thus quite unsuitable for activity allocation models. The predictions of the Venice model calibrated between 1951 and 1971 are good and this work promises to give unique insights into urban modelling through Systems Dynamics.

The Systems Dynamics philosophy has been used in other applications, in particular in the Susquehana River Basin Project by Hamilton *et al.* (1969) and in an economic model of Kent County, Michigan, by Swanson and Waldmann (1970). These applications are much more sensitive to related work in other fields than is the Urban Dynamics model, and could be regarded as only conceptually related to Forrester's approach. The approach is clearly of some importance if only for the fact that it has generated so much interest but, as Burdekin and Marshall (1973) remark in their useful review of this work, '...the model has been the subject of considerable comment but little practical use'. There is little doubt that any potential this approach has will be quickly realised in the near future.

Urban models based on economic dynamics

There is a class of urban models which has recently been stimulated by the work of economists such as Paelinck (1970), based on the specification of urban dynamics in terms of difference equations relating macro-economic phenomena. Economic base type models such as the one due to Czamanski (1965) outlined earlier can be treated in this way. In particular, emphasis has been placed on analysing the equilibrium properties of such models in analytic terms if possible, although simulation has also been used. To introduce this approach a simple model following ideas introduced by Paelinck (1970, 1972) will be presented.

The model is of the economic base type and can be stated succinctly in the following five equations where the notation is as defined in a previous section

$$P(t+1) = a_1 P(t) + a_2 E(t), \tag{11.29}$$

$$S(t+1) = b_1 P(t) + b_2 S(t), \tag{11.30}$$

$$E^l(t+1) = c_1 P(t) + c_2 E^l(t), \tag{11.31}$$

$$E^b(t+1) = d_1 E(t) + d_2 E^b(t), \tag{11.32}$$

and

$$E(t+1) = S(t+1) + E^l(t+1) + E^b(t+1). \tag{11.33}$$

Constants could be added to (11.29)–(11.32) if necessary in the estimation procedures. This system of equations can be represented in matrix terms explicitly as

$$\begin{bmatrix} P \\ S \\ E^l \\ E^b \\ E \end{bmatrix}_{t+1} = \begin{bmatrix} a_1 & 0 & 0 & 0 & a_2 \\ b_1 & b_2 & 0 & 0 & 0 \\ c_1 & 0 & c_2 & 0 & 0 \\ 0 & 0 & d_1 & d_2 & 0 \\ (b_1+c_1) & b_2 & (c_2+d_2) & d_2 & 0 \end{bmatrix} \begin{bmatrix} P \\ S \\ E^l \\ E^b \\ E \end{bmatrix}_t. \tag{11.34}$$

Equation (11.34) can be summarised as

$$\mathbf{p}(t+1) = \mathbf{Q}\mathbf{p}(t), \tag{11.35}$$

where $\mathbf{p}$ is an $n \times 1$ column vector of activities and $\mathbf{Q}$ is an $n \times n$ matrix of coefficients. Then by recursion, activities at time $t + \tau$ can be expressed in terms of time t by

$$\mathbf{p}(t+\tau) = \mathbf{Q}^\tau \mathbf{p}(t). \tag{11.36}$$

The theory of difference equations, as, for example, elaborated by Goldberg (1958), can be used to analyse the equilibrium properties of simple equation systems such as that given in (11.36). Paelinck (1970, 1972) effectively pursues this analysis for simple cases but for complicated systems, simulation is required.

In some respects, there is a direct correspondence between the linear, dynamic, Systems Dynamics, and economic dynamics equation systems presented here, for all these systems can be set up in similar terms. The real differences lie in notations concerning analysis, simulation and calibration-estimation. For example, Blokland, Hendriks and Paelinck (1972) have devised an economic dynamic model for simulating the effects of decline in an urban system. At present, the model is being calibrated to data for the Hague and a mixture of analytic evaluation, sensitivity testing through simulation, and estimation by trial and error iteration is being employed in model construction. One of the features of models whose spatial component is implicit rather than explicit, concerns their development in depth for in such models, there tend to be many more hypotheses to validate than in their spatial counterparts. Thus, although these models tend to be richer in detail, they are frequently more difficult to calibrate to any real situation.

These economic dynamic models seem extremely promising for several reasons. First, their hypotheses are usually grounded in fairly unambiguous economic theory which is familiar and acceptable. Second, emphasis on trying to determine whether or not such models converge to or diverge away from some equilibrium might lead to interesting insights into the behaviour patterns of urban systems. And third, estimation of the parameters of such models is a fairly well developed area in econometrics and thus, these models are probably easier to apply to real situations than the Systems Dynamics models. Developments in this field are likely to provide one of the most important areas of urban modelling in the next decade.

A comparison of dynamic urban models

There are many similarities between the models presented in this chapter although their different presentations and terminologies tend to highlight their differences. Perhaps the most critical difference lies in the way in which the spatial dimension is handled; it appears that spatial models substitute the richness of hypothesis-building characteristic of non-spatial models for the extensiveness of space. It becomes meaningless to compare spatial and non-spatial models through a count of equations for space adds a new dimension to models, which magnifies the number of equations by at least the square of the number of zones. Spatial models are essential for most urban situations where interaction and spatial organisation is the overt expression of underlying urban processes. Yet, there are as many non-spatial as spatial dynamic models, and in general, the concept of time has been handled more cogently by neglecting the influence of space. This then presents the challenge: to build a model which is both explicitly spatial and explicitly dynamic in terms of such criteria as Harris's Principle and notions governing relocator behaviour in the city.

It is not difficult, at one level, to extend static models by incorporating a dynamic sector. But it is difficult to produce dynamic models whose hypotheses are testable and whose organisation in the time dimension is focused around a relevant concept. In the models reviewed here whose key features are summarised in Table 11.1, hypotheses concerning dynamics are implicit rather than explicit. Ideas based on lags in perception and concepts of ageing and obsolescence do form useful organising principles, but these are not spelt out in the models in any detail, and if progress is to be made in this area, then a more explicit consideration of these factors is required.

TABLE 11.1. *A comparison of dynamic urban models*

Type of model	Main field of origin	Equilibrium properties	Mover pool and migration factors	Spatial component	Solution procedures	Key reference
Economic base type models	Macro-economics	Unspecified	Not identified	Non-spatial	Regression analysis	Czamanski (1965)
EMPIRIC – econometric models	Econometrics	Unspecified	Not identified	Spatial distributions over I zones	Two-stage regression analysis	Irwin and Brand (1965)
TOMM – Time Oriented Metropolitan model	Traffic and land-use planning	Unspecified	Operated through the stable land constraint	Spatial distributions over IJ zone pairs	Trial and error iteration	Crecine (1964)
Activity allocation models	Traffic and land-use planning	Unspecified	Operated through employment sector	Spatial distributions over IJ zone pairs	Trial and error iteration	This chapter and Chapter 4
Urban dynamics models	Systems Dynamics: management	Steady state oscillation	Formal migration rates between sectors	Non-spatial	Hypothetical simulation	Forrester (1969)
Economic dynamics models	Macro-economics: econometrics	Steady state oscillation or divergence	Not identified	Non-spatial	Analytic solution of difference equations	Paelinck (1970)

In the next chapter, a model of the urban system which attempts to meet some of these concepts will be outlined and applied to the Reading sub-region. The model is much more a simulation model in the technical sense defined earlier than any of the models outlined in previous chapters, and thus its hypotheses are more difficult to test in a formal fashion. Nowhere in this book is the critical problem of 'why modelling' more exposed than in this next chapter for here, the notion of calibration to a reality is under question. The idea that models are simply 'aids to imagination and under-standing' is an important rationale for this work but this in no way resolves the inevitable dilemma between modelling as prediction and modelling as explanation.

12. *Dynamic simulation of an urban system*

The various models of urban dynamics outlined in the previous chapter provide the context for the design and construction of a spatial dynamic model which is applied here to the Reading subregion. The model attempts to integrate both spatial and temporal behaviour of various locators and in particular, the concept of the mover pool, referred to previously, is widely exploited. Furthermore, the model is always in disequilibrium although an equilibrium can be reached in the absence of further stimuli through the model's input, thus satisfying Harris's Principle. In this chapter, the observational dilemma concerning the impossibility of monitoring change at its most elemental level, is faced directly. Even the most simple and crude of hypotheses to be built into the model are difficult to validate against data, thus demonstrating one of the major barriers to ambitious urban modelling.

The design for the macro-dynamic model to be outlined here is the result of many compromises. Although the model may appear a little rough around the edges and over-complex in some parts, the preliminary design appears to provide a promising approach to simulation in urban systems. In essence, the model is quite simple for it builds upon the ideas of spatial interaction described by Wilson (1970a) and upon an interpretation of the dynamic multiplier in macro-economic theory (Allen, 1967). Before the model is outlined, it is important to clarify the position of the model in the context of other research. To this end, Paelinck (1970) has suggested that modelling research can be organised under three headings; first, research based upon empirical analysis; second, research based upon mathematical analysis; and third, research based upon simulation. It is this third approach – the approach to modelling through simulation – which forms the method described in this chapter.

A model of urban dynamics

The design principles for a model of spatial and temporal interactions need further clarification. In previous attempts at macro-static modelling and in particular in the activity allocation model, the interactions or flows of activity between different areas have been central to the way in which different patterns of location develop. Activities have been modelled as summations of spatial interactions or flows (Cordey-Hayes and Wilson, 1971). It is also obvious that at any point in time, the distribution of activity represents the summation of changes in activity in previous time periods. Such a concept of temporal interaction is well developed in macro-economic theory where the stock of activity at any instant is a function of previous stocks. In particular, the concept of the distributed lag has been developed to deal with the effects which different levels of activity have in time. Distributed lags are also a central feature of Forrester's model where the difference equations describing change are to a high order.

Just as spatial interaction declines as distance or spatial cost increases from a point, the effect of activity on other activities declines as time increases from a particular instant. In dealing with changes in activity, dynamic modelling has considerably more potential for incorporating aspects of population growth and migration, which have been hitherto ignored in urban development models. Furthermore, an important component of change is due to the relocation of existing activities. This internal migration is dealt with in the TOMM and Forrester models but only net change is dealt with by the EMPIRIC model. It appears to be important to model the behaviour of relocators referred to as the mover pool.

In the model at any point in time, a configuration of activities called stocks can be derived by summing interactions over time and space. In economic parlance, the activities generated in any period of time are called flows, but to distinguish such flows from spatial interaction, they are referred to here as changes. The repercussions of activity in time are generated using a dynamic interpretation of the multiplier effect. As in many other urban models, the prime input to the model which starts the process is basic employment; in the dynamic case, the repercussions from basic employment are generated through time. The spatial interactions derived in the model are oriented around the location of activities. Activities are divided into three major types: residential population, services, and basic employment. Services are subdivided into consumer and producer-oriented groups and basic employment is broken down into employment dependent on existing employment, and unique locators whose location cannot be forecast by the model.

The unique locators provide the external stimuli to the model for although the total level of basic employment is exogenous, the other category of basic employment is distributed spatially using a linear model. Both population and service employment are allocated using production and attraction-constrained gravity models of the type derived by Wilson (1970a). These models attempt to simulate, albeit very coarsely, an

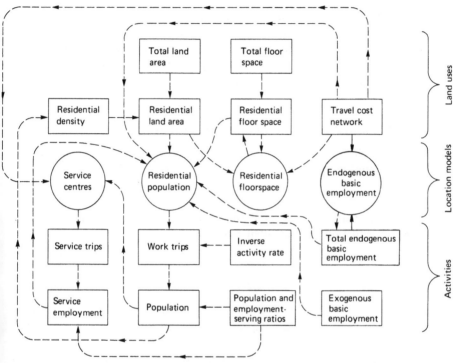

Fig. 12.1. The structure of activities and land uses in the simulation model.

equilibrium between demand and supply of activities although in the case of the residential location model, a further submodel has been designed to deal with the supply of residential land and floorspace. Figure 12.1 illustrates a schematic form for the model and the main relationships between the sectors. Both new locators and relocators, in terms of different activities, are allocated using these models. Although basic employment is exogenous to the model, other inputs include the transport system, various density limits on activity location, and the set of model parameters. The model begins with a complete configuration of existing activities and spatial interactions.

The way in which dynamics are modelled is different in this model from others and two dynamic effects can be recognised. First, there is the influence of previous stocks and changes in activity on the future distribution of activities in terms of locational attraction; this is an effect which all of the models described in the last chapter incorporate. Second, there are the repercussions from previous changes in activity which are still working through the system: this is an effect which is not explicitly embodied in the models described in the last chapter. To describe the detailed methods by which these processes are simulated, each part of the model will be first described separately, and then these parts will be assembled into the system of equations used in the model.

Modelling the distribution of activities in time

The approach to dynamics adopted in this model is through the concept of the multiplier and the economic base hypothesis. This concept has formed a basis for several models of urban development, in particular the activity allocation model, and has already been succinctly stated in four equations in Chapter 2. Without suggesting any dynamic interpretation, these four equations are rewritten as follows

$$P = \alpha E, \quad \alpha > 1, \tag{12.1}$$

$$S_1 = \beta_1 P, \quad 0 < \beta_1 < 1, \tag{12.2}$$

$$S_2 = \beta_2 E, \quad 0 < \beta_2 < 1, \tag{12.3}$$

$$E = E^b + S_1 + S_2. \tag{12.4}$$

The notation is as defined previously but is restated for convenience. P is total population and E is total employment, S_1 are consumer-oriented services and S_2 are producer-oriented services, E^b is basic employment, α is an inverse activity rate, β_1 is a population-serving ratio and β_2 an employment-serving ratio. The multiplier connecting total population to basic employment is derived as follows. First, it is necessary to express E in terms of E^b

$$E - (\alpha\beta_1 + \beta_2) E = E^b. \tag{12.5}$$

Note that $0 < (\alpha\beta_1 + \beta_2) < 1$. Then by setting

$$\mu = \alpha\beta_1 + \beta_2,$$

and

$$\gamma = 1 - \mu,$$

equation (12.5) can be rewritten as

$$E = \frac{E^b}{\gamma}. \tag{12.6}$$

Then it is obvious that the equation linking population to basic employment is

$$P = \alpha\frac{E^b}{\gamma}, \tag{12.7}$$

and $1/\gamma$ is the multiplier which features so strongly in macro-economic theory.

Equations (12.1)–(12.7) provide a static approach to urban activity analysis, and it is interesting to note ways in which this kind of analysis can be made dynamic. The classical method of macro-economic theory is largely concerned with tracing the growth paths of variables linked together by multipliers. For example, classical analysis could proceed by formulating (12.5) as a first-order difference equation (Allen, 1967)

$$E(t) - \mu E(t-1) = E^{\text{b}}. \tag{12.8}$$

Note that the bracketed indices t and $t-1$ denote time as before. The solution to (12.8) in terms of an initial level of employment $E(0)$ is found by recursion

$$E(t) = \frac{E^{\text{b}}}{\gamma} + \left[E(0) - \frac{E^{\text{b}}}{\gamma}\right](1-\gamma)^t. \tag{12.9}$$

As demonstrated in the last chapter, Paelinck (1970) has pursued this type of analysis in some depth, examining the equilibrium properties of a series of dynamic models. A similar analysis with a more empirical bias also described above has been made by Czamanski (1965). Equations (12.1)–(12.4) form the basis of his model which is strictly speaking an econometric model of Baltimore incorporating a second-order lag in (12.1) and a first-order lag in (12.2). Like Paelinck, Czamanski uses classical economic analysis to derive solutions to the model.

A different interpretation of the multiplier is suggested in this model and this can be regarded as a more disaggregated approach than that implied above. It is well known that under most conditions the multiplier can be expanded in the following way (Artle, 1961)

$$\frac{1}{\gamma} = \frac{1}{1-\mu} = 1 + \mu + \mu^2 + \ldots + \mu^n. \tag{12.10}$$

Given an increment of employment $\Delta E^{\text{b}}(t)$, where the difference operator Δ defines $\Delta E^{\text{b}}(t) = E^{\text{b}}(t+1) - E^{\text{b}}(t)$, the total population P generated from this increment is

$$P = \alpha \Delta E^{\text{b}}(t)(1 + \mu + \mu^2 + \ldots + \mu^n). \tag{12.11}$$

Economic analysis tends to treat the multiplier itself as a rate of change because often activity is multiplied up to its true level quite quickly. In other words, the repercussions associated with the multiplier quickly work themselves through the economy. From (12.11), however, each increment of activity generated from $\Delta E^{\text{b}}(t)$ is associated with a term in the series, and each term could be associated with a particular time period. This of course depends upon the length of the time period, but the hypothesis adopted here states that the repercussions traced by (12.11) are sufficiently large and take sufficiently long in urban systems to form a suitable basis for dynamic modelling.

Assuming a constant parameter μ and that each increment of activity is generated in successive time periods, any particular increment of population $\Delta P(t)$ is derived from an equation of the following form

$$\Delta P(t) = \alpha[\Delta E^b(t) + \Delta E^b(t-1)\,\mu + \Delta E^b(t-2)\,\mu^2 + \ldots + \Delta E^b(t-n)\,\mu^n].$$
(12.12)

Equation (12.12) shows that the lag is distributed over $n+1$ time periods, and this equation has similarities to the geometric distributed lag equation defined by Allen (1967). Each increment of activity generated by (12.11) need not be associated with a particular time period for it is possible to combine two or more terms of (12.11) into a particular time period. The time period has to be sufficiently short to detect the geometric series of (12.11) in a discrete fashion, and furthermore, it is likely that, after a given number of time periods, the multiplier effects will become insignificant. These considerations have led to the adoption of a one-year time interval within which two successive increments of activity are generated. It is also assumed that after ten time periods, the multiplier effects are small enough to ignore; in other words, in (12.11), n is never greater than 20. Table 12.1 shows the amounts of employment and population generated using this scheme.

From Table 12.1, the distributed lag equations for employment and population can be written as follows

$$\Delta E(t) = \Delta E^b(t) + (1+\mu)\,[\Delta E^b(t)\,\mu + \Delta E^b(t-1)\,\mu^3 + \ldots + \Delta E^b(t-n)\,\mu^{2n+1}],$$
(12.13)

$$\Delta P(t) = \alpha(1+\mu)\,[\Delta E^b(t)\,\mu^0 + \Delta E^b(t-1)\,\mu^2 + \ldots + \Delta E^b(t-n)\,\mu^{2n}]. \quad (12.14)$$

Equations (12.13) and (12.14) summarise the way in which activities are generated in time, although in the simulation model, employment and population are not formally generated in this manner for each time period is modelled separately. In more familiar terms, this process implies that the repercussions from changes in the location of basic employment in terms of services and the associated population would occur over *time* as well as over space. But at any one period of time, the amount of basic employment itself would be changing; therefore in a time period, change would be composed of a spectrum of changes originating from present and past time periods, as illustrated in Figure 12.2. If, however, the total of basic industry were to stabilise, then changes in the quantity of activity would gradually die away until an equilibrium were reached, thus satisfying

TABLE 12.1. *Generation of activity in successive time periods from* $\Delta E^b(t)$

Time period	Employment activity	Population activity
1st period	$\Delta E^b(t)(1+\mu+\mu^2) = \Delta E^b(t)+\Delta E^b(t)\mu(1+\mu)$	$\alpha\Delta E^b(t)(1+\mu) = \alpha\Delta E^b(t)\mu^0(1+\mu)$
2nd period	$\Delta E^b(t)(\mu^3+\mu^4) = \Delta E^b(t)\mu^3(1+\mu)$	$\alpha\Delta E^b(t)(\mu^2+\mu^3) = \alpha\Delta E^b(t)\mu^2(1+\mu)$
3rd period	$\Delta E^b(t)(\mu^5+\mu^6) = \Delta E^b(t)\mu^5(1+\mu)$	$\alpha\Delta E^b(t)(\mu^4+\mu^5) = \alpha\Delta E^b(t)\mu^4(1+\mu)$
.	.	.
.	.	.
.	.	.
nth period	$\Delta E^b(t)(\mu^{2n-1}+\mu^{2n}) = \Delta E^b(t)\mu^{2n-1}(1+\mu)$	$\alpha\Delta E^b(t)(\mu^{2n-2}+\mu^{2n-1}) = \alpha\Delta E^b(t)\mu^{2(n-1)}(1+\mu)$

Harris's Principle. In the above equations the ratios are shown as constants which do not vary through time. Although it is probable that such ratios vary, it would be difficult to detect such variation from data. Therefore, in the case of μ, it is assumed that

$$\mu = \frac{1}{n+1} \sum_{t=0}^{n} \mu_t.$$

Although this averaging implies a strong assumption, it is possible to vary μ in the simulation model over longer periods of time incorporating about 5 time periods.

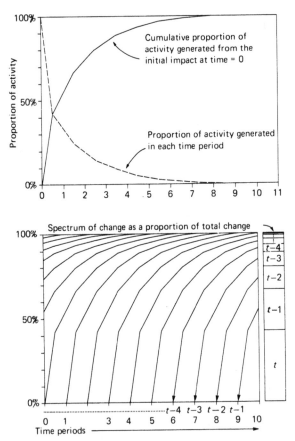

Fig. 12.2. Spectrum of changes in activity generated by the economic base mechanism.

Modelling the distribution of activities in space

The simulation model has been designed initially for application at the subregional scale, and is operated mainly through the location of activities rather than land uses. Figure 12.1 shows that three submodels exist to allocate activity to zones of the spatial system; basic employment endogenous to the simulation, population, and service employment are the three categories of activity which are modelled in spatial terms, and these activities can be treated in turn.

The basic employment location model attempts to predict the location of the growth in basic employment which depends upon previous levels of activity in the system. Declines in such employment are not simulated using this model which is appropriate only to a growth situation. Successful models of this sector have been built elsewhere using linear equation systems (Putnam, 1970) and it was decided to model this activity in a similar way. The model was built outside the main framework of the simulation by Cheshire (1970) and was fitted using stepwise regression analysis. The change in endogenous basic employment $\Delta Y_i(t)$, where $\Delta Y_i(t) = Y_i(t+1) - Y_i(t)$, is allocated as follows. Note that the i, j subscripts refer to zones as defined in all previous chapters. The model can be stated as

$$\Delta Y_i(t) = \sum_k a_k Z_{ik}(t) + \sum_l b_l \Delta Z_{il}(t-1) + g, \qquad (12.15)$$

where $Z_{ik}(t)$ is the stock of activity k in zone i at t, and $\Delta Z_{il}(t-1)$ is the change in activity l in i between t and $t-1$. a_k, b_l and g are parameters of the equation. At each time period, the total change in endogenous basic employment is input to the model and (12.15) is normalised before this activity is allocated.

The residential location model is perhaps the most complex of all the spatial submodels for a crude attempt has been made to model both the demand and supply of residential space. The model is based on some theoretical work by Schneider (1967) who argues that the attraction of an area to residential locators must be some function of both the land available and the existing residential floorspace. Schneider has proceeded to devise a model for the allocation of floorspace and he has further extended his research by fitting the model to data from Chicago (Schneider, 1969). A variant of Schneider's model has been adopted here as a simple model of the supply of floorspace which is in turn an input to the residential location model. The actual form of this model is similar to the potential model used by Lowry (1964) to allocate population. At each time period, total floorspace $\Delta F(t)$ which is exogenous to the model is allocated to zones as follows

$$\Delta^* F_i(t) = \Delta F(t) \, QX_i(t), \tag{12.16}$$

$$X_i(t) = \sum_j [F_j(t+1) + L_j(t-1)] f^1[c_{ij}(t-1)], \tag{12.17}$$

$$Q = \frac{1}{\sum_j X_j(t)}. \tag{12.18}$$

Note that in the following discussion, a difference operator of the type Δ^* shows that a change in a time period is *not* the net change between t and $t+1$. In the above equations, $\Delta^* F_i(t)$ is the expected rather than the actual change in the supply of floorspace in i, $F_j(t+1)$ is the expected supply of floorspace in j at $t+1$, $L_i(t-1)$ is the amount of land available for residential development in i at the end of the previous time period $t-1$, and $f^1[c_{ij}(t-1)]$ is some function of travel cost between i and j at $t-1$. Starting with $F_j(t)$ as a first approximation to $F_j(t+1)$, (12.16)–(12.18) are iterated until convergence, with the new level of expected floorspace at time $t+1$ being computed at each iteration from

$$F_j(t+1) = F_j(t) + \Delta^* F_j(t). \tag{12.19}$$

There are several problems connected with the development of this model and among those requiring further research are questions of overlap between the 'supply' of residential space predicted by this model and the 'demand' for such space which is simulated by the residential location model described below. Although floorspace and land in this supply model are measured in the same units, there are also problems of combining such variables as in (12.17) which need further investigation.

Floorspace from (12.19) and available land form the critical variables measuring the locational attraction of every zone j for residential purposes between t and $t+1$. Residential attraction $D_j(t)$ is calculated as follows

$$D_j(t) = \phi_j[\sigma F_j(t+1) + (1-\sigma) L_j(t-1)], \quad 0 \leqslant \sigma \leqslant 1, \tag{12.20}$$

$$\phi_j \begin{cases} = 0, & \text{if } P_j(t) \geqslant C_j(t), \\ = 1, & \text{otherwise.} \end{cases} \tag{12.21}$$

Note here that σ, and C_j have been redefined from their previous notation. σ is a parameter controlling the relative influence of land and floorspace on residential attraction, ϕ_j is a term which controls the overall level of residential attraction, $P_j(t)$ is population in j at t, and $C_j(t)$ is the population limit in zone j at t.

The residential location model is based on a production-constrained gravity model of the type outlined in Chapters 2 and 10. The model allocates a change in employment $\Delta E_i(t)$ located in i to place of residence in j

$$\Delta T_{ij}(t) = A_i(t)\,\Delta E_i(t)\,D_j(t)f^2[c_{ij}(t-1)], \qquad (12.22)$$

$$A_i(t) = \frac{1}{\sum_j D_j(t)f^2[c_{ij}(t-1)]}. \qquad (12.23)$$

$\Delta T_{ij}(t)$ is the change in work trips between i and j, and $f^2[c_{ij}(t-1)]$ is some function of travel cost between i and j at $t-1$. This model satisfies the constraint

$$\sum_j \Delta T_{ij}(t) = \Delta E_i(t), \qquad (12.24)$$

and the change in population $\Delta P_j(t)$ in j can be found by summing (12.22) over i and scaling the result by α, the inverse activity rate

$$\Delta P_j(t) = \alpha \sum_i \Delta T_{ij}(t) = \alpha D_j(t)\sum_i A_i(t)\,\Delta E_i(t)f^2[c_{ij}(t-1)]. \quad (12.25)$$

The land available for residential purposes at the end of the time period can be calculated by converting $\Delta P_j(t)$ to land area using a population density ratio δ_j

$$L_j(t+1) = L_j(t) - \delta_j\Delta P_j(t). \qquad (12.26)$$

The third submodel allocates the demand for service employment in j to service centres in i, and is formulated as an attraction-constrained gravity model. Service centre attraction in i is assumed to be a function of the previous demands for service employment in i, and at present, this attraction $V_i(t)$ has the following form.

$$V_i(t) = \rho\Delta S_i(t-1) + \rho^2\Delta S_i(t-2) + \ldots + \rho^n\Delta S_i(t-n), \quad 0 < \rho < 1. \qquad (12.27)$$

ρ is a ratio controlling the effect of previous changes in activity on attraction. The change in demand for services in i by the population living at j called $\Delta S_{ij}(t)$ is computed from the following equations

$$\Delta S_{ij}(t) = V_i(t)\,R_j(t)\,\beta_1\Delta P_j(t)f^3[c_{ij}(t-1)], \qquad (12.28)$$

$$R_j(t) = \frac{1}{\sum_i V_i(t)f^3[c_{ij}(t-1)]}. \qquad (12.29)$$

$f^3[c_{ij}(t-1)]$ is some function of travel cost between i and j at $t-1$. The model presented in (12.28) and (12.29) is subject to the constraint

$$\sum_i \Delta S_{ij}(t) = \beta_1\Delta P_j(t). \qquad (12.30)$$

The total change in service employment at i is calculated by summing (12.28) over j and adding the services generated from the change in employment at i

$$\Delta S_i(t) = \sum_j \Delta S_i(t) + \beta_2 \Delta E_i(t). \qquad (12.31)$$

As this completes the description of the spatial submodels, it is now necessary to outline the factors which affect the relocation of activity in the system. The previous equations are valid for the generation and location of new activities in the system but some slight modifications are needed to model the relocation of existing activities.

Modelling the relocation of existing activities

In the model, only existing population and service employments are allowed to relocate in each time period. This is consistent with the structure of the model in which basic employment is largely exogenous to the simulation. Yet the structure of the model poses many problems with regard to a first approach to the problem. As with the modelling of external changes in activity, the mechanism for relocating the existing population and associated services must be operated from the basic employment on which these relocators initially depend. In other words, it is necessary to identify basic employment associated with population and services and to relocate these activities from this point.

A further complicating feature of the model, but one which makes the simulation much easier to execute, concerns the relocation of activities in time. As with external changes in activities, the relocation of activity is lagged according to the multiplier effects. Reverting to a previous notation of postscripting variables to indicate time, the relocation of service employment between $t+1$ and t, called $\Delta S^m(t)$ and population called $\Delta P^m(t)$ is as follows

$$\Delta S^m(t) = \pi(1+\mu)\,[E^b(t)\,\mu + E^b(t-1)\,\mu^3 + \dots + E^b(t-n)\,\mu^{2n+1}], \qquad (12.32)$$

$$\Delta P^m(t) = \alpha\pi(1+\mu)\,[E^b(t)\,\mu^0 + E^b(t-1)\,\mu^2 + \dots + E^b(t-n)\,\mu^{2n}]. \qquad (12.33)$$

π is referred to as the mover pool ratio and $0 < \pi < 1$. This ratio indicates the proportion of the existing stock in previous time periods which is gradually working its way through the mover pool. Although π is likely to vary in time, it is assumed here that π is an average over the simulation period.

The most complex feature of the mover pool arises from a need to simplify the simulation. When the simulation is begun at $t = 0$ the ratios α, β_1 and β_2 are likely to be very different in the initial configuration of activities from the ratios used in the simulation period. It is extremely difficult, if not impossible, to take account of these differences, for at each time period, new activity generated using the new ratios is being added to the existing configuration, thus changing the actual ratios. Furthermore, new activities generated in previous time periods are also eligible for relocation in later time periods. These factors mean that for each activity, the ratio π must be modulated at each time period to ensure that the right amount of activity is reallocated. Taking the example of population, at each time period a new ratio $\pi(t)$ is computed from

$$\pi(t) = \pi \frac{P(0)\,(1/\alpha - \beta_2/\alpha - \beta_1) + \sum\limits_{t=0}^{N} \Delta E^{b}(t)}{E^{b}(0) + \sum\limits_{t=0}^{N} \Delta E^{b}(t)}. \tag{12.34}$$

Note that the summation of $\Delta E^{b}(t)$ is from $t = 0$ to $t = N$, where N is the previous time period. As the calculation of $\pi(t)$ is complex, it is necessary to explain the terms in (12.34) in more detail. The term $P(0)\,(1/\alpha - \beta_2/\alpha - \beta_1)$ converts total population in the system at the beginning of the simulation ($t = 0$) into a hypothetical amount of basic employment which is consistent with the ratios α, β_1 and β_2. This basic employment is likely to be different from actual basic employment $\Delta E^{b}(0)$ because the ratios α, β_1 and β_2 are averages pertaining to changes in activity over the simulation period, not to the structure of activities at the start of the simulation. At each time t, total basic employment consistent with these ratios is divided by actual basic employment, and this proportion is used to weight the mover pool ratio $\pi(t)$. This mechanism is purely a device to enable movers in the system to be reallocated according to the same ratios used to allocate changes in activity, and has been introduced solely to minimise computer time. In applying the weighted mover pool ratio $\pi(t)$, (12.33) now becomes

$$\Delta P^{m}(t) = \alpha(1+\mu)[\pi(t)\,E^{b}(t)\mu^0 + \pi(t-1)\,E^{b}(t-1)\mu^2 + \dots$$
$$+ \pi(t-n)\,\Delta E^{b}(t-n)\mu^{2n}]. \tag{12.35}$$

The rather unrealistic nature of the relocation procedure is seen quite clearly when space is considered. The ratio $\pi(t)$ is constant in each time period and for the whole system; therefore the numbers of trips which are affected by relocation are a constant proportion $\pi(t)$ of each i,j pair. This seems highly unrealistic for it is likely that $\pi(t)$ varies spatially. As yet no efficient way of incorporating a spatial mover pool ratio has been found; if a feasible method exists, it may be possible to make $\pi(t)$ endogenous to the model. At present, changes in travel costs and measures of locational attraction are the key determinants of relocation. A fairly elaborate accounting procedure which is dealt with in more detail later, is used to ensure that no double counting of activities occurs; relocation is essentially internal migration which is largely independent of the absolute growth of the system and in each time period the following equation is always satisfied

$$\sum_j \Delta P_j^m(t) = \sum_i \Delta S_i^m(t) = 0.$$

At this stage, the major components of the simulation model have been described and the task now is to assemble these components into the basic model. The equation system is outlined below in two parts: the equations concerned with generating and allocating activity in each time period are first discussed, and then the relationships used in accounting for net changes and total stocks of activity are outlined.

The equation system I: generation and allocation

At the start of the simulation, an initial configuration of activities and trips in the system is required. Although activities must be available, trip distributions are often difficult to obtain and therefore an option is built into the program to generate such distributions using production-attraction constrained gravity models. When $t = 0$, the distribution of work trips is generated as follows

$$T_{ij}(t) = A_i(t)\, B_j(t)\, E_i(t)\, P_j(t) f^4[c_{ij}(t)], \tag{12.36}$$

$$A_i(t) = \frac{1}{\sum_j B_j(t)\, P_i(t) f^4[c_{ij}(t)]}, \tag{12.37}$$

$$B_j(t) = \frac{1}{\sum_i A_i(t)\, E_i(t) f^4[c_{ij}(t)]}. \tag{12.38}$$

A distribution for $S_{ij}(t)$ is obtained using a similar model with $\beta_1 P_i(t)$ replacing $E_i(t)$ and $S_j(t)$ replacing $P_j(t)$ in (12.36)–(12.38). The parameters of the function $f^4[c_{ij}(t)]$ are approximated using formulae and numerical procedures derived by Hyman (1969) which were discussed in Chapter 6.

The constant ratios – the inverse activity, population-serving and employment-serving ratios – are calculated at this stage for the simulation period. Then

$$\alpha = \frac{\sum_t \Delta P(t)}{\sum_t \Delta E(t)}, \tag{12.39}$$

$$\beta_1 = \frac{\sum_t \Delta S_1(t)}{\sum_t \Delta P(t)}, \tag{12.40}$$

$$\beta_2 = \frac{\sum_t \Delta S_2(t)}{\sum_t \Delta E(t)}. \tag{12.41}$$

The summations in (12.39)–(12.41) are from $t = 0$ to $t = n$, where n is the end of the simulation period. At this point, the model begins to simulate changes in activity in each time period. The network of travel costs or distances is updated using a shortest routes program, and the equation modulating the mover pool ratio π is worked out

$$\pi(t) = \pi \frac{P(0)\left(\frac{1}{\alpha} - \frac{\beta_2}{\alpha} - \beta_1\right) + \sum_t \Delta E^b(t)}{E^b(0) + \sum_t \Delta E^b(t)}. \qquad (12.42)$$

Then endogenous basic employment $\Delta Y(t)$ is allocated to zones of the system using the basic employment location model

$$\Delta Y_i(t) = \Delta Y(t) \frac{\sum_k a_k Z_{ik}(t) + \sum_l b_l \Delta Z_{il}(t-1) + g}{\sum_i [\sum_k a_k Z_{ik}(t) + \sum_l b_l \Delta Z_{il}(t-1) + g]}. \qquad (12.43)$$

The measures of locational attraction for this time period are now calculated; first, the Schneider model which allocates the total change in floorspace $\Delta F(t)$ to zones is run. Accessibilities $X_i(t)$ are derived

$$X_i(t) = \sum_j [F_j(t+1) + L_j(t-1)] f^1 [c_{ij}(t-1)], \qquad (12.44)$$

$$\Delta^* F_i(t) = \Delta F(t) \frac{X_i(t)}{\sum_j X_j(t)}, \qquad (12.45)$$

$$F_j(t+1) = F_j(t) + \Delta^* F_j(t). \qquad (12.46)$$

As $F_i(t) = f[F_i(t)]$, (12.44)–(12.46) are reiterated until convergence. At the present time, Schneider's original model is being investigated in a separate program. With certain starting values and parameters, Schneider's model does not converge and therefore the variant described in (12.44)–(12.46) was adopted until further work has been done on the structure of Schneider's model. Next, residential attraction in each zone j is computed

$$D_j(t) = \phi_j [\sigma F_j(t+1) + (1-\sigma) L_j(t-1)], \qquad (12.47)$$

and then, the measures of service centre attraction are calculated from

$$V_i(t) = \sum_{r=1}^N \rho^r \Delta S_i(t-r). \qquad (12.48)$$

The total basic employment to be allocated including the basic employment associated with relocation is found from

$$\Delta^* E_i^b(t) = \Delta H_i(t) + \Delta Y_i(t) + \pi(t) E_i^b(t), \qquad (12.49)$$

where $\Delta H_i(t)$ is now the change in exogenous basic employment. The model now moves into an inner loop which is concerned with allocating and generating two increments of employment and population. This inner loop is referred to by an index m. The first increment of employment includes the change in service employment from the previous time period t to $t-1$ which has not yet worked its way through the system

$$\Delta^*E_i(t, m) = \Delta^*E_i^b(t) + \Delta^*S_i(t-1). \tag{12.50}$$

Employment is first allocated to areas of residence and scaled to population; then service employment demanded is derived and allocated to service centres using the following equations

$$\Delta^*T_{ij}(t, m) = \Delta^*E_i(t, m)\frac{D_j(t)f^2[c_{ij}(t-1)]}{\sum\limits_j D_j(t)f^2[c_{ij}(t-1)]}, \tag{12.51}$$

$$\Delta^*P_j(t, m) = \alpha\sum\limits_i \Delta^*T_{ij}(t, m), \tag{12.52}$$

$$\Delta^*S_{ij}(t, m) = \beta_1\Delta^*P_j(t, m)\frac{V_i(t)f^3[c_{ij}(t-1)]}{\sum\limits_i V_i(t)f^3[c_{ij}(t-1)]}, \tag{12.53}$$

$$\Delta^*S_i(t, m) = \sum\limits_j \Delta^*S_{ij}(t, m) + \beta_2\Delta^*E_i(t, m). \tag{12.54}$$

If m is less than the required number of iterations then

$$\Delta^*E_i(t, m+1) = \Delta^*S_i(t, m), \tag{12.55}$$

and $\Delta^*E_i(t, m+1)$ is substituted for $\Delta^*E_i(t, m)$ in (12.51). Equations (12.51)–(12.54) are reiterated until the condition is met: in the simulation here, two iterations are required. The process of generation and allocation is now complete for this time period and the model moves into the accounting framework.

The equation system II: accounting

First, the gross changes in activities and trips are easily calculated from the earlier equations: these changes are listed below

$$\Delta^*P_j(t) = \sum\limits_m \Delta^*P_j(t, m), \tag{12.56}$$

$$\Delta^*S_i(t) = \sum\limits_m \Delta^*S_i(t, m), \tag{12.57}$$

$$\Delta^*E_i(t) = \Delta^*S_i(t) + \Delta^*E_i^b(t) + \Delta^*S_i(t-1), \tag{12.58}$$

$$\Delta^*T_{ij}(t) = \sum\limits_m \Delta^*T_{ij}(t, m), \tag{12.59}$$

$$\Delta^*S_{ij}(t) = \sum\limits_m \Delta^*S_{ij}(t, m) \tag{12.60}$$

Equations (12.56)–(12.60) are gross changes in that they include activity which is relocating in the system. To avoid double counting, this activity must be subtracted. Furthermore, to obtain the net changes, the complex modulations of the mover pool ratio through time must be taken into account. The proportions of activity relocating at different periods from any point in time are easily calculated as in Table 12.2 and these proportions are also given below

$$\theta(1) = 1 - \mu^2,$$

$$\theta(2) = \mu^2\theta(1),$$

$$\theta(3) = \mu^2\theta(2),$$

$$\vdots \quad \vdots \quad \vdots$$

$$\theta(n) = \mu^2\theta(n-1).$$

TABLE 12.2. *Proportions of population and service employment allocated at each time period*

Time period	Population and service employment*			
1st period	$\dfrac{\mu^0(1+\mu)}{(1-\mu)^{-1}}$	$= (1-\mu^2)$	$=$	$= \theta(1)$
2nd period	$\dfrac{\mu^2(1+\mu)}{(1-\mu)^{-1}}$	$= \mu^2(1-\mu^2)$	$= \mu^2\theta(1)$	$= \theta(2)$
3rd period	$\dfrac{\mu^4(1+\mu)}{(1-\mu)^{-1}}$	$= \mu^4(1-\mu^2)$	$= \mu^2\theta(2)$	$= \theta(3)$
.	.	.	.	.
.	.	.	.	.
.	.	.	.	.
nth period	$\dfrac{\mu^{2(n-1)}(1+\mu)}{(1-\mu)^{-1}}$	$= \mu^{2(n-1)}(1-\mu^2)$	$= \mu^2\theta(n-1)$	$= \theta(n)$

* It can easily be shown that the proportions for service employment are the same as those for population.

These proportions are relevant to the relocation of population but must be modulated for service employment, work trips and service trips in the following way. The subscripts R, T and S denote service employment, work trips and service trips respectively

$$\theta_R(t) = \theta(t)\frac{P(t)\,(\beta_1 + \beta_2/\alpha)}{S(t)}, \tag{12.61}$$

$$\theta_T(t) = \theta(t)\frac{P(t)}{\alpha E(t)}, \tag{12.62}$$

$$\theta_S(t) = \theta(t)\frac{\beta_1 P(t)}{S(t)-\beta_2 E(t)}. \tag{12.63}$$

The main calculations for deriving net changes are given below; total stocks of activity at time $t+1$ need not be shown explicitly for their calculation is obvious. Note that $N = 10$

$$P_j(t+1)-P_j(t) = \Delta^* P_j(t) - \pi \sum_{z=1}^{N} \theta(z) P_j(z), \tag{12.64}$$

$$S_i(t+1)-S_i(t) = \Delta^* S_i(t) - \pi \sum_{z=1}^{N} \theta_R(z) S_i(z), \tag{12.65}$$

$$T_{ij}(t+1)-T_{ij}(t) = \Delta^* T_{ij}(t) - \pi \sum_{z=1}^{N} \theta_T(z) T_{ij}(z), \tag{12.66}$$

$$S_{ij}(t+1)-S_{ij}(t) = \Delta^* S_{ij}(t) - \pi \sum_{z=1}^{N} \theta_S(z) S_{ij}(z), \tag{12.67}$$

$$E_i(t+1)-E_i(t) = S_i(t+1)-S_i(t)+\Delta H_i(t)+\Delta Y_i(t). \tag{12.68}$$

Total quantities of activity in the system can be calculated by summing over i or j or both. There are also several other outputs from the model at each time period such as zonal activity rates, trip lengths and residential densities. Before the model goes on to simulating changes in the following time period, the land available for future residential development is calculated from

$$L_j(t+1) = L_j(t)-\delta_j[P_j(t+1)-P_j(t)]. \tag{12.69}$$

A new measure of actual floorspace in residential uses is also derived from

$$F_j(t+1) = F_j(t)+\Delta F(t)\frac{P_j(t+1)-P_j(t)}{\sum_j P_j(t+1)-\sum_j P_j(t)}. \tag{12.70}$$

A test is made to assess whether the constraints on population in each zone have been violated. The ϕ_j term is set as follows for the next time period

$$\phi_j \begin{cases} = 0, & \text{if } P_j(t+1) \geqslant C_j(t+1), \\ = 1, & \text{otherwise.} \end{cases} \tag{12.71}$$

If $t < n$, t is increased to $t+1$ and the simulation begins again at (12.42). Equations (12.42)–(12.71) are reiterated until all time periods in the simulation period have been modelled. A flow diagram of the main operations in the model is presented in Figure 12.3.

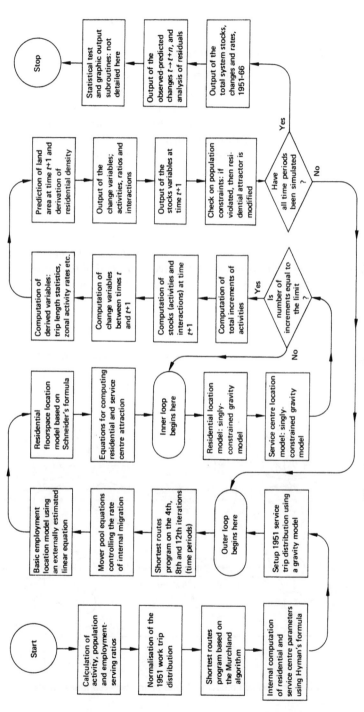

Fig. 12.3. Sequence of operations in the simulation model.

Restrictive assumptions of the simulation

Although the equation system describes the various feedback loops which operate in the model within and between time periods, a more direct presentation of these linkages is provided in Figure 12.4. At any point in time, the model is in disequilibrium in the sense that previous changes in the level of activity are generating further changes. These repercussions due to multiplier effects are assumed small enough to ignore ten time periods after the initial stimulus, and this means that in any time period, changes originally generated in the nine previous time periods are part of the total change in activity. Furthermore, when the simulation is terminated, there are still repercussions to work themselves out; there is also the problem of starting the simulation, for to preserve consistency the model should begin in disequilibrium. This could easily be achieved by adding the potential activity not yet generated at the end of the simulation, to the starting position. As yet this problem has not been dealt with, although in absolute terms, its effect on the system is quite small.

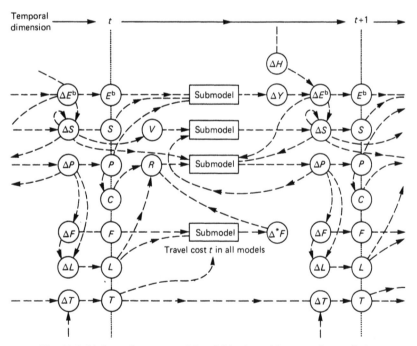

Fig. 12.4. Linkages between model variables in and between time periods.

The subdivision of the simulation period and the spatial system into discrete units is an important factor in detecting variance. As demonstrated in previous chapters, it was argued that spatial systems should be zoned to maximise the ratio of inter-zonal to intra-zonal interaction. A similar rule is necessary for fixing the length of the time period; the ratio of activity generated in the first time period to repercussions from that activity generated in later time periods, should be minimised. As the length of the time period increases, more of the multiplier effects from a change in activity are generated within that time period, and thus a time interval of one year is considered most appropriate here.

Although the activity parameters, α, β_1 and β_2 are taken as constant over the simulation period, it is possible to vary these parameters over periods of time longer than two years. Because of the nature of the multiplier, it is difficult to vary the parameters in each time period for this would change the form of the economic base relationship. This problem is largely one of estimating the parameters from data, and of accounting for different values of the parameters in the simulation. In future research, it may be possible to assume a trend in these parameters over the simulation period, thus implicitly recognising that the parameters vary. With regard to the mover pool ratio, this parameter can be varied over time, but it is much more difficult to vary the parameter spatially. This ratio should be partly endogenous to the simulation in that changes in the age–sex–household structure of the population are important determinants of internal migration. In future work, these relationships will be explored in more detail.

It is also necessary to comment on the recursive structure of the simulation model, and to assess its validity. In designing such a model, what appear to be simultaneous relationships in reality must be approximated by a sequence of relationships; this embodies certain assumptions as to the order of operations in the sequence. For example, the relationship between the supply and demand for floorspace is approximated in the following way. The expected supply of floorspace is derived using Schneider's model, and this becomes an input to the measure of locational attraction used in the demand model locating population. Population is then converted into actual floorspace which is likely to be different from expected floorspace. No iteration is used to establish consistency between the expected and actual supply of floorspace. This sequence of operations could easily be ordered so that the expected and actual demand for, rather than supply of, floorspace were computed. Such decisions with regard to ordering abound in the model, and it is assumed that the time period is short enough to make little difference to the order of operations.

Application and preliminary calibration

The simulation model is being run with data from the Reading area in Central Berkshire. This subregion has been divided into 18 zones and the simulation is from 1951–66 in one-year time periods; Table 12.3 presents

TABLE 12.3. *Major characteristics of the Reading subregion*

Total number of zones	18
Total land area in square miles	95.8250
Average land area per zone in square miles	5.3236
Total population	
(i) 1951	191 948
(ii) 1966	262 279
Average population per zone	
(i) 1951	10 664
(ii) 1966	19 577
Population density in persons per square mile	
(i) 1951	2 003
(ii) 1966	2 737
Basic employment	
(i) 1951	26 723
(ii) 1966	40 691
Total employment	
(i) 1951	76 712
(ii) 1966	109 405
Ratio of basic to total employment	
(i) 1951	0.3483
(ii) 1966	0.3779
Ratio of inter-zonal to intra-zonal work trips	
(i) 1951	0.6039
(ii) 1966	0.9586

the pertinent characteristics of this subregion. There is an immediate problem in collecting data for this model; although good cross-sections of activity and work trips exist for 1951, 1961 and 1966 from the Census of Population, very little data exist in yearly periods between these dates. Data on total employment by SIC are available for each year from the Employment Exchange Areas, and this provides the only time-series to guide the simulation. Consequently, many of the model's hypotheses cannot be validated in any strict sense. It is also clear that the model cannot be calibrated in the usual way, for gaps exist in the set of data which have been filled by assumption, or by outputs from other models.

The zoning of the subregion and the route network in 1966 are shown in

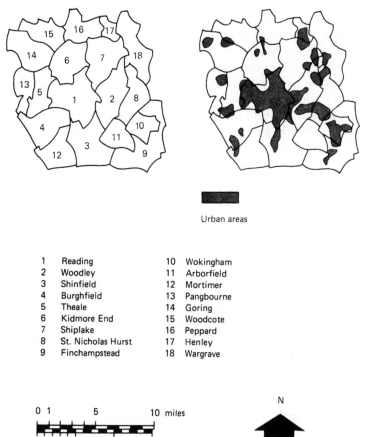

Urban areas

1	Reading	10	Wokingham
2	Woodley	11	Arborfield
3	Shinfield	12	Mortimer
4	Burghfield	13	Pangbourne
5	Theale	14	Goring
6	Kidmore End	15	Woodcote
7	Shiplake	16	Peppard
8	St. Nicholas Hurst	17	Henley
9	Finchampstead	18	Wargrave

0 1   5   10 miles

N

Fig. 12.5. Zoning of the Reading subregion.

Figure 12.5. Changes in the network and data on land use have been provided by the Local Authorities in the area and at present the model is being
run using a hypothetical time-series for basic employment. In general
terms, the mathematical methods developed for fitting and analysing time-
series are quite unsuitable for such a hybrid model as this. Furthermore, at
present this model is regarded as an exploratory tool for setting up experiments concerning urban growth processes and for refining and developing
existing theories of urban structure. The experimental approach is quite
consistent with the form of the model and the emphasis in the rest of this
chapter is on testing the sensitivity of the model's parameters and variables
to change. In this way, the key determinants of urban growth and structure

as simulated by the model, can be revealed. As a first step in this approach, reasonable values for the parameters need to be estimated using some short-cut techniques.

The basic employment location model was fitted to data from 1961-6 using stepwise linear regression analysis (Cheshire, 1970). Although there are more accurate and less biased methods for fitting such a linear equation to data consistent with a one-year time module (Rogers, 1968), the equations presented below are appropriate for experimental purposes

$$X_i^S(t) = \sum_j \frac{S_j(t)}{d_{ij}(t)}, \tag{12.72}$$

$$\Delta X_i^P(t) = \sum_j \frac{P_j(t)}{d_{ij}(t)} - \sum_j \frac{P_j(t-1)}{d_{ij}(t-1)}, \tag{12.73}$$

$$\Delta Y_i(t) = -0.7307 + 0.1215 E_i^b(t) + 0.0200 \Delta X_i^P(t) - 0.0119 P_i(t)$$
$$- 0.0264 S_i(t) - 0.0581 X_i^S(t). \tag{12.74}$$

All variables are significant at the 5 per cent level. $d_{ij}(t)$ and $d_{ij}(t-1)$ are distances between i and j in miles at t and $t-1$. Equation (12.74) is normalised in the simulation and total endogenous basic employment $\Delta Y(t)$ is allocated to zones. The coefficient of multiple correlation r^2 is 0.9899 for (12.74). Despite the apparent goodness of this fit, (12.74) is empirically determined, and has no theoretical underpinnings.

The following functions of travel time were assumed for the simulation and parameters were approximated using Hyman's linear interpolation–extrapolation method outlined in Chapter 6. Then

$$\left.\begin{array}{l} f^1[c_{ij}(t-1)] \\ f^2[c_{ij}(t-1)] \\ f^4[c_{ij}(t-1)] \end{array}\right\} = \exp\left[-\lambda_1 t_{ij}(t-1)\right], \tag{12.75}$$

$$f^3[c_{ij}(t-1)] = \exp\left[-\lambda_2 t_{ij}(t-1)\right]. \tag{12.76}$$

Travel time t_{ij} is used as a proxy for travel cost in the model. Note also that the service centre trip distribution model necessary to set up the distribution of service trips in 1951 uses parameter λ_2. The parameters λ_1 and λ_2 are functions of the associated mean trip lengths and Hyman's method generates an approximation from given means. The activity ratios α, β_1 and β_2 are estimated from data at the start of the simulation, and this presents no difficulties. A very approximate value of the mover pool ratio has been taken from data on internal migration in Berkshire recorded by the 1966 Census of Population between 1961 and 1966; the value of this ratio is 0.020 and has been computed from net, not gross movements.

A critical assumption has been made with regard to the form of the basic employment time-series between 1951 and 1966. The change in basic employment in each zone in each year over the simulation has been guided by the total change in basic employment in each year, available from the Employment Exchange Areas. The model has been run with the above assumptions and the results in the following section demonstrate the main

TABLE 12.4. *Statistical testing of activities*

	Stocks 1966		Changes 1951–66	
	Service employment	Population	Service employment	Population
Ratio of means	0.0061	0.0067	0.0232	0.0237
Ratio of standard deviations	0.0593	0.1162	0.2507	0.4349
Ratio of modes	0.0007	0.0265	0.0001	−0.4273
Chi-square χ^2	0.0003	1.0624	1.0004	9.7501
Coefficient of determination r^2	0.9991	0.9802	0.9703	0.0958
Slope of regression line	0.9419	0.8753	0.7392	0.1745
Intercept	203.8970	1737.1682	253.9523	3211.7998

NOTES: The ratios are formed by subtracting the predicted from the observed statistic and dividing by the observed value. The slope and intercept statistics are based on a regression of predicted on observed values of each activity.

TABLE 12.5. *Statistical testing of interactions**

	Total interaction 1966		Changes in interaction 1951–66	
Statistics	Service trips	Work trips	Service trips	Work trips
Ratio of means	0.0061	0.0074	0.0234	0.0223
Ratio of standard deviation	0.1079	0.1448	0.3631	0.4016
Ratio of modes	0.0021	0.0025	−0.0074	0.0014
Chi-square χ^2	1.0034	1.0045	5.0134	2.0032
Coefficient of determination r^2	0.9889	0.9871	0.2915	0.2187
Slope of regression line	0.8871	0.8503	0.3441	0.2809
Intercept	20.6652	48.5541	33.7124	71.3945

* Definitions of statistics are similar to those in Table 12.4.

features of the simulation. A summary of the model's performance in terms of various statistics is useful at this stage, bearing in mind the approximate and crude nature of the calibration. In Tables 12.4 and 12.5, statistics measuring the fit between the predicted and observed zonal and inter-zonal distributions of changes in activity between 1951 and 1966, and stocks of activity at 1966 are presented. Although the statistics measuring the fit of the stocks are heavily biased towards a good fit, the statistics associated with the changes in activity reveal that the performance of the model is fair in the light of the major assumptions.

Experiments in urban simulation

At the end of each time period, the model outputs a new configuration of the stock and new patterns of interaction; also, changes in the stock and in the interaction patterns, computed in the previous time period, are produced. Therefore, during each simulation run, a large volume of data needs to be quickly digested and to facilitate presentation, a crude graph-plotting subroutine has been developed. Changes and stocks of activity in each zone are plotted through the simulation period, and some of the following figures show this facility. With regard to future research, it is hoped that other means of graphic presentation such as computer mapping can be developed, for at present a large part of the output is being ignored on each run due to an inability to digest it all in a short time.

The trajectories of change in the whole subregion are shown in Figure 12.6. The important point to note from this graph concerns the sensitivity of endogenous variables such as population and service employment to changes in the exogenous variable – basic employment. Although activities on this graph and the following graphs are not to scale, Figure 12.6 shows that the endogenous variables respond almost immediately to external stimuli; this is to be expected from the nature of the simulation and the fact that much of the lag in the generation of activities is of the first order. As a large proportion of the change in activity is in the zone of Reading, this zone is the major determinant of the time-series in Figure 12.6, and as Figure 12.7 shows, Reading has a similar form of time-series to the system as a whole. An important characteristic of this zone relates to the change in population which is both positive and negative during the simulation period. The behaviour of this zone shows features typical of decentralisation and suburbanisation in that the ratio of changes in population to changes in employment is close to zero throughout the simulation. In Figure 12.8, the pattern of work trips generated by persons working in Reading and living in other zones of the system is shown for each time period of the simulation. It is interesting that the changes in activity in Figure 12.7 are also reflected in Figure 12.8: the two peaks in activity in 1953-4 and in 1961-2 are apparent in a peaking of the work trip distribution at these dates. Note also that the change in total stocks is also shown on each of these graphs thus demonstrating how quite large changes in stocks are smoothed when aggregated to total stocks.

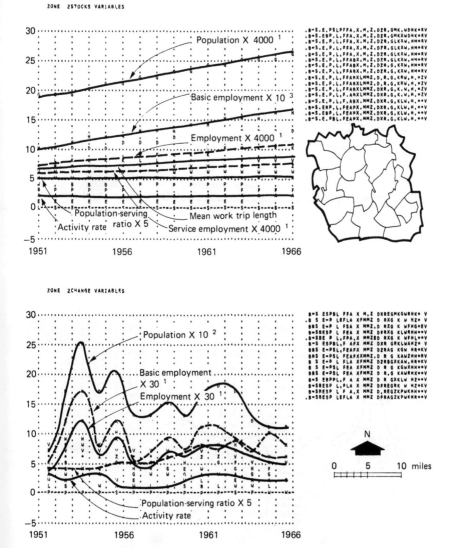

Fig. 12.6. Changes in critical variables in the subregion, 1951-66.

Two other zones in the subregion – Wokingham and Henley – show behaviour similar to that of Reading. In both these cases the change in the inverse activity rate is close to zero, which indicates that population generated in these zones is being largely located outside these zones. In the case of Wokingham, shown in Figure 12.9, the change in basic employment is similar to the system as a whole. In Figure 12.10 which shows changes in

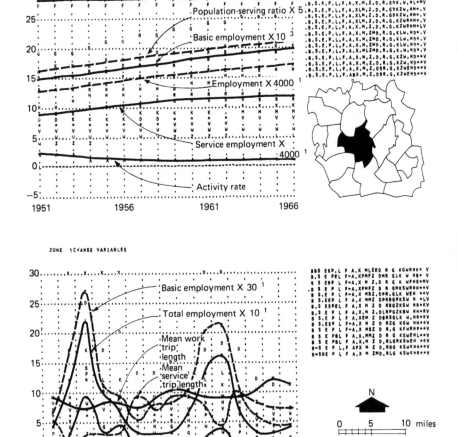

Fig. 12.7. Changes in critical variables in Reading zone 1.

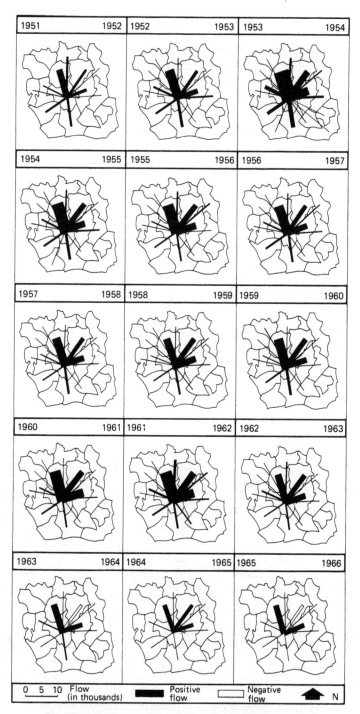

Fig. 12.8. Distribution of work trips from Reading, 1951–66.

Henley, marked peaking of the mean service trip length is due to the fact
that service employment increases in these years.

The experimental approach to urban simulation is clearly illustrated in
Figures 12.11 and 12.12 which show changes in the zones of Kidmore End
and Shiplake respectively. These zones both reveal behaviour patterns
opposite but complementary to zones such as Reading, for the changes in

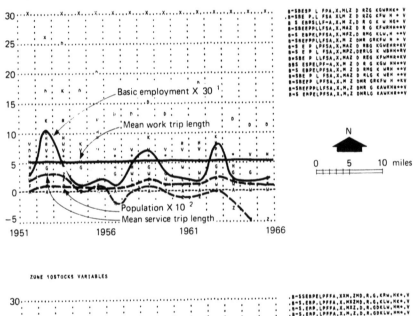

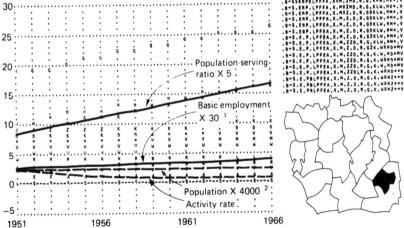

Fig. 12.9. Changes in critical variables in Wokingham zone 10.

the inverse activity rates are high, showing that these areas are growing from an incoming population which has its place of work elsewhere. In the case of Shiplake in Figure 12.11, changes in activity reveal the essential purpose of simulation in providing new insights into the structure of urban systems. The peculiar oscillatory behaviour which starts in Shiplake towards the end of the simulation can be accounted for as follows. In

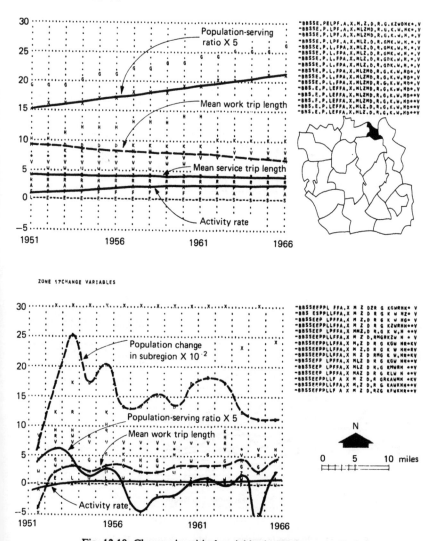

Fig. 12.10. Changes in critical variables in Henley zone 17.

terms of the performance of the model, Shiplake's population is growing too rapidly and in 1962–3 reaches the population constraint limit $C_j(t)$. When this limit is reached, the term ϕ_j is set equal to zero and the residential attraction in the following time period is also zero. Besides allocating new activity, the residential location model *reallocates* activity in the mover pool. In Shiplake, the attraction is zero and persons in the

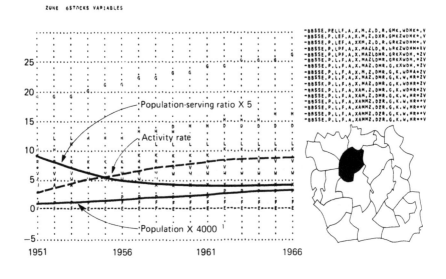

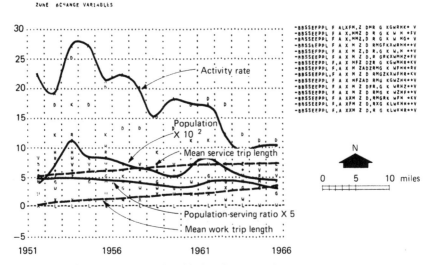

Fig. 12.11. Changes in critical variables in Kidmore End zone 6.

mover pool will not relocate in Shiplake although this may be their place of residence in the previous time period. Therefore, there is a net out-migration from Shiplake, this lowers the population which falls below $C_j(t)$, the residential attraction becomes positive and in the next time period, population flows back in.

In the simulation, these oscillations, although in absolute terms not

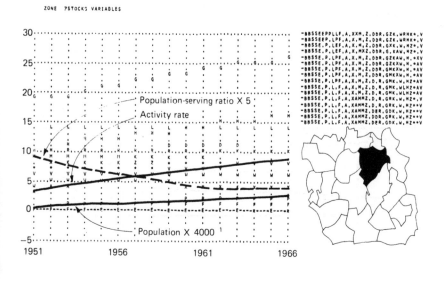

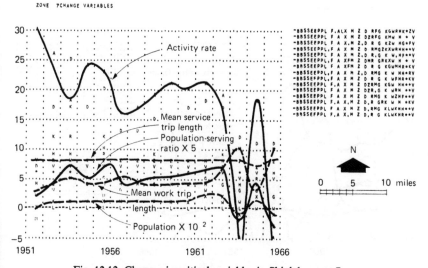

Fig. 12.12. Changes in critical variables in Shiplake zone 7.

large, can continue indefinitely. This may or may not be realistic dynamic behaviour, but as such behaviour was not anticipated *a priori*, this is certainly cause for further testing of the realism of this particular mechanism in the model. Figure 12.13 which illustrates changes in Woodcote, demonstrates the way in which lags are distributed in the system. A decline in basic employment is reflected in declines in service employment in later

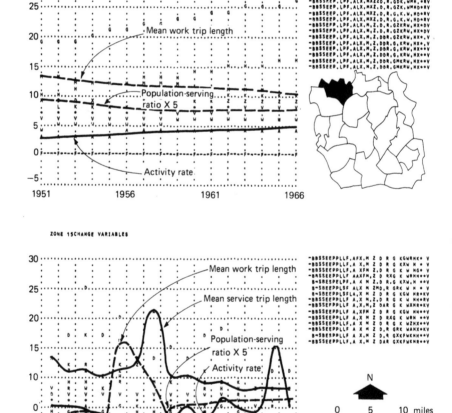

Fig. 12.13. Changes in critical variables in Woodcote zone 15.

time periods. This decline in services also has an effect in damping the measure of service centre attraction in later time periods. Such effects can easily be seen in Figure 12.13 where a major effect on the mean service trip length follows two periods after the decline in employment.

Changes in the zone of Rotherfield Peppard shown in Figure 12.14 demonstrate the sensitivity of various ratios to changes in employment. As

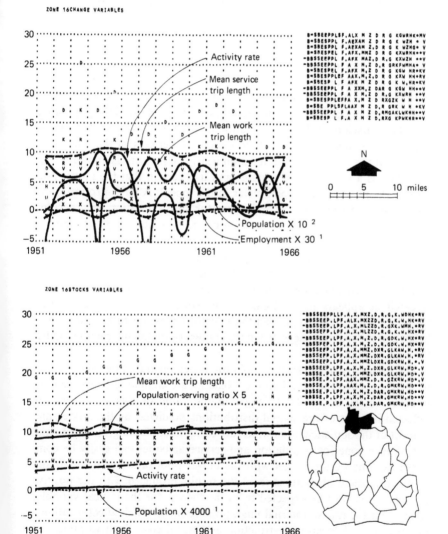

Fig. 12.14. Changes in critical variables in Peppard zone 16.

an example, when the inverse activity rate declines, the mean work trip length increases. Several different hypotheses can be advanced for this behaviour, but it seems that a more rigorous analysis of the model's structure and further experiments in sensitivity analysis are necessary before such relationships can be clarified. Already, in the case of Shiplake, the importance of relocator behaviour has been discussed. The experimental approach to relocation can be taken further and in the following section, some migration analysis based on the simulation is presented.

An approach to migration analysis

The importance of relocation in the simulation cannot be overstressed. As an example, consider those runs of the model in which the mover pool ratio is set at 0.02 of the population stock in each time period. Over fifteen such periods in a situation of no growth, about one-third of the population would turn itself over. In the simulation reported here where the growth in population between 1951 and 1966 is about 36 per cent of the population in 1951, of the total change in location nearly 50 per cent is due to relocation. This is a very high percentage, and it is certain that the mover pool ratio is the most sensitive parameter in the model. A large proportion of relocation, however, remains undetected for most relocation occurs within a zone, yet migration across zonal boundaries is quite high in absolute terms. In reality, the whole population never completely relocates for the propensity to migrate varies widely between different social, economic and age groups. The model, however, is too macro to account for this kind of detail; if a disaggregation of the population was to be considered in future research, it appears in the light of this work that such disaggregation would need to be closely related to relocator behaviour rather than travel behaviour as has been suggested in the context of spatial interaction models (Wilson, 1971 b).

The sensitivity of the mover pool ratio is demonstrated by Figure 12.15, where changes in the population of Reading are compared when the ratio is equal to 0.0 and 0.02. Changes in the value of this parameter are reflected in most of the spatial distributions predicted by the model, and in most of the statistical tests which are computed. Net migration into and out of each zone for population and service activities can easily be computed by running the model with the mover pool ratio equal to 0.0 and subtracting these predictions from the results produced with the positive constant: this is to be expected from the theory, for the critical variables which alter the rate of internal migration are those which affect location – the measures of locational attraction and travel cost. Such variables are not likely to vary very much from time period to time period. In Figure

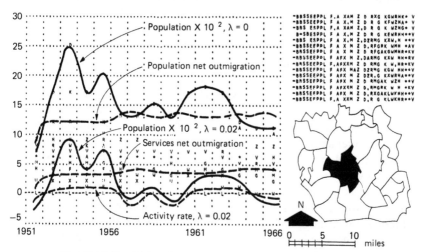

Fig. 12.15. Sensitivity of the mover pool ratio π in Reading zone 1.

12.15, the amount of net out-migration of population and services is shown for Reading. In the case of population, out-migration is constant whereas in the case of services, the level of out-migration gradually increases through time. The initial build-up in these rates is due to the fact that the simulation is not started in disequilibrium.

Spatial analysis of the pattern of net internal migration shows that in this model the mover pool ratio appears to be the critical parameter affecting the decentralisation of activity. This is apparent from Figure 12.15, and Figure 12.16 shows the net flow of population across different partitions of the subregion. This type of analysis was originally developed in Chapter 4 for projections with activity allocation models, but it is obviously relevant to dynamic modelling. The net out-migration from Reading, Wokingham and Henley demonstrates that the existing population is decentralising due to changes in the relative attraction of zones in the system. Areas of greatest net in-migration are typically suburban areas or rural areas with enclaves of exurban growth.

Future research in urban simulation

The approach to simulation outlined in this chapter represents some first steps in modelling the dynamics of urban systems. There are many mechanisms in the model which are unrealistic simulators of urban activity, and future research should be devoted to classifying and modifying the structure of the model in an experimental fashion. In particular, four research areas can be defined; these are labelled calibration, dynamics, structure and application, and are now discussed in turn.

The calibration described above is approximate in several respects. The degree to which such a model can be 'calibrated' in the traditional sense is an important area for research, and as yet, there are several sensitivity analyses of the model's variables still to be undertaken. Some calibration methods based on the theory of search and on numerical-iterative processes were described in Chapters 6 and 7 specifically for cross-sectional models of spatial interaction, and these methods could easily be adapted to the dynamic model. Yet it seems that the model is more useful as an experimental device for its validation would be extremely difficult statistically, and thus it is of conceptual rather than practical import. With regard to research into the model's dynamics, two major directions for study can be delimited. First, the specification of the model using a rigorous system of difference equations is worthy of further research, possibly in terms of the more theoretical approach such as that used by Paelinck (1970) described in the last chapter. Second, the concept of time as a one-dimensional continuum needs some exploration. In urban modelling, the temporal element is complicated by concepts such as expectation and uncertainty as in economics (Shackle, 1958); already, such concepts have been introduced as in the case of the floorspace location model, and it is probable that other mechanisms in the model can be made more realistic in this way.

Questions of structure are partly related to dynamics for the temporal as well as spatial relationships in the model form what is called structure. These relationships need to be explored in much more detail with regard to altering the sequential order of certain operations in the model, and modifying the balance between endogenous and exogenous variables. Finally, applications of the model could be extended in two ways. First, the model can be used to make short-term predictions of changes in urban activity and, in particular, the model is probably sensitive enough to forecast the impact of the new motorway system already planned for the Reading subregion. The second type of application is much more interesting for the model can also be used in a historical context; as the simulation is initially fitted to a previous span of time, it is possible to compare the present with predictions generated during the history of the simulation. This type of retrospective analysis could, for example, be used to compare the present with what might have happened if the course of recent spatial history had been slightly different.

This summary of future research reads rather like a catalogue but many of these areas can be explored in a straightforward manner. The concept of time certainly opens up a new dimension which has hitherto been

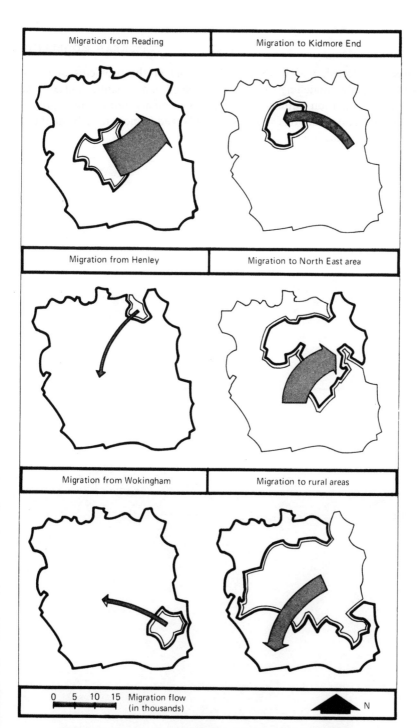

Fig. 12.16. Migration across different partitions of the subregion, 1951–66.

largely neglected, and it appears that many of the problems of cross-sectional static modelling can *only* be resolved in a dynamic context. The dynamic simulation outlined here appears to offer a promising approach to urban research and this should eventually lead to more realistic methods of spatial forecasting.

Conclusions

It seems appropriate to conclude this book by attempting to synthesise some of the themes which have been developed in these pages and to speculate on possible and necessary developments in urban modelling which are on the horizon. But first, it is worth while discussing some of the major criticisms directed against this type of work for therein lie many of the limitations in the theory and practice of urban modelling. One of the most widespread criticisms concerns the question of abstraction. Many argue that such models are so poor a representation of reality that they are often irrelevant to the problem in hand, whilst others argue, in a similar fashion, that urban modelling is a worthless task, for reality can never be described numerically. Both these views contain an element of truth. Yet the purpose of any model is to simplify reality, thus leading to greater understanding and to means whereby experiments can be made on the model in the quest to explore both the present and the future.

The simplification of reality is a cornerstone in the philosophy of science for all the theories and techniques used by urban researchers and planners involve a degree of abstraction by simplification. Furthermore, there are good and bad models, and models which are only relevant to certain situations. The model-builders, whether they be researchers or planners, can also contribute to the success of modelling by using models in a sensitive fashion and avoiding the temptations of pressing them to their limit. In the longer-term endeavour in urban research and planning, it is too easy to dismiss such techniques because they are limited in certain directions (Eversley, 1973). There is a need for a more liberal perspective on the state of the art by all involved in urban modelling, thus fostering the view that models are only aids to imagination in a wider process of design, problem-solving and decision-making in society at large.

Aids to imagination

Perhaps the real objection to urban modelling involves the clarity and apparent precision involved in such work, in contrast to the real world which, in the planner's eyes, is ill-defined and difficult to describe in any

detailed sense. Thus any mathematical representation of reality is suspect
to those who consider the world too complex to be so described. However,
pattern and order does exist and is fairly easy to identify at least on a super-
ficial level in urban and regional systems. As to whether or not an individual
agrees with the description of such patterns statistically is a matter of
opinion, and ultimately of faith in the fundamental ideas.

There is another view which states that analogies between the physical
and social sciences are irrelevant because the two areas of knowledge are
quite different substantively. This again is a matter of judgement and
experience for it presupposes that the physical sciences are based on ideas
which are right or wrong, whereas the social sciences are not based on such
logic. This seems to be a mistaken view of the physical sciences where
intuition, speculation, verbal description and other methods have as great
a part to play as they have in the social sciences. Modelling does not
confine the role of intuition and experience in understanding the present
and the future, but attempts to establish a framework for research or
practice in which the analyst involved can develop his intuitive powers. In
some senses, modelling provides an ideal environment in which research
or planning can evolve, thus aiding the analyst's imagination and focusing
his ideas on the problem under consideration.

The most sweeping criticism of modelling is usually directed against the
notion that models imply some crude technocratic determinism which is
incapable of accommodating any other idea. Again, this criticism depends
upon the way in which the model is used. If the model-user sees the world
solely in strict analytical terms, then those components which cannot be
rigorously analysed will be omitted, thus confirming the criticism. There
is however no necessary conflict between modelling on the one hand and
social justice on the other. Those who think that there is must elaborate
their argument by example.

Social process and spatial form

One of the basic dilemmas facing social science involves the problem of
integrating or synthesising obviously related streams of thought which are
described in different ways. The traditional dichotomy between micro and
macro has never been satisfactorily resolved in economics or in sociology
for the various contributions to each have often been developed using
different languages which are hard to relate. Furthermore, integration
between the various disciplines is urgently needed so that related ideas can
be developed together. This dilemma has recently been cast in a spatial
mould by Harvey (1973), who cogently argues that social processes are
rarely, if ever, represented by models of spatial form and vice versa. This
does not imply that researchers are unconcerned about the difficulty of

synthesis for the fact is that the various languages and styles used to develop ideas about social process and spatial form are almost impossible to reconcile. Urban modelling demonstrates this dilemma in a direct fashion for the models in this book have almost all been concerned with spatial form rather than social process.

The difficulty of integrating these two approaches cannot be over-estimated. What seems to be required is a new type of calculus which is able to handle quantitative and qualitative ideas, micro and macro concepts, behavioural and statistical approaches and so on. This is an enormous task and it is hard to see how it can be attacked using conventional strategies of research. There are however certain limitations in formally representing urban systems. The recent work by Winograd (1972) in artificial intelligence suggests that there are basic limits to computer representation of human processes due to our ability to draw on experience, a source of knowledge which cannot be represented in a computer. However, if the present impasse is to be resolved, a new approach to urban research and planning must evolve.

Data and computation

Throughout this book, the various models introduced have been applied using data from available sources. Thus, it is not surprising that there is a continuing demand for more and better data. Yet it is surprising what can be done with available data and, in certain instances, more data could easily confound a modelling project. In many of the North American modelling projects in the mid-1960s, the collection of data became an end in itself and several models never got off the ground. There are researchers who believe that the data problem is an irrelevant distraction. For instance Forrester (1969) states 'In the social sciences failure to understand systems is often blamed on inadequate data. The barrier to progress in social systems is not lack of data....The barrier is deficiency in the existing theories of structure.' There is some truth in Forrester's statement, for many theories and models would never have been proposed if data were a prerequisite. This book has also presented models based on easily available data, and at the present time, it seems that more work is needed on model structure and design rather than data collection.

Computation has also been a perennial problem in urban modelling. In spatial interaction modelling especially, the storage required increases exponentially with the number of zones into which the system is divided. In most computers, models with greater than 200 zones are impracticable unless external storage on tapes is used, but such external storage increases the running time sometimes prohibitively. Yet some dramatic changes have been made in computer size and speed of processing in recent years. Gibson

(1972) quotes the time needed to invert a 100×100 matrix on a series of IBM machines. On the early IBM 360/25, the time required is 23 minutes in contrast to 1.2 seconds on the 360/85. This incredible increase in speed in little over a decade has important implications for urban modelling, and during the next decade, it is likely that models larger than anything anticipated now will be made operational. Indeed, there are many computer scientists who are suggesting that the real problems in using computers in the future will not concern speed or capacity but will revolve around defining the appropriate problems by asking the right questions.

Existing problems in model design

Design issues concerned with zoning, locational attraction, calibration and a host of measurement problems have been discussed in previous chapters and perhaps the most intractable of these relates to zoning. As yet, only hints of an appropriate theory of zone size have been presented (Broadbent, 1970b) but it is clear that an immense amount of work is required in this area before an operational algorithm for constructing an optimal zoning system is derived. Furthermore, practical problems of data availability affect zone shape and size, and some way of integrating these factors into any such theory will be necessary. Another set of design problems relates to the form of equation system relevant to the model. Simultaneous relationships are difficult to represent in hybrid models such as those discussed here, and usually such relationships have to be structured sequentially. Any generalisation of these models such as that proposed by Wilson (1970b) is easier to make if the structure of the model is sequential. Often, factors such as computer capacity, speed, and availability of data determine the actual form of equation system feasible to the problem in hand.

Of the problems discussed in this book, the calibration problem has yielded best to research. Conventional procedures of non-linear optimisation and numerical analysis have been employed as a basis for estimation as described in Chapters 6–8. Yet this process of calibration cannot be seen as a process of validating the model, for validation is a much wider issue involving a range of factors outside the ambit of statistical fit. Calibration is only a process of determining the values of certain variables which relate to the particular area under study, or which are simply arbitrary factors used in tuning up the model. Validation, on the other hand, depends upon whether or not the structure of the model reflects reality to the desired degree. This question is of fundamental significance, for attempts to disaggregate models and make them dynamic reflect the search for model structures which are less abstract and more relevant to the real world. The models of the last three chapters are important in this context.

Urban research or design science?

Zwick (1962) defines three roles for urban models: the first relates to the design of models for research into spatial structure, the second for educational purposes and the third for spatial forecasting or planning. These three roles have all been stressed in one way or another in this book which has sought to show how models can be used to understand, to explore and to predict the spatial form of urban and regional systems. But there has been less emphasis on prediction than on understanding and exploration. The fact that to use any model in forecasting, one must design and calibrate the model first, means that prediction is inevitably left until last which often means that it is ignored. Furthermore, the construction of models in an academic environment means that there are no pressures on using such models to predict. Yet prediction with such models is of great importance and there are some who would argue that the sole justification of modelling is in terms of prediction. Thus, there is an urgent need for a more explicit use of models in forecasting, and also in the design and evaluation stages of the technical plan-making process.

This discussion raises the notion of normative factors in urban modelling. At present, there is a gap between the models attempting to explain existing urban structure and those attempting to change it in some optimal way. Just as there is a need to bridge the gap between micro and macro, inductive and deductive modelling, there is a need to synthesise normative with descriptive models. It should be possible to build models which explain urban phenomena and which can accommodate strategies which seek to change the same phenomena in the quest to optimise urban form. Rather than building models around the concept of linear programming, it should be possible to apply mathematical programming to descriptive models. Such a model would take on several roles within the planning process – in analysis, in description, in forecasting, in design and in evaluation. At present, it appears that this strategy might be the most fruitful development with respect to many of the models outlined in this book.

Development of the urban models presented here in the directions described above is an important goal for future work but there is perhaps a more important quest. There is a need for these models to be integrated in planning practice, for only then can their true potential be realised. Urban modelling is the logical outcome of a systems approach to planning, and if such an approach is to evolve and flourish, it will be necessary to accept its importance in the practical plan-making process.

Bibliography

Aitchison, J. and Brown, J. A. C. (1957), *The Lognormal Distribution*, Cambridge University Press, Cambridge.

Alexander, C. (1964), *Notes on the Synthesis of Form*, Harvard University Press, Cambridge, Mass.

Alexandersson, G. (1956), *The Industrial Structure of American Cities*, University of Nebraska Press, Lincoln, Nebraska.

Allen, R. G. D. (1967), *Macro-Economic Theory*, Macmillan, London.

Alonso, W. (1960), A general theory of the urban land market, *Papers and Proceedings of the Regional Science Association*, **6**, 149–58.

Alonso, W. (1964), *Location and Land Use*, Harvard University Press, Cambridge, Mass.

Andreski, S. (1972), *Social Sciences as Sorcery*, Andre Deutsch, London.

Angel, S. and Hyman, G. (1971), *Urban Spatial Interaction*, CES-WP-69, Centre for Environmental Studies, London.

Anthony, J. (1970), *The Effect of Income and Socio-Economic Group on Housing Choice*, L.U.B.F.S. Working Paper 51.

Apps, P. (1970), *Theoretical Structure for a Residential Model*, L.U.B.F.S. Working Paper 52.

Artle, R. (1961), On some methods and problems in the study of metropolitan economics, *Papers and Proceedings of the Regional Science Association*, **8**, 71–87.

Asimow, M. (1962), *Introduction to Design*, Prentice-Hall, Englewood Cliffs, New Jersey.

Avriel, M. and Wilde, D. J. (1966), Optimality proof for the symmetric Fibonacci search technique, *Fibonacci Quarterly*, **4**, 265–9.

Barras, R., Broadbent, T. A., Cordey-Hayes, M., Massey, D. B., Robinson, K. and Willis, J. (1971), An operational urban development model of Cheshire, *Environment and Planning*, **3**, 115–234.

Batty, M. (1969), The impact of a new town, *Journal of Town Planning Institute*, **55**, 428–35.

Batty, M. (1971), Modelling cities as dynamic systems, *Nature*, **231**, 425–8.

Batty, M. (1972*a*), Recent developments in land use modelling: a review of British research, *Urban Studies*, **9**, 151–77.

Batty, M. (1972*b*), Entropy and spatial geometry, *Area*, **4**, 230–6.

Batty, M. (1972*c*), A probability model of the housing market based on quasi-classical considerations, *Geographical Papers*, No. 18, Dept. of Geography, University of Reading, Reading.

Batty, M. (1973), *Concepts of Geographical Aggregation Based on Hierarchical Entropies*, Department of Geography, University of Reading, Reading.

Batty, M. (1974), Spatial entropy, *Geographical Analysis*, **6**, 1–32.

Baxter, R. (1971), *Urban Systems: The Development of a Cordon Model*, L.U.B.F.S Working Paper 47.

Baxter, R. and Williams, I. (1972), *The Second Stage in Disaggregating the Residential Sub-Model*, L.U.B.F.S. Working Paper 65.

Baxter, R. and Williams, I. (1973), *The Third Stage in Disaggregating the Residential Sub-Model*, L.U.B.F.S. Working Paper 66.

Beach, E. F. (1957), *Economic Models: An Exposition*, Wiley, New York.

Beardwood, J. (1972), *The Space-Averaging of Deterrent Functions for Use in Gravity Model Distribution Calculations*, TRRL Report LR462, Transport and Road Research Laboratory, Crowthorne.

Beckmann, M. J. (1969), On the distribution of urban rent and residential density, *Journal of Economic Theory*, 1, 60-7.

Bellman, R. (1957), *Dynamic Programming*, Princeton University Press, Princeton, New Jersey.

Ben-Shahar, H., Mazor, A. and Pines, D. (1969), Town planning and welfare maximisation: a methodological approach, *Regional Studies*, 3, 105-13.

Berry, B. J. L. (1961), City size distributions and economic development, *Economic Development and Cultural Change*, 9, 573-88.

Berry, B. J. L. (1964), Approaches to regional analysis: a synthesis, *Annals of the Association of American Geographers*, 54, 2-11.

Berry, B. J. L. (1967), *Geography of Market Centers and Retail Distribution*, Prentice-Hall, Englewood Cliffs, New Jersey.

Bertalanffy, L. von (1971), *General System Theory*, Allen Lane, The Penguin Press, Harmondsworth.

Black, J. (1966), *Some retail sales models*, A Paper presented to the Urban Studies Conference, Oxford.

Blokland, J., Hendriks, A. J. and Paelinck, J. H. P. (1972), *Elements for the construction of a simple model for a stagnating town*, A Paper presented to the Regional Science Association, Dutch Meeting, Rotterdam.

Bone, R. (1971), The Tyne-Wear model, *Proceedings of the Seminar on Urban Growth Models*, PTRC, London.

Bono, E. de (1967), *The Use of Lateral Thinking*, Jonathan Cape, London.

Booth, P. (1970a), *Model of a Town: Cambridge*, L.U.B.F.S. Working Paper 13.

Booth, P. (1970b), *Cambridge: The Evaluation of Urban Structure Plans*, L.U.B.F.S. Working Paper 14.

Boyce, D. E., Day, N. D. and McDonald, V. (1970), *Metropolitan Plan Making*, Regional Science Research Institute, Monograph Series, No. 4, Philadelphia, Penn.

Box, M. J., Davies, D. and Swann, W. H. (1969), *Nonlinear Optimisation Techniques*, ICI Monograph No. 5, Oliver and Boyd, Edinburgh.

Broadbent, T. A. (1968), *Calibrating Inter-Urban Generation-Distribution Models*, MAU-Note-106, Ministry of Transport, London.

Broadbent, T. A. (1969a), *Zone Size and Spatial Interaction in Operational Models*, CES-WN-106, Centre for Environmental Studies, London.

Broadbent, T. A. (1969b), *Zone Size and Singly-Constrained Interaction Models*, CES-WN-132, Centre for Environmental Studies, London.

Broadbent, T. A. (1970a), Notes on the design of operational models, *Environment and Planning*, 2, 469-76.

Broadbent, T. A. (1970b), An urban planner's model: what does it look like?, *Architectural Design*, 40, 408-10.

Broadbent, T. A. (1971). A hierarchical interaction-allocation model for a two-level spatial system, *Regional Studies*, **5**, 23–7.

Brown, H. J., Ginn, J. R., James, F. J., Kain, J. F. and Straszheim, M. R. (1972), *Empirical Models of Urban Land Use: Suggestions on Research Objectives and Organisation*, National Bureau of Economic Research, New York.

Buckley, W. (1967), *Sociology and Modern Systems Theory*, Prentice-Hall, Englewood Cliffs, New Jersey.

Bunge, W. (1966), *Theoretical Geography*, Lund Studies in Geography, Series C, No. 1, Lund.

Burdekin, R. and Marshall, S. A. (1973), *The Calibration, Potential Development and Limitations of the Forrester Model*, A Paper presented to the PTRC Annual Meeting, University of Sussex, Brighton.

Bureau of Public Roads (1968), *Calibrating and Testing a Gravity Model for any Size of Urban Area*, U.S. Department of Transportation, Federal Highway Administration, Washington, D.C.

Carrothers, G. A. P. (1956), An historical review of the gravity and potential concepts of human interaction, *Journal of the American Institute of Planners*, **22**, 94–102.

Casetti, E. and Papageorgiou, G. (1971), A spatial equilibrium model of urban structure, *Canadian Geographer*, **15**, 30–7.

Casey, H. J. (1955), The law of retail gravitation applied to traffic engineering, *Traffic Quarterly*, **9**, 313–21.

Catanese, A. J. and Steiss, A. W. (1970), *Systemic Planning: Theory and Application*, D. C. Heath and Co., Lexington, Mass.

Caulfield, I. and Rhodes, T. (1971), The use of an allocation model in the preparation of a structure plan for South Hampshire, *Proceedings of the Seminar on Urban Growth Models*, PTRC, London.

Cesario, F. J. (1973), Parameter estimation in spatial interaction modelling, *Environment and Planning*, **5**, 503–18.

Chadwick, G. F. (1971), *A Systems View of Planning*, Pergamon Press, Oxford.

Chapin, F. S. (1965), *Urban Land Use Planning*, University of Illinois Press, Urbana, Illinois.

Chapin, F. S. and Weiss, S. F. (1962), *Factors Influencing Land Development*, Institute for Research in Social Science, University of North Carolina, Chapel Hill.

Chapin, F. S., Weiss, S. F. and Donnelly, T. G. (1965), *Some Input Refinements for a Residential Model*, Institute for Research in Social Science, University of North Carolina, Chapel Hill.

Chapin, F. S. and Weiss, S. F. (1968), A probabilistic model for residential growth, *Transportation Research*, **2**, 375–90.

Chen, K. (1972), *Urban Dynamics: Extensions and Reflections*, San Francisco Press, San Francisco, California.

Cheshire, A. (1970), A note on a model for allocating basic employment, unpublished paper, Urban Systems Research Unit, University of Reading, Reading.

Chilton, R. and Poet, R. R. W. (1973), An entropy maximising approach to the recovery of detailed migration patterns from aggregate census data, *Environment and Planning*, **5**, 135–46.

Chisholm, M. and O'Sullivan, P. (1973), *Freight Flows and Spatial Aspects of the British Economy*, Cambridge University Press, Cambridge.

Chorley, R. J. and Kennedy, B. A. (1971), *Physical Geography: A Systems Approach*, Prentice-Hall International, London.

Christ C. F. (1966), *Econometric Models and Methods*, Wiley, New York.

Clark, C. (1951), Urban population densities, *Journal of the Royal Statistical Society*, Series A, **114**, 490–6.

Cliff, A. and Ord, K. (1973), *Spatial Autocorrelation*, Pion Press, London.

Cordey-Hayes, M. (1968), *Retail Location Models*, CES-WP-16, Centre for Environmental Studies, London.

Cordey-Hayes, M. (1972), Dynamic frameworks for spatial models, *Socio-Economic Planning Sciences*, **7**, 365–85.

Cordey-Hayes, M. and Wilson, A. G. (1971), Spatial interaction, *Socio-Economic Planning Sciences*, **5**, 73–95.

Costa, P. and Piasentin, U. (1971), *Un Modello di Simulazione dello Sviluppo Urbano di Venezia*, A Paper presented to the Symposium on Trends in Mathematical Modelling, UNESCO, Venice, Italy.

Crecine, J. P. (1964), *TOMM (Time Oriented Metropolitan Model)*, CRP Technical Bulletin No. 6, Dept. of City Planning, Pittsburgh.

Crecine, J. P. (1967), *Computer Simulation in Urban Research*, P-3734, RAND Corporation, Santa Monica, California.

Crecine, J. P. (1968), *A Dynamic Model of Urban Structure*, P-3803, RAND Corporation, Santa Monica, California.

Crecine, J. P. (1969), *Spatial Location Decisions and Urban Structure: A Time-Oriented Model*, Discussion Paper No. 4, Institute of Public Policy Studies, University of Michigan, Ann Arbor, Michigan.

Cripps, E. L. and Foot, D. H. S. (1969*a*), The empirical development of an elementary residential location model for use in subregional planning, *Environment and Planning*, **1**, 81–90.

Cripps, E. L. and Foot, D. H. S. (1969*b*), A land use model for subregional planning, *Regional Studies*, **3**, 243–68.

Cripps, E. L. and Cater, E. A. (1972), The empirical development of a disaggregated residential location model: some preliminary results, in Wilson, A. G. (Editor), *Patterns and Processes in Urban and Regional Systems*, Pion Press, London.

Czamanski, S. (1965), A method of forecasting metropolitan growth by means of distributed lags analysis, *Journal of Regional Science*, **6**, 35–49.

Davies, R. L. (1970), Variable relationships in central place and retail potential models, *Regional Studies*, **4**, 49–61.

Deutsch, K. W. (1963), *The Nerves of Government*, The Free Press, Glencoe, NY.

Dixon, L. C. W. (1972), *Nonlinear Optimisation*, The English Universities Press Ltd., London.

Draper, N. R. and Smith, H. (1966), *Applied Regression Analysis*, Wiley, New York.

Easton, D. A. (1965), *A Systems Analysis of Political Life*, Wiley, New York.

Echenique, M., Crowther, D. and Lindsay, W. (1969*a*), A spatial model of urban stock and activity, *Regional Studies*, **3**, 281–312.

Echenique, M., Crowther, D. and Lindsay, W. (1969*b*), *Development of a Model of a Town*, L.U.B.F.S. Working Paper 26.

Echenique, M. and Domeyko, J. (1970), *A Model for Santiago Metropolitan Area*, L.U.B.F.S. Working Paper 11.

Echenique, M., Crowther, D. and Lindsay, W. (1972), A structural comparison of three generations of new towns, in L. Martin and L. March (Editors), *Urban Space and Structures*, Cambridge University Press, Cambridge.

Edens, H. J. (1970), Analysis of a modified gravity demand model, *Transportation Research*, **4**, 51–62.

Eilon, S., Tilley, R. P. R. and Fowkes, T. R. (1969), Analysis of a gravity demand model, *Regional Studies*, 3, 115–22.

Elton, M. and Rosenhead, J. (1971), Micro-simulation of markets, *Operational Research Quarterly*, 22, 117–44.

Evans, A. W. (1970), Some properties of trip distribution models, *Transportation Research*, 4, 19–36.

Evans, A. W. (1971), The calibration of trip distribution models with exponential or similar cost functions, *Transportation Research*, 5, 15–38.

Eversley, D. (1973), *The Planner in Society*, Faber and Faber, London.

Farbey, B. A., Land, A. H. and Murchland, J. D. (1967), The cascade algorithm for finding all shortest distances in a directed graph, *Management Science*, 14, 19–28.

Foot, D. H. S. (1965), *The Shortest Route Problem: Algol Programmes and a Discussion of Computational Problems in Large Network Applications*, Discussion Paper No. 10, Department of Economics, University of Bristol, Bristol.

Foot, D. H. S. (1973), *A Comparison of Some Land Use Allocation/Interaction Models*, A paper presented to the PTRC Annual Meeting, University of Sussex, Brighton.

Forrester, J. W. (1961), *Industrial Dynamics*, Wiley, New York.

Forrester, J. W. (1969), *Urban Dynamics*, MIT Press, Cambridge, Mass.

Forrester, J. W. (1971), *World Dynamics*, Wright-Allen Press, Cambridge, Mass.

Furness, K. P. (1965), Time function iteration, *Traffic Engineering and Control*, 7, 458–60.

Garin, R. A. (1966), A matrix formulation of the Lowry model for intra-metropolitan activity location, *Journal of the American Institute of Planners*, 32, 361–4.

Gibson, J. E. (1972), A philosophy for urban simulations, in Chen, K. (Editor), *Urban Dynamics: Extensions and Reflections*, San Francisco Press Inc., San Francisco, California.

Ginsberg, R. B. (1972), Incorporating causal structure and exogenous information with probabilistic models: with special reference to choice, gravity, migration and Markov chains, *Journal of Mathematical Sociology*, 2, 83–103.

Goldberg, S. (1958), *Introduction to Difference Equations*, Wiley, New York.

Goldner, W. (1968), *Projective Land Use Model (PLUM)*, BATSC Technical Report 219, Bay Area Transportation Study Commission, Berkeley, California.

Goldner, W. (1971), The Lowry model heritage, *Journal of The American Institute of Planners*, 37, 100–10.

Golob, T. F. and Beckmann, M. J. (1971), A utility model for travel forecasting, *Transportation Science*, 5, 79–90.

Graham, A. K. (1972), Modelling city–suburb interactions, *IEEE Transactions on Systems, Man and Cybernetics*, SMC-2, 156–8.

Hadley, G. (1961), *Linear Algebra*, Addison-Wesley, Reading, Mass.

Hadley, G. (1962), *Linear Programming*, Addison-Wesley, Reading, Mass.

Hall, P. (Editor) (1966), *Von Thunen's Isolated State*, Pergamon Press, Oxford.

Hamilton, H. R., Goldstone, S. E., Milliman, J. W., Pugh, A. L., Roberts, E. B. and Zellner, A. (1969), *Systems Simulation for Regional Analysis: An Application to River-Basin Planning*, MIT Press, Cambridge, Mass.

Hansen, W. G. (1959), How accessibility shapes land use, *Journal of the American Institute of Planners*, 25, 73–6.

Harris, B. (1964), A note on the probability of interaction at a distance, *Journal of Regional Science*, 5, 31–5.

Harris, B. (1966a), The uses of theory in the simulation of urban phenomena, *Journal of the American Institute of Planners*, 32, 258–73.

Harris, B. (1966*b*), *Note on Aspects of Equilibrium in Urban Growth Models*, Department of City and Regional Planning, University of Pennsylvania, Philadelphia, Penn.

Harris, B. (1968), Quantitative models of urban development: their role in metropolitan policy-making, in H. S. Perloff and L. Wingo (Editors), *Issues in Urban Economics*, The Johns Hopkins Press, Baltimore.

Harris, B. (1970), *Change and Equilibrium in the Urban System*, Institute for Environmental Studies, University of Pennsylvania, Philadelphia, Penn.

Harris, B. (1972), A model of household locational preferences, in R. Funck (Editor), *Recent Developments in Regional Science*, Pion Press, London.

Harris, B., Nathanson, J. and Rosenburg, L. (1966), *Research on an Equilibrium Model of Metropolitan Housing*, Institute for Environmental Studies, University of Pennsylvania, Philadelphia, Penn.

Harvey, D. (1973), *Social Justice and the City*, Edward Arnold, London.

Henderson, J. M. and Quandt, R. E. (1958), *Micro-Economic Theory*, McGraw Hill, New York.

Herbert, J. D. and Stevens, B. H. (1960), A model for the distribution of residential activity in urban areas, *Journal of Regional Science*, **2**, 21–36.

Hill, D. M. (1965), A growth allocation model for the Boston region, *Journal of the American Institute of Planners*, **31**, 111–20.

Hill, D. M., Brand, D. and Hansen, W. B. (1965), Prototype development of statistical land use prediction model for Greater Boston region, *Highway Research Record*, **114**, 51–70.

Hoggatt, V. E. (1969), *Fibonacci and Lucas Numbers*, Houghton Mifflin, Boston.

Huff, D. L. (1964), Defining and estimating a trading area, *Journal of Marketing*, **28**, 34–8.

Huff, D. L. (1963), A probabilistic analysis of shopping centre trade areas, *Land Economics*, **39**, 81–90.

Hyman, G. M. (1969), The calibration of trip distribution models, *Environment and Planning*, **1**, 105–12.

Ingram, G. K., Kain, J. F. and Ginn, J. R. (1972), *The Detroit Prototype of the NBER Urban Simulation Model*, National Bureau of Economic Research, New York.

Irwin, N. A. and Brand, D. (1965), Planning and forecasting metropolitan development, *Traffic Quarterly*, **19**, 520–40.

Isard, W. (1956), *Location and Space-Economy*, MIT Press, Cambridge, Mass.

Isard, W. *et al.* (1960), *Methods of Regional Analysis*, MIT Press, Cambridge, Mass.

Isard, W. and Czamanski, S. (1965), Techniques for estimating multiplier effects of major government programs, *Papers of the Peace Research Society*, **3**, 19–45.

Kadanoff, L. P. (1972), From simulation model to public policy, *American Scientist*, **60**, 74–9.

Kain, J. F. (1962), The journey to work as a determinant of residential location, *Papers and Proceedings of the Regional Science Association*, **9**, 137–60.

Karlquist, A. and Marksjo, B. (1971), Statistical urban models, *Environment and Planning*, **3**, 83–98.

Keyfitz, N. (1968), *Introduction to the Mathematics of Population*, Addison-Wesley, Reading, Mass.

Kiefer, J. (1953), Sequential minimax search for a maximum, *Proceedings of American Mathematical Society*, **4**, 503–6.

Kilbridge, M. D., O'Block, R. P. and Teplitz, P. V. (1969), A conceptual framework for urban planning models, *Management Science*, **15**, B246–66.

King, L. J. (1969), *Statistical Analysis in Geography*, Prentice-Hall, Englewood Cliffs, New Jersey.

Kirby, H. R. (1970), Normalising factors of the gravity model: an interpretation, *Transportation Research*, **4**, 37–50.

Kirby, H. R. (1972), *A Comment on 'Normalising Factors of the Gravity Model: An Interpretation'*, Note HRK/72/02, Research Group in Traffic Studies, University College, London.

Kirby, H. R. (1974), Theoretical requirements for calibrating gravity models, *Transportation Research*, **8**, 97–104.

Klir, J. and Valach, M. (1965), *Cybernetic Modelling*, Iliffe Books Ltd., London.

Knos, D. S. (1968), The distribution of land values in Topeka, Kansas, in B. J. L. Berry and D. F. Marble (Editors), *Spatial Analysis*, Prentice-Hall, Englewood Cliffs, New Jersey.

Koestler, A. (1964), *The Act of Creation*, Hutchinson and Co., London.

Krolak, P. and Cooper, L. (1963), An extension of Fibonacci search to several variables, *Communications of ACM*, **6**, 639–41.

Kuhn, T. S. (1962), *The Structure of Scientific Revolutions*, The University of Chicago Press, Chicago.

Lakshmanan, T. R. (1964), An approach to the analysis of intra-urban location applied to the Baltimore region, *Economic Geography*, **40**, 348–70.

Lakshmanan, T. R. (1968), A model for allocating urban activities in a state, *Socio-Economic Planning Sciences*, **1**, 283–95.

Lakshmanan, T. R. and Hansen, W. G. (1965), A retail market potential model, *Journal of the American Institute of Planners*, **31**, 134–43.

Lathrop, G. T. and Hamburg, J. R. (1965), An opportunity-accessibility model for allocating regional growth, *Journal of the American Institute of Planners*, **31**, 95–103.

Lathrop, G. T., Hamburg, J. R. and Young, G. F. (1965), Opportunity-accessibility model for allocating regional growth, *Highway Research Record*, **113**, 54–66.

Lee, D. B. (1973), Requiem for large scale models, *Journal of the American Institute of Planners*, **39**, 163–78.

Lindsay, W. (1971), Using models for new town design, *Architectural Design*, **41**, 286–8.

Lowry, I. S. (1963), Location parameters in the Pittsburgh model, *Papers and Proceedings of Regional Science Association*, **11**, 145–65.

Lowry, I. S. (1964), A model of metropolis, RM-4035-RC, RAND Corporation, Santa Monica, California.

Lowry, I. S. (1965), A short course in model design, *Journal of the American Institute of Planners*, **31**, 158–66.

Lowry, I. S. (1968), Seven models of urban development, in G. Hemmens (Editor), *Urban Development Models*, Special Report 97, Highway Research Board, Washington, D.C.

Mackie, S. (1971), The calibration of spatial interaction models, unpublished M.Sc. Thesis, Department of Geography, University of Reading, Reading.

Martin, L. and March, L. (1972), *Urban Space and Structures*, Cambridge University Press, Cambridge.

March, L. and Steadman, P. (1971), *The Geometry of Environment*, RIBA Publications, London.

March, L., Echenique, M. and Dickens, P. (1971), Models of environment, a special issue of *Architectural Design*, **41**, 275–322.

Marquardt, D. W. (1963), An algorithm for least squares estimation of nonlinear parameters, *SIAM Journal*, **11**, 431–41.

Masser, I. (1970), *Notes on an Application of the Lowry Model to Merseyside*, Department of Civic Design, University of Liverpool, Liverpool.

Masser, I. (1971), Possible applications of the Lowry model, *Planning Outlook*, 11, 46–59.

Masser, I., Coleman, A. and Wynn, R. F. (1971), Estimation of a growth allocation model for North West England, *Environment and Planning*, 3, 451–63.

Masser, I., Batey, P. and Brown, P. (1973), *Design of Zoning Systems for Interaction Models*, A Paper presented to the 6th Annual Conference, Regional Science Association, British Section, University College, London.

Massey, D. B. (1969), *Some Simple Models for Distributing Changes in Employment within Regions*, CES-WP-24, Centre for Environmental Studies, London.

Massey, D. B. (1973), The basic: service categorisation in planning, *Regional Studies*, 7, 1–15.

McLoughlin, J. B. (1969), *Urban and Regional Planning*, Faber and Faber Ltd., London.

McLoughlin, J. B., Nix, C. K. and Foot, D. H. S. (1966), *Regional Shopping Centres: A Planning Report on North West England. Part 2: A Retail Shopping Model*, Department of Town and Country Planning, University of Manchester, Manchester.

McLoughlin, J. B. and Webster, J. N. (1970), Cybernetic and general-system approaches to urban and regional research, *Environment and Planning*, 2, 369–408.

McLoughlin, J. B. *et al.* (1969), *Leicester and Leicestershire Subregional Planning Study*, Volume 2, Leicester County Planning Department, Leicester.

Medawar, P. B. (1969), *Induction and Intuition in Scientific Thought*, Methuen, London.

MHLG (Ministry of Housing and Local Government) (1967), *Central Lancashire, Study for a City*, Consultants Proposals for Designation, H.M.S.O., London.

MHLG (Ministry of Housing and Local Government) (1968), *Central Lancashire New Town Proposal – Impact on North East Lancashire*, H.M.S.O., London.

Mills, E. S. (1972), *Studies in the Structure of the Urban Economy*, Resources for the Future and Johns Hopkins Press, Baltimore.

Milne, W. E. (1949), *Numerical Calculus*, Princeton University Press, Princeton, New Jersey.

Mischke, C. R. (1968), *An Introduction to Computer-Aided Design*, Prentice-Hall, Englewood Cliffs, New Jersey.

Mitchell, R. B. and Rapkin, C. (1954), *Urban Traffic: A Function of Land Use*, Columbia University Press, New York.

Montesano, A. (1972), A restatement of Beckmann's model on the distribution of urban rent and residential density, *Journal of Economic Theory*, 4, 329–54.

Mood, A. M. and Graybill, F. A. (1963), *Introduction to the Theory of Statistics*, McGraw-Hill, New York.

MOT (Ministry of Transport) (1966), *Portbury: Reasons for the Minister's Decision not to Authorise the Construction of a New Dock at Portbury, Bristol*, H.M.S.O., London.

Murray, W. and Kennedy, M. B. (1971), Notts/Derbys: a shopping model primer, *Journal of Town Planning Institute*, 57, 211–15.

Muth, R. F. (1969), *Cities and Housing*, University of Chicago Press, Chicago.

Naylor, T. H. (1971), *Computer Simulation Experiments with Models of Economic Systems*, Wiley, New York.

NEDO (1970), *Urban Models in Shopping Studies*, National Economic Development Office, London.

Nelder, J. A. and Mead, R. (1965), A simplex method for function minimisation, *The Computer Journal*, 7, 308–13.

Olsson, G. (1965), Distance and human interaction: A migration study, *Geografiska Annaler*, **47B**, 3–43.

Orcutt, G. H., Greenberger, M., Korbel, J. and Rivlin, A. M. (1961), *Micro-analysis of Socio-economic Systems: A Simulation Study*, Harper and Row, New York.

Paelinck, J. H. P. (1970), Dynamic urban growth models, *Papers of the Regional Science Association*, **24**, 25–37.

Paelinck, J. H. P. (1972), Alternative methods for the study of urban dynamics, in R. Funck (Editor), *Recent Developments in Regional Science*, Pion Press, London.

Papageorgiou, G. and Casetti, E. (1971), Spatial equilibrium residential land values in a multi-center setting, *Journal of Regional Science*, **11**, 385–9.

Parry-Lewis, J. (1964), *Mathematics for Students of Economics*, Macmillan, London.

Parsons, T. (1952), *The Social System*, Routledge and Kegan Paul, London.

Popper, K. R. (1972), *Objective Knowledge*, Oxford University Press, Oxford.

Porter, H. R. and Henley, E. J. (1972), Applications of the Forrester model to Harris County, Texas, in K. Chen (Editor), *Urban Dynamics: Extensions and Reflections*, San Francisco Press Inc., San Francisco, California.

Powell, M. J. D. (1964), An efficient method for finding the minimum of a function of several variables without calculating derivatives, *The Computer Journal*, **7**, 155–62.

Putnam, S. H. (1970), Developing and testing an intraregional model, *Regional Studies*, **4**, 473–90.

Rao, C. R. (1952), *Advanced Statistical Methods in Biometric Research*, Wiley, New York.

Redish, K. A. (1961), *An Introduction to Computational Methods*, English Universities Press Ltd., London.

Rees, P. H. and Wilson, A. G. (1976), *Spatial Demographic Analysis*, Edward Arnold, London.

Reilly, W. J. (1929), Methods for the study of retail relationships, *Bulletin No. 2944*, University of Texas, Houston, Texas.

Rhodes, T. and Whitaker, R. (1967), Forecasting shopping demand, *Journal of Town Planning Institute*, **53**, 188–92.

Rittel, H. W. J. and Webber, M. (1972), *Dilemmas in a General Theory of Planning*, Working Paper No. 194, Institute of Urban and Regional Development, University of California, Berkeley, California.

Robinson, I. M., Wolfe, H. B. and Barringer, R. L. (1965), A simulation model for renewal programming, *Journal of the American Institute of Planners*, **31**, 126–34.

Rogers, A. (1968), *Matrix Analysis of Inter-Regional Population Growth and Distribution*, University of California Press, Berkeley, California.

Schlager, K. J. (1965), A land-use plan design model, *Journal of the American Institute of Planners*, **31**, 103–11.

Schlager, K. J. (1966), A recursive programming theory of the residential land development process, *Highway Research Board*, **126**, 24–32.

Schneider, M. (1959), Gravity models and trip distribution theory, *Papers and Proceedings of Regional Science Association*, **5**, 51–6.

Schneider, M. (1967), Access and land development, in G. C. Hemmens (Editor), *Urban Development Models*, Special Report 97, Highway Research Board, Washington, D.C.

Schneider, M. (1969), *Transportation and Land Development – A Unified Theory and Prototype Model*, Creighton-Hamburg Inc., and U.S. Department of Commerce, Springfield, Virginia.

Seidman, D. R. (1969), *The Construction of an Urban Growth Model*, DVRPC Plan Report No. 1, Delaware Valley Regional Planning Commission, Philadelphia, Penn.

Senior, M. L. and Wilson, A. G. (1972), *Disaggregated Residential Location Models: Some Tests and Further Theoretical Developments*, Working Paper 22, Department of Geography, University of Leeds, Leeds.

Shackle, G. L. S. (1958), *Time in Economics*, North-Holland, Amsterdam.

Shannon, C. E. (1948), A mathematical theory of communication, *Bell System Technical Journal*, **27**, 379–423 and 623–56.

Simon, H. A. (1955), On a class of skew distribution functions, *Biometrika*, **42**, 425–40.

Simon, H. A. (1969), *The Sciences of the Artificial*, MIT Press, Cambridge, Mass.

Simon, H. A. and Chase, W. G. (1973), Skill in chess, *American Scientist*, **61**, 394–403.

Smith, N. J. and Sage, A. P. (1973), Hierarchical system identification of models for urban dynamics, *Socio-Economic Planning Sciences*, **7**, 545–69.

Solow, R. M. (1972), Congestion, density and the use of land in transportation, *Swedish Journal of Economics*, **74**, 161–73.

Spang, H. A. (1962), A review of minimisation techniques for non-linear functions, *SIAM Review*, **4**, 343–65.

Spendley, W., Hext, G. R. and Himsworth, F. R. (1962), Sequential application of simplex designs on optimisation and evolutionary operation, *Technometrics*, **4**, 441–61.

Stephenson, G. (1961), *Mathematical Methods for Science Students*, Longmans, London.

Stewart, J. Q. (1947), Empirical rules concerning the distribution and equilibrium of population, *Geographical Review*, **38**, 461–85.

Stewart, J. Q. and Warntz, W. (1958), Physics of population distribution, *Journal of Regional Science*, **1**, 99–123.

Stonebraker, M. (1972), A simplification of Forrester's model of an urban area, *IEEE Transactions on Systems, Man and Cybernetics*, SMC-2, 468–72.

Stouffer, S. A. (1940), Intervening opportunities: a theory relating mobility and distance, *American Sociological Review*, **5**, 845–67.

Stradal, O. and Sorgo, K. (1971), *A Model for Regional Allocation of Activities, Paper 1 – Formulation, Calibration, Verification*, Institute for National, Regional and Local Planning of the Swiss Federal Institute, Zurich.

Swanson, C. V. and Waldmann, R. J. (1970), A simulation model of economic growth dynamics, *Journal of the American Institute of Planners*, **36**, 314–22.

Tanner, J. C. (1961), *Factors Affecting the Amount of Travel*, Road Research Laboratory, Technical Paper No. 51, H.M.S.O., London.

Theil, H. (1967), *Economics and Information Theory*, North-Holland, Amsterdam.

Theil, H. (1972), *Statistical Decomposition Analysis*, North-Holland, Amsterdam.

Thorburn, A. *et al.* (1969), *Nottinghamshire and Derbyshire: Subregional Study*, Notts. Derbys. Subregional Planning Unit, Alfreton, Derbyshire.

Tobler, W. (1963), Geographic area and map projections, *Geographical Review*, **53**, 59–78.

Tobler, W. and Wineburg, S. (1971), A Cappadocian speculation, *Nature*, **231**, 40–1.

Tribus, M. (1969), *Rational Descriptions, Decisions, and Designs*, Pergamon Press, Oxford.

Turner, G. C. (1970*a*), The development of an activity allocation model for the Bristol subregion, unpublished M.Phil. Thesis, University College Library, London.

Turner, C. J. (1970*b*), *Severnside Shopping Model: A Discussion of the Calibration Procedure and Results*, Working Paper No. 4, Nathaniel Lichfield and Associates, London.

Ullman, E. L. and Dacey, M. F. (1962), The minimum requirements approach to the urban economic base, *Lund Studies in Geography*, Series B, Human Geography, **24**, 121–43.

Vorobev, N. N. (1961), *Fibonacci Numbers*, Pergamon Press, Oxford.

Wagon, D. J. and Hawkins, A. F. (1970), The calibration of the distribution model for the SELNEC study, *Transportation Research*, **4**, 103–12.

Walker, D. L. (1968), *The Direct Trip Allocation Model in SCOTS Modelling Process*, Cleveland-Seven County Transportation-Land Use Study, Cleveland, Ohio.

Walters, A. A. (1968), *An Introduction to Econometrics*, Macmillan, London.

Waugh, F. V. (1950), Inversion of the Leontief matrix by power series, *Econometrica*, **18**, 142–54.

Watt, K. E. F. (1968), *Ecology and Resource Management*, McGraw-Hill, New York.

Weiss, S. J. and Gooding, E. C. (1968), Estimation of differential employment multipliers in a small regional economy, *Land Economics*, **44**, 235–44.

Wendt, P. F. *et al.* (1968), *Jobs, People and Land: Bay Area Simulation Study (BASS)*, Special Report No. 6, Center for Real Estate and Urban Economics, University of California, Berkeley, California.

Wiener, N. (1948), *Cybernetics*, MIT Press, Cambridge, Mass.

Wilde, D. J. (1964), *Optimum Seeking Methods*, Prentice-Hall, Englewood Cliffs, New Jersey.

Willis, J. (1972), *Design Issues for Urban and Regional Information Systems*, CES-WP-71, Centre for Environmental Studies, London.

Wilson, A. G. (1968), Models in urban planning: a synoptic review of recent literature, *Urban Studies*, **5**, 249–76.

Wilson, A. G. (1969*a*), Developments of some elementary residential location models, *Journal of Regional Science*, **9**, 377–85.

Wilson, A. G. (1969*b*), *Disaggregating Elementary Residential Location Models*, CES-WP-37, Centre for Environmental Studies, London.

Wilson, A. G. (1970*a*), *Entropy in Urban and Regional Modelling*, Pion Press, London

Wilson, A. G. (1970*b*), *Generalising the Lowry Model*, CES-WP-56, Centre for Environmental Studies, London.

Wilson, A. G. (1971*a*), A family of spatial interaction models and associated developments, *Environment and Planning*, **3**, 1–32.

Wilson, A. G. (1971*b*), On some problems in urban and regional modelling, in M. Chisholm, A. Frey and P. Haggett (Editors), *Regional Forecasting*, Butterworths, London.

Wilson, A. G., Hawkins, A. F., Hill, G. J. and Wagon, D. J. (1969), Calibration and testing of the SELNEC transport model, *Regional Studies*, **3**, 337–50.

Wingo, L. (1961), *Transportation and Urban Land*, Resources for the Future Inc., Washington, D. C.

Winograd, T. (1972), *Understanding Natural Language*, Edinburgh University Press, Edinburgh.

Zwick, C. J. (1962), *Models of Urban Change: Their Role in Transportation Research*, P-2651, RAND Corporation, Santa Monica, California.

Author Index

Subject Index